Ursula Ganz-Blättler

Signs of Time

Medialität – Crossmedialität

Beiträge zur Fernseh- und Onlineforschung

herausgegeben von

Joan Kristin Bleicher

Band 4

LIT

Ursula Ganz-Blättler

SIGNS OF TIME

Cumulative Narrative
in Broadcast Television Fiction

LIT

Cover illustration: Visualisation of Paul Ricœur's mimetic cycle,
adapted by ugb.
© Annik Dubied 2004

Supported by the Swiss National Funds and the Research Commission
of the Zurich University

Accepted as habilitation thesis by the University of Fribourg in 2009

Bibliographic information published by the Deutsche Nationalbibliothek
The Deutsche Nationalbibliothek lists this publication in the Deutsche
Nationalbibliografie; detailed bibliographic data are available on the Internet at
http://dnb.d-nb.de.

ISBN 978-3-643-80273-6 (pb)
ISBN 978-3-643-85273-1 (PDF)
Zugl.: Fribourg, Univ., Habil.schrift, 2009

A catalogue record for this book is available from the British Library

© LIT VERLAG GmbH & Co. KG Wien,
Zweigniederlassung Zürich 2018
Klosbachstr. 107
CH-8032 Zürich
Tel. +41 (0) 44-251 75 05
E-Mail: zuerich@lit-verlag.ch   http://www.lit-verlag.ch
Distribution:
In the UK: Global Book Marketing, e-mail: mo@centralbooks.com
In North America: International Specialized Book Services, e-mail: orders@isbs.com
In Germany: LIT Verlag Fresnostr. 2, D-48159 Münster
Tel. +49 (0) 2 51-620 32 22, Fax +49 (0) 2 51-922 60 99, e-mail: vertrieb@lit-verlag.de
e-books are available at www.litwebshop.de

INDEX

A new beginning xi

1 Introduction 1
    1.1   Research interest and questions 8
    1.2   Acknowledgements 15

PART I: EPISODIC FICTION AS COMMUNICATION

2 The gaps of which communication is made 17
    2.1   Vilém Flusser and John Durham Peters 19
    2.2   Niklas Luhmann and the improbabilities of communication ... 21
    2.3   The role of mass media 32
    2.4   Communication as transmission and ritual 35
    2.5   Conclusion 39

3 Episodic narrative as communication 43
    3.1   Narrative as art 44
    3.2   Narrative knowledge 50
    3.3   Signs of time 54
    3.4   Only narration can narrate 59
    3.5   Narrative episodes 61
    3.6   The gaps of which episodic narratives are made 66
    3.7   The particularities of episodic narrative communication 70

4 Episodic fiction as entertaining communication 77
    4.1   The privileges of leisure time 78
    4.2   Entertainment studies 80
    4.3   The reality of entertaining communication 82

4.4	Wolfgang Iser on narrative indeterminacy and reader response	89
4.5	Episodic fiction and customary reader response	95
4.6	The spectacle / performance paradigm	100
4.7	Summary	104

5 Episodic fiction across media and genres 105

5.1	Narrative indeterminacy and questions of control	106
5.2	Serial production of commodity culture and the cost disease	108
5.3	Episodic fiction and cross-media ownership	112
5.4	Distribution modes and questions of access	124
5.5	Narrative conventions and questions of genre	126
	Excursion: A side glance at gender bias	130

6 Episodic television fiction as programmed program 137

6.1	The specifics of broadcasting	137
6.2	Two broadcast models for Europe and the United States	139
6.3	Television as a storytelling medium	142
6.4	Television as a *leitmedium* in transition	146
6.5	Like day and night: daytime serial vs. prime time series	151
6.6	Television fiction reread, rerun and recorded	156
6.7	Three eras of prime time drama: from the series to the quality serial	158

PART II: EPISODIC FICTION AS ART

7 The gaps of which episodic television fiction is made 167

7.1	Vacancies and blanks within broadcast television fiction	169
7.2	Openings and closures of segments	174
7.3	Acts and beats within segments of broadcast television fiction	182
7.4	Story arcs that extend beyond segments	187

| | 7.5 | Seasonal endings and series' runs | 188 |

8	The serialised series: a state of the art	191
	8.1	What happened until now	191
	8.2	Some preliminary remarks	195
	8.3	From series / serial dichotomy to series-serial continuum	198
	8.4	From unilinear to multilinear prime time fiction	200
	8.5	From "modular" to serialised prime time fiction	202
	8.6	Synthetic overview of approaches	204

PART III: THE CUMULATIVE NARRATIVE AS EPISODIC FICTION

9	From picaresque to cumulative narrative: Horace Newcomb's theory of *Magnum, P.I.*	209
	9.1	"As characters remember, so do we"	212
	9.2	Aspects of intimacy, seriality, and liminality	217
		9.2.1	Intimacy	218
		9.2.2	Seriality (was: Continuity)	219
		9.2.3	Liminality (was: History)	219
	9.3	Backstory wounds and character growth	221
	9.4	The example of *Magnum, P.I.*	229
	9.5	The example of *The X-Files*	233
	9.6	The example of *Six Feet Under*	235

10	Questions of diegesis	239
	10.1	Preliminaries	239
	10.2	Paradigms and syntagms	242
	10.3	Story and plot	245
	10.4	Narrative memory as diegesis	256

11 Cumulative narrative as memory in progress 259
    11.1 Diegetic memory and expanding story worlds 259
    11.2 Narrative models 261
    11.3 Expanded story worlds and narrative involvement 267
    11.4 The example of *Magnum, P.I.* 270
    11.5 The example of *The X-Files* 272
    11.6 The example of *Six Feet Under* 274
    11.7 Narrative uses of the past 275

12 Conclusion: End of story? 279

13 Abbreviations 283

14 Bibliography 285
    14.1 Dictionaries and encyclopaedias 285
    14.2 Primary resources 286
    14.3 Secondary and tertiary resources 287
    14.4 Playwriting / screenwriting resources 289
    14.5 Secondary literature 289
        14.5.1 Television and broadcast series / television fiction in general 289
        14.5.2 Television studies / broadcast studies in general 301
        14.5.3 Episodic narratives in other media / in general 306
        14.5.4 Narratology / ludology / genre theory / gender theory 306
        14.5.5 Fan studies / audience studies in general 313
        14.5.6 Memory studies 321
        14.5.7 Linguistics / semiotics / (post-)structuralism 322
        14.5.8 Communication studies / cultural studies / media economics 323

FIGURES

Figure 1: Narrative as artistic communication 49

Figure 2: Ricoeur's mimetic cycle applied to miscellaneous news 56

Figure 3: Ricoeur's mimetic cycle applied to narrative events 57

Figure 4: Ricoeur's mimetic cycle applied to stories 58

Figure 5: Ricoeur's mimetic cycle applied to episodes 63

Figure 6: Mimetic cycles from episodic stories as chains of events 69

Figure 7: Circle of mimetic "redundancy" 71

Figure 8: Eco's 70"typology of repetition" 72

Figure 9: Expressive reader response to mass-mediated source material 98

Figure 10: Technical and program costs of an average US TV station 111

Figure 11: Flows of money and product in the entertainment industry 113

Figure 12: Structurally coupled person with emphasis on systemic autonomy 133

Figure 13: Structurally coupled person with emphasis on social affiliation 134

Figure 14: Main divisions of a major US broadcast network 153

Figure 15: Model of European TV's broadcast history 161

Figure 16: Model of US-American TV's broadcast history 161

Figure 17: The plotted drama's "unity-of-action" structure 176

Figure 18: The classic drama series' four-act structure 184

Figure 19: The classic sitcom's two-act structure 185

Figure 20: Narrative model of the episodic segment / story arc 216

Figure 21: Narrative model of the cumulative segment / story arc 216

Figure 22: Story and plot 253

Figure 23: Narrative model of the "modular" segment 261

Figure 24: Narrative model of the "modular" arc show 262

Figure 25: Narrative model of the multistrand arc show 262

Figure 26: Narrative model of the episodic "cluster" 263

Figure 27: Narrative model of the classic (daytime or prime time) soap opera 264

Figure 28: The complex diegetic web woven on soaps 264

Figure 29: What the soap's characters actually do, and say 265

Figure 30: Model of the episodic cumulative narrative 265

TABLES

Table 1: Two views on communication 38

Table 2: Six stages of conversational narratives 46

Table 3: Literate and oral modes 67

Table 4: The second worlds of the *Alien* franchise 123

Table 5: Prestige correlating with program costs 155

Table 6: A (very) short history of US television 159

Table 7: The intervals structuring broadcast television fiction 190

Table 8: The *serialised series* on broadcast network television 205

Table 9: Broadcast history of *Magnum, P.I.* (CBS, 1980-1988) 230

Table 10: Broadcast history of *The X-Files* (Fox, 1993-2002) 234

Table 11: Broadcast history of *Six Feet Under* (HBO, 2001-2005) 236

Table 12: Paradigms and syntagms 244

Table 13: Narrative levels in literary (and film) studies 252

Dedicated to Caroline, Marlène and Thomas.
And to my mum, in loving memory.

A NEW BEGINNING

When Roger de Weck, the former director of Swiss pubcaster SSR, was asked by journalists to explain why he thought that storytelling mattered, he referred to the exchange of narratives as an existential human need. To make his point clear, he quoted "elementary" needs that are material, energy-driven, and "existential" needs that are immaterial and information-bound. Among the former he listed food, water and shelter. Among the latter: love, respect, and the deeply-rooted urge to engage in mutual storytelling.[1]

De Weck's list of basic emergency supplies differs significantly from Maslov's famous "hierarchy of needs" that provides a generalised priority list of what we – as individuals, and as society members – require to be taken care of so that we can feel comfortable and safe.[2] That needs can be objectified and graded is far from evident, though: Who is to decide which ones are addressed *first* within a life-threatening emergency like, say, an earthquake, the outbreak of war or another kind of brutal, unforeseen attack? What about the availability of (... trustworthy) news, as fuel for new hope and reminder of shared beliefs? Not to mention that reassuring capacity communication has when providing symbolical venues of shelter in toughest times.

This book draws from de Weck insofar as it describes storytelling as a fundamental, intrinsically motivating communicative operation that societies rely upon in order to a) articulate aspects of belonging in time and space and b) make sense of our fragile, and necessarily precarious existence as human beings.

The book differs from other theory-loaded books on storytelling in the choice of its topic (a hindsight look at broadcast network television fiction in an era of transition from television conceived as *mass* medium to more differentiated looks at *diffused*

---

[1] For the interview with de Weck see Simon (2016, 34).
[2] In his original article published in 1943, Maslov distinguished five sets of human needs, or motives: Physiological needs, security-driven needs, society-oriented needs, self-oriented needs and self-actualising needs (Maslov 1943, and 1954). In his later writings he differentiated these needs further and added the longing for transcendence as another important motivational set. His intention was not so much to priorise the different urges but to lay out the various aspects of what drives humans in general.

audiences and media uses, as Abercrombie / Longhurst suggest).[3] It also stands out with regards to its theoretical framework that aligns a Bakthinian perspective on communication as pluralistic dialogue with the multiplicity of viewpoints and shifting power relations proposed by Cultural Studies scholars. Added to the mix is a hefty dose of constructivism in the guise of Luhmann's system's theory that has some Ricoeur and Schütz interspersed for good measure.

Most of all it is the scholarship provided by Horace Newcomb that fuelled and guided me. His contribution reaches out to the heart of the matter at stake: What is meant by the term of the *cumulative* narrative, and what does accumulation as concept "do", for the analysis of narrative as communication and reflective stance?

Newcomb's conception of storytelling as referring back to events and episodes that are (long) past and gone guided this thesis from its sketchy beginnings as a fangirl's mission to assert *Magnum, P.I.* its rank as one of the best prime time series around right to its final chapter that recommends uses of diegetic memory (... of characters as well as interpreting communities making use of hindsight revelations such as *backstory wounds*)[4] as a powerful strategic tool for the developing, maintaining and further outreach of sustainable narrative worlds.

Cumulative narrative strategies are described as working on three levels of narrative reconstruction, and recognition:

1. They negotiate back references as "hooks" for applications of intratextual reflexivity, be it within some original media outlet or across media borders.

2. They cross-reference sections of fictional second worlds in terms of narrative episodes and thus allow for the respective diegeses (and editorial responsibilities) to interact, to merge or separate.

3. They carry the potential to deepen both the relationship between characters and some knowing readership and the relationship between narrators and narratees as co-tellers in a joint storytelling venture, as time goes by.

---

[3] The authors claim that the pervasiveness of media in our daily leaves audiences with no other choice but a certain media-savviness (... at least in technical terms) and the adoption of a distinctively participative stance toward contents and their distribution. On the other hand they are also inclined to shift in and out of attention, in response to the sheer amount of what is available *out there* in an enormous, and rapidly growing variety of consultable platforms.

[4] For the term, and the respective analysis of mainstream action cinema see Krützen (2004, and here, p. 210 ff.).

In view of the (mostly: post-)structuralist theories applied here I conceive the telling of entertaining stories as a notoriously "messy" and discordant form of conversation that is precarious, tends to be open-ended and ambivalent and has its weaknesses as functionally flawed process, in terms of social operation and playfully explored "identity kit". In consequence I do not consider narratives to be "neutral" or innocent since they can just as well build trust as lead astray, can courageously denounce mistakes and point out wrongdoings as they may obfuscate some truth and reinforce existing social taboos and power relations.

On a more idealistic note I also claim that narrative communication is by default media-savvy, participatory and highly reflexive (... in comparison of what was and what will be; and in comparison of what *is* and what *might* be, in some alternative universe of wishful thinking).[5] This underlying assumption renders storytelling so relevant, in my opinion – and hopefully this book worth reading.

There are many different ways of how stories have been conveyed over the course of human history, in reference to a long list of trusted *leitmedia* that followed in each other's footsteps and carried the torch as popular and widely shared tools for orientation and social guidance further.[6] Two of the more recently emerging leading media are, arguably, computer games (both in their offline and online variations) and that complex, gossipy web of *social media* that facilitates sociable talk as well as community-building among audiences of larger or smaller size, and greater or lesser intensity of participation.

The advent of computer games engaged narratologists and ludologists in a friendly banter over the question as to what extent complex gameplay was to be considered a *storytelling art* or not. The conflict has since been settled on a diplomatic note of *why not?* Of course it is possible (and highly recommendable) to introduce storytelling skills in games as well as the skills of gameplay into diegetic universes, as (ludologists) Jesper Juul and Espen Aarseth convincingly argue, in accordance with (narratologist) Marie-Laure Ryan.[7] When it comes to communicative engagement in the public sphere of social networks and a broad variety of asynchronous discussion boards, on the other hand, many typical features clearly indicate narrativity to be

---

[5] For a more elaborate reflection on this see Ganz-Blättler (2014).
[6] See Göttlich (2002, 193 f.): He defines as *leading media* those media outlets that shoulder – on their own or in a particularly significant combination – "a principal function in the constitution of social communication and the public sphere" (transl. ugb.).
[7] Juul (2001), Aarseth (2012), and Ryan (2009).

crucial, be it in the organisational structure of postings as "threads" or in the the various commentary functions, and netiquette rules evoking the conventions of conversational storytelling aptly described by Neal Norrick and Ellinor Ochs for various kinds of interaction in groups.[8]

Both examples, electronically enhanced gaming as well as electronically enhanced conversation, allow for the optimistic outlook that storytelling will maintain its historic role as a communicative *leit* principle also in information-drenched, globalised and digitised network societies that see uses and functions of old and new media shifting in unpredictable ways once more.

Storytelling conceived as a dialogic, thread-weaving process between various *knowing* and loosely connected partners is a particularly useful narrative model when applied to fiction as entertaining narrative communication. Here participation in a previously existing, serialised and heavily publicised, constantly evolving diegetic story-world ranges from reclaimed authorship (as showrunner, editing agency or distributor, to name just a few respectively entitled players) to involved audiences as stakeholders of all sorts. They may prefer to pay attention to just some of the material out there or wish to catch up on it all; while some choose to stay lurking in the background others happily engage in further imaginative talk. What results from such endeavours is not so much a *different story* than the one that originated the talk but a collaborative public domain of gossip and inquiry where alternative views and add-ons are produced, beginnings and endings daringly altered and re-shaped, inconvenient story parts edited out and particular sceneries, events and happenings reworked for whatever imaginative uses seems fit.

If looked at from a systems' theory perspective, this is exactly what narrative communication is about: Once narration keeps narrating (... following Luhmann's famous claim whereas only communication communicates with people relegated to mere elements *within* communication)[9] there is no longer any significant distinction between authorship and readership, between those engaging in a more active role and those that read, and reflect, and comment on the tale as such.

Serial stories do the telling in the form of instalments that follow each other in temporal sequence. The institutionalised breaks, or ellipses, in-between allow for

---

[8] Norrick (2000), and Ochs (2001).
[9] Luhmann (1992).

both ends of the communication-in-progress to regularly pause and a) re-process what happened and b) formulate new expectations, along the way.

When programmed as programs (within some recurring time-slot of a TV schedule, for instance) serial narratives multiply the reprocessing possibilities (with regards to what was told, at what particular moment of the telling) and the possibilities for anticipating what the narrative has in store for upcoming instalments, or seasons, or holiday specials, maybe. The regularity of publication works in two quite opposite directions: Complexity is reduced as one can count upon some content to be back, sooner or later. At the same time complexity is increased with regards to all the imaginable twists and turns out there – and in terms of the unforeseeable events and happenings that may interfere with the ongoing telling and hamper the production, distribution-and the consumption of the story-to-be.

The particular state of controlled uncontrollability is, arguably, one of the most endearing assets of serial narratives; it allows for conventional *and* inventive strategies to be put at work as required. In consequence initiated audiences can always hope for two opposed sets of expectations to be fulfilled – as long as the course of events moves forward and churns out instalment after instalment: There is redundancy versus surprise, safety versus risk, and continuation versus disruption. Also there is repetition versus change –and that is where the potential lies for serial narratives to integrate conceptions of time as flow and as interval.

In order to allow narrative progression over longer periods of time, the parties invested in a telling must agree to go that "extra mile" together. This is crucial for instances of institutional (for instance: broadcast) storytelling that involve complex ensembles of staff writers, producers, actors as well as funding instances that all rely on complex, densely clocked timetables. It is here, within the narrative context of mass media, where expectations are "doubled" (as Luhmann would say), and another set of relevant timeframes appear.

The following study addresses both sets of expectations – narrative communication in terms of ongoing conversation, and the narrative strategies employed to allow for the respective conversations to last within more institutionalised venues of storytelling.

> In Dreams Begins Responsibility.
> (William Butler Yeats, 1914)

1   INTRODUCTION

This is a book about, well, nothing. It is about the split-second of silence when we wrestle for words. About the gaps between what is said, and actually meant. And, mostly, about those unmarked spaces looming large between the more familiar, already-given-a-name-to realms of our everyday existence.

Following John Durham Peters,[10] there are many and variously meaningful gaps communication is made of. Some of them have been studied by Wolfgang Iser as located firmly within narrative fiction.[11] Their function is to allow our imagination to take flight. They also allow for meaningful misunderstandings to be co-creatively produced. This study follows Iser's earlier work on the gaps between what is said and what is actually meant. It is also indebted to Durham Peters when addressing the more fundamental abyss which separates me from you. Or *ego* from *alter*, as Niklas Luhmann might prefer to phrase it.[12] It is, in short, a contribution to a still underdeveloped field of study which I suggest to call *episodic narrative communication*.

As Alfred Schütz noted, we do not live and partake in one single world habitually addressed as "reality" and considered common to all mankind. Instead, we do inhabit – and collectively share – many different worlds. Schütz has mapped them out in an essay about the hazards and loopholes of scientific truth, calling them "provinces of meaning" and pointing to their intrinsic logic beyond everyday reasoning.[13] He saw them as necessarily limited, or finite (1945, 553; emphasis mine):

> "All these worlds – the world of dreams, of imageries and phantasms, especially the world of art, the world of religious experience, the world of scientific contemplation, the play world of the child, and the world of the insane – are *finite provinces of meaning*. This means that
> - all of them have a peculiar cognitive style (although not that of the world of working with the natural attitude);

---

[10] Durham Peters (1994, and 1999).
[11] Iser (1972, and 1974).
[12] See Luhmann (1992, for example).
[13] Schütz ([1945] 1962).

- all experiences within each of these worlds are, with respect to this cognitive style, consistent in themselves and compatible with one another (although not compatible with the meaning of everyday life);
- each of these finite provinces of meaning may receive e a specific accent of reality (although not the reality accent of the world of working)."

This is to say, basically, that no experience of ours is to be taken for granted. What we hear and see, touch and taste, digest and behold, and continue to remember in more or less significant bits and pieces, is what we learned to accept as part of our everyday (= *world of working*) conception of things. The acceptance results from a series of socialisation processes that make us grow into (fairly) well-educated, well-adjusted adults. But let us fall asleep, and we become wide-eyed foreigners once more, finding ourselves involved in the strangest possible endeavours. There is no doubt we can fly, run faster than the wind and develop supernatural sensory capacities we never thought to actually possess. And yet we do: Strange creatures are eager to meet and greet us (… or: eat us), and trees can talk and walk. Sooner or later we may find ourselves confronted by surprise visits from long lost beloved ones who may comfort or just as efficiently haunt us. In our dreams, that is.

We do not control our dreams since they belong to our subconscious. Neither have our dreams the power to control us. We may view them as some kind of highly personalised, creative "poetry slam" with a penchant for the absurd, or as purely escapist, sense- and meaningless offer of our imagination running wild while we get some well-deserved rest from our usual selves. Both assumptions confirm the (re-) creative potential of dreaming, in terms of therapeutic workout or time out. In dreams we are confronted with our innermost desires and fears. We get reminded of older times and civilizations when the world of dreams and the world of daily routines appeared far from separated.

By calling dreams and imaginary events "finite" within their own realm, Schütz accredits them with a cognitive and narrative logic of their own while nevertheless acknowledging their coexistence alongside each other. Passing from one realm to another asks for a transitory "shock" or "leap" (… of faith) and a transformation of our *attention à la vie* (ibid., 554). It means that the states of dreaming or being wide awake are related to each other as are the experiences we derive from everyday existence and those we seek elsewhere within some imaginary or virtual reality.

Our dreams represent the flip side mirror of our experiences, then, and reflect our hopes, desires and fears. This certainly becomes evident in the province of day-dreaming: When I click away those spam mails promising spiritual health, instant wealth and endless sexual pleasures only to find myself, hours later, swooning over

George Clooney riding his Harley through a murky paparazzi shot in an Italian people's magazine I become aware of my switching sides. Apparently our collective imaginary does need those scenic escape trips from what our illuminated forefathers mapped out in terms of rationality-bound provinces, some 300 or 400 years ago.

In other words: We all need dreams, and we crave fairy tales. They not only help us to face our inner demons while we transcend from childhood to adolescence, as Bruno Bettelheim (1976) famously noted. We also need them in order to feel whole. Throughout our lives we feel an insatiable appetite for the imaginary which fuels our self and keeps our spirits high. This appetite may be nurtured through religion and firm beliefs in some kind of afterlife. Through some sense of truth attributed to our wildest (... or wettest) dreams, or by the sheer expression of concern and emotional overflow when our favourite celebrity couple breaks up, when Ross and Rachel finally get together, or when a brave young wizard by the name of Harry Potter is about to face his final destiny.

According to the British author and screenwriter Hanif Kureishi (2005) our "stories, dreams, poems, drawings, enable us to experience ourselves as strange to ourselves. It is also where we think of how we should live" It is only when our dreams become stale and our trust in the soothing potential of the imaginary wanes that we start to lose the grasp of life itself.

Following David Carr (cit. in Meuter 1995, 249), human identity is best understood in terms of narrative identity. Narratives are cognitive artefacts born from associative activity and connections (Herman 2002), and thus constructed as well as constructing entities. Marie-Laure Ryan (2005, 344-348) emphasises this with regards to the role of memory and (the writing of one's own) autobiography as a metaphorical second chance: "[L]iving one's life and reflecting upon it is like writing one's life story: a continuous act of self-creation that involves at every moment choices, responsibilities, re-evaluations, and the addition of new chapters to the book-in-progress."

As *books-in-progress*, or narratives accumulated over time, human identities are necessarily procedural. They are produced, but also constantly reproduced through ongoing narrative activities. They are, according to Carr (ibid.), not "... a pregiven condition, but an achievement. [...] What we are doing is telling and retelling, to ourselves and to others, the story of what we are about and what we are. " Such an ongoing activity of telling and retelling includes synthesising what we were up to now, in terms of autobiographical reconfiguration – but also new stories about what we hope to be and achieve within our remaining lifetime. Norbert Meuter indicates the importance of "potential autobiography" when addressing the capacity of life stories to include what is not yet there and achieved (see Meuter 1995, 267):

> "Our identity contains ... not just who or what we are or have done so far, but implicates questions as to who or what we want to be. The identity of a person is not only defined by the security and stability of what this person has evolved into but also by the proposed prospect of eventually transcending the achieved in view of a new self-understanding."[14]

The potential of using past experiences for a prospective outline of future scenarios lies within all imaginative narrative activity. It is especially high in fictional storytelling – through all ages and life stages, and with regards to all media supports available. Fictional stories, and role-playing fictions performed individually or collectively on a public or maybe computer-based stage as "theatre" (Laurel 1993) allow us to express our dreams and fears in effective, yet relatively safe ways. Their imaginary status prevents us from actually having to face the consequences of our actions. However there is a "doubling of reality"[15] implied that leaves us with a possibility to succeed (or fail) where no one succeeded or failed before. Both implied consequences of fiction – the improbability of things to never, ever happen and the eventuality of the same things indeed happening one day – render the fictional prospect promising and tempting at the same time: We can try out the most eccentric scenarios and "test the waters" while the (virtual) options of alternative outcomes remain intact.

In other words: Whereas all narratives offer alternative perspectives how to see things, fictional narratives provide us with complete sets of imaginative possibilities how to experience things tentatively through the actions and observations of others. This is even more valid for fictional narratives providing us with sustainable, repeatedly accessible story worlds which can be explored once more next week, next month or a year from now ... as soon as more instalments of the franchise hit the

---

[14] Transl. ugb. Original version: "Unsere Identität besteht [...] nicht nur darin, wer oder was wir sind oder bisher getan haben, sondern impliziert immer auch Fragen danach wer oder wie wir sein wollen. Die Identität einer Person definiert sich nicht nur in der Absicherung und Stabilisierung dessen, was sie bisher geworden ist, sondern auch darin, ob und wie es uns gelingt, das Erreichte im Ausblick auf ein neues Selbstverständnis hin zu überschreiten."

[15] According to Luhmann (2000) all communication processes necessarily reproduce what we experience as "reality" but in distinct, generic ways.

air, arrive in the mail or wait for us at newsstands and in bookstores. This is about entering familiar fictional territory, about looking forward to further appointments with characters which we already know and enjoy having around. The reading (or listening or watching, or playing) experience leads us straight into a "room of friends", as Victor Watson notes with regards to children book series.[16]

Recurring fiction told in discrete instalments over a considerable amount of time differs significantly from other narrative fiction. Such narrative communication asks for considerable investments in terms of time, personal commitment and organisational skills (on both ends of production and reception). In return an extended, "accumulated" pay-off is offered, be it in the form of an especially loyal reader-, listener- and viewership, be it in terms of more exclusive pleasures – for initiated members only – that come with the more frequent visits to the fictional universe in question.[17]

There are arguably two models on which every episodic story told in discrete instalments is based: the episodic, or cyclic *series* on the one hand and the continuous, potentially never-ending *serial* on the other.[18] Whereas a series conventionally provides some kind of closure at the end of an individual instalment (for television think *Gunsmoke* or *Columbo* or, more recently, the various territorial adaptations of the *CSI* format), the form of the serialised serial is progressive and provides ellipses rather than endings as one instalment closes. However, some serials are (potentially) endless while others spiral towards some overall climax and closure.

---

[16] Watson (2000, v) quotes a former pupil of his, a sixth-grade boy, who expressed pleasure in reading series fiction. The boy explained how "starting a new novel is like going into a room full of strangers, but starting a book in a familiar series was like going into a room full of friends."

[17] The difference between *jouissance* and *plaisir* (Barthes 1973, see his *Oeuvres complètes* 2, 1521) is quoted by Ien Ang (1985, 83 ff.) to describe different kinds of pleasures tied-in with watching *Dallas* in Holland. See also Calbo (1998) for a further elaboration of the viewing pleasures derived from watching serialised fiction (and reality programs and talk-shows) on television.

[18] With regards to serial cartoon narratives see the following definition by Bill Blackbeard and Martin Williams (quoted by Hilmes 1997, 304, note 36): "[A comic strip is] a serially published, episodic, open-ended dramatic narrative or series of linked anecdotes about recurrent, identified characters, told in successive drawing regularly enclosing ballooned dialogue or is equivalent and minimized narrative text. " A television series might then be defined as a serially published, episodic, open-ended dramatic narrative or series of linked anecdotes about recurrent, identified characters, told in successive broadcast instalments through moving pictures, spoken dialogue, equally spoken (and / or written) narrative, atmospheric sound and music.

Mielke (2006, 46) describes as common traits of the two basic narrative forms – series and serial – the recurrence (in German: "Periodizität") of the publication and a *recurring framework* setting the instalments apart from other texts within the same media context. The difference lies in their presentation either as sets of separated, yet thematically linked stories or as one ongoing story which is told in subsequent, chronologically as well as logically interconnected segments.[19] The most popular representatives of the on-going form are the telenovela and the soap opera as designed for broadcast media (radio and television) within the first half of the 20th century. Soap operas provide as many mind-boggling, nerve-wrecking climaxes as they count narrative threads while the main story's closure (which could be a family's destiny or a specific community's future) is forever postponed (for this, see White 1994, and Spigel 1995).

Over the last decades and in a context of increased media convergence these two basic forms of episodic storytelling have come to be seen as complementary rather than antagonistic. At a closer look, *serials* just as regularly come to a halt and provide narrative closure (of specific storylines) as series do. On the other hand the episodic storylines of a *series* can be made to "go on" in various ways, be it by introducing partial continuity or by bundling them into distinct "story arcs" which extend over a specified number of episodes.

This also means that narrative endings within stories told in instalments no longer – or: not necessarily – correspond with the instalment's end: Closure may occur within an episode (while new storylines emerge and proceed) or, alternatively, interrupt rather than terminate some major action, be it at the end of an instalment or at the end of a predetermined number of instalments corresponding to a set of episodes as "season" (which, in the case of more recent television fiction, may soon be available in its entirety on DVD anyway).[20]

---

[19] See Mielke (ibid.): "Seriell ist das Erzählen, solange eine Geschichte noch nicht zu einem Ganzen kausal-logisch gefügt und beendet wurde und sie narrativ auf Endlosigkeit angelegt scheint. Erfolgt ein inhaltlicher Abschluss der Geschichte, so entspricht das Erzählen jedoch einem Zyklus. [...] Bei zyklischer Narration fügen sich die separaten Geschichten am Ende zu einer thematischen Einheit, die eine Rückkehr zum Ausgangspunkt darstellt, und die die Ausgangssituation der Rahmenhandlung beeinflusst und auf eine neue Ebene bringt. Beim seriellen Erzählen ist nicht die Kreisform beabsichtigt, sondern die lineare Bewegung der Reihe, die ein endloses Erzählen suggeriert."

[20] For the strategic braiding of storylines see Mittell (2006, and here, chapter 8), for the strategic timing of DVD reruns Adalian in *Variety* (22-01-2007, 16).

Episodic series drawing from both ends of the continuum are often addressed as *serialised series*. In European countries such as England or Italy the serialised series is used to describe a drama series consisting of fewer (usually six) seasonal episodes airing over consecutive weeks (see Nelson 1997, and Buonanno 2002). These seasonal arcs works like mini-series of its own and display inter-episodic (but not inter-seasonal) continuity. The Hollywood business paper *Variety* proposes the same term of the serialised series more generally for network prime-time series displaying continuous (individual or multiple) storylines.[21] The term is used particularly to describe the braided, multithread structure of the – often workplace-oriented and heavily populated – ensemble drama series as it originated on US-American networks in the early 1980's. The "MTM school" (see Feuer / Kerr / Vahimagi 1984, and Schatz 1987) can be traced back to the drama series *Lou Grant* (CBS, 1977-1982; a spin-off of the *Mary Tyler Moore Show*) and found its defining structure with the police drama *Hill Street Blues* by Steven Bochco (NBC, 1981-1987) and the medical drama *St. Elsewhere* by Joshua Brand and John Falsey (NBC, 1982-1988).

For this kind of particularly "thick" narrative other terms have been proposed as well: Robin Nelson suggests to call them *flexi-narratives* (Nelson 1997, 2000, and 2006), while John Corner opts for the term *multistrand narrative* (Corner 1999). More recent examples of this narrative model (which combines the traditional "case" structure with large ensemble casts and braided storylines) are *NYPD Blue*, *ER* and *Northern Exposure*, but also (to some extent) *24*, *Desperate Housewives* and *Lost*.

The description of narratives as "cumulative" is not to be identified with the aspect of multiple threads or perspectives (as described more recently by Allrath / Gymnich 2006). The term points to a particular structural characteristic and narrative strategy. Cumulative series focus on specific characters and their (back) stories. They rely on former story material and make use of what lies in the past in order to shape what is yet to come. Instead of concentrating on parallel life-courses they explore life-courses back in time and therefore, consequently, shift back and forth in-between various moments in time.

As *cumulative* counts a kind of television narrative which remains, for most of its characteristics, within the traditional action-adventure mould. Cumulative series are often distinctly quest-oriented and follow an episodic (or, more precisely, picaresque) logic. They focus on a limited number of (usually 1-2) main characters

---

[21] Michael Schneider in *Variety* (12-06-2006, 16, 18).

whose most remarkable quality is to *remember* (if only partially and selectively) what happened before, both within and outside of the series' explicit temporal framework.[22] The protagonists' memory, in terms of accumulated, cognitive as well as affective "personal baggage", does regularly transcend the diegesis of an individual episode, allowing for past narrative events to make an explicit comeback. What is brought back in an updated or revised version, however, is not restricted to characters and premises of the "case" in question (as may the recurring on-off guest appearances of a former adversary, client or "damsel in distress").[23] Instead it affects the major storylines and involves key characters, thereby shaping, influencing and transforming the original narrative concept as such (Newcomb 1985 and 1994, and Hoke-Kahwati 1990).[24]

1.1 Research interest and questions

This study deals with the cumulative aspects of episodic fiction in broadcast television.

The definition of narratives as stories in progression refers to the procedural aspects of such an endeavour: a story is never really "over and told" as long as there is some narrator or narrative instance left and ready to add further elements to the story or some new aspect to its meaning. This is especially true for cumulative narrative forms, where both author(s) and audience(s) – both tellers and "tolds" – are invited to add their five cents and round out or alter the course of events as they came to be, or have come to be told.

This study investigates US-American fiction as conceived for prime time network television in terms of broadcast or "free", advertisement-driven TV. Its focus lies on episodic drama series understood as a form of popular folk epic (for the term see Esslin 1975, Dupont 1991, and particularly Bleicher 1999). I am interested in ongoing storylines that emerge from episodic structures, and thus from distinct cases or

---

[22] With the turn of the century cumulative series have started to pertain to large ensemble casts as well; both *Lost* and *Heroes* were adventure series that employed multithread as well as cumulative strategies with regards to some complex overall mystery evolving over time.

[23] As for an example *MacGyver* features the protagonist's arch enemy Murdoc (played by Michael Des Barres) in recurring episodes; the same goes for a rarely seen friend named Jack Dalton (Bruce McGill) and a former love interest named Penny Parker (Teri Hatcher).

[24] Jeffrey Sconce (2004, and here, chapter 8) refers to the concept of the cumulative narrative without specifying the more distinct "memory functions".

"quests". Episodicity refers here to an organising principle whereby recognisable *tokens* of a specific franchise are moulded after an original format as *type* (Eco 1985).

The particular object are hybrid, "serialised" series that cross over generic borderlines, rely on continuous storylines, repeatedly evoke backstory events and thus provide the more experienced viewer with an increasing, indeed "cumulative" knowledge with regards to the main characters' whereabouts. Over the course of the last thirty years such drama series have become staple items within the prime time schedules of network (and cable) television, to the point that they are now – as Jeffrey Sconce puts it (2004, 98), "so ubiquitous in U.S. television that purely episodic programs are now almost as rare as live broadcasting and the long defunct anthology series".[25]

My research questions are thus the following:

What narrative features distinguish cumulative narratives from other conventional, institutionalised episodic narratives on network television and other media? What textual as well as contextual factors invited for the development of cumulative narratives within mass media? Where lies the (economic, cultural, but also political) potential of episodic narratives that provide a "wayback" function, considering the risks and chances implied for all participants in the ongoing communication process?

The larger context of this study is the negotiation of knowledge (which can be newly acquired or already "known" knowledge) in relation to the telling of time. I am more particularly interested in the cumulative forms of narrative and the processes of meaning-making because of their affinity to the construction of (individual, but also collective) memory. However: By the term "memory" I mean not to refer to sets of somewhat "stackable" and subsequently retrievable objects which simply need to be reorganised in order to make sense but instead to more malleable concepts of interwoven strands and overlapping layers of meaning that produce a dense "texture" ... or, indeed, another story-world constantly "in the making" (for this see Welzer 2002, Erll 2005, and Bittner 2006). Memories in this sense can take the form of stories. They also draw from stories which make us selectively remember things

---

[25] See Sconce (2004, 98). He summarizes Horace Newcomb's concept of the cumulative narrative in broadcast television, subsuming under the umbrella term *all* serialised series that feature continuous storylines, without specifying genres or particular uses of accumulated backstory with regards to character growth.

and keep them in mind over time or, alternatively, "dismember" and forget (for the role of selective forgetting Esposito 2002).

With regards to narrative knowledge the film theorist Edward Branigan (1992, 65) distinguishes declarative knowledge (that provides answers to paradigmatic *what? questions*) from procedural, skill-oriented knowledge that addresses syntagmatic *how to?* aspects of a problem at hand: "Knowing how involves the exercise of a skill in which something is achieved; it does not involve questions of truth or belief." Knowledge seen from a procedural perspective is always time-related and can pertain to aspects of *order* (with regards to events conceived within a logic succession of cause and effect), *duration* (in terms of reflection time needed to understand a specific phenomenon or problem) and / or *frequency* (for instance in relation to the repeated practise of the skills one needs to overcome a particular obstacle).

In this larger context my questions are the following: How do serialised (here: television) series as *stories in progress* generate, maintain and negotiate narrative knowledge over time? What keeps such communication running? Which factors determine the significance of a story, at what point of the telling, and by whose authority?

Narrative, knowledge and memory are key issues within the concept of the *cumulative narrative* and are addressed here, in the following chapters and paragraphs, with regards to television series as main example.[26] Needless to say that the concept leaves room for applications to other popular media narratives as well.[27] Horace Newcomb's ideas on narrative, knowledge and memory – not to mention his personal encouragement and critique – have remained a central source of inspiration over the full length of this study.

The story of this book began long before it became an academic research project – probably at a time when I started watching American television in the late 1960's.

Born in 1958, in a little town not far from the main motorway connecting Berne with Zurich and, on a bigger map, Geneva on the French border with St. Gallen on the German-Austrian border I grew up with Swiss and German public service television

---

[26] Examples are taken from long-lasting television drama series broadcast on American prime time television in the period stretching from the early 1980's to around 2005.

[27] As for a literary example see Thierfelder, Ulrike: The Magical Formula of Harry Potter. Master thesis, University of Lugano 2006.

only.²⁸ I learned to appreciate that voluminous box with the tiny, flickering screen only it when it began to tell me adventure stories – meaning stories to which I could, and would tune in week after week. It was an intriguing experience to see *Fury* and *Lassie* – and of course *Flipper* as well as that friendly, cross-eyed lion named *Clarence* – always come back for more adventures next week – same weekday, same hour.

When television entered our household I must have been about seven or eight years old. My father was of peasant roots, yet given the rare chance to study in order to become a catholic priest. Instead he chose to become a dentist. He was an avid "early adopter", enjoying the wonder years in the early sixties when Swiss economy boomed and early supermarkets displayed an abundance of consumer goods (see Brändli 2000). Virtually every consumer good seemed to be in reach, then: huge American cars, travels to far-away places (like Italy), but also a wide range of electronic gadgets manufactured to reduce the burden of domestic labour and illuminate the truly "modern" household.

I have two distinct memories from those wondrous years when television arrived: I used to watch boring programs made for grown-ups only for the rare privilege to watch it with my father. To cuddle up, feeling his hand stroking my hair and smelling the disinfectant of the doctor's coat still stuck in his hair was heaven. It compensated by far for watching some greyish indistinguishable figures with heavily-rimmed glasses talking about world politics while smoking endlessly.

On the other hand I used to watch children television together with my brother. He was four years my senior and took a wicked pleasure in lecturing his kid sister about the predictability of series' conventions. *Fury* never was the same again after he started teasing me with graphic descriptions of upcoming forest fires and tornadoes that would only leave bare soil behind – and a panting black horse, furiously kicking air. From then on, whenever the musical score started whispering "danger", I would inevitably jump "over the rail" and seek refuge behind the huge family sofa. This sensation of *angstlust* which I experienced long before knowing what it was called – that sure was heaven too.

---

[28] Regular television broadcasting in Switzerland began 1958 after a five-year test run in the local area of Zurich. The national public broadcaster SBC was founded in 1931. It held a monopoly until 1983, when 36 private radio-stations received permission to transmit on the (local) airwaves. Private television, either highly specialized or distinctively local, was introduced around 1990 (European Business Channel EBC).

What is curiously missing from my early television memories is my mother. She was the one telling us fairy tales and many other, more fantastic stories, and I can still picture her ironing large heaps of laundry while going on with her telling while we sat on our kitchen stools, quietly listening. However, that ironing world of the homemaker in the kitchen appears to be, in my memory, miles away from that male-dominated, adventurous television world out there in the living room.

All of my childhood series came in German-dubbed versions which were produced and broadcast by the two German public networks, ARD and ZDF. *Magnum, P.I.* was on every Tuesday night, and I simply loved the program – or rather it's major asset in my eyes, which was this heavenly built, wonderfully sensitive hunk played by Tom Selleck. He was not my first choice as male object of desire: Before Magnum there was Mannix (Mike Connors), and on *The Persuaders* I really had a hard time to decide whether I should fancy the American guy (Tony Curtis) or Roger Moore.

Only later I found out that most of the series I was watching were actually American, or British (like *The Avengers*), and that those funny moments when everybody on the screen seemed to hold their breath were due to a silent conspiracy – the blatant disrespect of most European television stations towards those little blackboard inserts telling broadcasters to "place commercials here". Back then in my teen years my competence in dealing with high-pitched danger music improved considerably, and so did my expertise in daydreaming. Looking back, I must have worked as a somewhat autonomous fan circle once I turned fourteen: I knew and collected everything I could about the shows and stars I cherished. I was keen not to miss any episode and had regular meetings with the only other fan I knew, telling *myself* all those great fan fiction stories I invented on a regular base.

My own private engagement as fan let me imaginatively take part in the stories as watched on TV; later on I would daydream them in slightly revised versions. Sometimes I acted as the rescuer to the hero who was in pain or life-endangering trouble.[29] Sometimes I would play the part of a lover-to-be, exploring that mysterious wonderland of attraction and seduction with no risk of making a fool of myself or getting hurt. It all happened in the backyard of my head, and it never occurred to me that I might not be the only one indulging in such forbidden pleasures.

---

[29] Sabucco (2000, 66 f.) lists several conventional genres for fan fiction; what I imagined corresponds to the *Mary Sue* genre, particularly despised by more experienced fanfic authors and / or readers because of their ample use of nondiegetic characters (i.e., thinly veiled auctorial *alter egos*).

Episodic narratives as stories in progress, or stories to be, deserve attention not just for their popularity with large audiences. The cumulative narrative in its industrialised form as television fiction follows storytelling principles that may seem uncommon when compared to more traditional traditions such as "high" literature and classical Hollywood cinema but are characteristic for all serially produced cultural artefacts:

1. The narrative proceeds in pre-defined segments, and at the same time also as a sequence of individual episodes or intertwined plotlines, without the author-producer(s) necessarily overseeing the narrative's progress from start to end and thus foreseeing and controlling its overall development.

    The principle of *recurrence* applies to all episodic series such as the hour-long drama series, the half-hour situation comedy and to all continuous serial narratives such as soap operas or telenovelas.

2. The narrative's fictional universe expands over time, with newly introduced characters and other plot-related elements (or existents) [30] likely to stay on and to be subsequently integrated into the overall meaning-making process.

    The principle of the *open-ended diegesis* applies to soap operas and telenovelas in particular, but also to hybrid series that display a flexi-narrative and / or cumulative structure.

3. The ongoing narrative is both intertextually and "intratextually" cross-referenced, meaning that recognition processes refer not just to various extra-textual resources, but also to what happened earlier on in previous instalments.

    This principle of *diegetic memory* applies to the cumulative narrative alone.

The initial goal of my research was twofold: I was curious to explore cumulative narrative fiction in broadcast television, in order to describe the strengths and vantage points the concept offers as well as its weaknesses and limits.

On the other hand I hoped to find out more about what kind of "social glue" narratives are, what their essential uses are and why we are so intrigued with the literally endless possibilities of experiences that await us in somebody else's carefully set-up

---

[30] Chatman ([1978] 1993^6, 9) distinguishes the "existents" of particular narratives from the "events" told in the story at hand, thus individuating the paradigmatic features (namely, characters and settings) from the syntagmatic features which structure the course of action. These terms are specified here, later on, p. 243.

narrative universe. And yet we rely on the reassuring perspective that these conventionally crafted or reconstructed story worlds are not really endless and allow us in time to "wrap up" and find our way back into our actual existence. This study describes narratives as world-constitutive and necessarily cumulative "systems". The argument is supported by social systems theory and a variety of other arguments picked from interdisciplinary narrative theory provided recently with regards to everyday storytelling (Neal R. Norrick and Elinor Ochs / Lisa Capps), literature (Monika Fludernik), cinematography (David Bordwell and Kristin Thompson) and interactive media (Marie-Louise Ryan, David Herman and others).

In structuralist contexts narratives are commonly described as text(s) and / or as discourse. As for stories which go on for lengthy periods of time an important question is how to handle both the episodic and the serial aspects (and the potential infinity) of such endeavours – with regards to each and every instalment, but also with regards to the text as a whole.

In a more economics-oriented approach, narratives are referred to as content or franchise. Here my question is what an analysis of (cumulative) storylines might contribute to an understanding of serial texts as "content" or "brand", especially with regards to content leverage – the distribution of licensed characters and narrative contexts on more than one media platform.

History, anthropology, sociology and psychology have set the foundation for linking different kinds of narratives to collective and individual pasts in terms of memory. The question here is how cumulative storytelling can influence such processes.

Finally, narratives can also be seen and understood as powerful means of accumulating and distributing knowledge within and beyond social systems – with the cumulative narrative form proposed as an especially "telling" and rich variation to be studied further.

This book is organised in three parts: The chapters in part I provide the reader with a discussion of some basic terms and underlying concepts such as "communication", "entertainment", "narrative" and "fiction", as well as with a cursory history of episodic fiction in mass media and broadcast television. Part II develops a formalist theory of the episodic narrative based on its two main characteristics: unpredictability and expanding story worlds. Here the specific potential of the cumulative narrative is traced back to its capacity to absorb *backstory* and to embed recurrent events – or a series of recurring events – as episodic, or modular tokens within the serialised narrative. Part III focuses on the uses of cumulative narrative in relation to imaginative world-making and characters' extended backstory as diegetic memory.

This study conceives narrative as communication and as art and, more specifically, as an ongoing communicative attempt at meaning making based on the circulation of knowledge about what is by default beyond reach; some "other". Narratives allow for symbolic access to (and symbolical participation in) other systems "out there".

In the first place, this book is a reflection on narratives in mass media, on "programmed" programs in broadcast television and the organisational principles that apply to scripted prime time drama series. As was stated before, the episodic drama series taken into account as illustrative examples stem from US broadcast network schedules of the 1980's and 1990's, with few exceptions reaching back into the 1970's and forward into the 2000's.

1.2   Acknowledgements

Books are not written in a day. This one was originally plotted in 1993, when a grant of the Swiss National Fund sent its author first to Austin, Texas, and then to Siegen, Germany. I went as a historian interested in television narrative – and I came back a media and communication scholar with a keen interest in all things called entertainment. Over the years of teaching and writing in that field, the book project simmered and was only occasionally stirred in order to not stick to the ground forever. It took a symbolic relaunch and two geographic moves from Zurich first to Geneva and then to Lugano to finally find the means – and the necessary determination – to conclude the project.

I am indebted to many individuals and collectives, to institutions as well as friends and colleagues. To name a few: Marlène von Arx, Los Angeles, and David Romas of "Magnum Memorabilia", Detroit, for providing me with the essential primary materials – video and audio tapes of *Magnum, P.I,* and those copies of *Magnum P.I.* fanzines. Caroline Schmidt for all things *X-Files*, and Thomas Christen for working with me on beginnings and, more particularly, endings over all these years. All the people offering online-transcripts of *X-Files* episodes under the following names: Vic Vega, Mark Rooney, JoLayne, CarriKendl, Dave Fox, Princess Leia, JFB Lilac, Deirdre Shelly, Leigh M, Debi Tuttle, Rob, Roni, Bentina, FMUlder, Starrrbuck, Al Ruffinelli, Dr. Weesh. The Swiss National Funds and the Research Commission of the Zurich University for financial aid, and trust. Thomas Schatz and others at the University of Austin, and Helmut Schanze and Reinhold Viehoff at the

Gesamthochschule Siegen. Brigitte Scherer, Monika Grosskopf and Ute Wahl for these highly entertaining collaborative efforts as self-made television scholars. Chris Anderson, Don P. Bellisario, Sue Brower, Paula Feldstein, John Hulsman, Sandra Idrovo, Chas. Floyd Johnson, David Marc, Cynthia Meyers, Linda Mizejewski, Megan Mullen, Donna Reiner and Mimi White "over there"; Joan Bleicher, Ingrid Brück, Spartaco Calvo, Udo Göttlich, Joachim and Julia Haes, Gerd Hallenberger, Susanne Herppich, Shelley Ann Mannion, Jonida Myftiu, Alex Repenning, Pat Schettino, Karin Wehn, Anne Yammine and many others "over here"; and Heinz Bonfadelli, Noll Brinckmann (for that Army-Air Force Song Book), Milly Buonanno, Yves Fricker, Jürg Häusermann, Kurt Imhof, Paul Michel, Ulrich Saxer, Michele Sorice, Kurt Spillmann, Franz Schultheis, Anna Lisa Tota and Uli Windisch for their most valuable support back home … wherever Kansas was.

I am indebted also to Antje Bratschi, Luis Calvo, Dorothea A. Christ, Sandrine Comment, Laura Crimaldi, Annik Dubied, Christine Erard, Sonia Ehnimb-Bertini, Alessandra Filippi, Matilde and Gianni Gaggini, Rolf Ganz, Irene Genhart, Waltraud Hörsch, Ruth Hungerbühler, Paul Michel, Samir, Beate Schappach, Sarah Sepulchre, Daniel Süss, Barbara Wenk and Ethel Wiener – for the interdisciplinary interest and those countless hours of patiently listening, and mutually watching obscure instalments of even more obscure television programs. Rick and TC never had to endure so much preaching from Higgins as you had from me.

Last, but not least my heartfelt thanks go to Ludmila Tataru and Ulrich Knellwolf (for gently nudging me towards giving this publication another try) and to Alvaro Baragiola, Diana Ingenhoff and Wilhelm Hopf for invaluable institutional support as closure approached.

PART I
EPISODIC FICTION AS COMMUNICATION

> Whatever we know about our society,
> or indeed about the world in which we live,
> we know through the mass-media.
> (Niklas Luhmann, 2000a, 1)

2   THE GAPS OF WHICH COMMUNICATION IS MADE [31]

Nobody is perfect. Humans are conceptually flawed beings, and so is communication between humans: a highly ambitious but nevertheless flawed project. Failure is not an option, but a rule of the game.

This chapter focuses on communication models which foreground the latent dysfunctionality of human communication rather than the chances (and necessary conditions) for success. This is not to say that all attempts to make communication "work" are denounced as futile and a waste of time. Quite the contrary: One of the most intriguing aspects of communication is that we absolutely need it to happen since we cannot do without. The question is whether the outcome must be as foreseeable and sustainable as we sometimes wish.

Human communication is usually said to involve two or more humans. That is not necessarily the case, though. Computers have taken over a fair share of our everyday communication via phone, mail and online resources. Pets can very effectively communicate with people. And we learn fairly early to successfully interact with guardian angels and dolls, the super heroes that zoom through some eclectic comic book realm and the current target of our highly ambitious teenage crush.

A good (albeit fictitious) example of this is Chuck Noland: After the crash of a freighter airplane the hero of the film *Castaway* (by Robert Zemeckis, 2000) spends four years alone on a deserted island. He survives not only by his improving hunting

---

[31] The title borrowed from Peters (1994). Note: References to works published first in another language than English are made with regards to the English version – with the original language edition included in brackets. My own translations are indicated as such.

(and medical), skills but also by his ongoing social (or is it parasocial?) interaction with a faithful companion named "Wilson": a stone-faced football washed ashore alongside Noland which will remain his sole conversation partner and friend over all this time.[32]

Communication is presented here as a precarious project with the potential to disconnect just as much as to connect people. Some default gaps remain to be minded rather than mended. Because we are, and we shall always be strangers to each other. We live side by side, confined by our own skin. What we feel towards each other is necessarily restrained by our limited capacity to reach out and get through. Yet we do live our lives as social beings and define ourselves through the company of others.

In many ways we resemble castaways that are stranded on separate islands: We keep our senses pointed towards the open waters in the vague hope to find other islands or shores out there, or at least some passing cruise ship or pirate vessel that might show signs of human life aboard.

In this study the term *communication* refers to all attempts at performing this search, in terms of elementary social operation. Some theorists describe communicative tools as *bridges* because of their supposed transmitting and relying power. Others view communication attempts rather as *crutches*, since only so much can be said, written or expressed at a time. But never all that might be said, written and mutually expressed.

As social beings we are asked to transmit, and we need to rely. And we give both endeavours our best shot. But there will always be at least two kinds of gaps left open: the gaps between my own existence and that of my neighbour, and the gaps in need to be constantly mended in order to make sense of our own existence. Because I relate my own life (both in prospective and in hindsight) to the life of others and to models derived from these lives. To put it in the words of the philosopher Odo Marquard: "Zukunft braucht Herkunft": All future needs an origin.[33]

---

[32] An intertextual inside joke is the fact that *Wilson* footballs belong just as importantly to US popular culture as the rock solid Hollywood marriage of Tom Hanks and Rita Wilson does.

[33] See the title of an essay collection published in view of the author's 75th birthday (Marquard, 2003).

2.1 Vilém Flusser and John Durham Peters

An idea derived from the *crutches* metaphor is incompatibility. While there exists an amazing variety of communicative tools and modes of address, there is no guarantee that the humans partaking in a given community will necessarily use these tools in perfectly corresponding or somewhat complementary ways.

Human communication is based to a considerable degree on speech acts and other What we describe as communication is based importantly on speech acts and other modes of conventionally coded and purposely meaningful behaviour. These other modes include glances, facial expressions, and gestures [34] as well as indirectly mediated forms of communication such as writing, drawing, photography, graphic design (and combinations thereof), telephone and radio messages and a fast growing variety of talking pictures that can be viewed and discussed in all kinds of public, semi-public or private settings.[35] These days, more and more of these message exchanges take place via Internet and within the realms of simultanously or remotely accessed online communities.[36]

Human communication is the result of multi-variant, complex processes of meaning-making and therefore not a "given". The highly coded, conventional default procedures imply experience and sophisticated knowledge as to how to read and interpret what was said, gestured, put on paper or programmed into some intelligently responding device supposed to talk or gesture respectively back to me. As the philosopher Vilém Flusser noted, the understanding of what someone else means to say by some kind of coded behaviour is far from evident. Because the codes need to be decoded (or: deconstructed) in order to become "natural" signs again (Flusser 2002, 35):

> "A code is a system of symbols. Its purpose is to make communication between people possible. Because symbols are phenomena that replace ('stand

---

[34] Klaus B. Jensen (2002, 3-4) speaks of media of the *first degree* and describes them as "biologically based, socially formed resources that enable humans to articulate an understanding of reality, for a particular purpose, and to engage with others in communication about it".

[35] Jensen (ibid., 4) refers to them as media of the *second degree*, in terms of "technically reproduced or enhanced forms of representation and interaction which support communication across space and time irrespective of the presence and number of participants".

[36] In Jensen's typology (ibid.) such media of the *third degree* translate as "digitally processed forms of representation and interaction which reproduce and recombine previous media on a single platform".

for') other symbols, communication is a substitute: It replaces the experience of 'that which it intends'. People must make themselves understandable through codes, because they have lost direct contact with the meaning of symbols. Man is an 'alienated' animal, who must create symbols and order them in codes if he wants to bridge the gap between himself and the 'world'. He must attempt to 'mediate'. He must try to give the 'world' meaning."

These coding and decoding processes can only lead to some kind of mutual understanding once some basic structure of what is supposedly signified has been set up and communicated earlier. Flusser (ibid.) evokes the example of pre-historian African anthropoids whose lives and daily experiences are set apart from ours by the temporal as well as spatial distance that separates us. While we may easily recognise the signifying practice in some elaborate arrangement of artefacts that was directed at a more contemporary audience we can only guess what exactly these early ancestors tried to say and express. All we can do is acknowledge the "meaning-giving intention" – and thus what is "artistic", and at the same time "artificial" [37] – in them.

Similar caveats apply to communication situations that are more familiar. Most attempts at communication are in fact lost on their audiences, be it because of linguistic and cultural differences, be it due to technical failure or temporary attention deficits. According to John Durham Peters the human condition is intrinsically linked to the precarious chances of communication to succeed (Peters 1994, 131):

> "We all tend to resist acknowledging the fundamental gap at the heart of all discourse, even though negotiating the gap is a daily accomplishment most adult language-users are quite expert at. The physical presence of another is no guarantee that 'communication' will happen. You can read love poetry to someone in a coma, never knowing if the words are 'getting through,' but the same doubt is just as relevant in other settings, as all teachers and parents know."

According to Peters' main argument (1999, 264) face-to-face talk is, and always was as "laced with gaps" as distant communication is. Once there is significant time and space in the way the differences between sender and receiver – and the resulting transmitting difficulties – just become more evident. Because the basic problem with communication is not distance but *difference*; at stake are the different faculties that people bring to the table when trying to read and understand what other people express and mean. In the words of an earlier essay of Peters (1994, 131),

---

[37] The German version of Flusser's text (1997, 23) refers instead to the term "artificial" (= künstlich): "Wir erkennen die sinngebende Absicht, das 'Künstliche' in ihnen."

"[t]he gaps of which communication is made are most visible at the margins of social life, in interactions with the mad and the aged, with children and strangers, and in free-floating academic seminars. The abyss dwells in all communication: 'normal' folks are simply more adapt at managing it (that may in fact be what 'normal' means), and the habits of daily life keep the potential of more spectacular misfires at bay."

The prospect of communication as being a flawed if not doomed human project may sound discouraging. If there is "[n]o distance ... so great as that between two minds" (ibid., 130), why should one try to get through in the first place? With the chances of our message reaching their designated target no bigger than an "... SOS in a bottle cast into the sea, a classified ad calling for love, a lost manuscript, or a text in an undeciphered script" (ibid.), what is the point in keeping up the good work, norwithstanding? Because as social beings we cannot do without, that is why.

2.2   Niklas Luhmann and the improbabilities of communication

The social sciences conceive communication and communication-related phenomena either as a social activity that can be traced back to individual agents and their (good or bad, and sometimes just misfired) intentions or as a complex system of socially constructed entities that, like modules wrought together into a prefabricated house, help build and shape society as a whole. In both the actionist and the systemic paradigm communication plays a central role. It can be seen as social glue that keeps humans as members of society connected and in touch or rather as some sort of social "grease" that keeps the social system running as such.

Niklas Luhmann and his German compatriot Jürgen Habermas have lead a lifelong debate (and friendly banter) over the conceptual differences between systemic and actionist thinking, with Luhmann pointing to the fundamental systemic nature of social networks and Habermas defending the idea of social responsibility that remains with every individual member of society and his or her capacity to make strategic, reason-based choices and decisions.[38]

The idea of communicative acts as individual performance that culminate in social action is based on the speech act theory developed by John R. Searle and others (Searle 1969). Cal M. Logue and Eugene F. Miller – two critics that have countered Peters' "gap-toothed" communication theory with an answer of their own (Logue / Miller 1996, 364). They maintain that

---

[38] For the actionist paradigm Habermas (1984); for the debate Habermas / Luhmann (1971) and Moeller's critical comment (2006, 187-191).

"[c]ommunication is not made of gaps but of more or less successful attempts to bridge the spatio-temporal and interpretive distances that attend our individuality as embodied beings. Starting from the idea that communication is an activity of sharing through the mediation of signs, we try to bring out its gap-bridging potential and to indicate why all communication presses towards completeness of sharing through interaction."

The same ideas of communication as social action have been outlined by Habermas with regards to a typology of human action that depends on address and intention (see Habermas 1984). In Habermas' theory of communication,

- *instrumental action* does serve a higher rational purpose and uses objects and subjects indiscriminately on that behalf. Instrumental action can be self-reflexive and directed at the agent him- or herself or directed at some object out there, like the shoe lace I purposely tie so to not stumble by accident. If my action involves other human subjects they are used like objects and for convenience purposes: a good example is the friend of mine I may briefly lean on when attempting to tie said shoe lace. In contrast to this instrumentalisation of subjects as objects,

- *social action* is always directed outbound and must by definition address other beings, be it in terms of *strategic* action that seeks the attainment of a more complex goal by way of a rational choice of tools and the following of rules, be it as *communicational* action that aims at some mutual understanding, in terms of a participative effort towards some shared communicational goal.

In Habermas' model communicational discourse is designed as a reciprocal giving and taking among individual agents that intents to serve the common interest of the collective as a whole. This is more or less what Logue / Miller have in mind when they define communicative sharing as "simply an activity by which one's thoughts and intentions may become known to others" (1996, 365). Such an activity benefits or harms others, depending on the intention which – according to Habermas – can be labelled communicational or strategic: "Sharing, as we use the term here, is not meant to connote unselfishness and benevolence or to serve as a synonym for generosity. [...] Communication may involve deception, i.e., when sharing is intentionally incomplete or illusory. In deceiving, lying, or dissembling, I share feigned thoughts or intentions in such manner as to disguise my real ones."

In Luhmann's functionalist system-oriented view, communication is not taking place between individuals as social agents but is conceived as basic operation of societies that need to observe themselves and their surroundings in order to maintain themselves and adapt to new developments. Alongside this social operation of *communication* there is another fundamental one: *perception* is conceived here as the basic operation of individual minds that need to observe themselves and what surrounds them to the same goal of systemic well-being, or maintenance. The two observational entities – the individual's consciousness and society's communication with itself – do exist and operate alongside, but they exist and operate within different spheres and unbeknownst to each other.[39]

Both operations – perception and communication – function thus in similar ways and work towards the same objective: that of making sense by way of linking one thing ("me" or "us") to another (what is "out there" and therefore out of reach). Since the "sense" at stake is not automatically fine-tuned to complement both the individual's consciousness and society's on-going introspection, however, the two operations can easily get into each other's way and thus create problems instead of resolving them.

According to Luhmann the human nature is far too complex for any known science to successfully transcend its default opacity. The conception of modern man as an individual – in terms of "undivided entity" – on the other hand entails the risk of oversimplification. From a Luhmannian (and thus systemic, functionalist) perspective humans are best seen as multivariate beings whose conception as "body", as "mind" or as some "element in a social communication" allows to assume more specific observational standpoints with regards to the research question at stake. As biological (living) systems we need energy, not information to survive. This means that we are fairly self-sufficient once our bodily needs are taken care of and appeased. As psychic systems that are provided with perception-, consciousness-based minds, we are constantly craving for outside stimuli in order to perform those linking operations that make sense, ultimately. The problem is, however, that we are not that well-equipped in collecting adequate information about our surroundings because as individuals we are *by definition* not able to foresee or predict what another individual mind is up to next. Interactions between two or more psychic systems are, therefore, necessarily based on mutual perception and rely on respective experiences and expectations.

---

[39] Structuralist systems' theory was introduced into sociology by Talcott Parsons. Luhmann rearranged some basic principles, adapting the theory to processual and systems of high complexity within Western society. For this see Luhmann (1995, and 1998) but also Giegel / Schimank (2003).

From the viewpoint of observable society, finally, humans (and this entails all representations of man in a somewhat humanoid and respectively expressive form) figure as components of social interactions only in our educated, socialised form and appearance as "persons" (for the use of this term see Luhmann, 1991) – but not in terms of autonomous agents (minds, or bodies) that can express some kind of individually generated or genetically programmed social conscience. As Hans-Georg Moeller explains (2006, 22), "social systems theory cannot accept the common assumption that society consists of human individuals – or of their minds or bodies. It consists, operationally speaking, of communication 'events' […]."

Moeller quotes a routine-based social interaction – the payment of a fast food meal between customer and cashier (ibid., 6-7) – to underline the specifics of a systemic view of communication. The respective interaction between two persons (one coded as paying patron, the other as employee expecting payment) can go on undisturbed while both minds are continuously engaged in a mobile phone conversation with third parties elsewhere. The patron is supposedly called by his boss, the employee by the spouse – and both phone calls are pursued as the monetary transaction takes place. Technically speaking, the unities engaged in communication are not four humans (two present, two absent) but three contemporarily led interactions that have a fair chance to succeed alongside each other in terms of communicative event.[40]

While the systems described by Luhmann – bodies, minds and social components taking some recognisable, and thus communicable form as "persons" – operate in three completely different spheres, they dispose nevertheless of sensorial antennae that can recursively link (in Luhmann's terminology: structurally couple) one system to the other. In the case of bodies and minds there exists a common system border in form of the five senses that function both in terms of organs and / or perceiving instruments. In the case of autopoietic minds and "persons" (that take part in communication events) the shared objective is "sense" that is either perceived by introspection or collectively produced by way of communication.

While humans as consciously programmed psychic systems cannot perceive what other humans as individuals are up to, the same humans as more or less successfully

---

[40] This is not to say that such complex communication events succeed by default. In the case at hand their precarious state is aptly illustrated by the sign forbidding mobile phones during payment that is mounted over many fast-food restaurant counters.

socialised persons can indeed predict or at least guess what some other (similarly educated and socialised) person will do next. Such assumptions are necessarily based on the presupposition that this "other" person is a component of the same (or the component of a somewhat compatible, again linkable) social universe.

This means that communication as basic *social* operation does structurally couple humans as persons that represent particular social roles to other persons that again represent particular (and hopefully corresponding, or complementary) roles. In this way persons function as the communicable "surface" of otherwise impenetrable individuals and can indeed respond to, and themselves be the object of social expectations.

According to Luhmann (1991, 174), persons are part of the organisational level of social systems; they reduce indeterminacies (in Luhmann's terminology: contingencies) by restricting the behaviour repertory of organised membership. Between psychic and social systems persons work as structurally coupling "frames" (to say it with Goffman, 1974) that allow for interpenetrations as well as for irritations to be observed and addressed from either side.

If we come back to the question of communication as social "glue" or "grease", the actionist paradigm comes to Logue / Miller's defense of the "common-sense idea that communication is a kind of sharing". In contrast, Luhmann's functionalist theory of communication backs up Peters' suggestion that communication is not mending the gaps but actually creating them – and is therefore not necessarily the remedy to be called for, but rather the sickness to be examined and diagnosed. A sickness we nevertheless have to live with and better acknowledge for what it is: an existential condition of human life (Peters 1994, 130): "The gaps at the heart of communication are not its ruin, but its distinctive feature."

Why do I recur to Luhmann for the purpose of this thesis on narrative fiction, rather than Habermas? The main reason stems from the different ways how the two communication theories account for relationships that take place between ego and alter. The respective partners are established either as socially active individuals or as socially coded persons (Horster 1997, 88 ff.): Habermas insists on individual efforts that need to be made to change perspectives, to adopt some "other" viewpoint and "see things from there". Social systems theory doubts that this is possible but believes instead in "double contingency". The term, established by Talcott Parsons, describes the double, bi-directional expectations that characterise communication attempts between ego and alter. According to Parsons ego does adapt its further behaviour to whatever behaviour can be expected from alter (that is either conceived as reliable or unreliable, and can be trusted or not). The same is true for alter, respectively, that adapts its behaviour in response to what behaviour might be expected from ego.

Contingency, in Luhmann's terminology, encompasses all the behavioural options that are waiting to be actualised within the range of what can be expected on the base of past experiences. Once choices are made an open contingency – in terms of *all* the possibilities out there – is transferred into a closed contingency (the possibility chosen). The interesting thing about double contingency is that it limits the range for social action rather than expanding it: The complexity of human behaviour can be significantly reduced by it since assumptions made about *ego* taking decisions based on observations of *alter*'s behaviour usually bring about fairly foreseeable results. The complexity of human behaviour can be significantly reduced by expectations based on expectations, or so it seems.

An illustrative example of this is the famous football kicking contest between Lucy van Pelt and Charlie Brown within Charles M. Schulz' *Peanuts* comic strip. The contest takes place every year in the coloured Sunday section and dates back as far as 1957. In its sixth annual edition (Sunday, 30-09-1962; see Schulz 2004, vol. 6, 274) both contestants base their decision explicitly on each other's behaviour as perceived *so far*. Detlef Horster (1997, 89) quotes the cartoon in full: [41]

> Lucy: Hey! Look what I have!
> Lucy: Could I interest you in a little "kicking-off" practice? (Charlie rolls his eyes.)
> Lucy: I'll hold the ball, Charlie Brown, and you come running up, and kick it.
> Charlie: Okay ... it's a deal.
> Charlie (to himself while walking): HA! I know what she's got on her mind!
> Charlie: Every year she pulls the same trick on me. She jerks the ball away just as I try to kick it.
> Charlie: Well, this time I think she has a different idea. I think she's going to try to fool me by NOT jerking the ball away!
> Charlie: This time she knows I know she knows that I know she knows I know what she's going to do ...
> Charlie (running towards Lucy, self-confidence radiating): *I'm way ahead of her!*
> Charlie (kicking air and just about to fall on his back, while Lucy jerks away the ball): AUGH!

---

[41] For a recontextualised history of the whole series of recurrent football jokes in the Sunday papers see Derrick Bang: The Football Gags, accessible at *www.fivecentsplease.org/dpb/football.html* (18-08-2017).

> Charlie (falls heavy on his back; the blow resounding with a thunderous "WUMP!")
> Lucy (standing over Charlie, lecturing him): I figured you knew that I knew you knew I knew that you knew I knew you knew, so I had to jerk it away.

Charlie Brown's and Lucy's mutual relation is clearly depicted as one of mistrust, and the outcome has one of the two participants in the encounter necessarily outsmarting the other (... with somewhat expectable results, in this particular case). What can be observed here is a long-term relationship sustainable enough for the social partners (as well as for us, the third-party observers) to make assumptions and maintain them over the course time.

This is exactly why double contingency is about. Once there is some predictability established with regards to the process of mutual assumptions these assumptions can, according to Luhmann, become the nucleus for a future system's auto-regulation. A "... system history" begins (Luhmann 1995, 131; for this see also Horster 1997, 91) that invites all participants in its telling to develop assumptions about the expectable behaviour of other participants. Such processes focus on mutual, ongoing reality constructions which can, in time, become stable enough to stabilise the system in return: There is no longer a recursive cycle of unrelated expectations that (in theory) allows "anything to happen" but instead a focused, common sensibility for specific options, specific actions to happen next (ibid., 131-132):

> "From the temporal perspective, double contingency works here as an accelerator of system construction. Beginning is easy. Strangers begin by reciprocally signalling each other indications of the most important behavioral foundations: the definition of the situation, social status, intentions. This initiates a system history that includes as well as reconstructs the problem of contingency. As a result, the system increasingly is occupied with arguments about a self-created reality: with handling facts and expectations that the system itself has helped to create and that also determine greater or lesser behavioural scope than the indeterminate beginning. Double contingency is then no longer given it its original, circular indeterminacy. Its self-reference has been de-tautologized. It has incorporated chance, has thereby grown, and appears against what is now determinate or still determinable only as 'being also otherwise possible.' This in turn lets the second self-reference, that of action as an element of a social system, come into play. Action acquires its selective determinacy together with the limited possibilities of being otherwise from its function as an element in the social system."

In other terms: Strangers that happen to share the sensibility for specific options to be more probable than other options can signal this to each other, in terms of common base of further action. Indicating one's status and intention suffices as identification of the respectively involved persons. This shared familiarity immediately produces "sense" and by this allows the system in question to develop some basic and recognisable structure.

According to Luhmann (ibid., 133) "[p]ersons never meet without some assumption, without some expectations about each other, and they can experience contingency in the sense of 'always being otherwise possible' only by means of behavioural types and expectations." This is why remarkably stable structures can result even from random, ephemeral encounters. Social systems are based to large extent on the shared sensibility for the system's needs that such conditioning processes engender. The same is true of society's central operation of self-observation – communication.

Niklas Luhmann's theory of social systems [42] is based in part on Talcott Parsons (1937) but differs significantly in that social systems are not considered the result of individuals' actions. Instead they appear as constructed and maintained through collective, system-immanent activities in terms of processes (such as the one just described) seen as "operations" of the system in question. Social phenomena are not conceived as directed towards some "other" (as would be the case if conscious beings as entities would act upon other conscious beings as entities) but towards the social entity as such. Individuals merely appear in their unmarked state as "psychic systems" relying on system-bound consciousness, or in their marked state as specifically socialised "persons": As such they can either perceive what other individuals as psychic systems based on *their* consciousness do (or fail to do) with regards to this psychic system's expectations, or assume a particular and socially observable role within an operation of the social system in question.

Only collectives can (and must!) communicate in order to distinguish themselves from other collectives. Their communications need other communications to precede and follow, in order to keep the social system running. What is communicated is necessarily rooted within a common ground of knowledge, which is then continuously actualised.

This is why "only communication can communicate" (Luhmann 1992, 251). And why communication should not be perceived as the product of social action, but rather

---

[42] For basic Luhmann texts in English see The Differentiation of Society (1982) and Essays on Self-Reference (1990), both New York: Columbia University Press; Social Systems (1995) and Observations on Modernity (1998); both Stanford: Stanford University Press. On communication also Luhmann (1992) and (2000a). For an introduction into functionalist systems theory Rasch / Knodt / Wolfe (1995), Rasch (2000), and particularly Moeller (2006).

as its necessary ground and condition (ibid.): "Communication is the basic operation by which societies are produced and reproduced."

The term of "choice" plays an important role not only in Habermas' theory of communicational action (as based on individual decisions), but in functionalist thinking as well. The term preferred by Luhmann is *selection*, however – it is not individuals choosing and deciding (... what to read or watch, for instance, or how to interpret and understand a certain message), but communication itself. Only communication as a social system ...

1. "chooses" some information over other available information (in terms of something that might be of particular interest when uttered),
2. selects what form the utterance takes (what kind of expressive behaviour applies),
3. decides what understanding (or misunderstanding) results from the operation.

Based on a particular understanding of what was given a closer look at and translated into such or such (type of) message the communication will be accepted or refused. In common sense terms: It takes place, or does not take place. On the base of these three premises communication either succeeds or fails.

Societies as systems must build upon operations of self-identification and differentiation. From a systemic view the other "out there" is everything that is – for now – not of interest and therefore not differentiated further. Communication is described as a process, but also as the basic system "invented" and "set in motion" by social systems for the purpose of what Luhmann calls *autopoiesis*, meaning self-reproduction.[43] This is why communication is not merely to be conceived as a dialogic "act" (or as a human "artefact", in the words of Vilém Flusser), but rather as a

---

[43] System theories differ from action theories in that there are neither subjects (actors) nor objects (to be acted upon) involved. There are merely systems "at work", with no particular entity authorising the "invention" or "setting in motion" of structures. Systems differentiate 1) the external world as "surroundings" (that are "of no particular interest to the system") and 2) a subsequent series of internal subsystems, designed to reduce overall complexity to manageable levels (see above), and assigned with specific tasks, or operations, with regards to the main system. The functionality or dysfunctionality of those subsystems depends on the viewpoint from which they are observed. In the present discussion, our viewpoint is that of a social subsystem purportedly searching for truth, namely, Science. From a systems' theory perspective, individuals are psychic systems, who base their "actions" on consciousness-related self-observation, while societies are social systems which base their operations on communication-related self-observation.

functional means of self-centered introspection – as a social systems' monologue with itself, so to speak.

Both Luhmann and Peters refer to the "gaps" of which communication is arguably made. Such gaps exist between individuals engaging in an interpersonal relationship but also between groups or communities that engage in a relationship supposed to extend beyond time and space. The functionalist approach of social systems theory differentiates between two perspectives as points of view: *Individuals* are conceived as psychic systems relying on *perception* to "scan" their surroundings. While *societies* (of which individuals are indispensable elements) rely on *communication* – for the same purpose.

This means: Whereas social systems must rely on communication when developing and maintaining their identity, psychic systems recur to their five (... or maybe more) senses to fulfil the same task. What we usually assume to be dialogic interaction between two or more individuals is conceived as retroactive expectation expressed by likewise monadic structures. The difference between perception (by individuals) and communication (by the same individuals as social beings) is made in order to explain that (Luhmann 1992, 243): "what another has perceived can neither be confirmed nor repudiated, neither questioned nor answered. It remains enclosed within consciousness and opaque for the communication system as well as for another consciousness." Perception appears as restricted to individuals (= psychic systems), while the same individuals may "communicate" as social beings – albeit not necessarily in accordance with what another social being in terms of persons. Only by way of (successive) communication, however, perception as such can be expressed and analysed and be further compared to similar experiences in order to become socially relevant as well.

Luhmann's description of communication processes is complex and difficult to accept since it excludes the individual "as such" from the actual social operation of communication. On the other hand he, rather than Habermas, accords each and every individual its uniqueness as an autonomous system, in terms of a largely self-sufficient "observation machine". His theory also corresponds remarkably well with Peters' statement (1999, 4) whereas "[o]ur sensations and feelings are, physiologically speaking, uniquely our own. My nerve endings terminate in my own brain, not yours. No central exchange exists where I can patch my sensory inputs into yours, nor is there any sort of 'wireless' contact through which to transmit my immediate experience of the world to you."

Seen from Peters' and Luhmann's monadic perspective, all interpersonal interacttion – in the sense of some individual "self" being expressed through speech acts shared with "other" (individuals) out there – will always remain an approximate task. Because the purpose of what is to be communicated (be it between individuals as observers or between groups, communities and whole societies as observing systems) can only be *autopoietic* and self-centered.

Contrary to action theories communication processes in functionalist-systemic thinking are not oriented directly towards "other" (addressing other social systems, or other psychic systems in the case of an interpersonal contact) nor intended to achieve some kind of mutual "exchange" (between these social or psychic systems). However, communication as well as perception, while being restricted to observations "within" a given system, can project enough self-centered assumptions to "other" areas out there in order to account for some understanding to take place. If only a tentative (mutual) attempt and (shared) illusion of understanding, maybe.

In the terminology of Luhmann the paradox of "communicating communication" is related to effects of what social systems theory understands as (see also here, further up) *double contingency*: Whenever two systems engage in a dialogic situation, they have to rely on the assumption that the other system shares same's own understanding of what is at stake. If the communication remains an illusory task then there is no problem as long as this illusion remains a shared one. It is the same paradox rooted in human nature that Flusser refers to in his earlier quote: If as *people* (in the sense of aggregated individuals) we cannot really communicate, but only as *members* of a specific group, community or tribe etc., then it is exactly by membership that our perception becomes distorted enough to produce (the shared, or mutual illusion of) some understanding.

As Peters puts it, and I repeat (1994, 131): The abyss dwells in all communication. Those considering themselves to be "normal" folks (in terms of adapted society members – or successfully socialised persons, in Luhmann's terminology) have learned how to cope with the resulting problems. Others struggle their whole life to get through, or simply give up trying.

No understanding is ever complete or exhaustive. This is why *successful* communication, in terms of an ambitious task of sharing (... information, a personal opinion, a common past or some future dream ...), is so unlikely to happen. As Peters puts it, with a bow to Emmanuel Lévinas (Peters 1999, 21): "The failure to communicate is not a moral failure, it is a fitting demise for a flawed project."

When taking into serious doubt the common-sense premise that communication ought to work as a kind of convenient tool kit allowing us to neatly bridge the abyss between humans (as psychic systems) or even succeed in mending the gaps between groups and communities, Peters and Luhmann point to *otherness* as a basic condition of human existence. Communication is seen as a smoke screen rather than as a source of enlightenment. For Luhmann, the social theorist, it is a system's operation designed to offer introspection and rhetorical means for constant self-assurance. While for Peters, the humanistic pragmatist, every smoke sign contains the implicit hope (if not the final satisfaction) to "reach out" and touch someone, at some point.

Both improbabilities – communication fulfilling its supposed destiny to successfully transmit information from A to B, and communication seen as the chance for two or more people to finally "become one" – have lead Peters to formulate much more modest expectations. The task may simply be (Peters 1999, 21) "to find an account of communication that erases neither the curious fact of otherness at its core nor the possibility of doing things with words." Or things with pictures and graphs and travelling sounds and video files and multivariant combinations thereof, for that matter.

2.3   The role of mass media

Luhmann argues in "Die Gesellschaft der Gesellschaft" (translated as "Society's society", published in the year of his death, 1998) that every social phenomenon can help to reduce the improbabilities of communication and thus assume the role of a medium. He suggests distinguishing three types of media with regards to their effectiveness in particular social situations (for a synthesis see Grampp 2006, 263-264). *Language* [44] is described as reducing the risk of misunderstandings, especially with regards to face-to-face communication where other sign-systems come into play as well. *Distribution media* (the term encompasses all means of telecommunication enabled to transcend space and time) are indispensable to ensure the larger registration of some communicative attempt beyond a limited, present audience. Then there are *symbolically generalised media* such as truth, money, love or power that ground in a common understanding of what kind of "sense" is at stake. Such media engender specific expectations that, in return, render particular communica-

---

[44]   Understood here as the underlying structure of *langue* rather than its actual use as *parole*.

tive options more probable than others.⁴⁵ Whenever attention is scarce or heavily contested (for instance in the case of a three-fold communication that was described by Moeller earlier on) such media can facilitate and accelerate the communication process at hand since no words need to be uttered or further explanations given.

As for the social system of *mass media*, it displays characteristics of all three types of media – such as second orality in terms of represented "presence", large registration and ample use of self-explaining code systems. It also fulfils a crucial role within society when providing its more specialised subsystems with common fodder for thought in the form of ongoing communication, respective expectations and recursively linked memories.

In his earlier reflections on the "Reality of the Mass Media" (2000a) Luhmann distinguishes between three socially agreed-upon communication genres, or "program strands" as the author prefers to call them, that have the potential to cut through system-specific borders with regards to language and distribution modes. Mass media genres structurally couple social sub-systems a) among themselves on an organisational level and b) these sub-systems again to the social system as such. Mass media genres are differentiated as

- recognised forms of *news and in-depth reporting*
- recognised forms of *entertainment* programs

    recognised forms of *advertisement*

Generic expectations and priorities may vary with regards to different media systems and institutional frameworks.⁴⁶ In their specific combinations within and across media platforms mass mediated news, entertaining programs and advertising

---

[45] See Moeller (2006, 26-28). This is where Habermas' idea of "instrumental" or "strategic" (social) action finds some corresponding match. Actions, however, depend on individual actors with specific intentions which may be judged as self-centered or altruistic whereas "communication communicating" relies on (more or less aligned) expectations on both sides of the exchange.

[46] This explains why news journalism is treated as a privileged subject in communications and social science departments of publicly funded universities. The various sub-genres of mass entertainment must compete with institutional attention given to other, more privileged, forms of the arts and humanities, while advertising is studied as a mere economic tool and "empty spot" which keeps the mass media system running as such. Ironically enough, says Luhmann (2000a, 44 ff.), it is advertising which supplies successfully socialised members of society with the fundamental distinguishing characteristics of "taste" and fashion sense.

define the outlook of complex modern societies – to the point where one might (reluctantly) agree with Luhmann's ironic statement (2000a, 1) whereas "[w]hatever we know about our society, or indeed about the world in which we live, we know through the mass media."

Luhmann defines mass media as means of communication which, for technical reasons, do not encompass direct interaction between the involved parties. Their social function is therefore necessarily ambivalent (Luhmann 2000a, and Grampp 2006, 264): There is on the one hand the provision and maintenance of a common stock of knowledge which allows for persons to maintain their identity features and thereby feel connected. On the other hand there is an ongoing production of new (meaning: unexpected, possibly disturbing or downright alarming) information that constantly challenges, actualises and modifies that same stock of knowledge. Mass media work as relaxing and disquieting communication "agents" at the same time: We expect them to exercise some integrative power, but we also expect them to watch out and to alert of imminent danger. By that double task of integration *and* irritation mass media keep, in Luhmann's own words (2000a, 22), "society on its toes. They generate a constantly renewed willingness to be prepared for surprises, disruptions even."

The difference between the three macro genres "news / reportage", "entertainment" and "advertisement" can also be expressed in terms of relation of trust or mistrust between the partners engaged within the communicative attempt: Audiences expect news and reportages to tell the "truth", while ad breaks and other forms of advertisement are well-known to "lie" by default. Entertaining program strands (and here, Luhmann singles out the subgenre of fiction) is based famously on Coleridge's definition of *willing, suspended disbelief for the moment* – and thus some fairly ambivalent program strand that has audiences oscillate between trust and mistrust.

The competing functions of social irritation and / or social integration are valid for all possible forms and combinations of these genres – and find an interesting correspondence in Cultural Studies theories such as Stuart Hall's "encoding-decoding" model (Hall [1974] 1980) or the "cultural forum" model proposed by Horace Newcomb and Paul Hirsch in 1983. All three concepts promote ongoing negotiation between various communication partners to be *the* crucial factor within public meaning-making processes, be it with regards to the divergent situational contexts the involved instances may bring to the table (in the case of Hall),[47] be it as a consequence of the plurality of opinions that leads to necessary ambivalences and conflicts within the follow-up communication they engender (for this, and the importance of an ongoing dialogic exchange within pluralist societies see Newcomb / Hirsch 1983).

Luhmann's ideas can be read as an invitation to have a closer look at the relation of trust and / or mistrust developed with regards to specific media, specific genres and more specifically conventionalised, institutionalised forms thereof.

On the other hand the curious alignment between Cultural Studies and constructivist thinking may also stem from the mutual understanding of individuals as "opaque" entities that are as unreadable as they are unforeseeable. This is why concepts of *otherness* (as discussed earlier with regards to Luhmann, Flusser, and Peters) offer themselves as starting points for poststructuralist just as well as for functionalist ventures into the realm of mass mediated communication.

2.4   Communication as transmission and ritual

Before I go on focusing on the social role of mass mediated narratives (see here, chapter 3) and the particularities of narrative mass entertainment (chapter 4 and 5) I would like to briefly compare Luhmann's model of mass media as based on irritation and integration with a similarly ambivalent communication model famously described by James W. Carey as "transmission" oriented and "ritual" oriented.

In his reflections on "Communication as Culture" (1988, 1992) Carey agrees to view communication as a flawed, since necessarily self-centered (or: soliloquious) project. Yet he insists on the meaningfulness of what we do when we actively pursue a conversation using words and other cultural (according to Flusser: "artificial") codes. Even if we would forever fail to "get through" we would probably keep on trying, again and again

According to Carey all communication attempts follow one of two basic patterns and strive to achieve one or another – and in most cases both – of the assigned goals: Classical *transmission* stands for communication processes which seek to

---

[47] Peters (1999, 52) links the encoding-decoding model of Hall to Kierkegaard, since both scholars argue that indirect communication encourages receivers to become "self-active". Peters also views the gaps between encoding and decoding as features of all forms of communication: "It often takes a new medium and its accompanying disruptions to reveal the gaps that were already implicitly there."

distribute information between "here" (a source) and "there" (a destination). Transmission as a metaphor can be understood as unidirectional and linear (meaning that authorised information wanders from *a* to *b*) or instead as a bidirectional dialogue (some information is transmitted from *a* to *b* in exchange for other information moving from *b* to *a*).[48] This also encompasses attempts at message transfers that are addressed at large and dispersed audiences – and in this case quite often correspond with the *irritation* function of mass media as described by Luhmann.

Successful irritation relies on information that is considered new and disquieting enough to prompt some receiving party to focus their attention on the news in question – to react, in other words. This kind of effective transmission is needed whenever targeted groups or communities ought to take specific (counter) measures within short intervals of time. Successful transmission of a message does not automatically guarantee for adequate behaviour at the other end: Whenever some specific reaction is expected (such as when imminent danger lurks, and the alarm signal might provoke confusion rather than initiate an evacuation), the transmission of the irritating warning is better complemented by established, reassuring rituals as to *how* to react within the said case of emergency.

If we consider the enormous complexity of such tasks, it seems no wonder that transmission issues have always been predominant subjects of worry within communication science. In the words of Peters (1994, 125): "A history of communication theory could be written in terms of the anxiety of messages being lost in transit."

On the other hand communication also seeks to fulfil what Luhmann addresses as *integrative* function: We are, as social beings, in constant need of reassuring ourselves where we belong. Communication, precisely, provides us with the means for symbolic belonging (Carey [1975] 1988, 18):

> "A ritual view of communication is directed not toward the extension of messages in space but toward the maintenance of society in time; not the act of imparting information but the representation of shared beliefs. [...] The archetypal case under a ritual view is the sacred ceremony that draws persons together in fellowship and commonality."

Some communication attempts may be directed at an effective message transfer rather than the establishing of mutual relations over time. A team of surgeons will

---

[48] In earlier writings (Luhmann, in Habermas / Luhmann 1971, 43) communication is described as a mutual actualisation of a shared common sense that provides information to at least one participant in the communication activity.

perform a series of tests to make sure that an organ donor's blood-type matches that of a hopeful recipient, while "bonding" between the surgeons or with the patient in question is relegated to a mere side effect. In other instances ceremonial aspects can take the upper hand – such as when the same surgeons get together and check on their patient years after the operation, just to find out how things moved on from there and to celebrate, hopefully.

In contrast to these model constructions of communication, most everyday communication situations do lack the framing cues which might be precise enough to prevent divergent interpretation in different situations by different communication partners.[49] According to Luhmann, the respective misunderstandings are – not surprisingly – a default option of communication rather than the exception.[50]

In a more recent article Peters argues that parasocial interaction – that is, conversation simulated in imagined relationships with well-known media protagonists – should be relieved from its stigma as a psychic disturbance (Peters 2006, 120):

> "Why is it a sign of mental illness to converse with entities that cannot quite reply – walls, books, oneself, or TV sets – when one-sided conversations are actually fitting for all kinds of settings, such as writings, prayers, reading, reverencing the dead and communing with babies, pets, or plants?"

In other words: While it may be futile to expect much significant news from a wall, a TV set, some dead person or a pet – or some mute basketball, for that matter – all of these entities can become perfect communication partners for the sake of relieving tensions and for feeling less alone in the world.

Carey's reflections on the ritual model envision those engaged in a communicative relationship not so much as "sender" and as "receiver" of a message (and thus as assuming more or less responsibility within the respective process) but as partners expressing some mutual interest in being close, be it through synchronised action or through the shared reference to a common ground (see here, Table 1).

---

[49] For examples see Tannen (1990; and here, chapter 5): She claims that women are socialised to emphasise relational, or ceremonial, aspects of communication while men are brought up to focus on the transfer aspects of communication (in order to be brief and effective). This implies that Carey's two notions of communicative goals can also be interpreted as (gendered) communicational "skills".

[50] Luhmann (2000a, 97): "Normally, ambivalences and misunderstandings are borne along as well, as long as they do not block communication; indeed, understanding is practically always a misunderstanding without an understanding of the mis."

Table 1: Two views on communication (Carey 1988, 14-18)

Transmission view	Ritual view
Transmission of signals or messages	Gathering
from A to B	of participants
in space	in time
to the purpose of control	to the purpose of sharing
at stake: imparting of information	at stake: representation of shared beliefs
for the sake of the message's extension [51]	for the sake of society's maintenance [52]

Carey's reflection can be interpreted as an explicit invitation to view the realm of popular culture as a secular, (post-)modern complement to what used to be the realm of religious worship, with its holy places, sacred times and the ordinary as well as extraordinary ceremonies of reverence and contemplation complemented by the respective universes of fiction and game-play. What Carey summarises as "representation of shared beliefs" is then easily recognised within the various forms of fan communities devoted to the analytical dissection and (more or less reverent) reproduction of popular culture phenomena. Equally telling examples of communities based on communication rituals are the moral panics that regularly follow up some mediated scandal (Carey 1998) and the standardised circulation of celebrity-oriented mythologies within the "people" columns and respective yellow press sections (for this see Turner 2004, and Dubied 2008).[53]

---

[51] Carey (1988, 14): "The transmission view of communication is the commonest in our culture – perhaps in all industrial cultures – and dominates contemporary dictionary entries under the term. It is defined by terms such as 'imparting,', 'sending,' 'transmitting,' or 'giving informations to others'. It is formed from a metaphor of geography or transportation. [...] The center of this idea of communication is the transmission of signals or messages over distance for the purpose of control."

[52] Ibid., 18: "In a ritual definition, communication is linked to terms such as 'sharing,' 'participation,' 'association,' 'fellowship,' and 'the possession of a common faith.' This definition exploits the ancient identity and common roots of the terms 'commonness,' 'communion,' 'community,' and 'communication.' A ritual view of communication is directed not toward the extension of messages in space but toward the maintenance of society in time; not the act of imparting information but the representation of shared beliefs."

[53] In societies based on democratic models consent is not a necessary condition for the building and maintenance of the community. On the contrary: Dissent is an

Carey conceives mass-mediated culture not as a "one way ticket" that is created to appease the masses than as the object and means of an ongoing dialogue that resembles interpersonal communication in its basic structure and function. Peters goes even one step further by suggesting that mass communication might be the more genuine – and the more user-friendly – of the two communicative forms: For him the "spreading of seeds" (in reference to broadcasting as his example) comes closest to what we usually do when struggling to "get through" to somebody (Peters 1999 and 2006). It is certainly the less obtrusive, or obliging way since feedback is possible yet remains optional.

Peters' "gaps" are understood here, again, in a fundamentally human sense and do not apply to long-distance and / or dispersed forms of communication alone. In Peters' view the line between face-to-face and mediated communication was blurred from the beginning (Peters 2006, 125): "Dialogue only lets one voice speak at once. If we are serious about finding democratic forms of communication, we should appreciate formats that allow many to take part at once: singing, voting, dancing, striking, worshipping, protesting, cheering, petitioning. Watching and listening can be intensely active practices – as audience researchers tell us – and they are collective forms."

2.5 Conclusion

Ritual aspects, as described by Carey, are an integral part of communication processes.[54] Following Peters, mass communication is not so different from interpersonal communication and not so much different from more recent forms of digital (synchronous or remote) communication either. Following Luhmann, conceptual differences between media systems need to be taken into consideration when analysing communicational forms and functions – but as differences in scale rather than principal differences. Carey's model sees society as shaped not only by strategic operations of information transfer across space, but also by processes of deliberate redundancy which produce common knowledge (in terms of common sense) through the continuous repetition of what is already known over periods of time.

---

indispensable precondition for testing some system's resilience and its capacity to handle core ambivalences.

[54] For interpersonal communication Goffman (1967); for mediated rituals also Becker (1995), Liebes / Curran (1998), Rothenbuhler (1998), and Sella (2007).

Communication works as a two-sided operation, then. At stake is control of access to symbolical goods that are considered valuable and / or dangerous (in the case of irritating information and its correct handling and understanding). At stake is also the production and maintenance of society itself, in terms of ongoing processes of inclusion and exclusion and symbolical belonging. Both endeavours are risky and necessarily hampered by in-built, systemic errors that relate to the human factor at work. This is why the chances of success are and remain scarce, and why there are always complex maintenance operations and repair works under way.

The wide range of conversational *and* disseminative forms of communication offered by digital media of the third level will certainly change existing media practises and expectations over the years to come. They will alter our perceptions of media and let us see traditional distinctions between more or less "dialogic" forms of communication in a more differentiated light.

As for the default operations of social interaction, we shall go on transmitting signs of understanding in response to what is uttered by some individual or social "other", even if there is no guarantee that such an understanding might indeed take place. This goes for both "perception" and "communication" – the two operations of closed autopoietic systems (more specifically, of individuals and social systems) seeking to establish contact while, at the same time, trying to maintain cohesion within the system-borders at stake. By way of such operations communication enables social systems to function, but also to vary and adapt those functions in response to social challenges and changes.

Seen from a systemic perspective it is not so important to know *what kind* of understanding results from such an operation as communicative process (or, what message is actually transmitted from *a* to *b*): Its success lies within the mutual agreement *that* some understanding has taken place.

With regards to the reality aspects of mass media Luhmann confirms that communicative efforts made by and through public media are just as risky and misleading as any other communicative attempt (Luhmann 2000a). Mass media add to the complexity of meaning-making tasks at hand, by the sheer amount of symbolical material they continuously (and also increasingly) circulate. On the other hand they also facilitate communication by organising that material according to easily recognisable themes and by providing us with generic models and respective "labels". This leads up to the question if mass communication – understood here as addressing unspecific and undifferentiated large audiences rather than specific targets – [55] can still reach heterogeneous groups in a more globalised society, and in ways that cause such groups to feel connected over time.

If the answer is an optimistic "yes" – at least for the time being – it is an answer grounded in the conviction that mass media, in terms of elaborated and complex sign systems, do not circulate random or "raw" material, but material that is constantly boiled down, processed and customised for cultural consumption on a larger scale. It is also based in the observation that for "virtual" communities to have a good reason to get together the program strands of mass media do still provide some basic source from which all further discourse emanates.

In other words: We are fairly aware of what to expect in terms of reading, listening and viewing before we open the book or newspaper in question, before we turn on the radio or television set or step over that threshold from the lobby into the (movie) theatre. It is this awareness, rather than the mediated text or event as such, which can assure us that we are about to engage with people – in terms of persons with a somewhat expectable behaviour – in a mutual process of sense-making with regards to what we read, or get to hear and see. As persons or "artefacts of social communication", as Luhmann puts it (1995, 72), we all will "[...] contribute to generating further communication – whatever the individuals involved might be thinking at the time".

Communication is not a linear process, then. It is not necessarily linking two (or more) ends, and neither is it solely transmission-oriented. Rather than on rational choices and successful hook-ups ("you have new mail!") it relies on shots in the dark and aborted tasks ("delivery notice failed!"). It is – in the words of John Durham

---

[55] In accordance with Carroll (1998, 12-13) I refer to mass-mediated contents – or "mass art", as he prefers – as industrially produced and broadly distributed materials available to different, and distinct aggregates of large and heterogeneous audiences. Carroll's definition for mass art as "easily accessible art" does not imply that all of the contents do reach (and automatically indoctrinate) masses of people within a limited territory such as a nation state or a linguistic region. In complex information societies relying on communication networks reaching beyond territorial boundaries the term of the "mass audience" can just as well refer to disparate aggregates of (smaller) audience segments sharing comparable cultural tastes and / or common interests and responding similarly to more individually customised, personalised offers. Carroll insists however that a significant part of industrially mediated content will always appeal to "vast majorities of people" (ibid., 13) and delineate some common cultural ground for targets identified, for instance, by age, gender or lifestyle.

Peters – *made of gaps*, but nevertheless exists as a social fact that rules our daily lives, lets us cope with our innermost hopes and fears and interferes with whatever we expect from some more or less significant other. Be it only for that essential need implied by Flusser, by Luhmann, Peters and Carey: to feel less lonely on our own personal island.

This is to be kept in mind when I turn now to narrative communication as a remarkably successful, variously tested and therefore sufficiently promising mode of knowledge transfer and ritualist knowledge assurance – or as a regulating operation that provides well-measured doses of irritation and integration.

3   EPISODIC NARRATIVE AS COMMUNICATION

This chapter establishes the characteristics of narrative communication and highlights the particular qualities of episodic narrative communication. The keywords are "knowledge" and "time", with *memory* described as observations backwards in time and *anticipation* described as observations forward in time. According to Paul Ricoeur these are the core elements allowing for narrative communication to happen.

What are narratives made of? One might claim with Seymour Chatman (1978) that "existents" and "events" are the core elements of storytelling – with the main questions pertaining to *what happens to whom, and why*. Others scholars point to the reflective stance of narrative communication recalling *what is past and gone* and can be recaptured only by way of narrative construction.

In the following chapter I maintain that action and reflection – or what actually *happens*, with regards to what is *left out* and must be inferred – account for the specific dynamics of storytelling. While an analysis of narrative action makes perfect sense within a theoretical framework based on social action, the analysis of "gaps" demands, by default a more reflection-oriented approach. It is here, within the undetermined spaces purposefully or accidentally left open for further reflection, where events become graspable as such, and narrative expectations rise. It is the stage where observation occurs and interpretive selections are made about what to remember and what to forget.

The functionalist framework of social systems theory does not offer ready-made theories of narrative communication. Instead it provides interesting implications that invite to be coupled with more explicitly reflection-oriented stances on narrative communication,[56] with the notion of "open texts" and, in the case of serial narratives, with many of the characteristics institutional indeterminacy has to offer.[57]

---

[56] See Ricoeur: Time and Narrative ([1983-85] 1984-88).

[57] See Barthes: S/Z [1970] 1974; Iser: Indeterminacy and the Reader's Response in Prose Fiction [1970] 1971; ibid.: The Implied Reader ([1972] 1974); and ibid.: The Act of Reading ([1976] 1978); and Eco: The Open Work ([1972] 1989); ibid.: Lector in Fabula ([1979] 1979); ibid.: Innovation and Repetition ([1984] 1985, 1990); and ibid.: Six Walks in the Fictional Woods ([1994] 1994).

3.1 Narrative as art

Narrative communication is widely acknowledged as "a semiotic phenomenon that transcends disciplines and media" (Ryan 2005, 344). It is also the most common art form there is. While most of us develop into skilled storytellers over the course of our lives, we would probably hesitate to call that cultural technology an "art".

A functionalist perspective frames storytelling as a social operation. Narratives invite participants to assume an observational stance that depends on institutional roles selected, and assumed, before the communication begins. There are two types of role-taking: A more hierarchic role-taking of narrator(s) versus narratee(s) assumes the imparting of knowledge to be at stake, with said circumstance mutually agreed upon by all involved of the telling. More collaborative forms of role-taking do invite co-narrator(s) as partners in an ongoing endeavour. The respectively framed communication is necessarily dialogic; it also infers the mutual inclusion (or: exclusion) of further parties expected to be worthy (or: not worthy) to participate. Both situations frame narrative communication as an ongoing process of anticipation and recollection. Rephrased in Luhmann's terms, it works as an operation of double contingency and aims at the subsequent transition of *open* (.... as yet undetermined) contingencies in *closed*, or determined, contingencies.

Such a perspective conceives storytelling indeed as an *art*, and namely as a second-order observation (i.e.: observation of observations) of what is recognised as narrative event (= some action, happening, or state) and *therefore* deemed worthy of being told.[58]

In the following reflection on the artistic function of narrative communication I maintain that such ventures are highly paradox. If storytelling has the potential to successfully reduce social complexity, then the necessary selections (of what to tell and what to withhold) must rely on complex codes and conventions. If the framework demands some critical distance ("Beware: story follows!") then the acceptance of particular roles (e.g. active narrator, interactive co-narrator or allegedly "passive" narratee) asks for considerable leaps of faith ("Listen, and ye will know!"). This double-bind structure is an important aspect of what renders narratives suitable for

---

[58] By interpreting narrative as "art" I do not claim that each and every type of story has that pedigree. In Luhmann's terminology "art" is a label assigned to (groups of) symbolically generalised media by initiated members as experts (see Luhmann 2000, and Baraldi / Corsi / Esposito 1997, 104): Labelling something as "art" is information enough for the initiated to understand and accept.

the social task to mend the gaps that arise from communication across disciplines and media – or, at least, to remind us of their existence.

Narrative gaps, when interpreted as yet unmarked spaces within some emerging tale, can be (re-)assigned particular meaning at any point in the telling process, and by any party involved in the communicative attempt. Viewed from Luhmann's perspective, narrative communication allows us to collectively perceive what individuals as psychic systems as well as social systems perceive – which makes it an exceptionally powerful tool, or lens for social reflection.

In an early essay (Habermas / Luhmann 1971, 43) Niklas Luhmann describes communication more generally as the mutual actualisation of sense that informs at least one of the participants within said communication.[59] In the case of narrative communication such actualisations arise not from some univocal claim of conveying information as a novelty, but from prior mutual agreements to rearrange narrative events in patterns that allow at least one of the involved parties to be surprised over the course of the telling. In this respect narrative communication can be understood as a (gradual, subsequent) leaking of knowledge from one participant in the communication process to other participants, based on reciprocal operations of anticipating and reassessing.

Further up, communication was described as based on *double contingency*, i.e., mutual expectations based on trust or mistrust: Ego can safely engage in communicative attempts with alter once some common ground has been established to start from and an assumed agreement (or: disagreement) reached with regards to the common goal of the encounter. In the case of storytelling such agreements are deliberately sought out and made explicit even before the telling begins and before the tale in question unfolds.

Whereas conversational, everyday narratives are concerned these conventional procedures help narrators "gain control of the floor", as Neal R. Norrick puts it (Norrick 2000, 1):

> "Generally, one conversationalist becomes the storyteller, while the others become listeners. The teller introduces the story so as to secure listener interest, gain control of the floor and ensure understanding. Then the teller must

---

[59] Trad. ugb. Luhmann's quote in German: "Kommunikation ist gemeinsame Aktualisierung von Sinn, die mindestens einen der Teilnehmer informiert." *Information* is understood here in Bateson's sense (1972, 381) as "a difference which makes a difference in some later event".

shape remembered materials into a verbal performance designed for the current context. This may include interruptions and comments from listeners; indeed, recipients may seek to redirect the story line, to reformulate its point or even to become full-fledged co-tellers of the story. In any case, story recipients can apparently understand and evaluate the story they hear rapidly enough to respond appropriately to it, perhaps with matching stories of their own."

According to William Labov and Joshua Waletzky (Labov / Waletzky 1967 and Labov 1972) the conventional procedures that lead up to the telling of a story (or a co-telling in situations where addressees are in grade to intervene of their own) do provide the intended audience with a thematic overview of the story and an orientation to *where* and *when* the events-to-be-told supposedly took place. This is followed by the actual telling.[60] At the end – meaning: before the telling is over – there is often some personal reflection offered regarding the moral of the story (e.g. "lessons learned") as well as a short concluding summary of what became of the protagonists, be it right then and there or in some later stage of their further life.

Labov / Waletzky's six stages of storytelling (here, Table 2) are not exclusive to everyday oral stories but apply to conventionally packaged media narratives such as novels, feature films, news bulletins and documentaries, and broadcast entertainment. Here, programs conventionally open and close with "paratexts" including credits, trailers, teasers, summaries, codas and / or epilogues (for the term Genette).

Table 2: Six stages of conversational narratives (Labov / Waletzky 1967)

Stage	Description	Type of text
(1)	*preview*	*narrative framework*
2	*orientation*	*narrative framework*
3	*exposition*	telling of events up to climax
4	*climax, coda*	remaining events told
5	*evaluation*	*narrative framework*
(6)	*epilogue*	*narrative framework*

---

[60] The overview establishes the narrator's authority as source of knowledge; it also allows prospective audiences members to quickly assess the potential benefits of their personal investment in the narrative encounter.

Narrative communication, including mass-mediated narratives and serial narratives told in regular instalments over time, can thus be understood as a conversational strategy based on culture- and media-specific reading contracts. What is pursued as narration is a dialogic enterprise involving two or more parties. The stories generated are not the product of a single mind and imagination alone: Instead, they are conceived within and originate from participatory narrative networks.

Again, this does not imply that there is (... or should be) equality for all partners involved in a telling: As Norrick observed within storytelling in everyday speech, participants in narrative conversation assume default roles from the beginning. There is usually an agreement as to who tells and who listens, with the teller at least initially in control of *what* is told and *how* the telling proceeds. What circulates within such networks, and is remembered and perpetuated through subsequent narrative communication, can be used to legitimise a mutually acknowledged state of art, with the teller leading the way to such understanding. But it can just as well be used to undermine and overturn that state of art. This is why storytelling is such a powerful tool for generating, reinforcing and (depending on the participants' ongoing negotiation) deconstructing ideologies. Finally tales can also emerge from these purposely "staged" communications, and be shared and traded simply for pleasure and the contagious joy of trading and sharing.

Luhmann describes artistic communication as relegated to a state of *second-order observation*. Instead of simply observing (or describing) what is at stake, art takes a stance and perceives from an outside vantage point what observations (or discourses) are taking place that concern the phenomenon at stake. Such processes can have irritating as well as integrative function and even transcend systems boundaries to a certain extent (Luhmann 2000b, 48):

> "Art makes perception available for communication, and it does so outside the standardized forms of a language (that, for its part, is perceptible). Art cannot overcome the separation between psychic and social systems. Both types of systems remain operatively inaccessible to each other. *And this accounts for the significance of art.* Art integrates perception and communication without merging or confusing their operations."

Second-order observations, such as from a social system's artistic or scientific vantage point,[61] allow the said system to observe itself. Participants in artistic communication can (and must) alternate between an inside and an outside view. While

---

[61] For a discussion of the scientific perspective see Luhmann, Niklas: Die Wissenschaft der Gesellschaft. Frankfurt: Suhrkamp 1990, 1992.

they are at it they cannot *not* acknowledge the artificial, constructivist stance they temporally assume.

The setup of a specific narrative stage for the occasion of storytelling has two distinct functions: It establishes a common ground of expectations, and it defines the role of the narratee as a more or less initiated and knowledgeable person – as someone who is more "inside" or "outside" of the telling process and can thus operate on several levels of observation.

A useful concept in the discussion of the reader's involvement in authorised texts is Eliséo Véron's "communicative contract" (Véron 1985, 1991, and Adam / Revaz 1996).[62] When entering a narrative world as readers, listeners or spectators we enter a communicative relationship with whoever helped create and populate the world in question. The contract is based on generic conventions, and its binding "signature" arises from shared expectations as to what can be expected from the unfolding story. It can suggest to follow the more authoritatively marked pathways (suggested in news journalism, for instance) but just as well invite for evasive strolls through the narrative undergrowth (Eco 1994). While obedient readers may want to align their commitment and take their pleasures from the cues offered for an intended or dominant reading, other, more unruly practices will bend the implicit rules of the reading contract and gain their pleasures from alternative or oppositional readings that are considered fit (see Hall 1980, and especially Fiske 1991). This can only occur once the narrative stance and the information at stake are understood.

Mutual assignment of the correspondent roles of narrator and narratee binds participants of a narrative conversation for the duration of the telling. It also clearly marks the tale as a rhetorical construction that bears little resemblance to what is actually represented or "meant" here. The doubling of roles at both ends of the narrative encounter is sometimes indicated by use of the terms "implied or model author" and "implied or model reader" (see Iser 1974, Chatman 1978, 28 and again Eco's various writings). It is within the context of this role assignment that mutual expectations with regards to the narrative process are negotiated and played out.

---

[62] Véron's concept is based on the analysis of press coverage (1985); in a later essay (1991) he suggests to include radio and television messages as well. Similar ideas regarding "reading agreements" are found in Umberto Eco's writings (1979, 1985 / 1990, see below for additional references): He distinguishes two levels: an "ingenuous" (first level) readership, and a critical (second level) readership. He also claims that serial fiction does establish a more intimate pact with more knowledgeable readers *by default*.

Narrative contracts expose ego and alter as *cast* in complementary and interdependent roles which point back to the observational stance of ego and alter. They also expose what is being told as *staged* for the occasion of the telling. Didier Coste's model of narrative communication illustrates these relations (Figure 1):

Figure 1: Narrative as artistic communication (Coste 1990, 78)

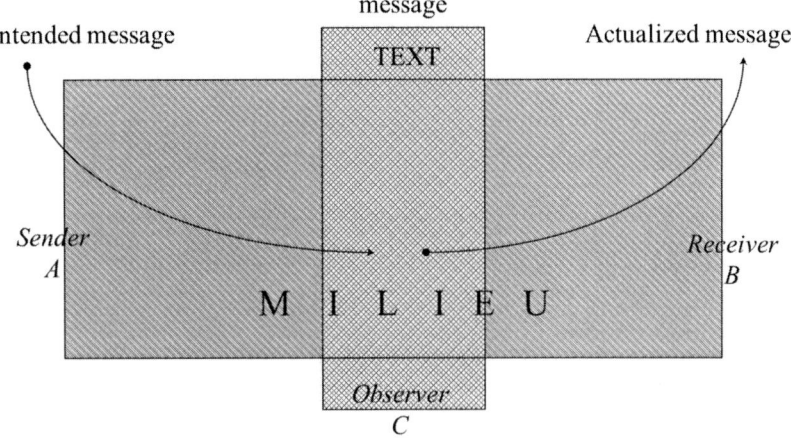

In Coste's model the "text" is conceived as the observable trace of the communication at stake; it stands as representative for some (mental) message intended on the sender's end and actualised on the receiver's end. "Sender", "receiver" and "observer" are seen as *functions* within the communicative situation, with the observer more specifically related to the text itself (since observation of the situation is only made possible in reference to a recording as material trace). Production and distribution of the text depends thus on a material support and – like all transmission – on a spatial distance between "sender" and "receiver".

According to Coste, four immaterial factors constitute the "milieu" setting the stage for narrative communication (ibid., 79):

- narrative rules which are combined within *codes*,
- narrative structures combined within *systems*,
- narrative needs (or desires) combined within dynamic *motivations*, and
- past communicative events combined within the *context* of the narrative situation at hand.

Coste's model reflects Flusser's semiotic stance as well as Luhmann's more constructivist view whereby all communication "bifurcates reality" (Luhmann 1992, 255) when providing conventionally coded cover versions of the world for the use of respectively socialised individuals as persons. However, while an action-oriented model of communication can always assume that social reality extends beyond communication (since communicative acts merely provide particularly meaningful representations of what is "out there") the functionalist paradigm is slightly more radical: Here communication produces a "yes" reality and a "no" reality, and what is left out of the communication simply ceases to exist – with regards to the selective observational behaviour of the conditioned persons, that is. In the case of narrative communication as rule-based structure all narration responds to particular narrative needs and expectations which are related to what was told before and earlier on. This means that what was left out by some telling is not necessarily lost and gone but can be understood as yet another invitation to anticipate and interpret further. In other terms: What is not narrated ceases to exist only when there is no more narrative communication to follow; in other words, when the story ends.

Narrative communication as a social art based on mutual expectations that are played out on a higher ground of self-consciousness can then succeed in integrating communicative action and communicative reflection. The gaps arising from this endeavour – i.e., narrative indeterminacies – allow for a reading as "unmarked spaces" hinting at more actions, happenings and states beyond what was made explicit, or made explicit *so far* in the telling. In terms of art, narrative communication reveals its constructivist condition and "blows the cover" of what is told, as it goes along.

3.2   Narrative knowledge

Narratives order events and put them in perspective. They relate to questions as to *what* came to be, *how* things happened, and (probably) *why*. According to the film theorist Edward Branigan (1992, 1), the telling of a story is a powerful strategy for making our world of experiences and desires intelligible: it is a fundamental way of organising data.

But storytelling is also a fundamentally creative activity and an effective means of world-making. In the words of Wolfgang Iser (1974, 280),

> "[n]o tale can ever be told in its entirety. Indeed, it is only through inevitable omissions that a story gains its dynamism. Thus whenever the flow is interrupted and we are led off in unexpected directions, the opportunity is given to us to bring into play our own faculty for establishing connections – for filling in gaps left by the text itself."

As the idea of the narrative "contract" or "agreement" implies, the imparting and (repeated, continuous) sharing of stories is a highly significant cultural practice within human societies. Narratives hold a central place in that large toolbox of operations devised to provide social irritation and integration and to negotiate collective identity over time. Pre-modern societies are said to be based on narrative discourse as the only means for knowledge transmission and knowledge preservation through time and space. In more complex societies, however, other systems of knowledge broking (such as science) came to substitute authoritarian and ceremonial storytelling as the primary source of information on the world "as we know it". If on the other hand, if Luhmann is right to assume the most relevant knowledge circulating within a more global network society concerns mass media events and personalities, then media narratives even more deserve our full attention with regards to what they selectively present as "world" and how they shape our understanding of the bits and pieces. Because, and I quote again Marie-Laure Ryan here (2005, 344), narrative is also "... what is left when belief in the possibility of knowledge is eroded."

In terms of etymology, the latin verb *narrare* is closely related to *gnare* ("to know, to make know"). As Nick Lacey (2000, 13) explains, the term is derived from the Indogerman root *gno-*, which is found in the Greek word *gignoskein* ("to know"), and in many other European languages where it relates to aspects of knowledge and / or recognition. This goes for French "connaître" / "connaissance" and Italian "conoscere" / "conoscenza", for English "(to) recognise" / "recognition", exactly, and for German "(er-)kennen" / "(Er-)kenntnis".

In his study on *Narrative Comprehension and Film* Edward Branigan identifies an initial "disparity of knowledge" as indispensable condition for what sets tales in motion and keeps the storytelling on track (Branigan 1992, 66):

> "Informally, one can grasp the importance of disparity by imagining a universe in which all observers are perfect and all-knowing. In such a universe, there can be no possibility of narration since all information is equally available and already possessed in the same ways."

Two forms of knowledge are to be distinguished, according to Branigan: *declarative* knowledge on the one hand (as a generalised form of "knowing that ...") and *procedural* knowledge on the other (i.e., pragmatic, applied "knowing how to ..."). But narrative knowledge depends also on what the narrative's characters (as agents) more or less explicitly anticipate with regards to the events at stake (ibid., 74-75): Ego as narratee expects and subsequently experiences as narrative action what specific characters do expect and experience with regards to particularly meaningful series of events.

Depending on how much story-related knowledge is subsequently leaked from narrators to narratees pertaining to the protagonists' whereabouts, choices and strategic decisions particular emotional responses are to be expected from more or less informed partners in the said communication: Alluding to crime stories (and Alfred Hitchcock's impeccably timed thrillers in particular) Branigan distinguishes between "mystery" (film viewers know just as much as protagonists, at any given moment in the evolving tale), "surprise" (viewers are left in the dark while protagonists already "know" and can act upon such major insight) and finally "suspense" (viewers are made to know slightly more than protagonists and can – or must – anticipate what is about to happen next).[63]

This means that mutual expectations between narrators and narratees do not simply emerge at the beginning of a tale and "catch up" once the tale's more or less convincing ending is imminent and closure attained. On the contrary: The narratees' expectations with regards to anticipated and subsequently revealed events vary in relation to what they can *momentarily* infer from the information available *up to that point* – be it from the unfolding story and interspersed clues, be it from the narrative framework or additional (for instance: genre-related) information, but maybe also from a prior reading or circulating rumours. The narrator's job is to cater to a variety of expectations, then, and to regulate the information flow so that anticipation can alternate with revelation in convenient doses.

An initial disparity of knowledge is usually established within the narrative framework, in terms of preamble of the communicative contract. It is what leads narrator(s) and narratee(s) to the *narrative surface* (a term coined by Monika Fludernik to describe the initial stages of a subsequent tale; see Fludernik 2006, 51 ff.) – and through that surface right to that first plotted, strategically set up event supposed to grasp the narratee's attention and keep it focused on the tale at stake.

A considerable part of narrative theory deals with the strategies a narrating instance – as the most knowledgeable party involved in the telling – applies when deliberately leaking *what kind* of explicit or implicit information *to whom* at *what point* in the unfolding narrative. The study of narration is also described as "the study of the

---

[63] In Hitchcock's *Rear Window* (USA 1954) viewers share the observational position of the protagonist who must, at one point, watch haplessly as danger closes in.

skills and procedures we apply in order to know narrative events" (Branigan 1992, 66).

Narrative communication results from the withholding of information just as much as from an imparting of information, then: What is not imparted (be it by deliberate omission or pure neglect) can nevertheless be inferred, based on former events and stoked anticipation.

In other terms: What is told by someone and thereby made knowledgeable to other persons partaking in the same narrative communication becomes valid only within concepts of *memory*. Narrative communication, both as an ongoing process of telling and as a resulting set of (intrinsically linked or loosely connected) tales, is about what a group, community or society wants or needs to be kept in mind.

Remembering is a loop-sided, biased process, though. A running theme or *leitmotif* within Luhmann's writing concerns memory's main function which is forgetting, to allow for even more information in terms of surprise, and irritation, to be processed and digested.[64] Only by ongoing selections of what to forget can we (as individuals, and as persons) go on to distinguish what is worth remembering. According to functionalist thinking the main asset of all recording devices is that they foster social amnesia: What is not recorded (or may have been recorded but was not sufficiently distinguished from other recorded material considered "rubbish") is just as lost for society as what was never uttered. Moreover (as with communication that cannot not communicate, according to Paul Watzlawick) it is not possible for individual or social memory *not* to make respective choices: What is made known by way of a telling draws from whatever has not been told – or has not been told *yet*.

What *is* remembered by way of a telling, though, is not to be taken for granted, once and for all: It is clearly applied, "natural" knowledge and as such comparable to a repeatedly reworked, well-digested manure. It can always be enhanced with further additives and once more dispersed as fertile ground for applications of shared beliefs, or collectively suspended disbeliefs. This understanding of narrative memory as "work in progress" goes for biographies and family histories – authorised or not – and for any form of institutional recording (and discarding) process that

---

[64] See Luhmann (1998, 579): "The main function of memory is to forget; to avoid the blocking of the systems once the results from former observations clot together." The same in German reads: "Die Hauptfunktion des Gedächtnisses liegt also im Vergessen, im Verhindern der Selbstblockierung des Systems durch ein Gerinnen der Resultate früherer Beobachtungen."

makes up for a particular group's, community's or society's official history. Especially for those ephemeral, necessary fragmented mass media memories (... in the sense of collectively explored and widely shared recognition processes) which I am particularly interested in.

According to Branigan, the narrative communication comes to its end when there is nothing (or, in Luhmann's terms: nothing of significance) left to be known further. But stories can also end based on an informal agreement pertaining to the communicative contract asking for some mystery, surprise or anticipated moment of nerve-racking suspense to remain unresolved and open-ended – at least *for now* and until some other agreement has been sought, and found.

3.3   Signs of time

Just as with narratives and knowledge, a close etymologic relationship exists between narratives and numbers.[65] "To tell" has the same linguistic root as the German verb "zählen" (= *counting*) or "er-zählen", (= *accounting for* or *re-counting*). Narrative communication as a telling of tales is also a counting of events. More precisely, a (selective) recollection of what actually or allegedly "happened" and emerges as series of events in hindsight and when all relevant telling, or counting, is done. This particular emphasis on narrative communication understood as a *retelling* rather than a *telling* or counting (of some knowledgeable facts or fictions) goes not just for the German language, and for its Italian ("contare" versus "raccontare") and French ("compter" versus "raconter") counterpart.

It is interesting to note that the procedure of "telling" refers in the English language to past events which are accounted for but also to the counting of numbers in relation to a monetary account. This means that "tellers" are not necessarily involved in

---

[65] There are, of course, other modes of artistic expression that rely heavily on mathematics, such as computer programming and music. While it is not that difficult to find affinities between music and mathematics (we need only look at the various notation systems for fixing some combination of melody and rhythm in time), the links between music and narrative are more complex. Often employed as a mnemonic device for narrative communication within oral cultures, music still has an essentially "bardic" function. It is used to convey slice-of-life-stories or as accompaniment to (or replacement for) spoken commentaries within audiovisual narratives (for this, see Levinson, 1996, and Kafalenos, 2004; for a discussion of the vocal and instrumental commentaries provided by *Miami Vice*'s musical score Buxton, 1994).

some storytelling but may just as well be professionals negotiating someone else's bank balance.

The common ground lies within the mathematical operation of "ordering" (events or sums) and in the "end result" emerging below the bottom line when all accounting is done and some end sum revealed.

Paul Ricoeur reminds us of the close relationship between the telling of numbers and the retelling of tales at the end of his trilogy on Time and Narrative where he suggests (Ricoeur 1984-1988, vol. 3, 241) that we "*take narrative as a guardian of time insofar as there can be no thought about time without narrated time.*"[66]

Ricoeur's statement points to an interesting dilemma: If time cannot be expressed other than as afterthought and in the guise of narrative reflection then narrative events are no longer likely to exist outside of a telling. Alfred Schütz came to a similar assumption earlier, with regards to the difficulties that we encounter when trying to grasp the very concept of individual action (Schütz 1945, 538):

> "In order to bring [actions] into view I have to turn back with a reflective attitude to my acting. [...] If I adopt this reflective attitude, it is, however, not my ongoing acting that I can grasp. What alone I can grasp is rather my performed act (my past acting), or, if my acting still continues while I turn back, the performed initial phases (my present perfect acting)."

Schütz distinguishes three stages of an individual's "action as an ongoing process": not only acting in progress (=*a ctio*) and action as performed act (= *actum*), and (ibid. 539) anticipated action as *projected action*, in terms of a "... rehearsing [of] my future action in imagination".

According to Schütz, and Ricoeur, human action is necessarily *reflected* action and related either to some psychic being's stream of consciousness (Schütz)or to a narrative recollection of some agreed-upon "order of events" as tale (Ricoeur). Communication of thoughts can consequently be described as a "... complicated mechanism of retentions and anticipations" (Schütz ibid., 543) and depends on mutually shared, conventional temporal settings in terms of civic, or *standard time* (ibid., 545).

---

[66] The original passage in French (1983-1985, vol. 3, 435) reads: "Sous forme schématique, notre hypothèse de travail revient ainsi à *tenir le récit pour le gardien du temps*, dans la mesure où il ne serait de temps pensé que raconté."

Narrative communication – and here I draw my own conclusions from Schütz and Ricoeur – can be described as a conveying of and mutual actualisation of (projected, acted out and finally reflected) actions with regards to conventional, time-bound settings within one of various shared and agreed-upon "provinces of meaning".

In his analysis of narrative communication Ricoeur offers a closer look at the individual stages of a telling with regards to some (projected, acted out and subsequently reflected) action. More specifically, he considers narrative events to be "prefigured" within the narrative framework leading up to some telling (*mimesis 1*), then "configured" within a particular text (*mimesis 2*) and subsequently "refigured" within the interpretive circles leading us to draw our own conclusions (*mimesis 3*).[67]

A model of this mimetic cycle pertaining to prefigured, configured and refigured events is proposed within Annik Dubied's doctoral thesis on miscellaneous news as narrative communication (Figure 2):

Figure2: Ricoeur's mimetic cycle applied to miscellaneous news (Dubied 2004, 130)

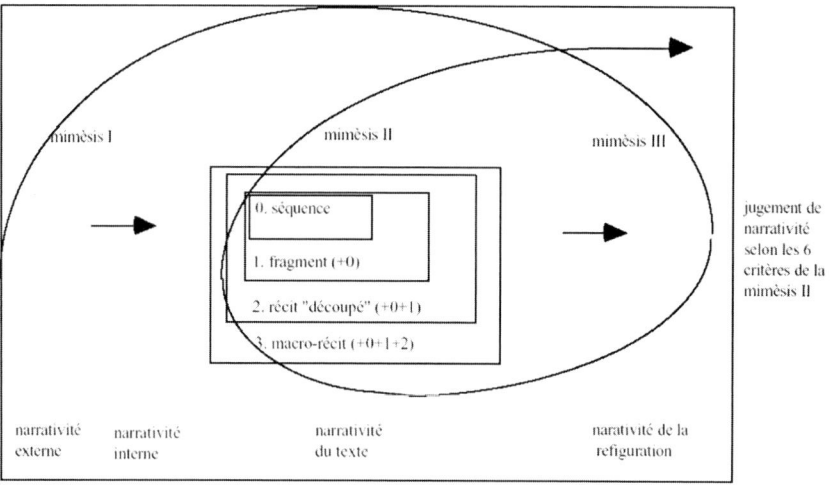

---

[67] *Mimesis* is a concept drawn from Aristotle's *Poetics* and translates as *imitatio*, the (artistic) rendering of a given concept. Luiz Costa Lima (1988, ix) precises the blueprint as "[r]ecognizable and acceptable according to the expectations engendered in the members of a given community by the criteria of classification in force in that community". According to Aristotle's teacher Plato (quoted in Chatman 1978, 111), *mimesis* specifies the present-bound performance of an imitative action, while *diegesis* is a narrative reflection on (past) action from a later vantage point. Distribution media of the second and third degree render the distinction between "showing" and "telling" increasingly difficult to behold.

What follows (here, Figure 3) is my own adaptation of Dubied's model with regards to narrative events:

Figure3: Ricoeur's mimetic cycle applied to narrative events

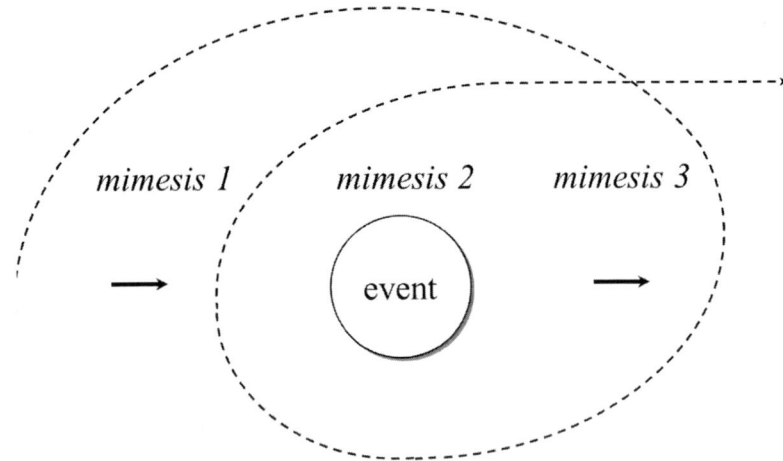

Aristotle's philosophical work served as Ricoeur's main inspiration here – just as it did for other Western media scholars venturing into areas of narrative theory and empirical application.[68]. The Aristotelian term for describing narrative anticipation is *prohairesis*, understood originally as "free will" or "reasoned choice" which alone makes human action possible. Wlad Godzich, in his foreword to Didier Coste's *Narrative as Communication* (1990, x-xi) refers to Roland Barthes' use of the term but interprets it further:

> "[Barthes] borrows the term prohairesis from Aristotle, who invoked it in the context of deliberative discourse to denote the future projection of a course of action, and simplifies its meaning to the rational determination of the result of an action. He recognises, however, that nothing is more difficult than to arrive at such a determination unless one knows beforehand what the outcome of the entire sequence of actions is going to be. Armed with this knowledge the analyst reads backward as it were and discards those elements that will prove unproductive, keeping only those that will contribute to the general result."[69]

---

[68] See Esslin (1987, *Aristotle and the Advertisers*), Hiltunen (2002, *Aristotle in Hollywood*) or Feyles (2003, *La televisione secondo Aristotele*). For an exhaustive analysis of Plato and Aristotle's contribution to the debate on entertaining fiction Stumm (1993).

[69] For an assessment of Barthes in regards to the *proairetic* and *hermeneutic* code see also Hagedorn (1995, 41 f.).

Stories, in Godzich's interpretation of Aristotle, come alive not simply as chains of "events" or "actions", but depend on complex processes of collective reflection. More particularly, stories are reconsidered and re-evaluated several times during a telling. With a nod to Coste's model discussed earlier we can identify these stages as

- the *tale that will be* (as announced within the narrative framework by a narrator as "sender"), then
- the *tale that is* (manifested within an observable "text"), and finally
- the *tale as recollection* which is subsequently actualised by narratees as "receivers" (within the conclusion of the narrative framework, and beyond).

If we refer once more to Ricoeur's model of mimetic cycles, stories emerge from ongoing reflections on narrative events within larger horizons of foreshadowing and recollection, as Figure 4 specifies (... all figures adapted from Dubied are my own):

Figure4: Ricoeur's mimetic cycle applied to prefigured, configured and refigured stories

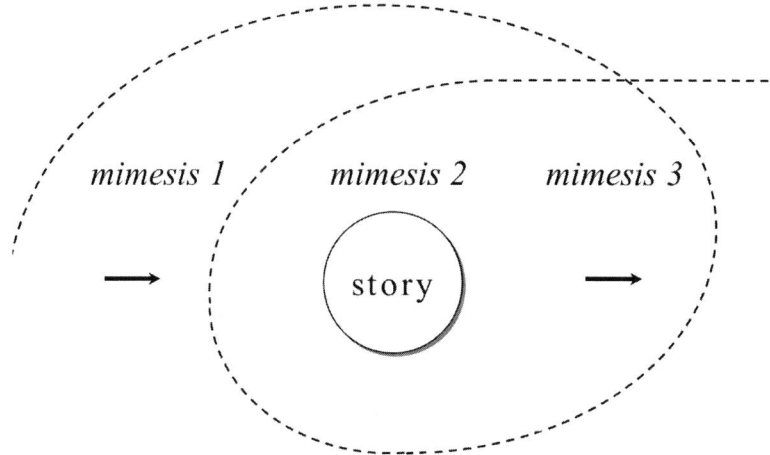

Ricoeur's (Aristotle-influenced) statement that there is no action possible (or: perceiveable) outside of a telling corresponds with claims made both by Schütz (for individual perception) and Luhmann (for social perception in terms of communication). Only within subsequent reassessments can an event become realised, and only within networks of narrative communication can (according to Luhmann 1992, 251) "... what we understand as action" emerge.

Plot-oriented theorists (such as Chatman, 1978) often underplay the reflective nature of narratives: As "events" do qualify *actions* and *happenings*. Both types of events supposedly relate to some decision-making within the set up of the narrative world.[70] Other theorists that are more particularly interested in character development over time – and thus in narrative reflection just as much as what is made explicit in terms of action – suggest to include descriptive *states* as well. Such states can refer to a character's introspection over time (Fludernik 1996) or to a simple penchant or predilection that sheds light on a particular character's personal motivation (Herman 2002).

3.4   Only narration can narrate

If Luhmann's assertion is to be believed that "only communication can communicate",[71] then we may just as safely assume that *only narration can narrate*. In the sense that only within narrative reflection can concepts of social action emerge and be realised – in hindsight. Can decisions be recognised as such and linked to specific "effects" as "causes". Can strategies be evaluated, and patterns of success and failure studied, and, finally, intentions inferred from (later) events in a telling – as motivated choices that lead up to some more or less responsible acting, with some more or less foreseeable outcome. In all of this narrative communication plays an indispensable role as structuring system and "telling" (= ordering as well as programming) social operation.

In one of his later conference papers Luhmann asks how decisions are supposed to be made within an emerging Information Society (Luhmann 1996). He defines as "decision" the opportunity to make choices between various alternative possibilities. Whoever decides transfers an open contingency into a closed contingency. At the same time a distinction is made between what was before and what comes after. Decisions "bifurcate" the flow of time – they set apart a *before* reality from an *after* reality and thereby allow to differentiate what is past (and observable as action) from what lies ahead (as yet unforeseeable and therefore unknowable future event).

---

[70] See Krützen (2004, and here, p. 211 ff.) for a discussion of backstory events and the way they influence decisions within mainstream Hollywood movies.

[71] See Luhmann (1992, 252): "[With regard to] the objection that ultimately it is the persons, individuals, or subject who acts or communicates, [...] I maintain that *only communication can communicate* and it is only within networks of communication that what we understand as action is created. [...] It is communication, not action, which is an unavoidably social operation and, at the same time, an operation that necessarily comes into play whenever social situations arise."

In order to have alternatives to choose from, social systems must activate specific memories (of a particular past that is chosen over other "possible pasts") and formulate specific expectations (that address a particular future, instead of other "possible futures"). Even if the operations cannot be accurate (for lack of reliable data) there is a fair probability that what is selectively remembered on the one hand "matches" what is selectively anticipated on the other. Meaning that we face another process of double contingency – here: over time – which can then lead up to sufficiently stable, fairly determined choices.

Narrative second-order observation demands us to make such choices continuously: We "bifurcate time" when we order narrative events in retrospect (i.e., what happens earlier in relation to what may be told later) and we set apart "pasts" and "futures" when identifying decisions as related to some character's motivation and reasons why.

The constructivist character of narrative communication goes beyond the bare facts told and beyond declarative knowledge. Whenever past events are connected recursively to other events it implies that some reasoned choice was made. Similarly, when further events are evoked which are more likely to happen than other imaginable events, their telling implies that the course of action is already, to some extent, determined. As soon as we "count" on something or somebody, we have practically inscribed this particular event(s) or agent(s) into an evolving narrative's course of action.[72]

The double contingency of the narrative contract is not one of a single, one-time anticipation, then: There are no narrators who *know*, once and for all, in contrast to narratees that *do not*. Instead, we should take into consideration fairly complex expectations pertaining to what can be known (... already, at that point) and what cannot be known (... yet), at specific moments in time and with regards to particular stages of an evolving tale. The resulting relations are "decision-sensitive" and procedural: They vary significantly with the kind of story at stake (which may be "finite" or still in full process) and vary with the narrative experience partners bring to the table as *cultural capital* (to quote Bourdieu, 1984). It is all about knowledge that

---

[72] Knudsen (2006, 81) questions how events might be operatively connected to other events within a system. The answer lies in two complementary operations: in recurrence to prior events and in the anticipation of following events. A system (here: a narrative) consists of such interdependent operations; it exists as "... a network of recursively connected operations" (ibid., referencing Luhmann's "Wissenschaft der Gesellschaft", 1990, 37).

circulated earlier – knowledge related to the story at stake, and knowledge related to generic conventions, and media literacy in general.

3.5 Narrative episodes

Because of its obviously constructivist stance narrative communication as art is hugely popular with overt constructivists, both in theory and practice.[73] Up to here narrative networks were presented as autopoietic systems in terms of "stories". Stories as social "systems" develop their sense-making potential only with regards to a telling. This is why narrative communication as a social operation depends on other narrative communication to follow. So far "stories" were described as well-ordered assortments of narrative events, with said "events" emerging from fairly determined, previously "plotted" stories. The construction of both relates to hermeneutic circles that have parties in a communication anticipate (or prefigure) narrative events which are configured within some material substrate and then reconfigured (or interpreted) in view of an emerging tale, or story.

What remains unclear is how such time-bound cycles of anticipation and recollection connect and can, at the same time, be linked to particular moments within an unfolding tale. From the thinking up of some action to the rethought action it may be a short step. But it is quite a leap from some more or less authoritatively prefigured set of events to some narratees' individual and collective reconfiguration and "ordering" of the storyline(s) at stake. Not just one "gap" to be mended or minded, but a multitude of gaping holes, or abysses!

This is where *narrative episodicity* lends itself as a helpful theoretical concept and analytical tool. The American Heritage Dictionary (1992) describes an *episode* as "... an incident or event that is part of a progression or a larger sequence" or, alternatevely, as "... one of a series of related events in the course of a continuous account." And, thirdly, as "a portion of a narrative that relates an event or a series of connected events and forms a coherent story in itself; an incident" (within a picaresque

---

[73] According to Nancy Spivey (1997, 78-79), "[s]tories are of special importance in the constructivist conception because they are so central to human meaning making and play such a major role in various activities and practices." More recent areas of application include the organisation of the workplace and the negotiation of managerial leadership; see, for instance, Seely Brown, John / Denning, Stephen / Groh, Katalina / Preisak, Laurence: Storytelling in Organizations. Oxford: Butterworth-Heinemann 2004, and Denning, Stephen: The Leader's Guide to Storytelling. Mastering the Art and Discipline of Business Narrative. San Francisco: Jossey-Bass 2005.

novel, for example). In another application of the term the particular subject matter of this book is more directly addressed as "a separate part of a serialised work, such as a novel or play."

The term can both refer to a significant, strategically plotted unit of action within a sequence of interrelated events and / or to a relatively autonomous unit making sense all by itself. According to Martinez / Scheffel (2006, 110) episodes refers in their general use to relatively closed narrative parts but also to "side plots" within a more coherent narrative context – which also implies that there can be more or less autonomy accorded to an episode in relation to some overarching story told.

Edward Branigan distinguishes three types of particularly organised data to be found within ongoing narratives (Branigan 1992, 19): He describes *heaps* as "random collections of data or objects assembled largely by chance" while *catalogues* are said to collect and present objects in their relation "to a 'center' or core" of the telling. *Episodes* differ from these types of data organisation by their explicit relation to time and an inherent logic: The elements contained within an episode can "show change" as they move forward; they develop and progress. This is why episodes offer themselves as mnemonic devices (ibid.): "Because the parts of an episode are defined through cause and effect, it is easier to remember an episode than to remember the miscellaneous parts of a heap or a catalogue."

An episode can stand alone as an "unfocused" chain of cause and effects ("... with no continuing center") or is instead cast within a "focused" chain of cause and effects, with some continuity of action implied from episode to episode. A "simple narrative" can then be understood as "a series of episodes collected as a focused chain", with closure expected to occur at the story's end (ibid., 20):

> "Not only are the parts themselves in each episode linked by cause and effect, but the continuing center is allowed to develop, progress and interact from episode to episode. A narrative ends when its cause and effect chains are judged to be totally delineated. There is a reversibility in that the ending situation can be traced back to the beginning; or, to state it another way, the ending is seemingly entailed by the beginning. This is the feature of narrative often referred to as *closure*."

An interesting aspect stressed by Martínez / Scheffel (2006) is that narrative episodes do not necessarily refer to particular segments within a linear sequence of events but can also address separate, parallel story strands which are only loosely tied in with the main action's continuity. Such side plots are classical narrative devices used to reinforce or vary some main theme, be it within a romantic opera, a situation comedy or a police procedural. More complex narratives, on the other hand, allow for an indeterminate numbers of plotted strands to take centre stage in alternation: This is the case with ongoing soap operas and other forms of ensemble-oriented drama such as Steven Bochco's *Hill Street Blues* or Robert Altman's *Short Cuts*: The stories can then be perceived as interwoven "plaids" of parallel, ongoing storylines extending over a part or the full length of a story told.

Within more linear narratives, however, an "episode" indicates some coherent unit of action, related either to what renders the contained events specifically meaningful or related to what said unit of action will eventually contribute to an overarching (in Branigan's terms: "focused") chain of ordered events. As the term "unit of action" indicates there are mimetic cycles pertaining to episodes as intermediate chains of ordered events within a (here: more or less focused, or strategically plotted) tale (see here, Figure 5):

Figure5: Ricoeur's mimetic cycle applied to episodes as chains of events

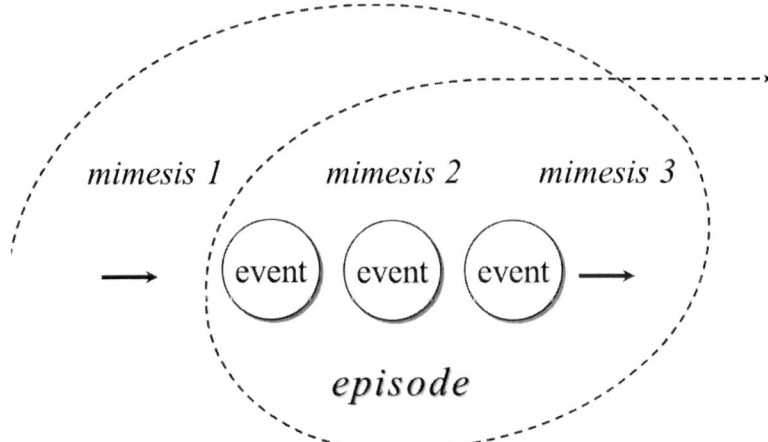

An episodic structure underlies all narrative communication. It is the visible trace of storytelling as manufacture. Depending on the time and care applied to finish and polish, the seams in-between episodes as textual unit can be more or less evident. Episodicity – i.e., a more overt manifestation of the seams – is characteristic for oral and less formal narrative communication (as well as narratives resulting from a participatory co-telling), whereas more literate, canonic and / or formalised narratives tend to emphasise the unity of the work as such.

As can still be sensed from the surviving transcriptions as written records, epic storytelling (such as Homer's narration of the fall of Troy and Ulysses' subsequent adventures) relied on verses and similes as mnemonic devices – and often some musical arrangements too (see for instance Ong 1980 and Havelock 1988, Honko 1995, Slatkin 1996, and Minchin 2001). The rhythmic structure of the "songs" provided both singers and listeners with regular pauses for reflection and thus helped to refocus in-between lengthy or winding passages.

If we browse through the history of episodic storytelling within Western literature, two distinct models emerge from the Middle Ages onwards: a "more focused" (or: goal-oriented) travelogue and "less focused" variations thereof. While pilgrims' accounts as well as other educational writings that were centred on religious topics appear organised in chronological chapters and clearly oriented towards a "continuing centre", the quest-oriented tales of medieval knights and minstrels followed a more autonomous and reiterative structure.[74] What results either as (auto-) biographically inspired account or as a series of chivalric exploits can be read as emergent literature between oral storytelling and the later novel (for details see Fludernik 1996, 115-128) or in the light of ideological undercurrents. Wolfgang Iser interpretes the courtly romances offered by Chrétien de Troyes as a literary reaction to radical changes unsettling the courtly society in 12th century France and undermined the feudal systems as a whole (Iser 1978, 77-78):

> "In order to reaffirm the courtly values, Chrétien [de Troyes] made his knights embark on various quests, in the course of which these values were tested and proven; the knights then returned home, thus stabilizing the courtly society which they had left. Isolation and reintegration form the pattern of all the adventures through which Chrétien presents both the departure of the knights from Arthur's court and their adherence to the values of that court. The adventures embody situations which are no longer covered by the social systems of the court. With its pattern of isolation and reintegration, the adventure fortifies the existing systems against the challenge of social change. Here, then, the function of literature is to remove a threat to the stability of the system."

It is interesting to note how various representations of the same chivalric genre have since – and especially within episodic literature from the 19th century onwards – been adapted from the same narrative *type* as particularly formatted *tokens* (in the

---

[74] For medieval pilgrims' accounts see Ganz-Blättler (1991), among other sources. Modern travelogues in literature and film seem to follow Branigan's "less focused chains of cause and effects". Their plot structure depends on the narrative's intention to either "go somewhere" or, alternatively, "go nowhere". Existential road movies such as *Easy Rider* (1969) and *Thelma and Louise* (1991) oscillate between these two forms, while many lightweight comedies such as the Italian movie *Tre uomini e una gamba* (1997) tend toward the less focused end of the spectre.

terminology of Umberto Eco, 1985 and 1990). This goes for printed magazines and newspapers (and the cartoon sections), early cinema film instalments, dime novels, radio plays and television series, more recently. Serial adventures referring to *Steve Canyon* as comic strip hero or the *Lone Ranger* (in radio and television), and *The Equalizer, The Renegade* or maybe *Walker, Texas Ranger* (not to forget *Hercules* and *Xena – Warrior Princess* as clearly postmodernist tributes to the original Greek and medieval ancestors) seem to just recycle upgraded versions of same traditional, semi-oral tales of wandering warriors and noble knights in shining armour. But they also had to learn how to assimilate new ideological undercurrents and how to integrate temporary irritations such as tough females kicking ass and displaying remarkable weaponry skills (for this, see Mizejewiski 1993, 2004, and Gwenllian 2000a, 2000b and 2004) or hefty doses of irony thrown in for good measure.[75]

While the finite, literary texts contained in written and electronic records such as books, audio books, videos or DVDs traditionally provide their readers, listeners and viewers with focused narrative chapters and a more distinct "sense of an ending" (to quote Frank Kermode, 1967), narrative role-playing games (both in their pen-and-paper- and computer-based variations) verge once more on the oral end of the storytelling spectre.

The heroic quests at the core of adventure games are not so different from their chivalric predecessors from the dawn of Western literature: Again, a chosen few of extraordinary gentle(wo)men face recurring challenges in the guise of action-packed and goal-oriented tasks. The obstacles do not necessarily follow a predefined chronological path as order of events, but can also appear randomly sequenced and may then be tackled at one's own pace and speed. If, however, there is some overarching, plotted logic programmed into the narrative world at stake, it will ask for decisions to be taken at particular moments within the evolving narrative which will further determine the course of action. Usually such scheming is revealed only at the end of the epic journey and in hindsight – which allows for players to assume different observing roles based on various levels of involvement, with regards to more than one visit, probably.

---

[75] For a discussion of the adventure genre and is essential ingredients see Cawelti (1976). For more on the particular structure of mythic journeys see Vogler (1993), based on Campbell (1949). Those "healthy doses of irony" do not necessarily originate with the popular text itself. In the case of *Walker, Texas Ranger* less respectful reconfigurations abound which have themselves achieved cult status (see http://en.wikipedia.org/wiki/Chuck_Norris_Facts (18-08-2017); kudos for the respective reference go to my late friend Alessandra Filippi.

The *pearl chain structure* of the typical action-adventure game is described by Aarseth (2004a and 2004b) as a series of unfocused individual quests that alternate with more focused, goal-oriented parts (the classical cut scene, for instance) which help newcomers to reassess the narrative scope of what is at stake. While experienced players may skip these time-consuming "detours" for extended periods of immersion within a virtual "here and now",[76] the less experienced player must nevertheless move back and forth – and pause – in order to understand the challenges at hand. Because at stake is not just action in terms of a playful *learning by doing* but, as always, reflection: here in terms of a gradual remembering and understanding of particular chains of causes and effects whose ultimate significance can be grasped only later on – once all episodes are known, and all levels of play mastered.

As this sketchy overview shows, episodes as particularly ordered chains of cause and effect can be oriented towards some macro or micro goal and appear more or less determined. They oscillate, in Luhmann's terms, between open and closed contingency. Suggested readings can presume focused or unfocused chains of events, and imply conformity to authoritatively prescribed dominant patters or foreground some ambivalent *double entendre* instead, depending on what narrative and social needs with regards to the handling of contingencies arise. The "gaps" of episodic storytelling are multifunctional, then: Episodic structure can significantly reduce narrative complexity when providing breaks as reflective pauses or, instead, add layers of complexity to simpler stories told, by way of some variation or focalisation.

Knowledge disparity within episodic narratives seems to be mostly negotiated at the "seams", then: It is here where (relative) *knowledge approximation* is provided.

3.6 The gaps of which episodic narratives are made

Episodic storytelling is usually associated with two types of narrative communication (Hagedorn 1995, 29): with *serial*, industrial texts as commodities on the one hand (i.e., media narratives widely distributed to attract and hook specific target groups) and with *conversational* discourses on the other (i.e., oral and informal

---

[76] Britta Neitzel (2005, 229) refers to Luhmann's concept of "expanded present", and I quote: "He assumes that the past sets in only from the point at which the changes resulting from a chain of actions are no longer reversible. Before that occurs, there is an expanded present in which certain tendencies for the future, though already introduced, could still possibly be steered in other directions. One could remain in this present, and possibly negotiate what should be. The future, then, would be open. in other words, a state of being is maintained, the result is not yet decided, and one is still in the process of fixing an outcome."

"everyday" storytelling). There is, however, a lack of scholarly reflection with regards to the functional similarities – and not just the structural differences – between the two realisations of narrative segmentation. This is possibly due to different research traditions established with either "literary" distribution media or "oral" communication in mind. Cultural Studies scholars were the first to bridge the gap and develop analysis models allowing for a critical assessment of segmentation across disciplinary and media borders.

Fiske / Hartley (1978) suggest to contrast the finite, or "literate", modes of cultural production with "popular" narratives that are constantly negotiated over time (see Table 3):

Table 3: Literate and oral modes (Fiske / Hartley 1978, 124-125)

Literate modes	Oral modes
Narrative	Dramatic
Sequential	Episodic
Linear	Mosaic
Static	Dynamic
Artefact	Active
Abstract	Concrete
Permanent	Ephemeral
Individual	Social
Metonymic	Metaphorical
Logical	Rhetorical
Univocal / "consistent"	Dialectical

Fiske's *Television Culture* reader (1987, 105-106) elaborates on the concept, considering *nowness* as an additional feature of oral narratives, understood in terms of
- a sense of the future that goes with an "unwritten" text,
- a direct, personalised address, and

- the production of a textual or cultural *experience*, rather than the accomplishment of a work of art.[77]

Instead of emphasising on yet another dichotomy (in his case: between finite and infinite artefacts) Horace Newcomb (1984) points to the basic dialogic nature of all narrative communication as *heteroglossia* (the concept was introduced by Bakhtin as synonym for "dialogism", 1981, and later translated by Julia Kristeva as "intertextuality"). For Bakhtin, and Newcomb, language is not the expression of one auctorial voice but of many voices, and inherently developed from cross-cultural and multimedia input. Plurilinguism applies to conversations as well as to mass media in general and is manifested in variations of genre and varieties of episodic instalments that follow similar moulds (which then allow for different characters with different problems to step into the foreground). The resulting impression is hardly one of discursive univocality (in the sense of ideological closure) but allows for a considerable bandwidth of voices to be articulated, heard, and understood, eventually.

Based on further reflections on the dialogic nature of mass communication as conversational art, the history of serial narratives has made remarkable progress across disciplinary and media boundaries (see for instance Hayward 1997, and DeForest 2004). However, an interdisciplinary history of *episodic* storytelling across media boundaries still waits to be written (for initial steps see Eco 1985 / 1990, for story cycles as "narrated narratives" Besson 2004, and Mielke 2006). This is also the reason why the very concept of episodicity within emerging and / or long-lasting storytelling practices is still best explained within common, "living" conversational narratives.

Elinor Ochs and Lisa Capps (2001, 6) point to open-endedness as an inherent property of informal narrative discourse. They conceive the difference between more authoritative reading contracts and more participatory storytelling agreements in terms of a "telling to" (from sender to receiver) and a "telling with" (... other participants as co-narrators). In both cases the position of narrator(s) and narratee(s) need to be negotiated within the "liminal space" extending between the individual consciousnesses involved.

---

[77] An example of an anthropological "reading" is offered by Florence Dupont (1991) with regards to the Homeric sagas and *Dallas*.

According to Ochs / Capps the episodic default structure of ongoing narrative conversations provides its participants with essential moments of temporary closure (ibid., 170):

> "Episodes have generally been treated as textual units consisting of an articulated chain of events that cohere around a focal character, topic, or goal. More recently, episodes have also been identified in terms of sustained organization of participants in the verbal interaction. In this perspective, episodes are jointly constructed by those involved in the communicative situation."

The ordering of events within narrative episodes is described as a collaborative effort inviting fellow interlocutors to "... knit actions, thoughts and feelings into an episode" and, subsequently, to "... weave episodes together into the narrative of our lives" (ibid., 170).

Ricoeur's suggestion to conceive narrative communication as a mimetic cycle of anticipation and recollection can once more be used as model here: Both the "knitting" and the "weaving" metaphor lend themselves beautifully to describe ongoing processes of prefiguration and refiguration, on the basis of events (micro level), of episodes (as focused or unfocused chains of events on a meso level) and of stories figured out so far (see here, Figure 6):

Figure 6: Mimetic cycles applied to stories emerging from episodic stories as chains of events

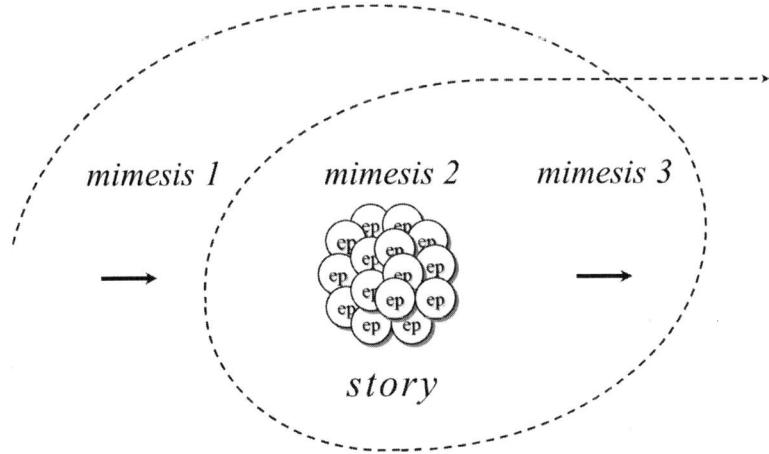

Narrative conversation, when conceived as a dialogic endeavour that transcends media and disciplinary boundaries (in terms of a "telling with", and in accordance with Fiske / Hartley), is just as much about episodes, about (more or less focused)

chains of cause and effects and the resulting (tightly or loosely knitted) textual units as it is about master narratives and seamlessly plotted arrangements of incidents. But the main asset of episodic narration lies in the space for reflection provided at the margins of each instalment and within the seams of the lingering narrative: Here is anticipation and recollection played out. And here is an overarching narrative logic – or, in functionalist terminology: some recursive connectivity of later events to former events – sequentially, and consequently established.

3.7   The particularities of episodic narrative communication

Whereas narrative *episodes* have been described as chains of events engaged in particular cause-and-effect relationships (with episodicity, as "visibility of the margins", characteristic for oral, ongoing and more informal narrative communication) *seriality* in general refers to (all) works of art "... published or produced in installments", as the Amercan Heritage Dictionary (1989) puts it. In theory, serial narratives do not depend on particular publishing dates; however *periodicity* is acknowledged as a main characteristic trait that distinguishes serial narratives from other (episodic) narratives. Because it is the repeated, ceremonially recurring announcement of "more to come" – at particular intervals and responding to a specific frequency of delivery – that makes interested readers, listeners and viewers collectively anticipate what is next in (the) store.

Academic enquiry on early publishing activities often uses the terms of *periodical* and *serial* as interchangeable synonyms (see for instance Meyers / Harris 1993). When contemporary storytelling is addressed the more general term is "serial" whereas references made to the "periodicity", as a recurrence based on regular publishing intervals, emphasise the frequency of the instalments and thus the distribution strategies applied to the case at hand. For the sake of this study I opt for *episodic fiction* as overarching term because the study does indeed focus on episodicity, and particularly on those gaps typical for recurring fiction that is distributed in distinct portions over time. In addition, the term *serial* has two distinct common meanings. It is used for the description of a *production mode* and, at the same time, for describing a particular *narrative form* (namely, the open-ended serial as distinguished from the closure-oriented episodic series). These terminological problems will be more specifically addressed later on in Part II of the present thesis.

Seen from the angle of an imparting as "telling to", serial (in terms of episodic, recurring) narration can be said to convey fairly similar "stacks" of knowledge over time. What results is not oriented towards some (new) information as surprise, but verges on the familiar, by this reproducing a closed cycle of narrative redundancy with each new instalment added (see here, Figure 7):

Figure 7: Circle of mimetic "redundancy" with regards to episodic narratives

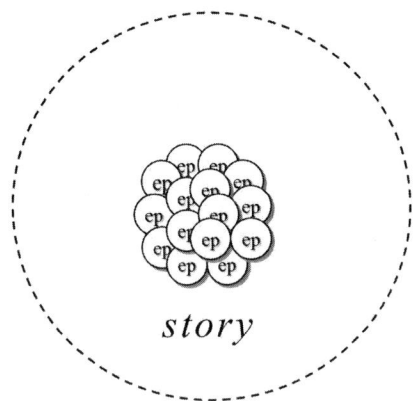

Narrative redundancy should not be seen as a vice, though. A ceremonial point of view conceives redundancy and the resulting bonds of familiarity (with the text as well as with partners involved in the communication) as an indispensable asset for the maintenance of communities Instalments providing "more of the same" (or rather: similar tokens as variations of an established type) may not convey much information as novelty and surprise. But they certainly produce knowledgeable readers over time. According to Umberto Eco (1990, 86), and in reference to "repetitive art" in general, the pleasures taken from mass-mediated series of (here: unfocused) narrative episodes stems not so much from the departure of the norm but rather from the constantly confirmed narrative scheme which remains largely invariant and can thereby cater to "... the infantile need of always hearing the same story, [that is] superficially disguised" (ibid.):

> "The series consoles us (the consumers) because it rewards our ability to foresee: we are happy because we discover our own ability to guess what will happen. We are satisfied because we find again what we had expected. We do not attribute this happy result to the obviousness of the narrative structure but to our own presumed capacities to make forecasts. We do not think, 'The author has constructed the story in a way that I could guess the end,' but rather, 'I was so smart to guess the end in spite of the efforts the author made to deceive me.'"

But gleeful recognition is only half of the story. Umberto Eco's ambition is two-fold: On the one hand he attempts to compile a "typology of repetition" – as the original Italian title of the essay reads – which results in the following Figure 8 (next page):

Figure 8: Eco's "typology of repetition" (1984, 21; adapted from original)

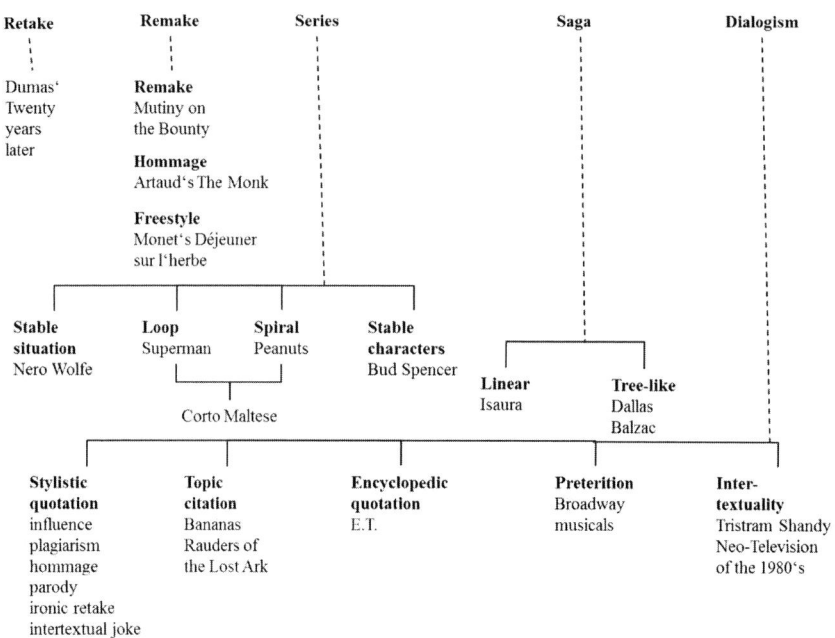

The comparison of various types of repetition across high-brow art (such as literature, classical music and the pictorial arts) and low-brow art (comic strips, mainstream film and television) serves merely to identify that very boundary as illusory. On the other hand it emphasises a shift in focus from the artist (in terms of what she or he might want to tell us) to the reader. As Eco himself admits (see 1985, 178, and 1990, 96), such "... a typology of repetition does not furnish the criteria that can establish differences in aesthetic values." Valorisation is instead negotiated in reference to the reader's prior acquaintance with the artwork in question which bears on what respectively cued reading will ensue, either as a more straightforward one that refers to a first level of observation while reconstructing what the author wants to convey, or as a more informed, more "knowledgeable" second-level reading that takes its cues from the privileged access to the ceremonial performance at stake.

In "The Role of the Reader" (1979) Eco already distinguished two variations of literature consumers as potential "lectores in fabula": One he describes as inclined towards the closed contingencies offered by more fully developed, "finite" literary texts (which Barthes, in S/Z, calls "readerly") and one instead quite content with the open contingencies provided by less determinate (or, "writerly") texts. From this earlier distinction Eco draws his own concept of the narrative contract, in terms of reading agreement between producers and consumers of serial narratives that must take into consideration the less acquainted tourist and the experienced series' regular who is fluent enough to operate from various observational levels (see Eco 1985, 174, and similarly 1990, 92):

> "Every text presupposes and constructs always a double Model Reader (let us say, a naive and a 'smart' one). The former uses the work as semantic machinery and is the victim of the strategies of the author who will lead him little by little along a series of previsions and expectations; the latter evaluates the work as an aesthetic product and enjoys the strategies implemented in order to produce a model reader of the first level. This second-level reader is the one who enjoys the seriality of the series, not so much for the return of the same thing (that the ingenuous reader believed was different) but for the strategy of the variations; in other words, he enjoys the way in which the same story is worked over to appear to be different. [Etc.]"

Postmodern art is said to address the sophisticated *connaisseur* more explicitly. This goes for Andy Warhol deliberately blurring the boundaries between high art and convenience food, and for any quality television series such as *Columbo* that knowingly exploits patterns of redundancy and variation while featuring the names of notable cinema *auteurs* as directors. But similar double readings can be expected from comic strips featuring superheroes that revel in recursive story *loops* and from Charles Schulz' *Peanuts* strips that play out repetitive patterns and only minimally adapted panels to knowing patrons in increasingly complex variations, or *spirals*, over time (for this see Eco 1985, 169, and similarly 1990, 87):

> "In the stories of Charlie Brown, apparently nothing happens, and any character is obsessively repeating his / her standard performance. And yet in every strip the character of Charlie Brown or Snoopy is enriched and deepened. This does not happen either with *Nero Wolfe*, or *Starsky and Hutch*: we are always interested in their new adventures, but we already know all we need to know about their psychology, their habits, their capacities, their ethical standpoints."

In the example of the *Peanuts* strips tension is built from a subtle interplay in-between later episodes and earlier, well-remembered ones where recursive connectivity emerges as an asset that distinguishes both episodic narratives from other, more seamless narrative forms, but also narrative communication from other forms of communication. Mutual contingencies of "normal" communication emerge transformed when long-lasting relations between communication partners are established that may still rely on trust or mistrust, but can count on a common base – namely, shared familiarity with narrative patterns.

Eco's discourse on "Innovation and Repetition" clearly focuses on redundancy and variations of textual types within recurring instalments as tokens. But there are implicit hints at further complications that may await the more knowledgeable consumer of episodic narratives. Once the gaps between separate episodes are acknowledged to be reflective pauses rather than voids (think of one *Charlie Brown* panel and the next – and one annual football-kicking incident and the already anticipated next one) they develop a remarkable creative potential of their own. This is why Roger Hagedorn (1995, 28) establishes episodicity as *the* crucial trait that distinguishes serial narratives from finite narrative texts, "… that is the single-unit realistic narrative, including the novel in book form, the feature film, the radio play, and so on." While such traditional narratives allow for consumption in their entirety, the serial presentation denies any such control; it "… places consumers at the whim of the medium that presents them (or, more precisely, at the whim of those who command the medium that presents episodic narrative texts)."

But narrative episodes do not just deliver audiences in regular intervals to media institutions (which explains why there are so many of the expensive audiovisual serials developed from commercial sponsoring activities). Narrative episodes also cater in ideal ways to narratees' expectations by regularly transferring open contingencies into closed contingencies. What could only be anticipated and guessed so far is now realised and known. But at the same time such freshly acquired knowledge only exemplifies all what cannot be known (yet) about the series' narrative course. According to Hagedorn (ibid.), serial narratives break with the three classical narrative unities established by Aristotle: Multiplying the elements of time, space, and character variation allows "for infinitely greater narrative complication", here. But serials also multiply "the number of narrative enigmas as well as partial answers, snares, delays, and so on that are activated in the course of the narrative."

All of this adds to the characteristic indeterminacy of serial storytelling – with the delays regularly provided at an instalment's end and across the narrative breaks (in the case of soap operas and telenovelas) contributing even further to the distinct sense of a suspended, or deferred determinacy. However, within the seams of a fading episode moments of (temporary, and approximate) equality of knowledge are reached and a recollection is possible with regards to what happened so far, while anticipation inevitably leads over to what is about to happen next. Chances are also offered for reassessing the assumed roles within the communicative contract – implying that roles are maintained for the time being, or shifted towards a more collaborative "telling with", or strategically usurped in the light of the textual units as "chains of causes and effects" yet to come.

This brings me right back to the beginning of this chapter. Narrative communication is often considered a linear and hegemonic enterprise, a "telling to" with the purpose to impart meaning from A to B. In Branigan's narrative model the story is over – and closure attained – when all story-relevant knowledge has been successfully imparted from sender to receiver, with both parties ready to step down from the communicative contract and move on with their lives. As long as the communication lasts, however, a negotiation of knowledge takes place, and someone is made *more* knowledgeable about particular chains of cause and effects.

The gaps between (more or less autonomous and distinct) narrative episodes serve on the one hand as orientation markers, like those emergency lighting devices supposed to guide us to the nearest escape route within a lengthy tunnel or a smoke-filled aircraft. As such they delineate recursive narrative outlets while at the same time inviting us for making use of our own recombining faculties. But episodicity is also a powerful narrative strategy that allows us to regroup (or: refigure) narrative events within larger sequences of causes and effects as particular units of meaning.

Depending on the observer's perspective and interest, such intersections of regrouped actions, happenings and states can be linked to other narrative units and thereby produce new meaning. And so forth: There is hardly a limit as to how more or less articulated chains of events can be "mimetically" refocused and subsequently integrated within further narrative communication, and what we perceive and communicate as social reality – i.e., Schütz' various "provinces of meaning" – can subsequently be episodically "mapped out" and explored (or analysed, from a second-order perspective) with a number of scales in mind. More specifically, narrative gaps can be said to refer

1. (with regards to evolving plots) to episodes in terms of narrative building blocks, or threads, that negotiate a structural middle ground between narrative events as basic unit of meaning and some overall story *so far,*
2. (with regards to story endings and beginnings) to the unmarked spaces between stories as units of meaning and an overall communicative program in terms of "master narrative",
3. (with regards to overall assessments of contradicting voices, finally) to the open space between communicative programs that are negotiated as units of meaning

within and in-between various institutionalised media and *this communication polyglot we know as society* (Newcomb 1984, 39).

Especially in the light of extended heteroglossia mass-mediated narrative "conversation" is not so much different from interpersonal peer-to-peer communication, or just so in scale. Not all of it is directed from a privileged source of knowledge to some heterogeneous "mass" of fairly ingenuous addresses. Instead, mass media narratives engage many knowledgeable (co-)narrators with many aspiring narratees in mutually shared anticipations and subsequent actualisations of narrative events and narrative episodes.

In the light of communication as a conceptually flawed project, the idea of episodicity as invitation to *think* (and invitation to *link*, recursively) is a very pertinent one. It aptly illustrates those "liminal spaces" Ochs / Capps evoke with regards to everyday narrative communication. The borderlands of episodic narratives can be metaphorically understood as common pastures for whoever engages in narrative communication over time and repeatedly "logs in" for the ceremonial purpose of some telling.

The default redundancies (i.e., repeated entry into the narrative contract and growing acquaintance with the mutually evoked narrative world) are multifunctional: They inform and initiate the more ingenuous readers, whereas the more knowing readers' increasing familiarity with the narrative's protagonists and whereabouts invariably produces fodder for further communication, in terms of collective anticipation and recursive connectivity. What results from these dialogic enterprises can indeed reduce the risk of communication failure considerably. But it will also unleash remarkable imaginative power and creative energies.

Narrative communication as reflective art and second-order observation is always open to interpretation (Eco 1979, 49): "*Every* work of art, even though it is produced by following an explicit or implicit poetics of necessity, is effectively open to a virtually unlimited range of possible readings, each of which causes the work to acquire new vitality in terms of perspective or personal *performance*." All dialogue-oriented forms of narrative communication – and that includes narrative serials referring to more or less focused (and more or less anticipated) instalments as episodes – must cater to expectations formulated on different levels of narrative knowledge involved. They oscillate between what can and what cannot be known, and they invite for collective narrative performances in various settings of double contingency.

> Of course it is happening inside your head, Harry,
> but why on earth should that mean that it is not real?
> (Albus Dumbledore to Harry Potter)

4 EPISODIC FICTION AS ENTERTAINING COMMUNICATION

This chapter leads over from the specifics of narrative episodicity to the characteristics of "indeterminacy" provided by narrative fiction, and to the gaps regarding episodic fiction in particular. Vacancies and "blanks" concern, for once, perceptions as operations of individual consciousness but also – since such perceptions nourish further communication as social operation – individuals as "persons" that choose to playfully perform selected identities within particular "second worlds" offered for imagining purposes.

So far narration has been described as an art and as a second-order observation (of society observing itself). In terms of "social thinking" narration relies on the gaps between what is said and what is meant just as much as on what gets conveyed as narrative event or episode. Chains of prearranged "cause and effects" must be recursively connected to other such chains to make sense – which is where our own capacities to link and associate, and to anticipate what is next, come into play. While narrative events may be best looked at from an action-oriented viewpoint, the reflective spaces in-between events, and in-between narrative episodes and stories are better suited for an analysis from an observation-oriented viewpoint – which is why I recur to systems theory for argumentative back-up.

So far narratives emerged as multifunctional endeavours: as time-bound negotiation of knowledge asymmetries on the one hand, and as ritual performance of shared common knowledge within networks of initiated persons (in terms of artefacts of the communication) on the other. To become sufficiently knowledgeable and / or admissible one must study and invest time and practice. This is why episodic narratives (both in their informal commonplace and more institutional, mediated and / or serialised varieties) produce different levels of critical readership, built on various levels of expertise with the narrative rule-work and applications.

Narrative communication can be observed as a dialogic enterprise bringing together narrators and narratees in exchanges of knowledge (or, more precisely: in ongoing negotiations of knowledge discrepancies) over time. Such dialogues takes place in various settings, with participants remaining in their position as narrator / narratee or swapping roles and become co-tellers while the telling lasts. Since mass-mediated narratives circulate in dialogic networks, the initiating and responding partners cannot observe entirely what (kinds of) tellings ensue. This is an important factor in what Peters describes as the "democracy" of mass media, here as constitutive element of what could be accordingly labelled the "democracy" of mass media entertainment.

4.1   The privileges of leisure time

When the Dominican Friar Felix Fabri wrote a German synthesis to a much more elaborate Latin pilgrimage account to Jerusalem, back in the late 15th century, he described the treatise as *[u]ber die mass kurtzweilig und luostig zu lesen* (= entertaining and amusing beyond all measure).[78] While the original travelogue [79] was directed at a limited circle of bible-literate fellow theologians, this abridged Reader's Digest version addressed instead Fabri's noble and rather wealthy co-travellers to the Holy Land. As Fabri makes clear in the introduction, his book was meant to be read to their "children, housewives, servants and maids" in their idle hours.[80]

---

[78]   The original title of the printed edition (1556) reads: "Ejgentlich beschreibung der hin unnd wider farth zu dem Heyligen Lanndt gen Jerusalem / und furter durch die grosse Wüsteney zu dem Heiligen Bergk Horeb Sinay / daraus zu vernemen was wunders die Pilgrin hin und wider auff Land und wasser zu erfahren und zu besehen haben / *Uber die mass kurtzweilig und luostig zu lesen* / sonderlich denen so der Heiligen schrifft ettwas erfarn sein." For a more recent (crime) novel drawn from Brother Felix' travels see Holman (1997).

[79]   Konrad Dietrich Hassler edited the three volumes of the original *Evagatorium* in Stuttgart (Bibliothek des Litterarischen Vereins Stuttgart, 1843-1849). The edition is accessible in a digitised version courtesy of Austrian Literature Online; see *www.literature.at/webinterface/library/ALO-BOOK_V01?objid=10897* (vol. 1), [...]=11028 (vol. 2) and [...]=11029 (vol. 3).

[80]   Quoted in Ganz-Blättler (2000, 269-270): "Aber so ich fürwar weiss / dass diss Büchlein kommen wirdt *ewern kindern und Haussfrawen / ewern dienern / knechten und mägden* in die hende / und wirdt ewern eigenen leuten vorgelesen / so hab ichs desto lenger gemacht. [...] Dabey hab ich auch etwann kindtlich / lecherlich sachen / die sich verlauffen haben in der reyse / hinzu gesetzt / und schimpliche Fabeln die ich gehört habe / und man saget / die da odder dort beschehen sein / das ewre kind / junge leut / knaben und töchter / desto lieber diss büchlein lesen / und bey den ernstlichen Heyligen Stedten / auch etwas frölichs fünden / damit sie lange weyle vertreiben. Wenn meine meinung ist nicht das jemandt diss Büchlein lese / in denen stunden so man ernsthafftig soll sein / und mit tapffern sachen soll umgehn. Aber so ein menschs sonst müssig gienge unnd zeit verlüre / Oder so ein Ritter des Heyligen Grabes wolt sein Walfarth wider in gedechtnuss bilden / so mag er in diesem Büchlein lesen."

What better way to woo an adolescent / female / domestic – as well as a male, noble – target audience than by way of hefty doses of "kindtlich, lecherlich sachen" (= childish, unimportant matters) and "schimpfliche Fabeln" (= juicy, unconfirmed rumours)?

As a black friar Felix Fabri understood narrative rhetoric, and he was an expert in marketing strategies. His German pilgrimage account has been published several times and made it, not surprisingly, into Sigmund Feyerabends "Reyssbuch" (1584), one of the most widely read travel compilations of the late 16th century (for details, see Simon 1998).

What Fabri also understood was the need of audiences to be entertained. If you were about to teach a lesson or two on how stepping into Jesus Christ's footsteps might save your soul such lessons were best tied in with some nerve-racking tale of the pilgrims' vessel narrowly escaping pirate attacks and, if possible, a detailed description of Middle East's more exotic inhabitants and wildlife.

The negative connotation of leisure as idleness is a relatively modern invention and thinkable only within societies that are, in one way or another, determined by the clock.[81] While the original Latin term of "otium" had a positive connotation of up-scale luxury, with the dictionary indicating a broad range of associations from the obvious (freedom of obligation and privacy) right to peace and political stability, literary interests and poetry. "Negotium" is the negative of it, in terms of busi/ness, political battle and hardship in general – whatever interrupts the blissful state of having nothing obligatory to do. Today's concepts of "free" time as "spare" time are still tied-in with concepts of work and responsibility: Such times are "idle" mostly in the sense that the "I" of the individual gets to decide what to do or not to do.[82] Exemption from social responsibility results in two options, in two kinds of activity or observational stance: There is the possibility to do something else then what is usually done or to do "nothing" at all and reflect instead.

Narratives told in leisure time have other social functions than narratives related to business matters and other social responsibilities. Jensen suggests to distinguish

---

[81] Hans Tucher, one of Fabri's travel companions, provides one of the earliest descriptions of a clock tower (for this see Herz, 2002).

[82] Distinctions drawn between "otium" and "negotium" are subjective, of course. Multivariate definitions of working time apply, with obligations seen as inflicted or chosen, The existence of leisure-oriented industries alone proves that one's otium is someone else's negotium – and vice versa.

between *time-in* and *time-out* culture (2002, 5): While time-in culture interacts with everyday life and its constitutive social structures (and thus includes circulation of mass-mediated news and in-depth reporting), *time-out* culture (in our case: mass-mediated entertainment) takes a more distant observatory stance.

> "Time-out culture places reality on an explicit agenda, as an object of reflexivity, and provides an occasion for contemplating oneself in a social or existential perspective, perhaps suggesting new avenues for agency. In this regard, mediated communication joins other cultural forms, from religious rituals to fine arts."

Time-in culture emerges from, constitutes and aliments everyday reality: It is here where procedures of social interaction are generated and played out. *Time-out* culture gives the everyday a break: Reality becomes an object of reflection and can be tentatively explored and played out.

Mass-mediated entertainment is an important program strand of modern leisure culture, besides a vast variety of "live" events and besides mass tourism that similarly allow to engage in *alternate* activities or *no* particular activity at all.[83] In contrast to education, from which modern entertainment culture evolved within Judeo-Christian culture, entertaining programs do not ask for a particular effort or for a concrete response. We are free to use the offer as we please: We can do nothing (of social importance) with it, or do something else then what we are supposed or suggested to do. In the case of entertaining narratives, pleasures can be taken from seemingly passive or "readerly" practices just as much as from (inter-)active, more "writerly" practices: The only thing not possible is to remain indifferent while being entertained.

If all narrative communication is dialogic, then all entertaining narrative communication is by default participatory. This is especially true for narrative fiction, or what Noël Carroll (1998, 273) defines as "stories that authors intend readers, listeners, and viewers to imagine".

4.2 Entertainment studies

When we consider fiction to work as a highly imaginative, playful communicative effort based on auctorial, creative first-hand inputs, authority over narrative

---

[83] For interactions of contemporary media culture with live events see Dayan / Katz (1992); for the transition from medieval pilgrim to modern tourist Bauman (1996); for mass tourism as social phenomenon Urry (2002).

knowledge is either assigned to identifiable individuals or collectives (for copyright reasons, maybe) or, alternatively, negotiated between stakeholders in the narrative franchise. According to Horace Newcomb (2004, 413), "[t]he 'work' done by narrative and genre can be understood as a process or rearranging the world for imaginative purposes. This imaginative activity occurs in at least two ways. First, the act of the one who [...] selects events and orders them, is an imaginative action. Second, the one who listens, who anticipates, who believes or disbelieves, who laughs or fails to laugh, [...] is also engaged in an imaginative process." He adds that the "freedom to participate in the constructed 'worlds' of narrative and genre" is probably one of the few common denominators all humans share.

When communication studies emerged within university curricula in Europe they did so within social sciences, not the humanist faculties). The disciplines were interested in educational and propagandistic endeavours, in news and investigative journalism and, maybe, advertisement (Meyen 2007, and Saxer 2007). In consequence transmission-oriented approaches and research methods were favoured, while ceremonial aspects of communication, allegedly trivial subjects and individual or collective pleasures taken from mass media were neglected.

Entertaining communication faced two types of institutional constraint: Invisibility on the one hand (since entertaining subjects were not considered relevant enough to be included in public educational curricula and examined in their social implications) but also lack of interdisciplinary collaboration – which is indispensable for coming to term with the subject's complexity.

Here is not the place to resume the more recent, and highly promising, developments of entertainment studies of the last few decades. According to historical overwiews (Bosshart / Macconi 1998, Bosshart 2006a and 2006b, Bryant / Vorderer 2006 and especially Vorderer 2006a and 2006b), two schools can be distinguished within social sciences and roughly described along the line of psychology (regarding private enjoyment and interior reflection) and sociology (concerning publicly displayed and collectively shared reactions to entertainment). While media psychology expresses a particular interest in what goes on in entertainment users' minds, sociology-oriented communication studies – clearly inspired by the Cultural Studies paradigm of the "inter/active" audience – explore more systematically the collective, communicative and performance-oriented practices tied in with entertaining programs. Differentiated views on entertainment uses have meanwhile overcome the stereotype of absorbing masses as "cultural dopes";[84] this is due also to increased collaboration with leisure-interested disciplines in other areas such as sociology, economy and (Christian) theology.

What the system-bound scepticism of serious academia towards mass-mediated entertainment (and mass culture in general) acknowledges, nonetheless, is that *all* narrative knowledge circulation directed at large audiences must rely, to some extent or other, on entertaining aspects in order to stimulate interest and activate the reader's, listener's or viewer's imaginative capacity. A pilgrim account written by a medieval Swabian monk was foremost an educational (and propagandist) learning occasion providing spiritual and material information on the Holy Sites in and around Jerusalem. The pirate-related incidents and exotic *bestiaria* merely served to get the message across. The same goes for other aspiring *leitmedia* of early modernity (for the term see the introductory remarks, p. xiii) such as scientific encyclopaedias that included popular myths on equally popular demand – and those serial periodicals that conveyed knowledge of the world no longer to privileged courts and convents but also to literate lay people socialised within the rising urban gentry.

More recent examples are 19th century's family-oriented variety journals such as the German *Gartenlaube* (Belgum 1998), but also daily newspapers in the wake of the 20th century and, of course, early cinema, radio and television: All of these distribution media provided material explicitly meant to divert (... from the more serious matters at hand) and make their target audience laugh, cry, wince, or wonder. The largely unanswered, and largely unanswerable question is, however, what people actually *did*, and produced in response to be able to laugh or cry or wince or wonder.

4.3 The reality of entertaining communication

Niklas Luhmann devotes a full chapter to entertaining communication in his reflection on the "Reality of Mass Media" (2000a). While he clearly sympathises with the concept some of his arguments remain fairly conservative. Entertaining programs fit

---

[84] The common misunderstanding of media entertainment inducing "passiveness" relates to the metaphoric reference world of the transmission model that relegates media users to the state of receivers or mere "containers". Receivers are meant to be filled (with useful information, for instance) and then emptied before they can be filled again. Seen from this angle entertaining fare corresponds to light-weighted packing material for more important and valuable goods "inside" (... including advertisement, depending on the viewpoint) but hardly considered filling, or otherwise rewarding as such.

the "time-out" pattern of media communication, they are part of leisure culture and meant "... to destroy superfluous time" (ibid., 51). As a "social game" they let the imagination roam free from the usual constraints that govern our everyday reality. Compared to other rule-based games there is even less social responsibility: When engaged in book-reading, watching a movie or listening to a radio play we are relegated to a "second world" for which specific conventions apply. One may choose to learn them and become more literate over time (and Eco's critical reader comes to mind here), but there is no social pressure to do so. Matters of taste do not interfere with one's feeling to be more or less satisfyingly entertained – an observation Luhmann shares with Fiske (1991) who also claims that popular taste is indifferent to the aesthetic criteria governing the appreciation of established, canonical cultural artefacts. The cognitive and affective investments in entertainment remain facultative and are beyond social control.

Luhmann shows no interest in classifying particular effects of entertaining efforts (ibid., 61):

> "What goes on in each individual viewer, the non-linear causalities, dissipative structural developments, negative or positive feedback messages etc. triggered by such coincidental observations, can simply not be predicted; neither can they be controlled by programme choices in the mass media. Psychological effects are much too complex, much too self-determined and much too varied to be capable of being included in communication conveyed via the mass media."

Instead the inquiry is about how reality is effectively doubled by such programs strands – and by entertaining fiction in particular. Whereas games are said to depend on socially agreed sequences of behaviour (ibid., 52), media entertainment provides entire alternative worlds which can be individually accessed and explored at will.[85] The respective "sub-worlds" and "provinces of meaning" (and I quote Schütz here, not Luhmann) develop their own peculiar reality state, with the social norms relegated to the stage of the doubled reality alone. Irritations may ensue between guides and visitors while the second world is held upright but this bears no consequences on the exterior, first-world behaviour of either party. Leisure time is by default exempted from the social constraints of everyday reality – meaning that once the alternate reality is left behind no need for further communication ensues,

---

[85] Ibid., 59-60: "It is extremely tempting to try out virtual realities on oneself – at least in an imagination that one can break off at any time."

whether in the guise of a reasoned answer or some other behaviour signalling that an understanding has taken place.

Luhmann uses literary and audiovisual fiction as main examples of his argumentation, but he also refers (2000a, 58) to televised "competitions of all kinds, such as quiz programmes or broadcasts of sporting events" and to talk shows in particular (ibid., 60). Whereas information provided by news reports and in-depth journalism is meant to irritate and / or integrate and seeks to provoke social reactions (namely, dissent or consent), there is no such behaviour expected from entertaining programs strands and no sanction of an eventual misunderstanding of story-relevant information ... except boredom, probably.

The only recursive – and nevertheless facultative – connection mass-mediated forms of entertainment suggest to make (since all successful communication can be expected to "make sense", in some way or another) concern the observer's own life and the freedom to associate what has been encountered to personal experiences and questions of identity (ibid., 61): "The 'trick' with entertainment is the constantly accompanying comparison, and [how] forms of entertainment [...] make use of world correlates: confirming or rejecting them, uncertain of the ending right until the very last moment or calmly with the certainty that that kind of thing cannot happen to me." And (ibid.): "Psychic systems which participate in communication through the mass media in order to entertain themselves are thus invited to make the connection back to themselves."

In contrast to news journalism that is supposed to hinge on unsettling novelty entertainment activates what is already subcutaneously present. Surprise is generated at minor levels of unexpected plot twists or "highly unlikely combinations" [of narrative elements], but takes care not to venture too far into uncharted territory (ibid., 58):

> "By being offered from the outside [for us to perceive], entertainment aims to activate that which we ourselves experience, hope for, fear, forget – just as the narrating of myths once did. What the romantics longed for in vain, a 'new mythology', is brought about by the entertainment forms of the mass media. Entertainment reimpregnates what one already is; and, as always, here too feats of memory are tied to opportunities for learning."

Luhmann's argument does not go into details of how such facultative "opportunities for learning" might be tied in with further "feats of memory". Since mass media forbid direct encounters between communication partners for technological reasons, no feedback possibilities are taken into consideration and theorised further –

and neither is the eventuality of further engagements with fellow visitors in entertaining follow-up communication (ibid., 57): "For entertainment means not seeking or finding any cause to answer communication via communication". The freedom not to have to recur to further communication is considered constitutive for leisure activities; it is an argument which makes Luhmann's ideas, at first glance, difficult to reconcile with the dialogic, more overtly participatory approaches suggested by Newcomb and Fiske / Hartley.[86]

What also emerges within Luhmann's argumentation is an overt scepticism towards narrative indeterminacy (which is considered "artistic" by default): According to Luhmann entertaining offers are better suited to closed readings, with narrative structure reducing surplus contingencies of the second world at stake and the lingering uncertainties finally resolved within the cyclic form of a "new mythology", as he calls it.[87] Narrative closure is to be expected from every single entertaining piece, as a clear signal that the second world is now ready be left behind and one's own life course resumed safely (ibid., 56):

> "If the story aims to satisfy certain basic requirements for its own consistency [...], the way it unfolds must be able to refer back to the beginning of the story. In any case, the elements needed for resolving the tension have to be introduced before the end, and only the reader or viewer is left in the dark. This is why it is not worth reading something twice – or it is only worth doing if the reader wishes to concentrate instead on admiring the writer's artistic skill or if someone watching a film wants to focus on the way it has been produced and directed.
>
> For a text or story to be exciting and entertaining, one must not know in advance how to read it or how to interpret it. People want to be entertained each time anew. For the same reason, every piece of entertainment must come to an end and must bring this about itself. The unity of the piece is the unity of the difference of future and past which has been allowed to enter into it. We know at the end: so that was it, and go away with the feeling of having been more or less well entertained."

---

[86] The concepts of (a) double contingency and (b) the binary trust- / mistrust-dichotomy help to define narrative communication between implied authors and implied readers as (equally implied) dialogue. I am not familiar enough with the growing bulk of functionalist, systems-oriented literary studies to assess the state of the art in that area. But it should be highly rewarding to relate Luhmann's perception of the necessarily "monadic" consciousness to reflection regarding *parasocial* interaction (Horton / Wohl, 1956 and 1957, and Auter, 1992).

[87] Luhmann echoes arguments expressed earlier by Kracauer (on film communication Kracauer 1947, and 1960) and, later, by Barthes (in: Barthes 1972, 109 ff.). For a poetics of grand myths shaping television narratives Bleicher (2002, and 2007).

If one agrees that *people want to be entertained each time anew*, some repetition can hardly elicit the same pleasures as the original experience did. Whereas Eco, and similarly Barthes point to the particular enjoyment resulting from repeated, more "knowing" and sophisticated readings of fiction,[88] such practices appear, in Luhmann's argumentation, relegated to a quite different ballpark – that of artistic communication.

Luhmann and Jensen refer to the same *distinction* (to quote Bourdieu, 1984) between media entertainment and "fine art" when describing the extensions of time-out culture. However, the shared argument is not so much concerned with artefacts that might deserve our attention or not, according to criteria based on individual taste, but more with ways of observing. One and the same experience can be viewed differently and provoke different reactions. The question is just if what has finally gained transparency as some kind of "art" (... or attained the cult status commonly associated with "religion", as Jensen might be quick to add) can nevertheless be enjoyed as pure and unabashed entertainment.

If we consider social interaction to be grounded in double contingency rather than physical proximity between two or more communication partners, then both individual and "collective" uses of mass media entertainment can certainly elicit further (here: further *enjoyable*) response. Luhmann himself describes follow-up communication as constitutive of mass communication in general (Luhmann 2000a, 99); but he seems hesitant to extrapolate from this description that entertaining communication within mass media might just as well *stimulate ongoing communication* – by default.

Corroborating evidence must therefore be sought elsewhere, with Cultural Studies the most likely candidate (see for instance Radway 1984, Ang 1985, Livingstone 1990, Dayan 1992, Brown 1994, Abercrombie / Longhurst 1998, Alasuutari 1999, Calbo 1999, Ross / Nightingale 2003; with strong support from McQuail 1997). In fact, the growing field of popular culture studies, and particularly "fan" studies, point to a

---

[88] Luhmann certainly speaks for the more protective fans of serial narratives that resort to "spoiler spaces" in order to prevent accidental slips of story-related information. But narrative pleasure (admittedly of a more wicked variety) can also be derived from aggressive in-group fights and strategic knowledge disclosure, as controversies surrounding the publication of each of the seven *Harry Potter* instalments prove, or the spoiler battles fought among fans of the ABC television series *Lost* (Gray / Hills, 2007).

broad variety of apparently enjoyable reader response from and among variously initiated audiences.[89]

Luhmann's argument finds support in Cultural Studies insofar as the era of the mass media, especially in the 19th and 20th century, is identified in both cases as one of increasing incorporation and "embourgeoisation" of entertaining practices. The technical distance introduced between performers and audiences participating in entertaining communication can then be read as an indicator rather than a reason for the increasing *social* distance applied at various levels (for a discussion on the two related arenas of theatre and soccer, see Abercrombie / Longhurst 1998, 47 ff.).

A predominantly private media use comes as a logical consequence thereof: The silent reading of novels, Edison's invention of the kinetoscope, drive in cinemas – and particularly radio and television relegating media users to predominantly domestic settings – do not so much follow from technical constraints forcing physical distance upon performers and audiences of mass-mediated content but from more general tendencies of individualisation. Individualised narrative experiences certainly limit the possibilities for audiences to engage in pleasurable follow-up communication if conveniently knowledgeable partners must first be sought out and contacted.[90]

What Luhmann identifies as imaginative daydreaming (in terms of what *we ourselves experience, hope for, fear, forget*) is certainly the foremost, most widely enjoyed reading practice by those attending to mass mediated cultural commodities. But it is not the only one: Depending on one's disposition (and determination) there are *other*, more outbound and socially engaging discursive possibilities how to enjoy an entertaining travel into alternate realities.[91]

To draw the line between observation of a communicative phenomenon as second-order ("art") or as first-order (gleeful, unabashed amusement) means to reproduce

---

[89] Harrington / Bielby (1995) distinguish practices of soap fans, based on their visibility, as *fanship* (individual, perceptive, private) and *fandom* (collective, communicative, public).

[90] This is one of the central problems strategic scheduling – or what is more recently called content leverage – seeks to resolve: Timed access not only heightens audience expectations but also increases the chance to spread the word and organise collective attendance and / or follow-up discussion.

[91] Interestingly Luhmann refers also to "body games" when discussing physical reactions to highly stimulating program genres such as thrillers, horror stories, or pornography. He just does not address that social arena in particular, here.

institutional, systemic distinctions which cannot sufficiently account for the complexity and functional equivalencies characterising today's saturation with popular culture and the responses played out on various levels of audience agency.[92] I suggest to opt instead for an inclusion of various observing stances within one system of "narrative art" that extends from market-tested, customised *mass art* (in the sense of Carroll, 1998) right to experimental vanguard forms of artistic expression, and from open narratives, and individually or collectively experienced "writerly" pleasures right to "mythical" narratives and the more "readerly" practices of those that follow the author's lead, "... plunged into a kind of idleness".[93] This allows us to align what is individually and collectively imagined within the narrative borderlands of entertaining communication while taking into consideration different levels of narrative knowledge and various concepts of pleasure.

Instead of insisting on the distinction between *otium* and *negotium* (a distinction difficult to maintain for domestic settings and more private pleasures) we better take a closer look at how narrative worlds are collaboratively constructed and maintained over time, with particular attention given to narrative gaps as reflective spaces and how they invite for various kinds of reader response.

---

[92] For a critical discussion of Luhmann's entertainment concept see Görke (2001), Liebes (2002), and especially Saxer (2007, 20-21): „So ist zum Beispiel die Luhmannsche Konzeption von Massenmedien als operativ geschlossenem funktionalem Subsystem, das gemäss dem binären Code Information / Nichtinformation operiert [...], gerade für die Erfassung von Phänomenen der Unterhaltungsöffentlichkeit nur wenig ergiebig. Der für deren Verstehen zentrale Aspekt von Institution und Gegeninstitution taucht ja in dieser wie in systemtheoretischen Öffentlichkeitskonzeptionen generell nicht auf. Unterhaltung ist vor- oder auch gegeninstitutionelles Kommunizieren und sonstiges Handeln, das aber selber auch institutionalisiert und damit instrumentalisiert werden kann. Auf jeden Fall ist der prekäre institutionelle Bezug für das Phänomen konstitutiv."

[93] The quotes from Barthes (1974, 4): "Our literature is characterized by the pitiless divorce which the literary institution maintains between the producer of the text and its user, between its owner and its customer, between its author and its reader. This reader is thereby plunged into a kind of idleness – he is intransitive; he is, in short, *serious*: instead of functioning himself, instead of gaining access to the magic of the signifier, to the pleasure of writing, he is left with no more than the poor freedom either to accept or reject the text: reading is nothing more than a *referendum*. Opposite the writerly text, then, is its countervalue, its negative, reactive value: what can be read, but not written: the *readerly*. We call any readerly text a classic text."

4.4 Wolfgang Iser on narrative indeterminacy and reader response [94]

When Umberto Eco defined modern art as "open work" (1962; see Bondanella 1997 for details), he stirred quite a controversy among Italian literary theorists. Eight years later Barthes' S/X followed, representing for many observers a more general shift of French structuralism towards poststructuralism. Also in 1970 German literary professor Wolfgang wrote an essay on prose fiction, introducing narrative indeterminacy as a key factor triggering imaginative reader response ("Die Appellstruktur der Texte. Unbestimmtheit als Wirkungsbedingung literarischer Prosa"; the English version edited by J. Hillis Miller, 1971). Iser significantly broke with the tradition of literary criticism to "pigeonhole" the meaning of a given text so that it might fit already existing frames of reference. Instead he focuses on the intersection between text and reader, since "a text can only come to life when it is read" (Iser 1971, 2). The basic question for Iser is how the reading process relates cues taken from the text to the individual reader's mind and consciousness.

He starts out from a bundle of premises:

- Indeterminacy embodies an elementary condition for readers' reactions.
- The more texts lose their determinacy, the more strongly is the reader shifted into the full operation of their possible intentions.
- If indeterminacy exceeds a certain toleration limit, however, the reader will feel strained "to an almost intolerable degree" (and lose interest, or change the reading mode).

Three research questions result from these premises, namely (1) What distinguishes literature from other (narrative) texts? (2) How can different levels of indeterminacy be described? And (3): What explanations may be given for the rise of indeterminacy in modern narrative literature, since the 18th century?

An initial reflection on the complex relation between fiction and everyday reality leads Iser to assume that fictional events need to be aligned with our own life experiences (ibid., 8 f.): "There are two extremes of reaction that can arise from the con-

---

[94] I am indebted to Milly Buonanno (2008, 123) who quotes Iser as pointing to the "strategical interruptions" of serials that provide spaces for imaginative work, and to Vorderer (2006b, 77) who mentions indeterminacies of "polyvalent", open texts as constitutive for readers' enjoyment. Similarly, on episodic television fiction and soap opera in particular, also Allen (1985, 75-81, and 1995, 17).

frontation between one's own world and that of the literary work involved: either the literary world seems fantastic, because it contradicts our own experience, or it seems trivial, because it merely echoes our own."

Since there cannot be a full overlap between what we recognise as familiar from our everyday reality with what we acknowledge as fictional reality out there in the text, we must determine which is which and continue to "counterbalance" the two conflicting realities. A perfect alignment would let us question the fictional quality of the narrative reflection; a stark contrast probably irritate us to the point where we choose between "throwing the book away" or reconsidering our own preconceptions.

Indeterminacies tend to disappear / to become invisible once we project our own perceptive standards on the text and construct its meaning from there. The same happens when we seek to understand "what the text wants to convey" (thus striving for successful communication). The fictional, or *literary* state of the text stems from its halfway position between two worlds, and from the need for continuous negotiation: The "act of reading" is described as an attempt (ibid., 10) "to pin down the oscillating structure of the text to some specific meaning."

In a second step Iser points out the impossibility of fictional objects to ever become fully determined: While there may be certain "schematized views"[95] offered for how we should read particular parts, this does not apply throughout the narrative. Some of the connections remain implicit and must be inferred.

Iser uses the metaphor of film editing to describe these "schematized" views (ibid., 11): "The sequence of views has the appearance of being dissevered here and there, resembling a cutting technique." He also recurs to a rather cinematic example when evoking multiple plot threads that are supposed to run simultaneously but must nevertheless be dealt with one after another. Indeterminacies, then, arise in the "no-man's land" between such views – and they become only more obvious by the effort invested to make them appear *determined*:

"Gaps are bound to open up, and offer a free play of interpretation for the specific way in which the various views can be connected with one another.

---

[95] The term coined by Roman Imgarden – whose concept is described by Iser as helpful, but limited. Imgarden sees the reader as merely completing the work of the artist (and is quoted in this by Luhmann 2000a, 82-83), thereby fulfilling the artistic, as Imgarden calls it, "desire for polyphonic harmony". It is this classic view differentiating between "true and false realizations of a literary text" that Iser refuses to adopt.

> These gaps give the reader a chance to build his own bridges, relating the different aspects of the object which have thus far been revealed to him. It is quite impossible for the text itself to fill in the gaps. In fact, the more a text tries to be precise (i.e., the more 'schematized views' it offers), the greater will be the number of gaps between the views."

In other words: What is not formulated by the text itself is filled in by the reader's own imaginative capacities, and by the reader's prior knowledge of what is expected to happen next (ibid., 12-13):

> "On a second reading, one has considerably more knowledge about the text, especially if the first reading was only a short time ago. This additional information will affect and condition the meaning-projection, so that now the gaps between the different segments as well as the spectrum of their possible connections, or repair, can be applied in a different or perhaps more intensive way. The increased information that now overshadows the text provides possibilities of combination which were obscured in the first reading. Familiar occurrences now tend to appear in a new light and seem to be at times corrected, at times enriched, but for all of that, nothing is formulated in the text itself; rather, the reader himself produces these innovative readings. This would, of course, be impossible if the text itself was not, to some degree, indeterminate, leaving room for the change of vision.
>
> In this way, every literary text invites some form of participation on the part of the reader."

Texts with minimal indeterminacy "tend to be tedious" since they leave the reader with no choice but acceptance or refusal. Chances given for active participation in the meaning-making let the fictional events appear "real". Concluding this second part of the argument Iser identifies indeterminacy as (ibid., 14) *the fundamental precondition for reader participation*.

The following example leads Iser towards his third area of investigation: indeterminacies within modern literature, and serialisation in particular. Serialised novels in the 19th century were delivered to the reader "in carefully measured doses" and worked as auto-advertisements for readers that were lured back for more. Dickens and other serials' authors took a great interest in their audiences since they wanted to find out how readers "visualised" the story's development, over time. The testimonials quoted by Iser reveal highly heterogeneous reading experiences: While many readers seemed to prefer the novel read by instalments to reading the integral story in book form, others confessed that they could not bear the building tension of the wait. Frequency was considered an important strategy factor for serial success, with weekly access to new instalments proving more effective than monthly intervals.

The intense, often enthusiastic reaction should not be blamed on strategy alone. Iser takes this as living proof for how indeterminacy elicits reader response (ibid., 17):

> "The reader is forced by the pauses imposed on him to imagine more than he could have done if his reading were continuous, and so, if the text of a serialized novel makes a different impression from the text in book form, this is principally because it introduces additional gaps, or alternatively accentuates existing gaps by means of a break until the next installment. This does not mean that its quality is in any way higher. The pauses simply bring out a different kind of realization, in which the reader is compelled to take a more active part by filling in these additional gaps. If a novel *seems* to be better in this form, then this is clear evidence of the importance of indeterminacy in the text-reader relationship. Furthermore, it reveals the requisite degree of freedom which must be guaranteed to the reader in the communication act, so that the message can be adequately received and processed."

Iser also quotes other examples of "indeterminacy", outside of serialisation. One technique refers to Dickens' *Oliver Twist* and concerns the narrator's address of the audience (ibid, 19-20): "Instead of offering the reader a single and consistent perspective, through which he is supposed to look on the events narrated, the author provides him with a bundle of multiple viewpoints, the center of which is continuously shifted. These comments thus open a certain free play for evaluation, and permit new gaps to arise in the text."

The third part of Iser's investigation of narrative gaps serves as a preamble to what followed a few years later as a more systematic examination of modern literature (*The Implied Reader*, English version 1974). Quoting more examples from prose fiction he examines particular forms of author-reader relationship and the specific role reader response plays in each case. In the closing argument of the 1971 essay, he affirms (ibid., 43) that "the reality of a literary text lies within the reader's imagination" and insists on the power of fiction that will, due to its undetermined state, "transcend the restrictions of time and written word and thus give to people of all ages and backgrounds the chance to enter other worlds and so enrich their own lives."

In his subsequent books Iser examined the imaginative relationship between implied authors and readers further (1974) and developed his own theory of reading as particular form of speech act (1978). Again, the reader's participation emerges as crucial for the construction of fictional universes and essential for experiencing pleasure (1974, 275) while overtly didactic text where "everything is laid out cut and dried before us" are dismissed as boring (ibid., 277). He also stresses the impact of cumulative reading and the respectively acquired narrative knowledge over time: What events are individually remembered while the reading goes on, is essential for how recursive connections are made. One can expect different stories from different readers, and from repeated readings by one and the same reader (ibid., 278-279).

Aspects of narrative knowledge and memory are further explored in *The Act of Reading* where Iser examines the reading process closer in its temporal dimensions. Particular attention is given to how narrative revelation interacts with anticipation, and how meanings shift as the reader's recognition slowly builds (1978, 149):

> "As meaning develops along the time axis, time itself cannot function as a frame of reference, and hence it follows that each concretization of meaning results in a highly individual experience of that meaning, which can never be totally repeated in its identical form. A second reading of the text will never have the same effect as the first, for the simple reason that the originally assembled meaning is bound to influence the second reading. As we have knowledge we did not have before, the imaginary objects accumulating along the time axis cannot follow each other in exactly the same way. The reasons for this may lie in the reader's own change of circumstances, but all the same, the text must be such as to permit of such variations."

Here, and based on textual gaps as *potential* connection, Iser develops a classification system of reader response (ibid., 182 ff.). The need to align or *combine* (of what emerges as the text's reality with what is brought into play from outside) is confronted with the idea of a *completion* of the text's meaning (as Imgarden saw it). This leads to the identification of three literary strategies: While the pedagogic "roman à theses" merely asks for completion, both the serial narrative (for commercial reasons) and the modern literary work (for aesthetic purposes) allow readers to roam free and eventually become *co-authors* (ibid., 191; the serial cliffhanger technique again quoted as example).

In his concluding chapter on the "functional structure of the blank" (ibid., 195 ff.) Iser points to the similar uses of blanks in literature and cinema and identifies the reader's "wandering viewpoint" as central instance where heterogeneous perspectives (of the real and implied author, of competing narrators, and various characters) are brought together. The resulting "field of vision" then constitutes the referential territory against which subsequent revelations are projected as the reading proceeds.

In contrast to "blanks" – as term used for interpretive spaces that serve to individualise the narrative experience – textual "vacancies" (ibid., 198) structure the overall narrative and suggest how story segments relate to each other. Vacancies refer to the reflective spaces in-between narrative events and episodes (or "themes", as Iser calls them): They enable the reader "to combine segments into a field by reciprocal modification, to form positions from those fields, and then to adapt each position to its successor and predecessors in a process that ultimately transforms the textual perspectives, through a whole range of alternating themes and horizons, into the aesthetic object of the text."

Whereas *blanks* invite readers to either dutifully complete what is suggested as "lesson to be learned" or (alternatively) to combine what commercially oriented serials and aesthetically ambitious modern artworks leave up to the reader as coauthor to develop further, *vacancies* work as structural devices. A specific position is metaphorically put on hold until it is occupied according to expectation, with the "theme" in question (once more) recursively linked to other "themes" within the overall chain of cause and effects. In other terms: Vacancies make sure that coherence ensues. Here Iser joins Ricoeur in what is clearly a hermeneutic understanding of the interpretive process (ibid., 201):

> "Once a theme has been grasped, conditioned by the marginal position of the preceding segment, a feed-back is bound to occur, thus retroactively modifying the shaping influence of the reader's viewpoint. This reciprocal transformation is hermeneutic by nature, even though we may not be aware of the processes of interpretation resulting from the switching and reciprocal conditioning of our viewpoints. In this sense, the vacancy transforms the referential field of the moving viewpoint into a self-regulating structure, which proves to be one of the most important links in the interaction between text and reader, and which prevents the reciprocal transformation of textual segments from being arbitrary."

Iser's theory of narrative indeterminacy helps to explain divergences that result from variable access to declarative and procedural knowledge and, just as importantly, from imaginative applications of readers' everyday experiences. Jerome Bruner suggests the term of *meaning 'performance'*. The term identifies readers as actors in a (co-scripted) play when exploring fictional, alternative worlds (Bruner 1987, 27). The argument has also found strong support in cognitive psychology and media studies in general. Richard J. Gerrig describes the same phenomenon as *transportation* to a virtual stage (Gerrig 1993, Green / Brock / Kaufman 2004, and Bilandzic / Kinnebrock 2006 for entertaining communication), with the imaginative use of narrative gaps is seen as indispensable for the readers' immersion in the narrative world at stake. In a typology similar to Iser's Gerrig distinguishes *inferences* (that is: everything brought in to support the story logic) from *participatory responses* (whatever allows readers to individually connect with the events at stake).

4.5 Episodic fiction and customary reader response

The most prolific supporter of Iser's ideas on reader response is, not surprisingly, Umberto Eco. His Harvard Lectures of 1994 (published as *Six Walks in the Fictional Woods*) represent a more accessible, easy to understand summary of the author's earlier arguments on open works, reader roles and how individual interpretive stances account for divergences in the production of meaning. Eco starts out with "blanks" (as Iser would call them) that are alimented by individual memories. What results as daydreaming lets readers "... move within the narrative woods as if it were our own private garden" (Eco 1994, 10). The literary examples quoted include Edgar Allen Poe's *Narrative of Arthur Gordon Pym*, Carlo Collodi's *Pinocchio* (originally published as a series of fifteen instalments in the *Giornale dei bambini*, 1881), and Mickey Spillane's *My Gun Is Quick*.

In the following five chapters, or "walks", Eco returns to the concept of the more knowledgeable second-level reader and explores the narrative contract between model author and model reader. According to Eco narrative detours open up possibilities for alternative strolls through the undergrowth. As long as "disbelief is suspended",[96] viewer perspectives oscillate between real-life models (that are brought into play by the reader's memory) and alternative models based on familiar, conventional schemes (that recall Imgarden's "schematized views"). Sometimes conflicts arise at the intersection between the two realms, and readers appear disconcerted or lose track altogether. This seems to be the prize one has to pay for "the opportunity to employ limitlessly our faculties for perceiving the world and reconstructing the past" (ibid., 131).

Neither Iser nor Eco, Bruner or Gerrig do overturn Luhmann's argument on media entertainment but complement it in important ways. Fiction is said here to emerge from implicit agreements between communication partners that are based on (commercially or aesthetically motivated) invitations to imagine and willingly suspend disbelief for the moment.

However, while Luhmann conceives narrative indeterminacy as a problem rather than a chance (... which is why he suggests to restrict the resulting contingencies, in

---

[96] The famous quote from Samuel Taylor Coleridge (1814; see Coleridge 1985, and 2004) describes the relation between authors and readers of fiction as based on *poetic faith*: Readers do not actually "believe" in what they experience as second world but let go of their belief in everyday reality – over a certain time ("for the moment") and voluntarily ("willing").

one way or another) here the "gaps" are hailed as particularly gratifying since they personalise the narrative experience.

Readers, listeners or viewers of mass-mediated narrative fiction are getting more involved in the unfolding story once narrative events are kept on hold: With the communicative contract sealed between implicit, "model" authors and readers as co-authors, readers can venture freely beyond the seams of what was made knowledgeable so far– and switch position from observer to performing agent and back at one's own leisurely pace, while disbelief suspended not once and for all, but *each time anew*.

All of this supports Hagedorn's claim whereas voluntary, recreational investments made in recurrent, episodic fiction will only become more rewarding over time. What Luhmann does not take into consideration, apparently, is the suggestive power of narrative conversation that builds on indeterminacy and imaginative reader response over time – with regular appointments, growing numbers of participants and an increasing variety of discursive arguments to be negotiated.

Determined *romans à thèses* with clear-cut beginnings and endings may still be found within contemporary mass media (and serial fiction most certainly provides many colourful examples), but they are not necessarily entertaining communication's first choice. More characteristic for popular entertainment seem episodic structures with lingering ambiguities and largely undetermined reality states that are based on sporadic, and eagerly awaited encounters between implied co-tellers that engage in recurring *day trips* to second world territory which consequently becomes more common, more "residential area" over time.

Serial narrative fiction does not streamline the imaginative experience in any way. On the contrary – extensive narrative gaps just provide further opportunities for audiences to activate their own completing, combining and inferring faculties. Victor Watson (*Reading Serial Fiction*, 2000) tells the story of an English schoolboy who was asked to tell the difference between serial and other children's literature. His response described the reading experience aptly as entering *a room full of friends* or, instead, *a room full of strangers*. That sense of familiarity does not stem, apparently, from the written text but from the hard labour of prior reading and from the affective engagement over time. Hayward reports similar statements of comfort from readers of newspaper cartoons and soap opera viewers: two forms of institutional narrative fiction best known for their commercially determined, strategic use of narrative indeterminacy. Here again, the regular observers "virtually create the story out of narrative gaps", as the author puts it (Hayward 2000, 86).

I do not blame Luhmann for lapsing back into an actionist paradigm when discussing narrative fiction in terms of entertainment. He may have been more into action-oriented and plot-driven visits to clearly delineated second worlds, as an experienced narratee, and maybe not acquainted enough with progressive newspaper cartoons (that serve to illustrate some of his arguments, as we have seen) or radio / television soap opera. Had he been familiar with Iser's arguments as much as Imgarden's, functionalist systems theory might by now extend to sustainable narrative worlds and how to maintain them as collective endeavour over time, based on poetic faith and individually reworked as well as collectively negotiated contingencies.

I agree with Luhmann in that what individual viewers perceive and experience (and develop as personalised relation to narrative entertainment over time) is hardly predictable or controllable, not by the industry nor by media psychologists. What can be observed with regards to serial as an *institutional* form of narrative entertainment are the more extravert expressions of customised follow-up communication between participants at both ends of the implied author / reader spectrum, in terms of "interactive" dialogue but also "intertextual" reflection. Fandom studies as still growing sub-disciplinary bulk of interdisciplinary entertainment studies (see for instance Bacon-Smith 1991, Lewis 1992, Jenkins 1992, Jenkins / Tulloch 1995, Harris / Alexander 1998, Colaiacomo 1999, Baym 2000, Le Guern 2002, Hills 2002, Volli 2002, Scaglioni 2006; not to mention studies of specific narrative universes such as the *Buffyverse* or the *Potterverse*) is about to chart a territory that was always "there" but becomes only now more visible as traditional mass media converge and allow narrative stakeholders to meet in new (... public as well as private) venues.

Costello / Moore (2007) provide many examples of active audiences engaging with the text of their favoured television series in creative and more or less canonical ways ranging from online debates, fan fiction and aggressive campaigning (in order to keep the program running) to direct interaction with those responsible for the program behind the stage (be it on- or offline). Veruska Sabucco (2000, 54) offers a genealogy of more conventional reader response in her comparative study on Japanese and Western *slash* culture (Figure 9, next page):[97]

---

[97] *Slash* fiction is fan-fiction written about (more often: male) characters that are described or depicted as engaging in (more often: deviant) romantic and / or

Figure 9: Expressive reader response to mass-mediated source material (Sabucco 2000, 54) [98]

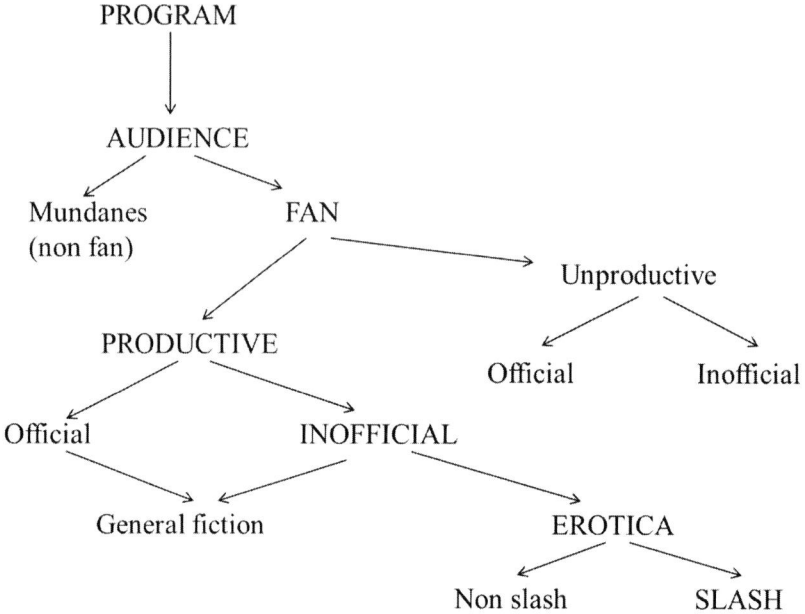

While most audiences of a specific (here: television) program engage in what Sabucco calls "mundane" everyday practices of occasional daydreaming (with or without social components) *fans* – and this term includes here whoever takes a more specific interest in a particular entertaining program or subject over time – get more involved in the story world over time, cognitively and affectively. This involvement is either expressed by what Sabucco calls "productive" fan practice: Readers becoming explicit, variously prolific *co-authors* that partake in imaginative and creative story extensions of their own (for a fine-tuned list of such activities see ibid., 66-70). Other expressive (here distinguished as "unproductive") behaviour is not concerned with expanding or manipulating the second world in question but

---

sexual relationships. For the term Bacon-Smith (1991) and Green / Jenkings / Jenkins (1998); for the anime-based variety known as *Shonen Ai* Sabucco (2000), and also Wikipedia (*http://en.wikipedia.org/wiki/Slash_fiction*, 18-08-2017).

[98] Fan culture is so omnipresent in the Web 2.0 era that it has spun off its own parodistic spoofs. For an example of a more humoristic fan typology see Lore Sjöberg's *Hierarchy of Geeks* (*Brunching Shuttlecocks* website, archived at: *web.archive.org/web/20160710215816/http://brunching.com/geekhierarchy.html* (18-08-2017).

instead focuses on (more or less regular) exchanges of topical knowledge among variously prolific expert gossipers as *co-discussants*.

Collective reader response is still considered a somewhat eccentric topic within mass communication studies while being recognised as constitutive for other forms of popular entertainment within media of the first and third degree. Theatrical and musical performances have always made use of the possibility to invite patrons to participate, re-enact and compile selected materials further, with topical knowledge negotiated in extensive intertextual networks.[99] Mass media may have helped to restrict these channels of immediate feedback, but instead opened up new venues for imaginative re-creation. The particular pleasures of serial fiction as mass communication derive from the winning combination of multiple gaps with sustained suspension of disbelief for weeks, or years or (in the so far unprecedented case of soap opera) decades to come. The price is high and much *superfluous time* destroyed (according to Luhmann) before increased familiarity with characters, places and events can pay off in narrative expertise paired with a strong sense of belonging.

As Jennifer Hayward resumes, Milton Caniff's strip *Terry and the Pirates* reached more than thirty million readers in 300 syndicated newspapers, 1934-1946. The author relied on cinematic framing / editing techniques to transport his readers into the exotic scenery of his serial stories. It took him more than a year "to get the average reader really to become vitally interested in a new strip, to read it every day and talk about it to his friends" (quoted in Hayward, ibid., 105). The successful launch of the strip involved two stages: First a general interest stirred by startling plots and sustained tension as hooks, but also (Hayward, ibid.) "the ritual of serial consumption, the depth and development of characters and a compelling narrative".

During the twelve years of the serial's original run Caniff received more than 100'000 letters from devoted fans – and invested considerable time and energy in efforts to write back. Many readers sustained the importance of the serial to launch conversation, and there were college reading groups as well as soldier groups gathering in regular collective readings during World War II. On the other hand Caniff received (just as Dickens and other serial writers did in their time) hundreds of

---

[99] The referencing of popular culture is not restricted to postmodernity. Bakthin (1981) mentions parodies of Homeric songs, and "classic" composers such as J.S. Bach regularly quoted, and mocked contemporary music. For popularisations of Shakespeare's plays in American playhouses of the 19th century see Levine (2001).

reading experts' suggestions how to develop storylines, and what alternative narrative routes to pick up, or strictly avoid.

Female romance readers taking a time-out from their domestic chores (Radway 1984) and gathering in reading circles for regular updates (Long 2003), the "serial craze" surrounding early weekly film serials and strategically planned magazine tie-ins (Stamp 2000, and Singer 2001), letter campaigns to networks and (individual or collective) engagements in fan fiction are all examples of regular audience behaviour with regards to popular culture in general and serial narrative fiction in particular. Customary audience agency always was a crucial ingredient of serial storytelling within mass communication and ranges from the private to the public and from the canonical to the apocryphal or heretic, as Sabucco's (and Sjöberg's) typologies indicate.

However: To enable audiences to become agents of their own, professional entertainment within traditional media have yet to come up with representative models and usable projections in the first place. Auctorial impulses are necessary triggers for what eventually results in individual and collective reader response. This also means that the idea of the commercially oriented franchise as cultural commodity will not go away anytime soon. The same can be said for the "conflicts over meaning" (Agger 1992, 1) that manifest themselves in struggles over intellectual property rights, and other discursive arenas too.

4.6 The spectacle / performance paradigm

Rob Cover introduces a brief history of media audiences in an article on *Audiences inter/active* that was written in 2006. Starting out from more current forms of reader response that has mass media content "affected, resequenced, altered, customised or re-narrated in the interactive process of audiencehood" (Cover 2006, 140), he traces such practices back to older forms of theatre; that is, before the Victorian stage model relegated audiences to silent onlookers of a *finished* work (ibid., 149) that were no longer encouraged "to control or interrupt the unfolding, real-time text". Cover identifies the introduction of recording media as a main factor that increased distance between content providers and content users but refutes a respective technologically determinist approach. As the example of the theatre stage suggests, it is up to audiences to accept or question a restraining order; more influential than any (technically supported) hegemonic need for control appears what Cover defines as "... cultural – that is, popular – demand for the democratisation of control over the text". The invoked examples (Reality formats in television, text message voting systems, and "swiffer" applications that can unlock protected content from online sources) do not refer to traditional forms of recorded media content. However Cover admits the possibility for any "closed" television text to (ibid., 152) "actually open to a greater number of 'aberrant' decodings by non-average readers, since such texts have, as a minimum requirement, a sociologically 'average' reader in mind."

According to Cover (and similarly Dery, 1993) the urge for readers to express themselves proves more influential for the activation of reader response then any industry effort triggered by commercial reasons. Audience agency remains in the audience's responsibility and is said to depend on user demand rather than on the technical and social possibilities offered. What opportunities are snatched up and put to imaginative and creative use (usually by media literate geeks that act as early adopters and agenda setters in a particular field of expressive interaction) *can simply not be predicted* (as Luhmann maintains), and neither do they cater to specific expectations that media executives might harbour.

As for mass-mediated entertainment, distinctions made between "open" and "closed" texts seem to be a matter of perspective, after all. Narrative indeterminacy is not well-suited for a discussion of power relations within what Abercrombie and Longhurst term the "Incorporation / Resistance Paradigm", or IRP for short (1998, 15). Matters of control and subversive appropriation – what Fiske / Hartley introduced as "politics of pleasure" – remain important issues on a research agenda that pertains to media as cultural battlefield. But the same media conceived as expressive playgrounds (here: for the imaginative and creative exploration of complex narrative worlds) ask for an analysis of audience agency in a slightly softer, more diffuse light (ibid., 31): "In the idea of playful readings any notion of the audience being constrained by the text is starting to disappear."

Instead of debating what (kinds of) reader response to what (kinds of) texts correspond more to some dominant or oppositional stance, and agenda, Abercrombie and Longhurst suggest to apply what they call the Spectacle / Performance Paradigm (or SPP), thereby acknowledging the "*disorder* of actual reader response"; that is, a "disorder of *unpredictability* not of *resistance*" (ibid., 32).

The paradigm shift Abercrombie and Longhurst propose derives largely from what they observe, and describe in detail as significant changes in the relationship between media texts and media readers:[100] Increasingly sophisticated, but also highly "diffused" and distinctively *modern* audiences find themselves courted by the mass media and suggestively asked out to engage in playful performances of spectacle and narcissism (ibid., 77 ff.). The possibilities to respond depend, however, on what resources (in terms of material and cultural capital) can be activated – with "[a]nalytical performance intrinsically related to emotional attachment" (ibid., 177).

It seems to me that the suggested metaphor of spectacle and performance – or mimetic play, as ludologists might prefer – suits the largely *unpredictable* practices that surround *indeterminate* (serial) fiction particularly well. Agency arises here from the gaps as reflective spaces and the perception-related, more or less consciously assumed freedom to imagine. What results from such practices as daydreaming pertains to largely private uses of mass media narratives but also public forms of interactive and intertextual participation for expressive purposes. For this see also Göttlich 2004, 35: From an actionist viewpoint media can be conceived as transitional "nodal points" for social, communicative everyday practices."[101]

In terms of spectacle and performance media entertainment can function both as a finite ("closed") or infinite ("open") game (see Carse 1986 for the difference, and Hague for a respective analysis of the mystery series *Twin Peaks*, 1995). The popular program strands offered by mass media delineate a vast topography of virtual and actual playgrounds for meaning-making activities and reflection.

When invited by authors to imagine – as readers, listeners or viewers – one can either partake in the spectacle "as it is" and try to complete the story (as Imgarden suggested), or take on narrative responsibility of one's own, fleshing out the blanks according to intentions less congruent with the auctorial standpoint and adding unforeseen creative supplements. Who is willing to invest even more and assume an auctorial stance instead, is free to peruse the narrative world and select elements

---

[100] Abercrombie / Longhurst quote earlier examples of star-audience relationships in the case of melodramatic cinema of the 1940s. In relation to Iser we can assume that particular media induced such changes at particular moments in time: Novels "did it" in the 19th century, while entertaining cinema experimented with performance-oriented address forms practically since its beginning as vaudeville attraction. Serialisation seems to have had a hand in this, and so has the explicit address of more "diffuse" audience segments such as women, or adolescents (... as Felix Fabri intuitively knew).

[101] Trad. ugb.; in German: "Durchgangspunkte sozialer bzw. kommunikativer Alltagspraxen" (for this see also Göttlich, 2007).

while leaving others to oblivion, deliberately altering appearances, genre characteristics, and storylines.

To illustrate such imaginative cut-and-paste compilation techniques I would like to refer to the *Harry Potter* heptalogy (Rowling, 1997-2007) and a particularly popular fan-based adaptation thereof.

In the *Potterverse* (for the term and its development see Thomas, 2007) the canonical territories are delineated by the seven books but also by a series of films in the making (Warner Bros., 2001- 2011). The carefully nurtured franchise became imaginative "fodder for thought" for individual fans as well as reading communities worldwide, with network-based translations of each and every instalment a constitutive, and particularly telling sign of collective reading practices. Among the many spin-offs and spoofs of the Potter saga is a series of short video skits by Neil Cicierega (2003 ff.) that featured real, but also in part animated hand puppets. According to the number of viewings indicated by the video platform *YouTube*, these short films did take a mostly adolescent fan community by storm. Thousands of commentaries left on this and other social media sites were only part of the phenomenon There was also an impressive number of recorded amateur performances emerging online,on which more follow-up performances were promptly modelled.[102]

Neil Cicierega's *Potter Puppet Pals* draw of course from Joanne K. Rowling's original characters (Snape, Dumbledore, Ron Weasley, Harry Potter and Hermione Granger, not to forget "Voldy" Voldemort) Cicierega went on to spin off his own narrative sub-world (or *Potterpalverse*), with co-tellers following his invitation to imagine and adding their own faithful re-enactments, creatively combined re-narrations as well as *resequenced, altered, customized* adaptations. A theatrical (and musical) spectacle of the original *Potter Puppet Pals* company before a Boston-based live audience (December 2006) elicited participatory response not unlike the *Rocky Horror Picture Show*, with delighted screams from the audience in response to particular details of the puppets' performance.

---

[102] For the original skits *www.youtube.com/user/potterpuppetpals*; 18-08-2017), for more information I suggest the Neil Cicierega fanpage at *https://illemonati.com/* (18-08-2017); the heavily debated re-enactments also found on *www.youtube.com* (search for "potter puppet pals").

4.7 Summary

Mass-mediated fiction depends on auctorial input that invites audiences to imagine and participate. Second-order observation of narrative events is relegated to the mimetic stage of co-created second worlds. As in other narrative communication events and episodes are prefigured, configured and refigured, with recursive connections realised in-between events and episodes. However, fictional narratives also open up "blank" spaces that can be recursively connected to one's own memories, hopes, and fears. Serial fiction is literally made of such gaps: Recognisable patterns of events and episodic rearrangements of events alternate with institutionalised waiting periods that provide ample space for imaginative and expressive performances of narrative knowledge.

As the example of the *Potter Puppet Pals* illustrates, serial narrative communication offered by mass media invites for prolific varieties of reader response. This is due to the accumulation of narrative knowledge over time and the repeatedly renewed invitation to imagine at the margins of instalments and episodes. Public access to reader response as "user-generated content" is clearly a result of new media technologies and rapidly increasing band-width which allows those aspiring performers to meet their audiences in conveniently furbished arenas. But the potential for these daydreaming activities derives from the imaginative freedom warranted by mass media, and entertaining narrative art in particular.

Serial entertainment is *interactive* because of the regularly anticipated and repeated entry in already familiar second world territory. Serial narrative communication pushes the envelope of sustained disbelief significantly further into areas of willing *participation* over extended periods of time, as Janet Murray (1997) notes.[103]

With episode endings read as "open" or "closed" and pertaining to "focused" or "unfocused" storylines serial narratives allow for more readings than meets the eye of the first-level observer. While serial presentations of fiction place consumers at *the whim of those who command the medium* (Hagedorn 1995), the control of content does not extend to equally controlled meanings. Narrative worlds as playgrounds for audience agency may (as Luhmann claims) come with somewhat "finite", socially determined borders and institutionally suggested roadmaps. But there are, and always were, more ways how to get involved and play along.

---

[103] Murray (1997, 40 ff.) has more examples for audience agency expanding into playful performances supported by computer technology. For media of the third degree see also Brenda Laurel (1993) and Mark S. Meadows (2002).

5   EPISODIC FICTION ACROSS MEDIA AND GENRES

Up to here narrative indeterminacy emerged as necessary precondition for narratees prepared to participate in entertaining fiction and waiting to be transported (in Luhmann's words) to narrative second worlds beyond the realm of everyday reality. The other precondition is willing suspension of disbelief, or (again in Luhmann's terms) second-order observation of one's own being transported. The need for audiences to "want to believe" in some alternative reality, for the moment and in the controlled atmosphere of playful communication, is a basic condition of social existence. Constructivist thinking sees reality states as depending on (socially negotiable) observational stances. To have alternatives to choose from is a prerogative for one's own everyday reality to become meaningful as such. The multiple second worlds of fiction can then be seen as society's training ground for the construction of sense – in terms of negotiation of what is "real" and what is not – within a given context. Part of this is and will remain play and "pure" entertainment. But part of it is also hard work and agony and entails the risk of failure (to make sense, exactly).

At stake is always the ambiguous reality state of narratives: What is mutually prefigured, configured and refigured as series of "events" within some co-created story world results from imaginative reassignments of narrative gaps (Iser's "vacancies" that are alimented from within the story world) but also from recursive connections linking voids (Iser's strategic or accidental "blanks") back to previous everyday experiences that are remembered, reassessed and put to work.

This is why narrative fiction produces different readings depending on motivations and investments in the second world at stake - different readings by different narratees, and different readings by narratees caught reading at different moments in time. Because memories of previously (lived or told) "stories" will interfere with later re-tellings: they merge and emerge from constantly rearranged, variously alimented narrative "streams". Over the long run (which may be: the course of one's lifetime) the two realms of knowledge blur and blend over, with blanks being reread as vacancies and vice versa, and with the collectively imagined feeding back into the experienced.

This study argues that entertaining fiction is an important part of such ongoing negotiations of reality states (in terms of narrative self-management of persons and organisations) and should not be dismissed as somewhat eerie, deceptive flip side of our common everyday reality. In Horace Newcomb's words (2004, 426), "[t]he significance of narrative and genre is the permission granted to consider alternatives to our own states of being".

Once narrative fiction emerges from episodic instalments the narratees' involvement can take on the dimension of some long-term engagement within the second world at stake. Chances are the world's ideated parameters will grow more familiar over time, with expectations building towards a reflexive stance that might indeed "know better" than to insist on suspended disbelief. Luhmann views reflexivity as problematic once it is applied to entertaining communication – because entertainment is not to be confounded with "art". I, however, take sides with Iser and Eco: Why exclude more knowing narrative stances that stem from an extended investment in playful worldmaking from the pleasureable experiences media do provide? In contrast to Luhmann I sustain that collaborative fiction is highly functional as entertainment as long as either side of the contract – narrators as well as narratees – are equally willing to boldly go where no one has imagined before, and work the stage for further narrative communication to ensue.

As has been previously stated this study is interested in the changes that affected serialised narrative communication within US-American prime time television from the 1980's onwards, with cumulative narrative strategies (Newcomb 1985) analysed more closely in part II and III (chapters 7 ff.). Seriality is analysed not so much in terms of aesthetic principle and expressive mode *sui generis* (of which dodecaphonic "Zwölftonmusik" and Chris Ware's graphic art might be more telling examples) but as an economic principle of commodity culture, or what is called "convergence culture" (Jenkins, 2006). This is why, in this chapter, the focus lies on questions of commodity and convergence – and more specifically on narrative control, on the *cost disease* affecting the cultural industries, on media shifting strategies, on aspects of distribution and, finally, on the symbolically generalised genres that regulate narrative expectation and are constantly negotiated between cultural industries and their clients, in terms of those variously knowing and responsive audiences.

5.1 Narrative indeterminacy and questions of control

As long as Catholicism, in the Western world, provided a largely uncontested literary canon in terms of "historical truth" there was no need for further distinction between narratives based on common knowledge as "truth" and other narratives referring to other sources of knowledge (... that were promptly identified as "lies"). If fictional works existed – and indeed they did, for educative as well as entertaining purposes – their authors did not face criticism, left alone the suspicion of heresy, as long as they convincingly claimed that their story belonged to the canon and deserved to be acknowledged as such.

This paradox situation is described by William Nelson (1973, 27 f.) as an

> "[...] accommodation of two conflicting attitudes: on the one hand, the insistence of the Judaeo-Christian tradition on veritable report, testified to as by witnesses in a courtroom; on the other, a sense that in tales of the past truth mattered little in comparison with edification or even entertainment. It must be concluded [...] that the accepted decencies forbade an author, not to make up stories, but to admit that he had. People, evidently, were delighted by stories and rewarded those who told them well. But there was no legitimate category of literature into which the verisimilar fiction could fit."

In consequence the study of medieval and renaissance literature does not refer so much to *fiction* (which is understood as describing a distinctively modern phenomenon), but rather to *secular* literature that emerged and evolved, in distinct varieties, from various genres of *sacred*, or religious writings.

In his book "Converting Fiction" (1998) David H. Darst traces back the measures taken by the Counter Reformation (a hegemonic cultural movement launched by the Roman Catholic Church against protestantism, in the wake of the 1563 Council of Trent) in its futile attempt to "streamline" what emerged as Spanish secular literature over the 16th and early 17th century. Popular works, in terms of early "bestsellers", were reassessed and *divinised* by a series of repurposing strategies which clearly foreshadow later acculturation techniques such as format adaptation, the "dubbing" of indexed passages, commissioned rewrites and plain censorship (for this see Darst 1998, 16).

What emerged from these radical rewritings of early fiction into "good", in terms of "valuable", reading material was supposed to foster the unsuspecting reader's conversion. In order to lure audiences back into what we may call catholic mainstream the responsible church officials relied on a well-known dramaturgical device – narrative closure. Forced endings came in three convenient variations that had unsuspecting protagonists either ...

- *baptised* (religious goal of conversion), or
- *married* (social goal of conversion), or
- *dying* (ontological goal of conversion).

For this see Darst (ibid., 10):

"In all three closures, the outcome is usually unexpected by the participants (although not by the readers / spectators / listeners), who view their ends as remarkably different from the expectations they as individuals had held. The works thus have a 'programmed' quality about them that demonstrates an 'agenda' of action leading inexorably to the appropriate closure, which in turn accommodates all those personages who have willingly reached a role of passive compliance with the directing forces in their lives."

One needs to distinguish here between *religion* on the one side (a system of believers' practices staking out the cultural dimensions of what is considered "real", in terms of believable versus unbelievable) and a monopolistic *knowledge structure* on the other – this is, a set of dogmatic positions which felt endangered by whatever temporary suspension of disbelief was playfully suggested by a competing "belief" system, namely secular fiction.

In their attempt to achieve what Luiz Costa Lima describes as "Control of the Imaginary" (1988) the Spanish inquisition took refuge within the same dramaturgic device that characterised adventure stories in earlier times of chivalric identity crisis. Narrative closure was seen as an effective means to restrain narrative indeterminacy. At stake was always a threatened monopoly of knowledge or, alternatively, an alleged "diverting" of audience attention from social matters considered more moral, more serious or just more rationally viable.

In the Victorian era the reading of novels was already a widely spread (as well as highly gendered) leisure activity (for this see Basch, 1974). At this time church officials were particularly worried about the gentry's well-educated daughters that might get involved with melodramatic fiction to the point where their fathers' authority was seriously threatened. Contemporary editors were fully aware of the paradox role their social engagement played: While they saw themselves as socially responsible mediators between authors and readers, willing to distribute acclaimed works of fiction to a large and dispersed audience, they also functioned as representatives of society's higher power and felt entitled to defend whatever puritan morale and bourgeois values prevailed at a given time.

5.2 Serial production of commodity culture and the cost disease

The industrial production of commodified cultural artefacts must, according to a widespread belief, follow Taylorist and Fordist principles of advanced capitalism (for this see Gramsci 1971 and Doray 1988) and is exploitative *by default*. Another remarkably pertinent argument is upheld likewise by overtly pessimistic sociologists and overtly optimistic advertisers: It sustains that serial narratives advance by their very nature as industrial goods the *massive* accumulation of profits through *massive* output of unspecific *mass* (or: trash) culture driving hapless *mass* audiences into conspicuous *mass* consumption (see Adorno in Bernstein, 1991, and MacDonald [1957] 1998; in response Brantlinger 1983, Miège 1989 and Carroll 1998).

From an economist's viewpoint, however, serial production – in terms of the streamlined assembly of easily recognisable, branded "tokens" in the mould of an approved, working "type" of product – belongs to a bundle of managerial tactics to keep rising production costs at bay.

According to Baumol et al. (Baumol / Bowen 1966, Baumol / Baumol [1984]1997, and Baumol 1997; for a synthesis also Kiefer 1998) all cultural industries face an indeed *massive* problem which is cost disease. At the core of what the authors also define as "cultural dilemma" lies the fact that the performing arts firmly root in handicraft as an invariably cost-intensive economic resource. The result is a comparatively low productivity that is compensated only in part by technological innovation.

A string quartet (to quote a favourite example of William J. Baumol) will always need the same amount of time to perform a specific piece of music – and not agree to play faster in order to compensate for rising salary costs. These activities become inevitably more expensive over time when measured by the standards established for economic growth in other sectors. The reason lies not so much with slow manpower (as one might assume) but relates to the increasing gap between technology-intensive production (where output is constantly accelerated while costs diminish over time) and less productive branches (where production output stagnates while the costs rise – in relation to the technology-intensive areas, that is).

This "disease" of stagnant productivity can be observed wherever production depends on human creativity and / or handiwork – not just within live performances of music, opera, theatre plays and other events understood as "art", but also within education, the legal system and health care: All of these sectors fight a constant battle for technological improvement and / or additional (for instance, governmental) funding, in order to remain competitive within the marketplace.[104]

It has been argued that the distribution of cultural artefacts by way of technology-enhanced mass media drastically diminishes, or even heals, the disease which seems

---

[104] For an application of the "cost disease" model to other and similarly cost-intensive social sectors see Baumol, William J.: Children of Performing Arts, the Economic Dilemma. The Climbing Costs of Health Care and Education. In: *Journal of Cultural Economics* 20 (1996, 183-206).

so obviously tied in with live (and local) performance. Instead Hilda and William Baumol went on to claim that hybrid cultural sectors – such as the film or broadcast industry – depend just as much on "live" investments of time and creativity as they do on technical innovation permitting cost reduction (Baumol / Baumol [1984] 1997, 112-113):

> "Broadcasting is a prime example of an activity which we call initially-progressive. It has two basic components: (1) programming, that is, the writing, set design and construction, and performance (acting, playing the music, etc.) of the actual programs, and (2) transmission, the delivery of the programs to their distant audiences. The first is extremely stagnant in its productivity growth; it is, indeed, virtually identical with live performance on a theatre stage. The second, electronic and high tech in character, is highly progressive. These are the defining attributes of an initially-progressive activity – the progressivity of one of the two dominating inputs and the stagnancy of the other, and the relatively fixed physical proportions of the two inputs – one hour of performance (with some flexibility in rehearsal time) and one hour of transmission per one-hour broadcast."

While the costs in an initially-progressive production sector appear to be decreasing right after some timesaving new technology has been put in place this is due to the said technology's rapid amortisation and therefore misleading. On the long run the stagnant activity will always "take over" and – once no more follow-up attempts at cost reduction ensue – account for up to 100% of the overall investment.

Serial production in the cultural sector (in terms of manufacture of preformatted items and the streamlining of the productive processes) and content leverage as "windowing" (the distribution of the respective product in planned stages) do work as effective counter measures against the cost disease. But they nevertheless provide only temporal relief.

When comparing the technical and program expenses of an average (local) US television station over 20 years in a row the Baumols found the thesis of the cultural dilemma confirmed: While in 1960 program costs accounted for 72% of the accumulated expenses (239.1 Mio $ of a total of 332 Mio $), by 1980 the percentage had gradually risen to 80% (1588.3 Mio $ compared to 1978.3 Mio $). The graph on the next page (Figure 10) is reproduced from the authors' original work and serves to illustrate the disproportionally rising costs within the broadcast sector.

According to Baumol (1997, 288) the main difference between initially progressive activities and stagnant, handiwork-based production lies in the limited potential for innovation of the latter. Mediating the cost disease results thus in a "mixed bag" of innovative and imitative measures, in most cases. Regarding live performances numbers of cast members can be reduced and repertoires somewhat "mainstreamed" in order to satisfy expectations of larger – or more diversified – audiences (Heilbrun, 2003). In the example of television entertainment (a classic hybrid sector, according to Baumol et al.) program executives may also choose to rely on reality programs and casting shows in order to exploit nonprofessional talent. Here the acquisition and / or adaptation of some ready-made program format replace elaborate, costly in-house research and development procedures.

Figure 10: Technical and program costs of an average US TV station (Baumol / Baumol [1984] 1997, 119)

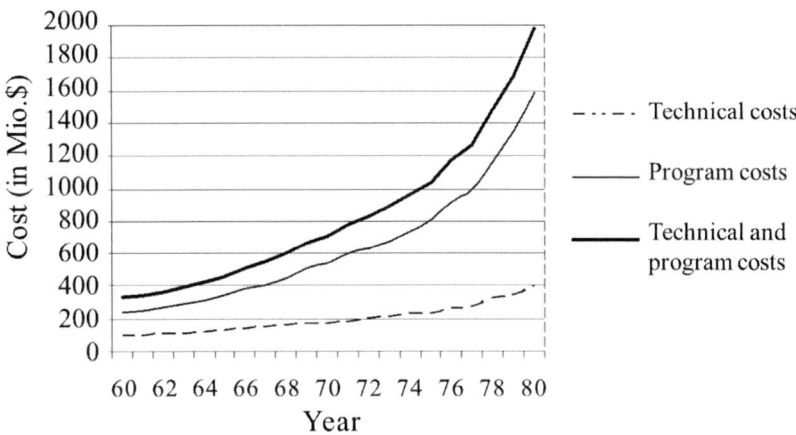

In a more recent analysis of capitalism and the free-market in terms of "innovation machine" (2002) William Baumol underlines (ibid., 271-274) the innovative role of R&D processes for television stations that must continuously scout for new content and promising talent. At stake is the willingness to risk and invest in long-term (human) resources which keeps competitors "on their toes" and in the marketplace while any attempt at safe play (i.e.: the choice to rely on preformatted content) would invariably result in a loss of profile. R&D activities may thus not always be rewarding in financial terms. But they entail the chance to accumulate knowledge which is an indispensable condition for both qualitative and quantitative growth.

According to the Baumols' diagnosis the successful management of cultural performances (... and other, similarly stagnant activities) depends on well-measured doses of innovation and imitation within the creative sector, in combination with a reasonable use of new production and distribution technologies. This is why industrial art follows conventional, recognisable recipes as "formulas" that leave room for the unforeseeable to happen. Any more radical cure applied to eradicate the cost disease (think of an exclusive investment in pre-tested programs while riskier activities are outsourced and / or substituted by investments in reproduction technology) might look good on a profit and-loss sheet but easily kill the patient, sooner or later.

5.3 Episodic fiction and cross-media ownership

While seriality in terms of narrative principle is as old as storytelling, seriality as production mode bears all the characteristic traits of modern commodity culture. According to Richard Dyer (1997, 14), "... [i]t's clear humans have always loved seriality. [...] However it is only under capitalism that seriality became a reigning principle of cultural production, starting with the serialisation of novels and cartoons, then spreading to news and movie programming. It's value as a selling device for papers and broadcasts is obvious."

Serially produced fiction published in discrete instalments over time works on two communicational levels, then: in terms of cultural artefact that invites for the circulation and further actualisation of meaning, and in terms of commodity that invites for further circulation within the system structures of cultural industries – and is invariably shaped, formatted also by these structures. While it is possible to analyse narrative fiction as text among other (narrative, fictional) texts, taking into consideration just the contexts that help to assess its meaning making capacity grasps only half of the story. The historical analysis needs to take into consideration the industrial contexts and the narrative traditions, as Roger Hagedorn suggests (1995, 29):

> What is lacking is the production and distribution of fragmented narrative in a mass medium that is consumed at regular intervals. Historically, for this to occur, one needs a social context characterized by three essential elements. A market economy, a communications technology sufficiently developed to be commercially exploited and, as [Roland] Barthes suggests, the recognition of narrative as commodity.

Fragmented storytelling within commodity culture works as an organisational device that binds authors of media narratives, their publishing and distributing agents and, finally, their audiences into a vertically controlled "assembly line" of production and consumption. Again, this does not exempt the resulting communication from being observed and enjoyed as what it is – art.

Systems theory allows for both perspectives as observational stances to co-exist: If some financial transaction at the fast food counter can go on despite two phone calls that are pursued simultaneously at both ends of the exchange (the example stressed by Moeller 2006, 6-7), all three communications may be equally "valid": the (successful) money versus receipt exchange flanked by two conversational talks at both ends. The same goes for an ongoing narrative conversation which is pursued by some auctorial collective at one end of the assembly line and an implied audience at the other: Immersion, sustained disbelief – and some collaborative production of meaning – ensue regardless of the economic prerogatives enabling that particular narrative conversation.

The following figure (Figure 11) is borrowed from Taylor (1993, 1) and illustrates the complex communicative endeavours pursued within the entertainment industry in the 1980s and 1990s, in view of some "text" as collaborative endeavour. Things have not changed much, since – except for the rising complexity at stake with regards to more media outlets available, in the wake of an increasingly globalised market and digitalisation.

Figure 11: Flows of money and content in the entertainment industry (Taylor 1993, 1)

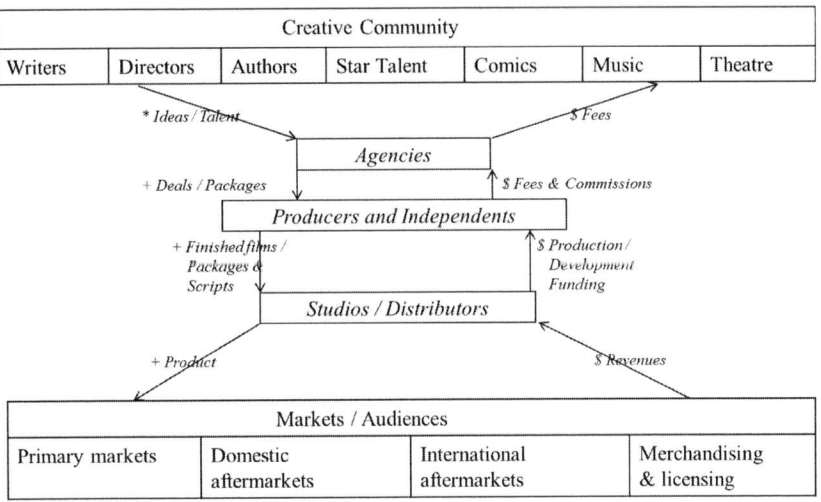

The Hollywood manufacture with its streamlined production of A and B types of content and strategic temporal windows opened towards primary and secondary markets relies on an interdependent web of institutional players including
- the *creative artists* performing (highly differentiated) tasks in view of some cultural good as commodity waiting to be published within a particular medium or a succession of particular media outlets over time,
- the main *publishers* and *distributors*; but also *agents* as middlemen stepping in that represent creative talent within crucial moments of deal negotiation, and

- the *merchants* delivering convenient packages of content to audiences, but also convenient packages of audiences to advertisers within specific territories and / or mediascapes.

In the context of the manufacturing process resulting from these interdependencies the principle of seriality allows for complexity reduction on various levels: Talent is hired on a long-term base instead of engaged "on occasion". Seriality formats content according to generalised expectations and delivers conveniently packaged doses of content, and audiences to markets. Not coincidentally the two basic formats of serially produced narrative communication within mass media – the autonomous ("unfocused") episode and the "focused", logically bound storyline within some overarching chain of cause and effects – were developed for paper periodicals. From written instalments they moved to early cinema; and from comic strips to broadcast radio and television.

Because of their potential to aggregate listeners, readers and viewers as loyal affiliates of particular contents, episodic narratives became staple goods within all distribution media, over time. The publication of novels in regular instalments did not involve a highly complex production infrastructure (apart from the technology Gutenberg invented some 500 years earlier). There was the publisher as commissioning instance (in terms of commercial / ideological risk-taker) on the one side, and the writer(s) who regularly engaged with personally known readers and / or reader communities on the other. Dickens' "serial stories" (see Iser 1971, and 1978, 191) should not be confounded with books that were merely retold in bits and pieces after some earlier publication as integral oeuvre had ensued. It makes a difference if auctorial control is applied *before* or *after* public reading, and assessing, sets in.

In the case of serial story distribution the media organisation (say: a newspaper or magazine editor) could determine non-negotiable entry deadlines based on the publication date and assign preformatted slots within the publication. Consequently, authors of ongoing stories published in successively submitted instalments were arguably just as much "at the whim of those who command the medium" as readers were – and also, to a certain extent, "at the whim" of the more expert readers that felt entitled to claim implied third party rights as co-tellers and co-authors.

The further differentiation of commercially viable organisational structures for book production and distribution confronted authors with the eventuality of lucrative long-term deals, but also with specific expectations as to what contents and narrative conventions were considered suitable. Successive publication of chapters of existing novels in local magazines was a strategy publishers employed to affiliate a predominantly female readership. Whereas Charles Dickens readily complied and adapted his works for episodic publication (and also started to write more frequently for this format) other contemporary writers did not want to hand over artistic control to their publishers and / or their audience. George Eliot (in private life: Mary Ann Evans) is a telling example of this, as Susanne Ostwald reminds us (2002, 75):[105] The author refused serial publication of her novel *Adam Bede* in the "Blackwood's Edinburgh Magazine" because she was in doubt about the legitimacy of her readers' expectations. She is quoted as following: "Unfortunately, I am as impressionable as I am obstinate, and as much in need of sympathy from my readers as I am incapable of bending myself to their tastes."

There is a particular kind of conflict over "control of the imaginary" at stake here: While secular authors in counter-reformatory Spain did not have a choice to resist what seemed to be an undisputed institutional demand, modern literature's commercial distribution system placed authors in-between publishing houses (as representatives of society, but also commercially interested enterprises) and an abstract readership on the other. Instead of death or expulsion as penalty for insubordination these writing professionals faced a complex set of constraints which was as subtle as it was binding. Instead of political censorship ruling there was an implicit commandment whispering: "You shalt not displease".

Hagedorn (1995, 30) argues that one of the early incentives for bit-by-bit distribution of literary fiction in daily newspapers was a legal loophole in regard to publishing taxes. The English Stamp Act of 1712 demanded a payment of one penny or 12 shilling for any full-sheet paper and of 6 shilling for any half-sheet paper, while so-called "pamphlets" (more than one page and less than book length) were only 2 shilling per page. Publishers took advantage by printing their daily news on one and a half page while filling up the remaining blank spaces with reprints of fiction. When the Stamp Act was revised in 1724 the practice of episodic publication of (existing) literary works stayed on since publishers grew aware of the fact that "readers had developed a taste for daily installments of fiction" (ibid.).

In the following years France became the most important European market for literary fiction published in distinct segments, because here the opinion press (which served specific party interests, in terms of a citizen-oriented, but not necessarily pluralistic "public service") gave way to more commercially oriented media

---

[105] Susanne Ostwald: Ende gut, alles gut. In: *Neue Zürcher Zeitung* (13-04-2002, 75).

structures far earlier than in other countries. The other main reason favouring the establishment of episodic fiction – which could then attract a returning, increasingly affiliated readership – already mirrored the single most important characteristic of private entrepreneurship: competition. While publishers of classical opinion press titles would aim for an utmost *difference* (of opinions expressed and point of views offered) publishers of commercially oriented press titles would rather try to go for *similarity*, either by adapting their selling strategies to what already seemed to work, or by simply stealing their rivals' ideas. This was the case with the parallel launch of Paris newspapers "La presse" (published by Emile de Girardin) and "Le siècle" (published by Armand Dutacq after he had – always according to Hagedorn 1995, 30 –initially collaborated with Girardin, during the planning phase of his paper.

The publication of fiction in consecutive instalments, if possible in association with a well-reputed brand name such as Honoré de Balzac (... whose *La vieille fille* began its run in de Girardin's "La presse" half a year after the launch of the newspaper), ought to guarantee quality as well as, yes, distinction (from other, similarly structured products).

Once the innovative turn towards episodic fiction linked renowned author names such as Charles Dickens, or Honoré de Balzac and Eugene Sue, with commercial success, episodic distribution of fictional narratives was firmly established as publishing principle. It was a matter of time until new, visually enhanced media just like the comic strip and the film serial jumped on the bandwagon. Not surprisingly, these were launched by severe competition in the publishing sector.

Comic strips were the main form of episodic entertainment licensed by newspapers or magazines from the turn of the 20th century onwards, with syndication (the subscription to a central right-holder conveniently organising the flow of content and fees) a far-reaching innovation for distribution (Hayward 1997, 93). Syndication of successful strips allowed for strategic programming of the funny pages, with characteristic scheduling patterns catering to various target audiences. There were the regular readers of the "dailies", but also the more occasional readers coming back only for the (more lavish, and often coloured) Sunday cartoon section. This is to say that both the middlemen and the original authors needed to consider different reading practices, with various levels of "ingenuous" or "knowing" readership.[106]

---

[106] For the history of the US-American comic strips see Inge, M. Thomas: Comics as Culture. Jackson: University Press of Mississippi 1990; Harvey, Robert C.: The

Episodic comic strips giving way to more complex forms of "graphic novels" over time foreshadowed the development of commercial television fiction in the late 20th century: Tight schedules and rigid spatial requirements asked cartoonists to adapt, but also to improvise and innovate.[107] As competition grew there were few viable alternatives for aspiring cartoon artists: either the imitation of already working models in terms of panel organisation and / or textual formula – or a more innovative use of the already established "multimedia" codes so typical for this hybrid art (think of writing styles, signature visuals, framing and editing of "movement", black and white alternating with colour, etc.). It fell to the responsible programmers of syndicates and individual newspapers to decide what narrative structures were offered to the weekend patrons instead of the daily strip patrons, and to what extent the respective reading patterns should be synchronised or not. What these graphic stories had in common with their written predecessors, however, was the relatively low degree of technological complexity which allowed readers (... at least in theory) to come up with their own written and / or drawn adaptations and extensions of auctorial input.[108]

Newspaper strips evolved from full-scale drawings containing scattered chunks of written text into the more common arrangement of (a predetermined number of) panels, with or without explicit frames and with or without textual "bubbles". Cartoon reading is not considered to demand extended alphabetical skills but it certainly requires specific skills with regards to the filling of vacancies and recursive linking of narrative blanks. This concerns both the gaps in between actions, events

---

Art of the Funnies. An Aesthetic History. Jackson: University Press of Mississippi 1995; Rohode, M.G.: The Commercialisation of Comics. A Broad Historical Overview. In: *International Journal of Comic Art* 1 (1999) 2, 143-170; and Wright, Bradford: Comic Book Nation. The Transformation of Youth Culture in America. Baltimore / London: Johns Hopkins Press 2001.

[107] An interesting example for both is David Lynch's vanguard strip featuring the *Angriest Dog in the World* (*L.A. Reader* et al., 1983-1992): Each panel consisted of three identical sketches of a house with a garden and a dog that leans in on a tight leash and snarls menacingly; the fourth was a night view. For the strip's author being notoriously absent and sending in the bubble text (for the dog-owners that speak from within the house) by mail or fax, this was an unorthodox as well as convenient way for keeping the comic strip running. For examples see *www.lynchnet.com/angrydog/* (18-08-2017).

[108] Research on literacy with regards to serial novels and comic strips that would extend to reader response offered and / or solicited over the course of time is still scarce – alas. Such practices can easily be found among a young readership, with abundant examples of drawings inspired by comic and cartoon models (and Disney characters, more particularly) found on as well as off school.

and states depicted from panel to panel and the gaps-between instalments as such (Hayward 1997, 85-86):

> "By taking a story and dividing it up into separate, isolated instants, comics annihilate the seamless 'flow' of narrative, forcing viewers or readers to subjectively justify leaps from frame to frame across temporal or spatial gaps. The reinvention of text / reader relations is troubled by the additional requirement that these disjunctive little boxes can only appear four at a time. This requirement has two consequences: creators are forced to leave out large chunks of narrative as they compress their stories, and narrative flow must be continually interrupted, frame to frame as well as day to day. Because of the gap signified by the thin line separating one frame from the next, the genre gradually developed conventions to signal any transitions that had been made in time, space, or subject. By actively interpreting these relationships of cause and effect, time, and space, comic-strip readers virtually create the story."

Another outlet for illustrated adventure stories were dime novels, also known in terms of *pulp* fiction. The output pertains to just about every adventure genre imaginable (for a history of the pulp genres and questions of readership see McCracken 1998; for a historical overview also DeForest 2004, 109-147). These two popular forms of serially produced and regularly displayed entertainment became known to wide audiences as "funnies" and "pulps". The third important outlet for episodic adventure stories were movie theatres, with the early "serials" explicitly addressed at female audiences. In the United States this phenomenon was intrinsically linked to an urban lifestyle and owed its success to the boom of the East coast metropolis at the turn of the 20th century. Here innovative newspaper editors such as Randolph Hearst commissioned weekly or bi-weekly cinema presentations that were usually 30 minutes in length and bore so titillating titles as *The Perils of Pauline* or *The Hazards of Helen*. But the same episodes were also reproduced – right before or right after they ran in cinemas – in the weekend supplements of the commissioner's newspapers or, alternatively, within specific fan magazines.

According to Jeremy Tunstall (1994, 69) the establishment of the US-American film serial resulted primarily from a "newspaper circulation war" fought between the "Chicago Tribune", the "Chicago Herald" and the publications owned and operated by Randolph Hearst:

> "The famous serial movies such as *The Adventures of Kathlyn, Lucile Love* and *Perils of Pauline* all resulted from a Chicago newspaper circulation war in 1913-14; the serials ran both as weekly film episodes and as newspaper serials (in the 'Chicago Tribune', the 'Chicago Herald' and the Hearst chain respectively). These film and newspaper serials were forerunners of soap operas for both radio and television. At least four such film serials were circulating in Britain by 1915. Before the blockade of 1918 they were also shown in Russia."

These conveniently "tied-in" newspaper serials were often lavishly illustrated and extended to elaborate photo plays (an earlier version of the Italian, also movie-indebted, *fotoromanzo*). Page examples can be found reprinted in Ben Singer's reflections on the subject (Singer 1993 and 2001).

According to Singer the parallel publication of instalments, both in movie theatres and as written episodes, had explanatory character and helped to compensate for a still rudimentary narrative language considered characteristic for the films of the time. Disoriented readers could then take their time and reassess the screen experience within the much more familiar form of a pictorial representation. Consequently Singer attributes the tie-in's decline (around 1917-1918) not only to paper shortage in the wake of World War I but also to the fact that the narrative language of cinema had evolved sufficiently to render these cueing devices obsolete (Singer 1993, 495):

> "As the classical Hollywood style developed, and film makers gained a better command of its codes of filmic narration (and a better understanding of its limitations), perhaps tie-ins were no longer needed as narrative guides. As movies became more intelligible (and longer), film-makers and spectators might have had less need of ancillary texts to elucidate subtleties of plot, motivation and psychology."

Shelley Stamp (2000) contests Singer's theory and insists on the early serials' narrative strengths rather than their weaknesses. If cinematic instalments worked as an intermediate form of audiovisual fiction between the earlier, mixed variety performances and the later feature-long presentations,[109] then reading practices could equally borrow from both forms of spectacle and knowingly integrate information provided by other media outlets. She suspects that the female moviegoers targeted by the "blood-boiling" adventures were savvy enough to enjoy the enhanced possibility to revive the narrative experience *again*, before or after access to the cinematic version.

---

[109] Philip Rosen (2001, 163) retraces the history of the mixed film program from the practice of the newsreel back to earlier, news-oriented "topicals" as a sort of *visual newspaper*. He claims that the fictional and factual parts of film presentations were always clearly distinguished and viewed differently– with television the first medium to actively blur the boundaries and establish what might nowadays be called "docudrama". For examples that are taken from early British television, with a nod to blue collar, working class soap opera such as the still-ongoing *Crossroads*, see Kerr (1990).

Rather than preparing audiences for the authoritatively predetermined dramaturgy of feature films (as Singer suggests) these movie serials successfully resisted ideological closure; they represented, according to Stamp (2000, 102-103), "... a marked departure from increasingly normative trends: issued in two-reel instalments usually over a period of months, serials were neither feature films nor traditional shorts; their multifaceted tie-in publicity encouraged intertextual viewing practices that were distinctly at odds with models of spectatorship becoming standardized in classical narrative."

Following Stamp's argument, these stories were not so difficult to understand (by expert readers of blood-boiling fiction, that is) but instead resisted the general tendency towards longer formats, with their imposed narrative closure and the silent, concentrated reading demanded of higher culture. It was, in other words, just so pleasurable to "go there" in order to become immersed all over again. Serials successfully subverted the ongoing trend towards *decorous femininity* as it was "celebrated in other promotions to would-be female filmgoers" (ibid., 103).

The phenomenon of parallel publication within different outlets is explained by Stamp in narrative but also economic terms, and here as serving promotional goals in terms of word-of-mouth (for this see also Hediger 2003, 71 ff.). Rather than providing additional occasions for readers and viewers to "get the message", once and for all, this industrial practice produced synergies between the economic and the narrative system by allowing consumers "at the whim of those who command the medium" to be transported one more time to the second world of a still lingering adventure story or, alternatively, to a narrative stage where memories of past adventures could be revived while the trailer already announced further attractions waiting to be coming to a theatre nearby, within a week or a fortnight from now.

The first film serial (*What Happened to Mary?*, 1912) was based on the fictitious portrait of an ideal American woman which was also depicted on the cover of the Hearst's monthly "Chicago American" supplement called "Ladies' World" and featured inside the magazine. From the second chapter of Mary's fictional biography onwards readers could follow her monthly adventures both in the "World" and in local movie theatres. And, once all of the 12 instalments of *What Happened to Mary?* had been screened, a sequel of six more episodes followed (*Who Will Marry Mary?*). At the same time the "Chicago Tribune" (owned by Cyrus McCormick) published in its own weekly sunday supplement another serial story called *The Adventures of Kathlyn*, which became a bi-weekly movie serial too.

From these early tie-ins between press and theatre releases the pattern spread over to other such collaborations and ignited what was soon talked about as "serial craze". Film serials such as *The Exploits of Elaine* (instalments screened on a weekly base) or *The Perils of Pauline* (published bi-weekly) drew audiences in apparently overwhelming numbers to the movie theatres. Most of these narratives were conceived as "serials", exactly, with an ongoing story and conventionalised cliffhanger structure, while closure was only expected to occur at the end of some heroine's frequently interrupted run towards wealth, or the detection of a long-lost sibling, or marriage. A few were "episodic series", however, with narrative closure provided at the end of every segment screened.[110]

Filmed live action drama – the medium favoured by the publishers of Ladies' supplements and magazines – was cost-intensive and depended on highly differentiated technical and artistic skills. These lavish and often spectacular second worlds had to be built from scratch, with the scripted narrative events played out by actors that were cast in the roles of recurring or guest characters and staged within theatrical settings adapted to the needs of cinematography. These complex procedures of world-making helped two of the institutional phenomena most typically associated with "Hollywood" – the studio system and the star system as interrelated, commercially driven manufactures of collective daydreaming – to evolve from these early adventure serials (for details see Schatz 1988 and Staiger 1995; for the star system also Gledhill 1991, and Stacey 1994).

Stamp describes in detail how the early movie star cult developed at the time, encouraging viewers to identify both with the female protagonists and the actresses playing them.[111] As her analysis of the opening "teaser" to one of the Pathé serials

---

[110] For a dubious case see Hagedorn (1995, 44, note 16): "There is a certain amount of confusion over the exact status of *What Happened to Mary?* While many historians regard it as a series film, others [...] have dubbed it the first serial, arguing that it followed a continuing main character and general story-line. Given the fact that the film no longer exists, it is difficult to determine if it constitutes a film series or serial. It seems very likely that [it] was yet another Edison series similar to its 1913 offerings, *The Chronicles of Cleek, Mr. Wood B. Wedd's Sentimental Experiences, The Adventures of Andy,* and *Octavius, the Amateur Detective,* and that most or all of these series were structured around some basic equilibrium which is repeatedly disrupted."

[111] Examples of (author- or viewer-induced) fan activities with regards to silent and early sound cinema are reassessed in Gledhill (1991), with ready-made fashion drawn from movie costumes and home couture activities a particularly interesting domain studied by Herzog / Gaines (in Gledhill, ibid.).

(*The Mystery of the Double Cross*, 1917) illustrates, many of these stories invited viewers to literally join the action – forerunning what Woody Allen humorously reconstructs as fictitiously lived out symbiosis of multiple realities in his nostalgic film comedy *Purple Rose of Cairo* (1985).

The star of the *Double Cross* franchise (Mollie King) is first seen reading the original adventure book, visibly excited and exclaiming (via intertitle) that she would love to "play this". She is then literally drawn into the book and appears briefly superimposed on its pages before the separate images of the reading actress and the playing actress dissolve into the book's heroine in full regalia. Assuming the role of the protagonist King turns to the audience, looks straight into the camera and invites viewers "… to come with me through my adventure and try to solve the Mystery of the Double Cross" (for this see Stamp, 103).

As this early example of intertextual as well as "interactive" reader address shows mass media borders were as readily transgressed as the "fourth wall" – which is more commonly associated with social distance. With media ownership extending from one narrative outlet to other strategic, text transfer from one medium to another appears to have been the rule rather than the exception. Just as film serials were tied-in with periodicals that conveniently retold a week's episode to an extended audience, the heroes of serial strips made their appearance within other economically linked media outlets as well.[112] Radio adventure series such as *The Shadow* switched to pulp magazines and back to radio, with a "side trip into the comics", as De Forest (2004, 158) puts it.[113] The radio western *The Lone Ranger* (1933-1956), for instance, spawned "novels, movie serials and comic books before eventually jumping to television" (ibid., 150).[114]

Radio performances brought to this thriving landscape of mediated serial fiction a new sense of theatrical "live" atmosphere that the movies lacked, for several reasons. The broadcasting technology provided what Ong calls "second orality", in

---

[112] The *Peanuts* strip from Tuesday 17-02-1953 pokes fun at the cross-over practice (see Schulz 2004 -, vol. 2, 21): Shermy asks Charlie Brown out to the (movie) theatre. The film in question is *Ivanhoe* (this must be *Sir Walter Scott's Ivanhoe* from 1952, with Robert Taylor and Elizabeth Taylor). Charlie Brown declines, arguing that "I don't like to see a movie before I've read the comic magazine".

[113] For the original magazine adventures see *www.thepulp.net/theshadow.html* (18-08-2017).

[114] Original episodes of *The Lone Ranger* can be listened to at the Old Time Radio Researchers Group; see *https://archive.org/details/OTRR_Certfied_Lone_Ranger* (18-08-2017).

terms of an illusion of direct address and peer-to-peer communication. On the other hand the domestic setting provided a much more intimate framework for reader response than earlier public reception modes did. A response that became not suddenly "passive" by such transitions but certainly less visible from the outside.

With the new outlet of broadcast radio added to the multimedia mix of movie theatres, pulp fiction and newspaper cartoons (and, not to forget, live theatre), the collaboration beyond media borders extended to the content-hungry radio schedules. Synergy effects did exist between radio and early cinema (for examples see Breitinger 1992, and Hagen 2005), and comic strips appear to have influenced the narrative structure of early radio serials (for this see Hilmes 1993, and 1997).

The same strategies that adapted comic strips to the radio waves, and to television screens in the early 1950s, can be observed in more recent attempts to tie-in long-lasting television series with feature films, or successful adventure movies with computer games. Of all the various collaborations the most sustainable varieties are probably found in theme parks that employ architectural sites and offer a multitude of occasions for immersion within the respective second world.[115] At the other, more ephemeral end we find as many *table top* and *handheld* solutions (think of board games, card games and applications for handheld devices) as there are playful and / or performance-oriented activities derived from all these successful franchises.

A telling example for *spin-offs* and *cross-overs* is provided by Angela Ndalianis (see Ndalianis 2004, 37-39) in a study drawing from Omar Calabrese's aesthetic concept of the "neo-baroque" (Calabrese 1992): She lists all the movies, sequels, comic books, games and other media that 20th Century Fox spun off in-between 1979-2004) from Ridley Scott's highly popular film franchise *Alien* (here, Table 4):

Table 4: The second worlds of the *Alien* franchise (Ndalianis 2004, 37-39) [116]

Franchise (year)	Property rights	Medium	Genre
Alien (1979)	20th Century Fox	cinema	horror
Aliens (1986)	20th Century Fox	cinema	horror
Alien 3 (1992)	20th Century Fox	cinema	horror

---

[115] Two recent examples: *The Wizarding World of Harry Potter* opened in Orlando (Florida) in 2010, *Pandora – The World of Avatar* (as curated by James Cameron) in Summer 2017.

[116] Some additions provided by the author of this thesis.

Alien Resurrection (1997)	20th Century Fox	cinema	horror
Aliens: Earth War (1991)	Fox / Dark Horse	comic book	horror
Aliens: Book One (1992)	Fox / Dark Horse	comic book	horror
Alien War (1992)	20th Century Fox	role-playing game	horror
Aliens: Stronghold (1994)	Fox / Dark Horse	comic book	horror
Aliens: Music of the Spears (1994)	Fox / Dark Horse	comic book	horror
Aliens: A Comic Book Adventure (1995)	20th Century Fox	computer game	horror
Superman vs. Aliens (1995)	Fox / Marvel	comic serial	horror / scifi
Alien Trilogy (1996)	20th Century Fox	computer game	Horror
Batman / Aliens (1997)	Fox / Marvel	comic book	horror / scifi
Alien vs. Predator (2004)	20th Century Fox	cinema	horror / scifi

The example of the *Alien* franchise illustrates what Umberto Eco suggests to call a "citizenship in the real world" (Eco 1994, 126) for fictitious characters of a second world that are allowed to extend their action space and "free [...] themselves from the story that created them" – thanks to media shifts, franchise migration, and continuously extended story worlds. Eco, however, referred to an earlier fan-based story combining elements from two existing cinema franchises, namely *The Maltese Falcon* (1931, and remade 1941) and *The Third Man* (1949), by this anticipating the important role (... if not the truly massive scope) of fan-based story extensions-to-be.

5.4   Distribution modes and questions of access

Mass media, in terms of distribution media, are said to address "massive" aggregates of listeners, readers and viewers as dispersed participants within "massive" communicative attempts. This involves an indeed "massive" output of discernible programs which are produced and circulated within increasingly "massive" – that is, horizontally and vertically integrated – media industry outlets. Notwithstanding the type of institutionalisation (for instance, public or private) and inclination towards one or another form of structural convergence these media do still function as *distribution* media to this day: Communication takes place between participants over distance, with complex media technologies providing controlled access to particular contents within various public and / or domestic settings.

According to a distribution typology suggested by Bordewiik / Kaam (see McQuail / Windahl 1993, 209, and Jensen 2002, 185) distribution media are best differentiated by their operation mode, by the controlling agency at work (of the original database / of individual items within the database) and by the various access modes (to the original database / to selected items) they provide. What results from the respective reflection are four different types of "reading contracts" based on spatial and temporal accessibility:

- *Allocution*, meaning central control of database and temporally limited access to items (broadcast model),
- *Conversation*, based on a dispersed database that is hosted in remote places, with unlimited access to items (filesharing model),
- *Consultation*, based on the same dispersed database in remote places but with limited access to items (dispenser, or newsstand model),
- *Registration*, meaning central control of database while access to the items provided remains unlimited (library, or subscription model).

Narrative *allocution*, in the case of episodic fiction, leaves the initiative by default with the providing institution / right holder while imaginative uses of the provided materials are up to the users' interest and playfulness. This leaves both sides, narrators and narratees, in the dark about who else might indeed participate or not, in what particular function and to what end or understanding.

Narrative *conversation* takes part between dispersed co-tellers taking turns and referring back to each other. Whoever delivers input can expect to be noted, or addressed back by other members of the conversational network established for the telling.

Narrative *consultation* asks from involved audiences to seek and obtain doses of content from official outlets within a given time frame. The original provider issues limited "contracts" that may or may not refer to the further uses eventually made from the sought-after content.

Narrative *registration* leaves the control of the communication process with the issuing institution but the binding move of registration necessarily with (... highly interested, and identifiable) narratees as participants. It is the most elaborate of all four contracts, with elaborate rules established and patrons probably lectured on the "do's and don'ts" with regards to their perusing of premises.

In the era of (hand-held) computer devices digital distribution has significantly blurred the distinctions between access modes, just as it has the distinctions between the various ends of some conversational co-telling. For once, sneaking (= consulting) patrons do leave traces back to their computers, or debit cards, just as officially registered patrons do. It also means that audience feedback within dispersed (fan) circles, or networks, is fairly easily consulted / monitored by authoring institutions, be it for inspirational or control purposes.[117]

Seen from the perspective of end users, episodic narratives always venture beyond some "mass" allocution towards conversation and registration because of the substantial reader involvement at stake. I suggest that the far-reaching investments required on both ends of the communicative attempt lead to an aggregation of authors and knowing, *smart* second-level readers (following Umberto Eco's terminology) while, at the same time, segregating these initiated audiences both from non-observers (that are not interested in episodic fiction as such or not interested in the narrative world at stake) and from the first-time readers' more innocent, or unsuspecting reading stance.

The narrative contract is volatile, then, and oscillating between *conversation* and *registration* for experienced readers, with random *consultation* (or, alternatively, complete *abstinency*) among the options for less interested audiences. While allocution may still remain the basic model for serial "mass" address – and as such corresponds to institutional needs and strategic goals – this nevertheless results in highly heterogeneous and differentiated reading patterns.

5.5   Narrative conventions and questions of genre

Jim Cullen (2001, 5) defines *genre* as a form which can exist in more than one medium and "has more specific expectations surrounding it". Textual genres circulate freely among distribution media, but are in need to be constantly negotiated within

---

[117] When Adorno wrote his essay on television, and more precisely on serial television fiction ("How to look at television", 1954) he took the mainstreaming effect of serial allocution for granted – whereas Iser (1971) points to the gaps ripping open *because* of institutional attempts at determining some meaning. What emerges as individual interpretation depends from the listener's, reader's and viewer's willingness to accept (or dismiss, or negotiate) some dominant reading just as much as from the respective, more or less explicit institutional agenda.

two parallel communication contracts – the one existing between media institutions and content providers, the other existing between the same providers as narrators and authors (journalists, writers, producers) and their audiences as co-narrators and co-authors. If we look at the example of the generic macro category "fiction" the subcategories foster anticipation and recognition towards specific narrative events which are prone to happen in one specific second world as province of meaning rather than in other, just as imaginable provinces.

From the viewpoint of the cultural industry used to levering content within that first communication contract just mentioned, generic patterns help to define product types within the manufacturing process of cultural artefacts.[118] From the viewpoint of storytelling as art, however – and this regards communication processes in terms of participation in narration as second-order observation – the same generic patterns organise narrative knowledge and help to tell apart "ingenuous" newbies from "expert" readers.

As the work-in-progress character of generic classifications already indicates, there is no firmly established terminology among communication scholars and practitioners how to delineate the uses of the term "genre". Cullen (2001) and Grignaffini (2004) both suggest to differentiate between the economic and logistic aspects of textual types as "formats" and their cultural side as "genres", in an attempt to tell the two different communication processes apart – the one providing stakeholders with *content* (and fighting cost disease, along the way) while the other provides narratees with *stories*. Formats refer here to "the specific organization a form takes within a medium" (Cullen 2001, 5) and are defined by organisational parameters such as the outer limits of an instalment (in the case of episodic communication), the temporal arrangement within a given number of instalments (be it as "story arc" or "season") and the interruptions provided for sponsors as commercial advertisement spaces-to-hire.

According to Giorgio Grignaffini (2004) the distinction between one-hour dramas and half-hour sitcoms is format-related (at stake is the duration of an episode, the number of commercial breaks and the arrangement of one or several instalments

---

[118] For the example of classical Hollywood cinema see Schatz (1981), for the example of television Creeber / Miller / Tulloch (2001) and Mittell (2004); for the organisation of television schedules in respect to genres as "basic building blocks" Ellis (2000, 130 f.).

fitting into a given timeslot), while the label of the same episode as "police procedural" or "domestic sitcom" defines the program in question in terms of genre.[119]

John Fiske proposes a terminology that conceives "genre" as the more general term and distinguishes two aspects of generic communication as economic "formula" and cultural "convention". References to *formula* describe the commodity aspect, while references to *convention* relate to aspects of recognition (Fiske 1987, 110):

> "Conventions are the structural elements of genre that are shared between producers and audiences. They embody the crucial ideological concerns of the time in which they are popular and are central to the pleasures a genre offers its audience. Conventions are social and ideological. A formula, on the other hand, is an industrial and economic translation of conventions that is essential to the efficient production of popular cultural commodities and should not be evaluated by aesthetic criteria that dismiss it as mere lack of imagination."

All of these terms are used, in various way, to (a) reflect on the constructivist principles of generic classification and to (b) provide practitioners such as schedulers, producers and screenwriters with some basic rule-work for distinctions that is as rigid as necessary and as flexible as possible.

Newcomb (2004, 424) sums up the benefits of generic classifications for the film and television industries, and more precisely for the "knowing" professionals that are involved in the manufacturing process and must rely on easily identifiable blueprints in all stages of production stages:

> "The stories / plots – the narratives – defining (and defined by) the genre are [...] predictable. This enables producers who fund, distribute, and schedule the works to rely on an available pool of talent and technique. Writers who specialize in specific genres can provide material in line with the producers' expectations. Similarly specialized directors are skilled in managing the production process on tight schedules and precise budgets. Actors, despite their unwilling-ness to be typecast, are often identified with specific roles or role types and play to generic definitions. Locations can be used repeatedly or entire sets constructed for use in multiple productions. Props, such as costumes, weapons, vehicles, and decorations, can be purchased once with costs amor-

---

[119] The English language does not distinguish between more generalising aspects of formats as content "types" and more particular (for instance: legal) aspects related to the trade of program formats (Moran, 1998). In Grignaffini's terminology the Italian term "format" is used to describe formatted programs (of any kind), while the English "format" stays reserved to the discussion of program formats, copyright issues and questions of cultural adaptation.

tized over many years and uses. In one way, then, genres are best understood as examples of industrial efficiency."

As Fiske emphasises, genres work in terms of culture-specific modes of reflection on various levels of the narrative communication.[120] Entertaining second worlds offered by mass media share with other expressions of time-out culture (among them all sorts of games, the fine arts and especially religion) that they circulate generalised models of how to assign meaning to alternative world territories, and possible future scenarios, while providing practical projection screens for looking back at one's own life and everyday reality.[121] Just as art, truth, love, power or money, genres can thus be seen as *symbolically generalised media*, in terms of communication devices that are used among initiated literati as affiliates of a specific social (sub-)system.

Similarly to other such social "currencies" (say: *art* attributing meaning to particular oeuvres, *truth* defining relations within the science system, *love* circulating within the intimacy system, *power* negotiated within political system, and *money* lubricating the economic system) they render other means of communication obsolete – within the scope of the said system, anyway.

Seen from this Luhmannian angle, genres provide classification systems as modes (or "moulds") of observation for complex phenomena that are fitted into simpler categories based on predetermined criteria. The respective labels delineate forms of common knowledge and corresponding expectations in terms of double contingency. Distinctions made between entities are here based on flexible and (in theory) negotiable criteria – and may just as well stratify psychic systems as "persons", according to socially determined criteria (such as "race" or "gender"), or distinguish particular text types from other (significantly different, or nondescript) text types in

---

[120] For the concepts of genre-specific convention and invention I refer to Cawelti (1970, 27-28): "[A]ll cultural products contain a mixture of two elements: conventions and inventions. Conventions are elements which are known to both the creator and his audience beforehand – they consist of things like favorite plots, stereotyped characters, accepted ideas, commonly known metaphors and other linguistic devices, etc. Inventions, on the other hand, are elements which are uniquely imagined by the creator such as new kinds of characters, ideas, or linguistic forms. Of course it is difficult to distinguish in every case between conventions and inventions because many elements lie somewhere along a continuum between the two poles. Nonetheless, familiarity with a group of literary works will usually soon reveal what the major conventions are and therefore, what elements are unique to an individual work."

[121] Not coincidentally, narrative patterns are said to relate to religious traditions that provide culturally specific concepts of *afterlifes* (for this see Kermode, 1967).

accordance with system-external criteria and categories. This also means that genres necessarily draw from overgeneralisations and conveniently stereotype certain parameters of the represented, in the case of psychic systems "personalised" world (for this see Lippmann 1922, and Seiter 1986).

Narrative conventions are neither universal nor given, then. They emerge from cultural habits and corresponding learning processes (for this see Cawelti 1997, and Newcomb 2004 – for television genres also Feuer 1992, Mittell 2004 and Edgerton / Rose 2005). That goes also for distinctions made between "fiction" and what often remains unspecified as "nonfiction" (for this see Hallenberger 2004, for a discussion of "documentary" and "realistic" modes Corner 2000, Rosen 2001 and Jerslev 2002) – or for conventional story beginnings, and endings (again Kermode 1967, for a more general discussion of the topic; for feature films Neupert 1995 and Christen 2001).

Excursion: A side glance at gender bias

According to constructivist thinking generic formulas are taught and internalised within the phases of primary and secondary socialisation (Berger / Luckmann 1966). In this context Luhmann (2000a) points to the increasingly important socialising role of mass media's multi-faceted referential models.

So far there is no gender-sensitive theory of narrative communication that sheds light on the complex relationship between "genre" (in terms of classification system for cultural artefacts that become recognisable as "works of a particular type") and "gender" (in terms of classification system of particularly socialised personae that become recognisable in terms of communicative behaviour).

The unison translation of both terms as *genre* in the French language and *genere* in Italian indicates a relationship that is hardly coincidental. Some narrative genres address gendered target audiences explicitly: Japanese animation films for young people exist in "shonen" variations for boys and "shojo" versions for girls; for this see Sabucco, 2000. Other genres refer to traditionally gendered roles and domains as their central subject and theme – this is the case of "action adventure" and "romance", for instance.

The problem is to find some valid common denominator within both classification systems that accounts for the coincidence and can explain why some types and forms of allegedly generalised narratives seem to cater to persons of one socially determined category rather than the other. When it comes to story protagonists as role models the respectively ascribed (professional, or personal) range of manoeuvre is indeed an important indicator of particularly "gendered" narratives as well as respectively gendered spaces in one's "paramount reality" (to quote Schütz). However, the look at existents (i.e., the protagonists / their place in society) can hardly account for structural differences that are expressed on syntagmatic levels (in terms of acting versus being acted upon, or "closure" versus "openness") and may result in bipolar schemes such as the *series* versus the *serial*. I claim that the common denominator is arguably found within communication as social operation and respectively gendered expectations towards communicative behaviour on all (macro, meso and micro) levels of observation.

While it should be possible to analyse gendered roles, communicative strategies and social differentiation in the light of systems theory, there has not been any respective attempt yet, to my knowledge.[122] From a functionalist perspective all genres (and here I include the classification system pertaining to social "persons") work as socially determined "observational modes" that read and distinguish particular (for instance: biological: psychic or narrative) items as "texts". This is to say that all generic expressions of time-out culture (within entertainment, the fine arts or religion) are necessarily linked to some "gendered" social category – and naturalised (= rendered invisible) as long as the respective combination appears to "makes sense".

According to the sociolinguist Deborah Tannen (1986) conversational styles were always – and remain, to a certain extent – highly gendered. She claims that dialogic communication relies extensively on gendered patterns that transform predetermined (namely, "public" and "domestic") spheres into telling soundstages for persons that engage in more or less socially approved everyday performances.[123]

Tannen's findings from the mid-1980's suggest that *masculine* conversational styles, understood here in terms of stereotypical communicational behaviour that follows cultural standards and caters to expectations, express tendencies towards

1. eloquence in public spheres contrasted with domestic, often awkward silence,

---

[122] Luhmann was rather old-fashioned in this regard and did not consider gender differences to be relevant enough to account for the shaping of modern societies and expressed severe scepticism towards feminist social criticism (for a discussion of Luhmann's position see Hellmann, 2004). This may be why systems theory only recently engaged in gender issues (see Kampmann / Karentzos / Küpper, 2004, and especially Weinbach, 2004).

[123] Among the first to theorise communication as social performance was Erving Goffman (1959). For the approach of *doing gender* (the term coined by Candace West and Don H. Zimmerman in 1987) see Kotthoff / Wodak (1997), Romaine (1999), and Speer (2005).

2. efficient message transfer, with ritual preliminaries often considered secondary,

3. status negotiation as an indispensable prerogative to engage within communicational contracts.

Feminine conversational styles (in the same social and cultural context) are said to verge accordingly towards

1. eloquence in domestic spheres contrasted with public, often awkward silence,

2. establishment of intimacy as communicational goal, with message transfer often considered secondary,

3. status ambiguity, flexibility and fluidity seen as unproblematic when engaging in communicational contracts.

The second worlds of narrative and game-oriented mainstream fiction are, of course, not exempt from such stereotypical behaviour since they borrow heavily from everyday reality and common sense. According to Fiske (1987, 215), "[w]ork patterns, narrative form, and the meanings given to gender difference are all constructs of the same patriarchal culture so it is not surprising that they are based on the same structural play of similarity and difference."[124]

An interesting correspondence emerges between what Tannen identifies as gendered conversation styles and Luhmann's ambivalent conception of humans as closed psychic systems on the one side but also structurally coupled "persons" on the other. If socialisation processes work as distinctions that mark individuals (which remain otherwise impenetrable) as somewhat recognisable "persons", then gender is arguably the very first distinguishing criterion to come into play here – from early ultrasound scans onwards, practically.

Seen from a systemic angle the main difference between *masculine* and *feminine* conversational styles lies in the attention typically paid to either one or to the other side of the distinction – either to the psychic system's autonomy that is sustained and catered for or, alternatively, to the person's affiliation with its environment that is encouraged and rewarded.

---

[124] Fiske (ibid., 215-223) gives an overview of the paradigmatic, gendered differences made within the televisual narratives told in daytime and prime time relates the strive for climaxes and closures within Western culture to respective patriarchal power struggles. For the gendered concepts of "productivity" and "reproductivity" see Agger (1998).

What results as systemic interpenetration and mutual irritation between the categories of the respective "gender system" is best interpreted in the light of status / role negotiation, as Fiske suggests. Because the establishing of system borders and what results as structural couplings is pursued as every day task and mirrored within very many "typically" gendered patterns that range from playing preferences among rivalling boy groups and girl groups to more implicitly gendered categories in adult life, such as the distinction between "hard" news and "soft" news. Tannen's typology of conversational styles can be read here as a map of how such perceptions are conventionally negotiated (a) within gendered domains and (b) episodic everyday communication but also (c) within communicative situations of a higher complexity where understanding may depend on the attention given to the social borders at stake.

What results as gender bias can thereby be (metaphorically!) described as a somewhat naturalised socialisation of men as (solitary) "trees" and women as (interconnected) "grass". The difference with regards to social affiliations is exemplified in the following two figures (Figure 12, here, and Figure 13, next page):

Figure 12: Structurally coupled person with emphasis on systemic autonomy

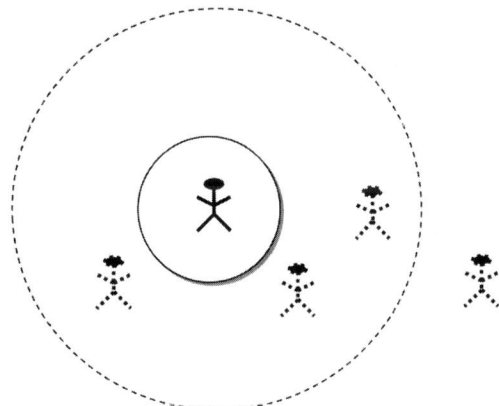

While such analytical distinctions work as second-order observations of stereotypical first-order observations – and thus entail a certain risk of further naturalisation of the discrimination, as Bourdieu warns (2002) they do indeed help to explain gendered phenomena and social problems related to psychic systems' borders – they are more than "skin deep", proverbially spoken.[125]

Figure 13: Structurally coupled person with emphasis on social affiliation

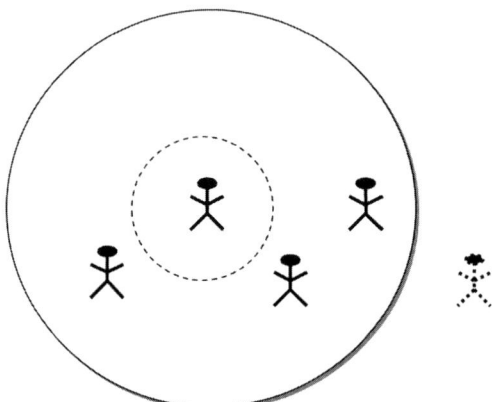

As mentioned before stereotypical (pre- as well as re-)constructions of the public sphere as "masculine" and the domestic sphere as "feminine" have produced a broad variety of respectively marked genres – most significantly *action adventure* on the one hand (for this see Carey, 1976) and *romance* on the other (Ang 1990, Byars 1991, and Kaplan 1992).

But Tannen's categories do allow for some more generalised re-readings of gendered communication, with priority assigned either to the attainment of predetermined objectives (in the case of "masculine" conversation) or to sustained intimacy (in the case of the "feminine" counterpart) and with regards to gendered social skills within complex communicational networks (that are to be understood as vertical orientation within hierarchic communication and horizontal orientation within communication among participants viewed as equals).

Marshall McLuhan was arguably the first explicitly feminist media scholar to satirically comment on such bipolar structures with regards to mass mediated fiction (McLuhan [1951] 2001, 154-157). In his merciless look at contemporary feature films as "horse opera" and radio daytime fiction as "soap opera" he dismisses the Wild

---

[125] Striking examples of this may be found within public beauty discourses – but also in other arenas where the appearance of women is under public scrutiny, with aspects of femininity related to ideals and according life style choices.

West stereotypically represented in contemporary movies (and comic strips, as one might add) as sheer, nostalgic illusion:

> "[T]he idea of the West that appealed to the patrons of 1894 and still lives in the imagination of French, German, and English boys is the West not of Gary but James Fenimore Cooper; that is, a world of fantastic adventures and noble savages. It was directly related to the romantic ideals of revolutionary France and the attack on feudal civilization.
>
> The celluloid West still plays something of that role in our imaginations. It offers equestrian dash and characters of ruthless and exuberant individualism to a population bedraggled by mechanical routine and befuddled by complex economic and domestic changes. [...]
>
> Even a casual glance at horse-opera heroes suggests that they share with the ideal businessman and the athlete certain qualities of muscular asceticism and harshness. The puritanical rigor of the celluloid frontier appeals to those who have espoused other kinds of rigor in their business and social lives. So the cowboy is as non-erotic as the hard-driving executive. He is emotionally hardened and unresponsive to any but a tiny area of experiences. He can act, but he cannot feel. Therefore he cannot be cast in a lover role any more than the businessman. Both are rigidly adolescent and non-receptive to experience. So Hollywood has to import its screen lovers, and often the women to whom they make love, as well."

On the other hand he doesn't hide his sympathy for the domestic, suburban (second) world of soap opera (ibid., 157):

> These dramas are more realistic than horse opera, since the situations they present are often very close to ordinary domestic experience. Moreover, they suggest that the bogus cheerfulness of business bounce and optimism 'where never is heard a discouraging word' doesn't quite overpower the millions of housewives who are daytime serial fans. The Pollyanna philosophy of the *Reader's Digest* and the *Saturday Evening Post* simply doesn't impress the home-town scepticism of the soap-opera adherent. Cheerfulness as normal extrovert behaviour, necessary for keeping things humming, is not very appealing to American women, it would seem.

McLuhan ends on an ambivalent note towards the gender differences expressed within popular culture:

> "Horse opera and soap opera, then, embody two or the most important American traditions, the frontier and the home town. But the two traditions are split rather than fused. They show that radical separation between business and society, between action and feeling, office and home, between men and women, which is so characteristic of industrial man. These divisions cannot be mended until their fullest extent is perceived."

To come back to the issue of "genre" it may be added that generic knowledge (referring here to classifications of personae as well as classifications of narrative texts) is learned by doing, with serially reproduced generic patterns a particularly prolific training ground. What is commonly addressed as "media literacy" is often genre-bound literacy – with the respective conventions trained and respective reading habits internalised over time. But that is only half the story since media literacy also produces knowing, second-order observation-savvy readers developping more specific expectations towards labelled texts and drawing from a significantly greater repertory of intertextual reference material beyond the ingenuous, "innocent" reading patterns.

Serially produced, episodic fiction does not need to follow already established generic patterns. While a series' pilot episode will work as a generic prototype or "format" it will spin off recognisable "tokens" based on similarity. But episodic fiction can also promote new genres from a yet nondescript premise, with examples ranging from the "dysfunctional family business" (*Six Feet Under*, HBO 2001-2004; with *Brothers and Sisters* an idoneous successor from 2006 onwards) to the "slice of life" advertisement (for this and other advertisement genres see Corner 1999, 112 ff.). It can alternatively draw from more than one established genre and produce hybrids such as the "mystery thriller", the "docusoap" or the "dramedy" in television – by this notably enhancing narrative indeterminacy while catering to already existing generic expectations.

If genre distinctions do indeed regulate mutual expectations on various levels of institutional, organisational and narrative communication such playing with generic formulas allows both for an enhancement and a reduction of narrative indeterminacy. Amplifications of indeterminacy can then result from systematic or accidental alterations of paradigms but also pertain to syntagmatic cross-over techniques that subvert stereotypical behaviour sequences in favour of formulaic patterns deriving from some other generic second world "out there". Both intertextual strategies will activate the playful, imaginary co-authorship of more genre savvy listeners, readers and viewers while leaving less knowing audiences guessing. And / or, presumably, coming up with particular, cultural-bound readings that ring closer to home.[126]

---

[126] Liebes / Katz (1990) provide an overview of cultural appropriations of *Dallas* in the U.S., Israel, and Japan; other examples of extrapolation refer to *Rambo*'s legacy within Aboriginal viewing communities in Australia (mentioned by Fiske 1987, 316) and *The Young and the Restless* scoring high with fans in Trinidad (Miller, 1992).

Theater is life. Film is art. Television is furniture.
(Slogan read on T-shirt, Austin 1993)

6 EPISODIC TELEVISION FICTION AS PROGRAMMED PROGRAM

6.1 The specifics of broadcasting

Publishing houses and film studios ship out specific quantities of copies (of an original periodical, manuscript, or movie) that are distributed in response to anticipated market demands.[127] In contrast broadcast media address their dispersed audience by electronic signals that stem from some central point and are "read" by receiving devices placed not only, but primarily in the addressees' own home. What resembles a "sowing process" is to be understood in more than one metaphorical sense as such (Gripsrud 2004, 211):

> "The word 'broadcasting' is an agricultural metaphor. It originally referred to the sowing of seeds by hand, in as wide (half) circles as possible. The metaphor, in other words, relies on the existence of a bucket of seeds – that is, centralized resources of information, knowledge, creative and technical competence, and the like – that is, to be distributed as widely as possible in a certain 'field' or territory. 'Broadcasting' is thus an optimistic, modernist metaphor: successful sowing will, given the right conditions of growth, yield a rich harvest some time in the future when universally distributed information, education, and entertainment (the classic formula for John Reith's public service broadcasting at the BBC) results in an enlightened, socially and culturally empowered, and presumably quite happy, population."

What Gripsrud quotes here is Raymond Williams' ground-breaking study "Television. Technology and Cultural Form" (1974) when comparing the similarities and differences of two eras of imminent change – the one Williams faced in his times, in terms of multiplication of outlets, and the one we have faced since under the name of the "digital turn".

According to Williams ([1974] 1992, 13) new media technologies are never invented out of the blue and at random. Instead they are "foreseen [...] not in utopian but in

---

[127] For the differentiation between the *publishing logic* of exchanged cultural goods in material copies (including CDs and DVDs of previously broadcast programs) and the *flow logic* more characteristic for broadcasting itself see Miège (1989, 12); for a critical discussion Kiefer (1998, 103-105).

technical ways – before the crucial components of the developed systems had been discovered and refined." New communication systems such as television – or the Internet – are thus considered an "intrinsic outcome" of the earlier transformations of industrial production, and as answer to the social changes that are induced by it.

Williams points to a significant ambivalence at the core of radio and television history (ibid., 17-18): While both media technologies were, right from the start, referred to as "mass communication" – by its' innovators as well by as its fervent critics – they were envisioned to reach their audience in individual homes. To Williams it is no coincidence that (ibid.) "the only developed 'mass' use of radio was in Nazi Germany, where under Goebbels' orders the Party organised compulsory public listening groups and the receivers were in the streets".[128]

The "mass" to be addressed by the sowing metaphor, then, is not to be identified with an anonymous "mob", but rather with large numbers of individuals to which messages are delivered simultaneously, by the move of the spreading hand.

The only thing "new" and significantly different from other mass communication techniques such as the press or the cinema was the fact that investments went primarily into distribution, not into content. Williams uses the term "parasitical" (ibid., 19) in order to describe the very first programs that were *sown* by broadcast media – not as original productions but as renderings of "state occasions, public sporting events, theatres and so on." Unlike previous communications technologies, radio and television were (ibid.) "systems primarily devised for transmission and reception as abstract processes, with little or no definition of preceding content." Not only preceded the supply of broadcasting facilities the actual demand – "it is that the means of communication preceded their content."

In other words: While the newspaper and feature film industry "knew" from the start what contents were available as well as suitable (since technologies grew out of distributing demands rather than distributing opportunities) radio and television had, just like the Internet in our time, yet to find some specific profile as media outlets that could make a difference. The distinctive feature did not refer to what was broadcast but instead to the distribution technology accounting for events

---

[128] For a history of German television in the era of the Third Reich see Uricchio, William (ed.): Die Anfänge des deutschen Fernsehens. Kritische Annäherungen an die Entwicklung bis 1945. Tübingen 1990 (= Medien in Forschung und Unterricht A 30), and Zeutschner, Heiko: Die braune Mattscheibe. Fernsehen im Nationalsozialismus. Berlin: Rotbuch-Verlag 1995.

heard and seen "here" (where people actually lived) and "now" (in real time). This is why the "blind spot" implied in the image of the sowing hand is not so much the targeted territory (in terms of dispersed audience) but rather the seed itself.

For the first time in media history the owners and providers of a new mass media technology *first* had to find out and define what their sowing purpose might be, in order to legitimate the process as such.

6.2 Two broadcast models for Europe and the United States

The widely recognised distinction between "public" and "private" service refers to different organisational models, or ideals, with regards to the distribution of common goods such as education, transportation or, in our case, mediated content. Traditional mass media systems in Western societies are either predominantly "public" or "private", with regards to ownership, regulation and agendas. But they can also be mixed, on different levels and to different degrees.

Government interest in broadcast regulation is historically based on two aspects: distribution of wavelength frequencies (which were relatively scarce, in the beginning) and mode of payment. Broadcast materials are not counted and paid "per view" or "per play" such as movies or concerts, or discs, cassettes, books and individual newspapers; they are available in the home and at virtually any time, "[...] at the turn of a switch, like gas, water or electricity" (Scannell 1990, 11). As the word indicates, broadcast materials are not aimed at individual or collective targets – they are "disseminated" in order to reach whoever happens to tune in at that very moment of dissemination, either by intent or by accident.

Not knowing beforehand who may get "hit" at the exact moment of media exposure confronts those being (or: feeling) responsible for the seeding with two remarkable dilemmas: How to ensure that specific audience members are exposed to only those materials actually considered suitable? And how to make sure that reception is dutifully paid for, be it by everyone in reach or by those actually interested? In the case of the public model, payment is either collected via taxes or subscription fees which must be renewed on a regular base (with the government determining the level). If reception is free of charge, in the private model, producers must make sure to get their income secured elsewhere, such as by selling individual program slots (or "dissemination hours") to advertisers.[129]

But the differences go further than that. Public broadcasting asks from the provider (or: the media system in question) to represent and actively pursue interests of the common good, and not just those of the system / the organisation itself. The idea to have providers fulfil needs rather than to spread content according to audience taste reflects both the urge to exert control and the urge to assume responsibility (in a paternalistic way) for those considered too fragile or malleable to resist possible harmful side-effects caused by those ephemeral voices and sounds, or pictures.[130] Private broadcasting, on the other hand, translates as a medium's, or a conglomerate's main interest in its own organisational well-being, implying that financial success will automatically lead to better product, and services.

If one looks closer, the two concepts reveal to be anything else than antagonistic. Two points of view often get confounded here, either for need of simplicity or for strategic reasons: One is the normative level of public vs. private domain, with legislation and policies applied to specific functions, privileges and constraints of one or the other type of provider, the other an informal level of the public vs. the private as social spheres. "Public" transport, in terms of service, is more about general access and reasonable fares than it is about large vehicles with an abundance of seats. "Private" cars, on the other hand, do circulate in the same open spaces as do trains and coaches. "Public" schools are supposed to be open to everyone, with school rates as low as possible, while private schools can afford to be highly selective, in terms of fees as well as with regards to whom admission is granted.

While the examples of transport and schooling helps to illustrate the differences between the two models, they shed light also on the problems of differentiation.

---

[129] Peters quotes David Sarnoff, later to become director of NBC, as one of the first to envision commercial use for broadcasting, right after World War I. When he described radio as a "household music box" (1999, 207-208) he did not think of actual product advertisement yet, but of large quantities of (Westinghouse) radio sets targeted to large quantities of potential consumers.

[130] One of the main reasons for differentiation between normative regulation of the (printed) press and (stricter) normative regulation of broadcasting in Switzerland lies (according to Krummenacher 1988, 15-16) in the different uses of time. From a consumer's viewpoint information by "the press" is defined as a number of individual selections one does make, namely of the content to be read and of the *actual moment* when to read it. Once the process is bound by a framework of restrictions as to what is available to large numbers of individuals tuning in at *what moment in time* the information in question is labelled as "broadcast".

"Public service" doesn't necessarily imply state ownership or state- (or community-) based funding. In the case of private-owned and market-oriented train lines, or taxis, it may be only "public access" which defines the "public" of the service, in terms of the common good as an equally available good. When it comes to broadcasting the change from one national provider to competition in the field, from a monopolistic to a dual or pluralistic system, and from state-funding to a variety of financial resources – or vice versa – does result in specific convergence (or adaptation) processes. While private competition forces public stations to act and behave in more market-oriented ways, a strong public contender is "contagious" insofar as it may lead private rivals to emphasise more on cultural status and integrative strengths.

What does "public" mean, then? In terms of domain, it is, in the first place, the shared assumption of responsibility for what people might "need" which is at stake. Respective responsibility can be assumed by legislative, executive and jurisdictional forces but also by explicit efforts of individual "haves" sharing resources with those out there who "have not" – economic and cultural capital, that is.[131] With regards to sphere, it is the sheer number of people sharing one (actual or virtual) space, while going there and / or being addressed within. Spheres are not as explicitly specified as domains; the borderline between the "public" and the "private" is as fluid as the one between what one might consider "private" or, instead, "intimate".

In terms of sphere, it is individual autonomy which is at stake, since higher visibility ("out there" in the public eye) implies a higher degree of social control. Domain and sphere do, however, refer back to the same historical and cultural roots: Whenever shared "public" and individual "private" spheres fell into each other – just as times of "work" and "leisure" did, for that matter – the two notions of "needing each other" and "knowing (about) each other" became intrinsically linked.

As many critical analysts of the bourgeois concept of the "public sphere" have argued,[132] both sets of categories – domains and spheres – are far from being universal or "natural"; they are related to specific ideological backgrounds and imply tacit

---

[131] PBS (Public Broadcast Service) in the United States is funded in part by taxes, in part by private sources.
[132] See Habermas (1989), Calhoun (1992), Crane (1996), and the feminist critique of the concept as expressed in Herbst (1992), Brooks Gardner (1994) and McLaughlin (1998).

rules as to *who* got access to the "public" as domain and *who* is entitled – under what circumstances – to "privacy" as a sphere of (relative) individual autonomy.

It is with regards to social concepts of access and freedom, then, that the conceptual line between domain and sphere gets blurred – and more so in relation to mass media as public phenomena which, at least in theory, allow for expression of virtually any interest and, and for extreme exposure, in terms of audibility / visibility.

There are several categories by which to distinguish the two basic models for broadcast media in Western societies, based on structural as well as functional criteria. Profit-orientation (as established within the US system of broadcast networks) leads to emphasis on professionalism and institutionalised control of output and success while the "common good" of state-controlled public service (as established, in variations, in most West European countries) is emphasised by an array of explicit and non-profit-oriented social functions that need to be fulfilled, or at least striven for.

The easiest way to tell the two models apart is to go by self-declaration of providers as well as providers' declarations of what their ideal clientele looks and acts like. As citizens of a state or of a community we are expected to be informed and educated by media – in return for a moderate fee which we pay in the name of social responsibility. As members of a capitalist consumer society we are expected to prefer entertainment to all other kinds of mass media content; in return, we are sold by numbers (rating points and market shares) to specific program sponsors whose main interest is to saturate "our" free programs with advertisements for consumer goods and services (Ang 1991, 26-32).

A large number of people reading this may have, like me, grown up with a radio and television monoculture, which was (in most countries of Western Europe) public in the sense that there were few advertisements in-between programs, but monthly fees to be paid and distinct broadcast guidelines to be respected. Or they were (in the United States, I presume) private – meaning that regular timeslots were reserved for advertisement, programs were available *free to air*, with distinct broadcast guidelines to be respected nevertheless.

6.3 Television as a storytelling medium

Broadcast network television is undoubtedly one of 20th century's "central storytelling systems" (Newcomb / Hirsch [1983] 2000, 571). This does not prevent the leisurely watching of television from being reflexively dismissed as a waste of time which might be put to better use . Up to this day, television mobilises remarkably vast and heterogeneous audiences, both within nationally confined societies and beyond. Television is an integral part of modern lifestyle and does, as such, keep society "on its toes" (as Luhmann put it). This means that television – in combination with other major storytelling systems such as the press, mainstream cinema and radio – aliments society's subsystems with fodder of thought for ongoing irritation and integration.

Horace Newcomb and Paul Hirsch describe television as a *cultural forum*, by this term (synonymous with the Greek "agora", the public place of political debate) pointing to the heteroglossic and ambivalent "texture" of the television message (ibid., 571):

> "Our model is based on the assumption and observation that only so rich a text could attract a mass audience in a complex culture. The forum offers a perspective that is as complex, as contradictory and confused, as much in process as American culture is in experience. Its texture matches that of our daily experiences. If we can understand it better, then perhaps we will better understand the world we live in, the actions that we must take in order to live there."

The role of "forum" refers here not to networks or programs but to television as a complex and often contradictory communication system that circulates "a multiplicity of meanings rather than a monolithic dominant point of view" (ibid., 564). John Fiske (1987, 84) confirms the unstable state of the television message that needs to be constantly negotiated between narrators and narratees – but also between what Fiske calls "... forces of closure, which attempt to close down its potential of meanings in favor of its preferred ones, and forces of openness, which enable its variety of viewers to negotiate an appropriate variety of meanings."

The multiple levels of meaning-making are characteristic not just for television systems within modern society but for all of its formative textual genres: news and reportages, advertisement and entertainment (such as fiction, quiz and talk shows, and what is more recently understood as "reality" programming). Most of these genres derive from other popular storytelling media such as theatre and literature, the periodicals, cinema's early variety programs, and radio. They find themselves combined in characteristic patterns of episodic narrative communication within the television schedule, thereby emphasising the chameleonic ability of this composite medium to adopt features from other media's typical narratives into its own textual arrangement as "flow" (Williams 1992, and Jensen 1995, 110).

According to Manfred Rühl (1995) broadcast media provide audiences with *programmed programs*. The term refers to a complex assortment of communicative contracts that do not just involve producers and audiences of a specific broadcast narrative as co-tellers and / or co-authors but refer to larger contextual frameworks. There is the underlying *social project* as defined by the responsible stakeholders (such as political institutions and citizens), whose contracts refer to media functions on a macro level of society, with more specific agreements pertaining for instance to a network's operating license or to the jurisdiction regarding property rights. What is negotiated between social partners bears upon *what* is broadcast and *how*, in terms of suitable information and preferred expressive modes. On the other hand there is the *temporal project* of the broadcast schedule that narrows down the access to radio and television programs to specific moments in time (in terms of what Bordewijk / van Kaam define as *allocutional* mode of address). This is where the *when* and *where* of the authorised input's (further) transmission is regulated – with direct consequences for the preproduction, production and postproduction of recurring programs such as newscasts, ad breaks or (here) episodic fiction.

While the social project is negotiated on a macro level and informs about the institutional role(s) accredited to mass media,[133] decisions with regards to programming principles are negotiated on a meso level between publishers on the one hand (here: television networks and affiliate stations, but also media conglomerates as network owners) and the creative talent that is solicited to provide a given time slot with what can be perceived either as specifically formatted "content" (from the publisher's view) or as part of a specific generic "story world" (from the artists' perspective). It is here where Fiske's "forces of closure" and "forces of openness" come into play and delineate the stage for the narrative communication between (implied) authors and (implied) readers to be played out, in terms of time-out culture and mutual invitation "to imagine".

In this chapter three eras of US-American broadcast television – often labelled as "network", "cable" and "digital" era [134] –are briefly examined regarding the develop-

---

[133] According to the "Four Theories of the Press", a model developed by Siebert / Peterson / Schramm in 1956 (for the project's background see McQuail 1994, 124; for a critical discussion Nerone, 1995), a medium "[...] always takes on the form and coloration of the social and political structures within which it operates. Especially, it reflects the system of social control whe-reby the relations of individuals and institutions are adjusted. We believe that an understanding of these aspects of society is basic to any systematic understanding of the press."

[134] Historical periods are model constructions that help to reduce phenomenological complexity. They identify structural differences i.e., (either organic or imposed) change. For the three-partite scheme suggested as TV I, TV II and TV III see Rogers / Epstein / Reeves (2002), but also Reeves / Epstein / Rogers (1995)

ment of episodic television fiction. Special emphasis is given to the increase of narrative indeterminacy during the periods of TVI, TV II and, more recently, TV III. Particular attention is called to

- the social project at stake,
- the scheduling principles involved, and
- the reading contract negotiated between authors and variously "knowing" audiences as readership and co-authors."

Two guiding hypothesises lead me to assume that what emerged as significant change within the narrative structure of episodic television prime time fiction over the course of TV II is related to (1) the successful adaptation of the daily daytime serial into the weekly prime time schedule, with early examples being *Dallas*, CBS, 1978-1989, and *Dynasty*, ABC, 1981-1989, and to (2) the increased access to episodic fiction in the form of reruns, or *reprogrammed* programs on the one hand, but also extended remote access to individually *reprogrammable* programs on the other; the second in response to increasingly personalised access to recording media such as video, DVD and the various "streaming" techniques of the digital age.

The changes these new technologies brought upon television as a popular medium may not have had some immediate impact on audiences' viewing habits, in terms of enhanced narrative performance and co-authorship. But they certainly nurtured expectations both on the institutional level of project estimation and appreciation and on organisational levels of content leverage and schedule planning. What resulted is – supposedly – a mutual encouragement in-between contractual partners on all three levels of communication contracts to opt for more indeterminate, "open" narratives, in terms of a greater intergeneric variety and permeability, increasingly contingent storylines and enhanced recursive connectivity to what occurred in other generically related second worlds or within the same narrative parameters earlier on.[135]

---

and Reeves / Rogers / Epstein (1996). Marc / Thompson (2004) and Edgerton (2007) follow instead Todreas' (1999) classification system of *network era* (ca. 1950-1975), *cable era* (1975-1995) and *digital era* (1995 – date). Another possibility is to distinguish between *network* era (from the late 1940's through the mid-1980's) and *post-network* era (from the mid-1980's onwards; see Newcomb 2004, 426). Amanda Lotz's proposition to view TV II as *transition era* in-between network and post-network era would have fitted this study pefectly (see Lotz, 2007; the revised version 2014).

[135] For examples see the original television series *Star Trek* (1966-1969) whose science fiction formula already permitted for subtly subversive extensions of more

First, however, let me briefly re-evaluate television's status as leading storytelling medium within modern Western societies in the second half of the 20th century.

6.4 Television as a *leitmedium* in transition

In the Luhmannian tradition mass communication is conceived as social operation, but also as a social system in its own right. As autopoietic systems media depend on continuous communicative input for sustaining themselves. This explains, for instance, why media systems increasingly communicate about their own whereabouts and engage in speculation about their most indispensable environment as mass media system – people.[136]

Lorenz Engell (2006) defines any mass medium as *leitmedium* that is legally and / or habitually entrusted by social systems to regulate the production and circulation of meaning. *Leitmedia* do not just repurpose customary "master" narratives in more conveniently formatted versions (... for which the knightly adventure story and its various revenants are a good example) but assume defining power over what meanings do generally circulate within a given society.[137]

What Engell addresses as "meaning" corresponds to Luhmann's definition of the term and grounds in a conceptual difference between "what is *actually given* and what can *possibly* result" from some communicative attempt (Luhmann 1995, 74). Meaning must transcend what is currently and conventionally "said" by words,

---

conventional scenarios, in an attempt at what Catherine Johnson (2005a) calls "regulated innovation". Recursive connectivity can be found within the second world of the *Peanuts* cartoons, in reference to the annually recurring football kicking incidents that build on each other or – in some rare moment of non-scheduled "memory flash" – when Snoopy, in full surfer regalia, regretfully dismisses a former love interest (strips 06-08-1965 to 13-08-1965; see Schulz 2004 -, vol. 8, 94-97) after his chivalrous attempts at wooing her failed earlier on, over a fortnight of ice-skating episodes (strips 22-01-1966 to 06-02-1966; ibid., 10-16).

[136] In systems' theory the term "environment" refers to all other systems "out there" that can only be speculated upon, for lack of reliable references. A good example is the *yellow press* whose operative task is to chronicle the public sphere through continuous reports on the whereabouts of public persons. In terms of autopoietic system the same papers strive to sustain themselves by way of a continuous recycling and repurposing of mass media personalities as "celebrities" (for the phenomenon see Fowles 1992, and Turner 2004, for the people press as communication Dubied 2009).

[137] I use the German term for "leading medium" here, in the sense that Engell suggests (2006, 49): "Leitmedium ist dasjenige Medium, dem die Aufsicht über die Sinnproduktion übertragen wird und das letztlich Sinn nach seinen Möglichkeiten definiert."

some written passage, or moving sounds or images, and adapt itself to alternative or further actualisations of what is shared as sense.

Systemic thinking distinguishes three dimensions of what is – eventually – actualised as meaning. At stake are (ibid., 75):

- the *fact* dimension that regulates distinctions between the "inside" and "outside" of what is observed. This is here identified as paradigmatic dimension of a given story world and said to pertain to characters and settings as *existents*.
- the *temporal* dimension that regulates distinctions between what is observed as past or future "event". This dimension is identified here as syntagmatic dimension and said to pertain on the one hand to (prefigured, configured, refigured) actions, happenings and states and episodic "clusters of events", of course. Also, with regards to broadcast narratives in their characteristic form as "unfocused" and / or "focused" episodes, to the *scheduling process* of the clusters which John Ellis aptly describes as "editing on an Olympian scale" (Ellis 2000, 131).[138]
- the *social* dimension that regulates distinctions between "ego" and "alter". In the case of narrative communication this dimension arguably concerns questions of perspective; it pertains to the points of view that emerge as viable and acceptable and thus regulate our "taking of sides" and what is granted social relevance as narrative "truth".

Engell suggests that television inherited its status as social *leitmedium* from the cinema as cultural institution and industry. With the example of cinema in mind he distinguishes three theoretical stages of how leading media first develop "forms" (in terms of specifically structured narratives) that become more flexible (or: less structurally coupled) over time and, in consequence, less susceptible to define what can any longer be generalised as meaning, or socially relevant "truth". The following is paraphrased from Engell (2006):

---

[138] See Ellis (2000, 131-132): "Scheduling is nothing other than editing on an Olympian scale. Instead of combining shots and sounds into a sequence and sequences into a programme, as an editor does, the scheduler combines whole programme units into an evening's flow, whole evenings into a week, whole weeks into a season, and whole seasons into a year. The principles involved are broadly similar, combining variety and connection, repetition and originality into harmonious and mutually supporting arrangements."

First stage: Development of a structurally coupled narrative form, in terms of content prototype. In the case of cinema Hollywood's star and studio system is identified as guiding instance that generated specific narrative formulas based on the seamless integration of economic and cultural expectations. What resulted were stringent, focused narratives that could be observed and understood as "stories", in accordance with functional sets of filmmaking principles.

Second stage: Typical is a "mediatisation" and subsequent erosion of the form. The classic cinema narratives became more malleable and allowed for irritation as well as interpretive openness, at the same time revealing their character as construction and artefact. Indicators for this process are various "auteur" movements, but also an increasing visualisation of formal aspects within the dominant narrative currents. Indicators for this process are a higher narrative complexity, with multiple storylines and alternative viewpoints mirroring the loss of one "defining" perspective (for multilinear narratives in more recent cinema see Tröhler, 2007).

Third stage: Its signature trait is an increasingly playful proposal of reality states with more possibilities to recombine narrative levels. Form and mediatisation fall into one and allow – within Engell's interpretation – for nearly limitless possibilities of meaning-making processes and actualisations. "Meaning" emerges no longer from an unquestionable auctorial instance such as Hollywood (... or God, or a church or a national state – to name a few other examples of *leit* institutions) and can therefore no longer be identified as a source of univocal "truth". Instead meaning must be actively sought and constructed from the wilful as well as skilful application of narrative "toolkits" that invite for individually tailored, custom-made adaptations of what can always be told alternatively and "fitted" otherwise.

Engell's cinema-derived model invites for a closer look at other media's histories in terms of *leitmedia* discourse. Chapter 5 can be read here as a reminder how Western literature, the press, and broadcast radio all served as important narrative role models for television, just as cinema did.

From the earlier periodicals television apparently inherited the winning combination of episodicity, generic expectation and formatted manufacture. Newspaper cartoons arguably paved the way to more contingent forms of story development when navigating between "forces of openness" and "forces of closure" – as Hayward's chapter on Milton Caniff's *Terry and the Pirates* (Hayward 1997, 84-137) demonstrates. Radio perfected the narrative form of the ongoing serial – the *soap opera* within US-American daytime schedules, but also the *telenovela* as Latin

America's leading storytelling instance, thus allowing for the very epitome of narrative indeterminacy (which is: sustained gossip within extended narrative networks) to become a major asset of commodity culture.[139].

What Engell's scenario lacks is a reflection on mass media synergies and complementary functions. The author's main interest apparently lies with his theoretical claim that meaning-making within media follows three stages from (1) an initial stabilisation of an expressive form to (2) the medium's autopoietic reinvention and to (3) what Luhmann describes as "unity of a difference" between form and medium.[140] It is a scenario that comes compellingly close to what Wolfgang Iser (in Iser 1974) described as the development of Western novel from Bunyan to Beckett, earlier on.[141]

While it is tempting to extrapolate from Engell's observation some kind of Darwinian rule-work that explains how leading mass media took turns in defining society's common sense, such a view needs to be complemented by an economic reasoning regarding media ownership, copyright issues and distributing synergies. This is why

---

[139] For a history of radio soaps see Breitinger (1992), and Hilmes (1993, 1997 and 2004); for soap opera viewing communities Brown (1994), Stempel Mumford (1995) and Baym (1997, 2000).

[140] Engell (2006, 49): "Diese drei Phasen unterscheiden sich danach, dass sozialer Sinn zunächst als Form, dann als Medium und schliesslich als Einheit der Differenz von Form und Medium begriffen und in Umlauf gesetzt wird." For the underlying concepts of "form" and "medium" and the possibility for forms to become media and vice versa see Moeller (2006, 254 ff.).

[141] Iser conceives the novel as a literary genre rather than a medium. He describes its development in terms of (implied) author-reader relationship (Iser 1974, xiii-xiv), mirroring Engell's stages perfectly: "While the eighteenth-century novel reader was cast by the author in a specific role, so that he could be guided – directly, or indirectly, through affirmation or through negation – toward a conception of human nature and of reality, in the nineteenth century the reader was not told what part he was to play. Instead, he had to discover the fact that society had imposed a part on him, the object being form him eventually to take up a critical attitude toward this imposition [...]. The process has become even more complex in the twentieth-century novel, for here the discovery concerns the functioning of our own faculties of perception. The reader is meant to become aware of the nature of these faculties, of his own tendency to link things together in consistent patterns, and indeed of the whole thought process that constitutes his relations with the world outside himself. This means that the novel no longer confines itself to telling a story or to establishing its own patterns, for now it also deliberately reveals the component parts of its own narrative techniques, separating the material to be presented from the forms that serve its presentation in order to provoke the reader into establishing form himself the connections between perception and thought."

Instead of an analysis focused on particular media outlets and how they mirror Engell's logic I opt for a more generalised, more generic view of modernity as communicative *leit* project; a project which found its master expression within mass-mediated, streamlined, dialogic and yes, episodic, narrative communication. Seen from this angle, the characteristic shift between determinacy (in terms of what is recognised as a given "form") and indeterminacy (the invitation to playfully explore what is considered "up for grabs") is an incentive to work with formulas that are flexible, and yet "connectible" enough to produce sustained irritation and integration beyond factually, temporally and socially defined parameters of meaning.

Changes in media technology did certainly play an important role in that differentiation of code-related repertoires and recognisable styles – as Ben Singer sustains for the case of early cinema, and Caldwell (1995, 2000) elaborates for the case of television. But just as important are discursive shifts that pertain to social *leit* differences such as "gendered" roles in patriarchal societies, or "religion" and other belief-systems. Because the changes that affect social projects on a macro level necessarily bear upon strategic decisions made on the organisational level of media ownership and content scheduling. And they leave traces on the narrative contract, with regards to the forces of closure and openness that are mentioned by Fiske.

When it comes to the acceptance of serial indeterminacy (in the sense of Iser's original assessment of Dickens' work, 1971), mainstream television proved to be more flexible and innovative than mainstream cinema, over the long run. While the movie industry discarded serials in favour of more clearly delineated traditions of storytelling and authoritatively "given" meanings (... as Shelley Stamp argues), television immediately picked up what had already become radio's signature trait – namely, institutionalised narrative indeterminacy within the daytime schedule. This, if anything, allowed television to become the first audiovisual medium to come to terms with socially viable "forces of closure" and "forces of openness" at the same time – but within different timeslots.

The two major social projects involved in this were, as hinted before, the Fordist prospect of an optimistic and radically consumer-oriented postwar society (for this see Gramshi 1971, Doray 1988 and Gitlin [1983] 2000) – and the early domestication of the medium, in correspondence and in syntony with the domestication of the American suburb (for this see Spigel, 1992).

6.5 Like day and night: daytime serial vs. prime time series

In the beginning of radio broadcasting most fiction broadcast in distinct, recurring instalments was scheduled in the evening. Many scholars see the reluctance of the industry to address domestic audiences as a reason for this; in the words of Simon (1998, 15-16) there were no daytime programs simply out of fear that "... housewives would not be able to concentrate on a program while performing their chores". Later, however, sponsors began to advertise domestic products directly to female patrons within specialised afternoon programs such as *The Womens' Magazine of the Air*. This made sponsored fiction a viable option for the afternoon ... or what was soon to be known by the nickname of the "soap opera". A similar development is confirmed by van Zoonen for early television (1992, 76):

> "During the postwar years, advertisers and networks once more viewed the daytime market with skepticism, fearing that their loyal radio audiences would not be able to make the transition to television. The industry assumed that, unlike radio, television might require the housewife's complete attention and thus disrupt her work in the home. Indeed, while network prime-time schedules were well worked out in 1948, networks and national advertisers were reluctant to feature regular daytime programs. Thus, in the earliest years, morning and afternoon hours were typically left to the discretion of local stations, which filled the time with low budget versions of familiar radio formats and old Hollywood films."

The newly formed (fourth) television network Du Mont was the first to produce fictional programs specially devised for the daytime market, while the other three networks hesitated to put their investments in daytime radio at a risk. Only in 1951 began CBS, NBC, "and, to a lesser extent, ABC [...] to colonise the housewife's workday with regularly scheduled network programs" (ibid., 77).[142]

Three communication partners needed to closely work together to make these narrative fictions happen, day after day: the programs' sponsors / owners in the first place, then the distributing network's responsible schedulers, and innovative, prolif-

---

[142] Spigel's argument echoes McLuhan's feminist stance on *horse operas* and *soap operas* from 1951 (Spigel 1992, 98): "Indeed, sexual difference, and the corresponding dynamics of domestic labor and leisure, framed television's introduction to the public in significant ways. The television industry struggled to produce programming forms that might appeal to what they assumed to be the typical housewife, and in so doing they drew an abstract portrait of 'Mrs. Daytime Consumer'. [...] This 'ideal' female spectator was thus the very foundation of the daytime programs the industry produced. But like all texts, these programs didn't simply turn viewers into ideal spectators; they didn't simply 'affect' women. Instead, they were used and interpreted within the context of everyday life at home."

ic authors such as Irna Phillips (*The Guiding Light*, 1937 – 2009). Innovation does not just refer to the invention of suitable second worlds with a believable population and a sufficient variety of storylines but also to the development of basic ruleworks that allowed for streamlining the tightly scheduled production process within increasingly differentiated and specialised teams of writers and speakers (for this see Rouverol, 1984).

In television, just as in radio before, both narrative forms of episodicity – the serial with its characteristic overarching focus and the series with its autonomous, self-sustained "case" structure – came to co-exist under the same roof of larger network structures. But as before they developed within neatly separated social spheres, both in terms of cultural commodity and "domains of meaning". Because one of these forms was organised as daily daytime serial, the other as weekly prime time series (Newcomb 2004, 421):

> "Most early fictional television programs did, in fact, follow the classic structure – beginning, middle, end; goal-oriented hero; and equilibrium disturbed but restored in the 'conclusion'. Thus, each week, the central recurring character of a western would defeat the violent intruder, or the police detective would solve the current crime.
>
> The primary alternative to this narrative pattern was found in the fictions of 'daytime television,' the soap opera. Originally developed for radio, the soap opera was designed to attract female listeners / viewers, and, as the nomenclature suggests, many early programs were produced by the advertising agencies of their sponsoring domestically identified products such as soap powders. These narratives were programmed in short, usually 15-minute, episodes. But neither the story nor the plot was concluded in a single episode. Indeed, the longest running soap opera, *The Guiding Light*, began on radio in 1937 and continues in television at this time."

The parameters that set the primetime series and the daytime serial apart, over the first 25 years of their co-existence within television broadcast schedules, become more evident when contextualised within the organisational structure of a major US broadcast network (Taylor 1993, 17; and next page, Figure 14).

It comes as no surprise that the entertainment division in this model of a commercial, *free to air* television network outweighs the *news* and *sports* division. Timeslots translate directly into target audiences as market segments (… or numbers of "eyeballs", from a sponsor's / advertiser's perspective). The three types of entertaining programs "in development" refer to (a) children as target audience, to (b) daytime (with the proverbial homemaker as target) and to (c) a much more complex arrangement of prime time programs subdivided as "drama", "situation comedy", "motion pictures", and "specials".

Figure 14: Main program divisions of a broadcast network (Taylor 1993, 17)

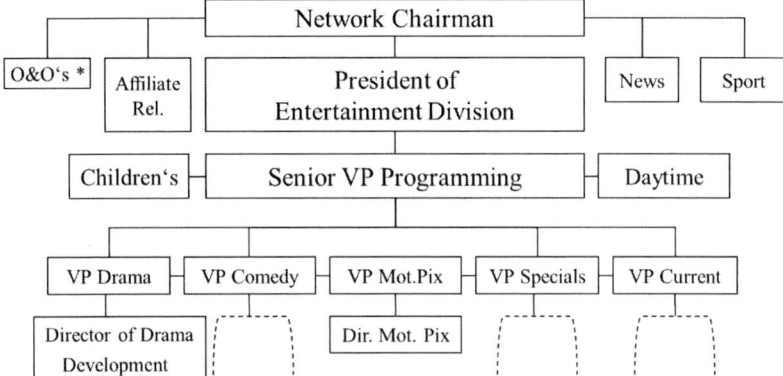

When looked at closer the unspecific term of "daytime" translates as *soap opera* and as *daytime talk*. The more specified subdivisions of "prime time" address the –more cost-intensive – processes of research and development towards the network's future prime time, with hour-long drama series and half-hour situation comedies the main concern. While "drama" and "comedy" development are strategic departments foreshadowing tomorrow's content, the term "current" refers to the operational business regarding drama and comedy series that are, as currently produced works in progress, either *on air* or *on hiatus*.

Prime time works thus as the network's primary showcase and shop window. Here a program's success depends just as much on strategic timing (in terms of opposition or complement to other programs aired at the same time, and continuity of what is aired before and after) as it does on narrative structure, the talent featured and other production-oriented values (for this see Bielby / Bielby 1994, and Lin 1995).

Daytime and children's programming (but also news and sports) are considered less critical departments because communication is supposed to work on the base of pre-established patterns and expectations: Audiences are seen as comparatively "sure bets" that allow sponsors to target their products accordingly – for instance toys in the case of kids' programs (Seiter 1993, 1995), and domestic products such as household appliances for the typical audience of "daytime" programming.[143]

The different expectations of network executives towards the function of daytime and prime time fiction, and towards the roles allegedly assumed at both ends of the narrative contract are described by Kreutzner / Seiter 1995, 235-236:

> "As a commercial medium, US network television is primarily interested in the production of profit by selling the largest possible audience to advertisers. In order to materialize this goal, the medium developed three main strategies for addressing the audience, each of which depended on placing given shows within the network schedule. The first of these strategies addresses the television audience as female. This strategy clearly dominates network television's daytime production and determines the characteristics of daytime texts. Although daytime shows (such as soap operas) are actually watched by women and men, interviews with network researchers and production personnel of daytime soap operas in 1987 showed that producers and network executives (still) consider the male audience during daytime as negligible. The second strategy addresses the television audience as a familial one. This mode of address dominates the early evening hours. [...] The hours after 10.00 p.m. are determined by a third strategy which constructs the audience as 'adult'. [...] Up to the second half of the 1970s, this slot was dominated by the crime, detective, and lawyer genre, that is by generic texts culturally coded as 'male'. In terms of the narrative form preferred within these time slots, the television serial – with its characteristic resistance to closure and its multiple plot structure – was and is the dominant fictional narrative on daytime television. Until the second half of the 1970s, prime-time slots used to be the exclusive domain of the episodic series."

The distinction between daytime and prime time is thus clearly related to questions of power. While the underlying social project does not necessarily consider all programs for children and housewives to be "laughable matters" and "juicy rumours" (as the German Dominican Felix Fabri put it, in his earlier attempt to repurpose educational content for more domestic audiences) there is less attention given to that kind of programming as to what addresses the "familial audience" or the "adult" – and, until the late 1970s, supposedly male – breadwinner. This finds its reflection also in the economic flow of product and money.

Jeremy Tunstall analysed the relation of production costs and prestige in a comparison of British program genres that is quoted in Kiefer (1998, 107, and here, Table 5).

---

[143] Bonner refers to this as "ordinary" television (Bonner 2003) because programming here does not involve particular efforts to be innovative and is perceived as part of everyday routine by most of its casual viewers.

Afternoon and early evening soaps emerge as the most prolific (and: least expensive) fictional genre. And, not surprisingly, as the program genre accredited with the lowest reputation.

Table 5: Prestige correlating with program costs (Tunstall 1993, cit. Kiefer 1998, 107)

Format	Audience	Prestige	Eps/year	Time slot	Min. shot per day	Cost per hour (in 1'000 £)	Cost per audience hour (p)
Soap	large	Low	104-156	<8.30 pm	15 min.	100-150	1
Contin. series	large / medium	Medium	6-15	8.00< pm	5 min.	300-800	5-10
Mini-series	medium	High	3-8	9.00 <pm	3-5 min.	500-700	10-15
Single drama	small	High	1	9.00 <pm	3-4 min.	400-800	15-25

The consideration of the domestic afternoon drama as "less important" or "less meaningful" resonates with Marshall McLuhan's earlier critique regarding the *frontier* presented in Western movies, and radio's *domestic sphere* as represented in the daytime schedule (McLuhan 1951, 157):

> "[W]hen you consider that soap operas are written and acted quite as well as the ordinary evening radio drama, it will appear that they have been the object of a good deal of irrelevant criticism. The fact that evening shows feature well-known stars in radio versions of Broadway or Hollywood successes seems to have beguiled a number of critics into quite pointless abuse of the daytime serials."

Over the course of the 1970's and 1980's, however, the particular "gender gap" between US-American daytime and prime time fiction began to narrow, and what was earlier connoted as stereotypically "male" drama opened up towards traits deemed more characteristic of soap operas and talk shows. New dramas focused more on intimate subjects, with premises based on relational instead of professional skills, and ensemble casts (instead of solitary protagonists) asking for multiplied, braided storylines (Schatz, 1987).

All of this happened in prime time and was framed "adult" television, with a newly found emphasis on "more serious" drama. What was earlier dismissed as unstructured "chaos" was now appreciated as "narrative complexity" (for this see Chisholm 1991, and Mittell 2006). And what appeared, in its original domestic context, as "trashy" if not downright deviant audience behaviour (such as: listeners and viewers collectively gushing over adorable or cutesy "personae", the endless exchange of gossip within networks of friends and initiated strangers, not to mention all kinds of imaginative re-enactments of familiar scenes from favourite second worlds),[144] was now faced with an increasing respect as socially relevant "expert" discourse.

In 1990 the *Soap Opera Digest* asked writers, producers and actors of different daytime and prime time shows in a series of interviews if they felt what they wrote, produced and played was "soap" (Kahwati 1990, 24-29). Many of the interviewees reacted defensive, and one actress of *Thirtysomething* (NBC, 1987-1991) denied the allegation altogether ("We're on at ten"; quoted ibid., 27). Bernard Lechowick, then among the head-writers of *Knots Landing* (CBS, 1979-1993) explained the reluctance to admit the soap opera's legacy as such (Kahwati 1990, 28-29):

> "No show that uses a continuing story is going to call itself a soap, because of the widespread glib, gratuitous damnation of soaps that they're all lowbrow [...]. There's as much misogyny in that assessment as there is critical thinking. It's women's programming; ergo, it's not important. You just use continuing story and you don't call yourself a soap. If I had to do it again, I'd call us, for critical purposes, a serious continuing drama. There's a tendency for critics to write off something they can call a soap. It behooves anyone knowing the value and importance of continuing story to say they're anything but a soap."

6.6 Television fiction reread, rerun and recorded

As discussed before, narrative communication as entertaining "art" relies on redundancies that stem from former narrative knowledge which is currently re-circulated and repurposed for further use in other meaning-making contexts.

In popular fiction such extended narrative knowledge derives by default from two areas of study – official, canonical sources of information, and privileged access to apocryphal (= alternative) sources. The first category entails repeated viewings of narrative bits and pieces that are rebroadcast or accessible in recorded versions, and extends to paratexts issued by copyright holders ... such as the *Soap Opera Dig*est, in

---

[144] See Hayward (1997) for examples of soap fan behaviour; for an assessment of early research on radio soap listening Brunsdon (2000) and Liebes (2002).

the case of afternoon programming (1975 – present). The second refers to word of mouth and thus more to the relational aspects of oral, ritual communication, with discriminations made between different levels of knowledge according to the respective viewing community's structure, and dynamic.

In the case of soap opera alternative sources of wisdom preceded the official sources by many years. There was practically no institutional recording of instalments until the late sixties when production modes switched from live broadcasts to video (Simon 1998, 32). The narrative indeterminacy of the soap opera was consequently handled as an "internal affair" among circles of variously initiated audiences.[145]

Laura Stempel Mumford gives a vivid picture of how narrative memory is cared for and carried on by variously initiated soap opera audiences (1995, 5):

> "Because so much of the soap opera audience has, as I do, a long history with the genre and with particular programs, it is crucial to distinguish the specific expertise that arises from such a history from the more generalized competence – what Charlotte Brunsdon calls 'the culturally constructed skills of femininity' – that might be needed to make sense of the genre in the first place. For that reason I want to begin by outlining a typology of soap opera viewing competence, ranging from the inexperienced or incompetent viewer – one who has never watched a soap – to the expert, who has a long history with the genre as a whole, and with one or more individual shows. The incompetent viewer, who knows nothing of soap opera convention or history, will understand little of an episode, and because of its self-referential, nonlinear structure, may not even be able to make sense of it in the most superficial way. An expert, on the other hand, will bring a wealth of historical memory and detailed information to the viewing experience, and therefore will, if she watches attentively, understand nearly everything she sees: the characters, their motivations, the relationships among them, and thus the background and potential consequences of particular narrative developments.
>
> In between those two poles I would place, in order of increasing expertise, the novice, also a newcomer to the genre, but one whose interest in learning its rules marks her difference from the incompetent viewer; the casual viewer, with some experience of the form, but no particular history with or commitment to any specific shows; the irregular viewer, who may have a long history but watches infrequently, or whose habitual viewing may be interrupted for long periods of time (by, say, a change in work or domestic routine); and the competent viewer, who has regular viewing habits and some history, but lacks the detailed historical memory conferred by years of experience."

---

[145] Robert Allen (1985, 83) refers to Eco's more sophisticated "model reader" who, in the case of *The Guiding Light*, is more likely to be a working-class woman than a male literary critic.

Mimi White also focuses on applications of these "skills of femininity" in her reflection on women's memories and television reruns (White, 1994). While extensive viewing oscillates between increased familiarity (with characters and settings) and an increased critical stance (towards inconsistencies and auctorial decisions deemed absurd or downright silly) such narrative ambivalence (ibid., 344) accounts, eventually, for the acceptance of contradictions that result from sudden transformations and reversals in actors, characters and plots, "even as these transformations rupture the internal consistency and verisimilitude that ground a realist reading and account for identification and textual absorption."

What results is a constant rewriting of the soap's own history which is actively pursued at both ends of the narrative communication, namely by authors that must narratively come to terms with organisational decisions on the level of hiring, and firing talent and by co-narrating audiences that have to "recursively reconnect", and imaginatively recombine what "really" happened, according to some master plan that is forever in danger to become obsolete.

Over the long run soap operas produce "what might best be described as memory without nostalgia" (ibid., 350). The ongoing accumulation of event-related knowledge is not supposed to result in stable "facts" of a given history – even if this history is testified by knowing viewers and can be "video-proofed" by recurring to recording technologies and written sources of all sorts.

Prime time fiction, on the other hand, was accessible in filmed reruns from the early 1950s onwards and found ample reuse within the expanding network schedules over the course of the 1970's and 1980's. Viewers' use of recording devices became more common from about 1985 onwards and allowed (in theory) for storage of episodes within (institutional or private) libraries. Commercial video collections and DVD boxes in the 1990s finally allowed for the full reconstruction of a series' history in terms of coherent, and authorised "work", with further consequences for the series' narrative structure, or what emerged as more distinctively focused seasonal "arcs" around the turn of the 21st century (for this see Kompare 2006, and Mittell 2006).

6.7 Three eras of prime time drama: from the series to the quality serial

Jamie Medhurst's "(very) short history of television" (2006) focuses on the parallel development of television as a cultural technique in the United States and Europe. His tripartite scheme comes remarkably close to Engell's *leitmedium* scenario and invites for a closer look at the parameters of change in terms of Rühl's "social project" (see here, Table 6):

Table 6: A (very) short history of US television (Medhurst 2006, 123)

Era	TV I	TV II	TV III
Viewer choice	scarcity	availability	plenty
Regulation	state control	deregulation	market-driven
Focus	broadcasting	narrowcasting	niche programming
Organisation	limited terrestrial channels	cable and satellite	multichannel
Range	national	national / internat.	global
Technology	analogue / black+wh.	analogue / colour	digital / HDTV
Access	live	video	DVD
Audience env.as	passive viewers	mass viewers	interactive viewers
Program mode	restricted broadcasting	rigid schedules	TiVo (DIY scheduling)
Characterisation	experimentation	"Golden Age"	debates around quality

Medhurst's synthesis is based on Rogers / Epstein / Reeves (2002, for organisational aspects) and Ellis (2000, for aspects of access to programs and viewers' choices). Another source is Umberto Eco's satirical look at the transition from "paleo" to "neo" television in Italy – an article originally published within the scholar's weekly column in *L'Espresso* (see Eco 1983; for an abridged English translation Eco 1988).

Eco's seminal paper is arguably the single most quoted text by Italian television scholars and has become the cornerstone of most reflection on deregulated television in Italy.[146] The program-based analysis fits neatly into Engell's *leitmedium* discourse and invites for adaptation to all television histories shaped by deregulation.

---

[146] Casetti, Francesco: Tra me e te. Strategie di coinvolgimento dello spettatore nei programmi della neotelevisione. Torino: RAI-ERI (1984, 1988); Barlozzetti, Guido: Il palinsesto (Italian for "schedule"). Testo apparato e generi della neotelevisione. Milano: Angeli (1986); Casetti, Francesco / Odin, Roger: De la paléo- à la néo-télévision. Approche sémio-pragmatique. In: *Communications* 51 (1990, 9-26); Bruno, Marcello W.: Neotelevisione. Dalla comunicazioni di massa alla mas-

Eco insists on the contractual address of television and how the expressive modes of programs mirrored both the medium's self-image and use of audiovisual vocabulary.

According to Eco's original essay of 1983 – what he calls a "small dictionary of mutating television for a public of mutants" (Eco 1988, 19) – the frantic competition for viewer attention and audience loyalty lead Italian TV programs of the late 1970's and early 1980's to increasingly seek the viewers' complicity and active participation. In consequence shows became more chatty, but also more tongue-in-cheek and self-ironic; they revealed their artificial, constructed character at any given moment and thus contributed to the medium's quasi-complete autopoiesis, in terms of narcissistic self-observation of itself being observed by its audience (ibid., 23):

> "Paleo-TV wanted to be a window that looked out from the most far-flung provinces onto the wide world. Independent Neo-TV [...] points the TV cameras on the provinces, and shows the public of Piacenza the people of Piacenza – which has gathered together to listen to a Picenza [sic] watchmaker's advertisement, while a Piacenza presenter makes coarse jokes about the 'tits' of a Piacenza woman, who takes it all incomplainingly so that she can be seen by the public of Piacenza while she wins a pressure cooker. It's like looking through the telescope from the wrong end."

Later, Jean Louis Missika (2006) proposed to complete the scheme of Eco's two eras by the introduction of a third era he called "post television". Its main characteristic is the medium's newly achieved "ordinariness" that allows *ordinary people* to raise their voice, not just institutional speakers and "expertsε" (... as was the case in the patriarchal, government-funded system of paleo TV). There is also an increased urge to display "intimacy" (a typical trait of Eco's neo television) to be applied to practically every domain, every program genre and program format available.

If we compare European and US television of the *paleo* and the *neo* era there are striking differences as well as similarities. The main distinction lies in the initial set-up of the national broadcast systems either as a legal monopoly of state-funded public service channels or as a factual oligopoly catering to privately owned, commercial media enterprises. The following two figures allow for a comparison of the defining parameters of television as a social, temporal and narrative project over the three eras of "scarcity", "availability" and "plenty" in Europe and in the U.S. (see here, next page: Figure 15, and Figure 16).

---

sa di comunicazioni. Messina: Rubbettino (1994); Stella, Renato: Box populi. Il sapere e il fare della neotelevisione. Roma: Donzelli (1999).

Figure 15: Model of European TV's broadcast history (adapted from Zaccone / Medolago, 2000) [147]

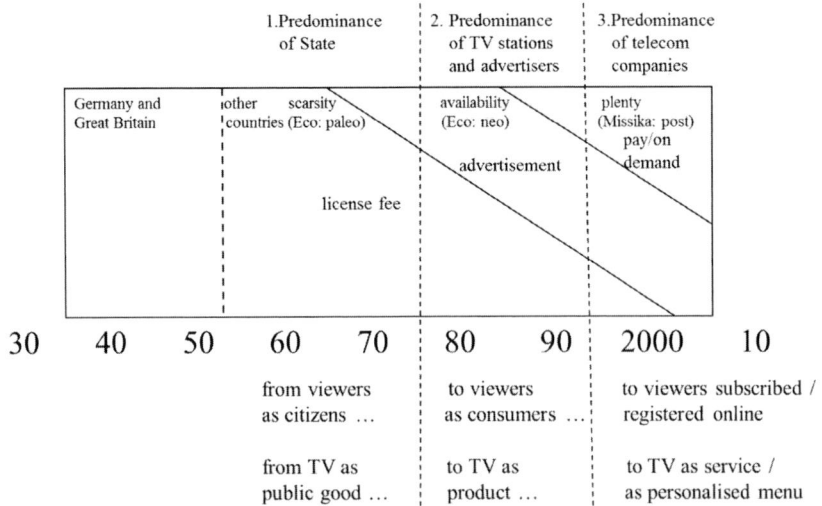

Figure 16: Model of US-American TV's broadcast history (adapted from Rogers / Epstein / Reeves, 2002)

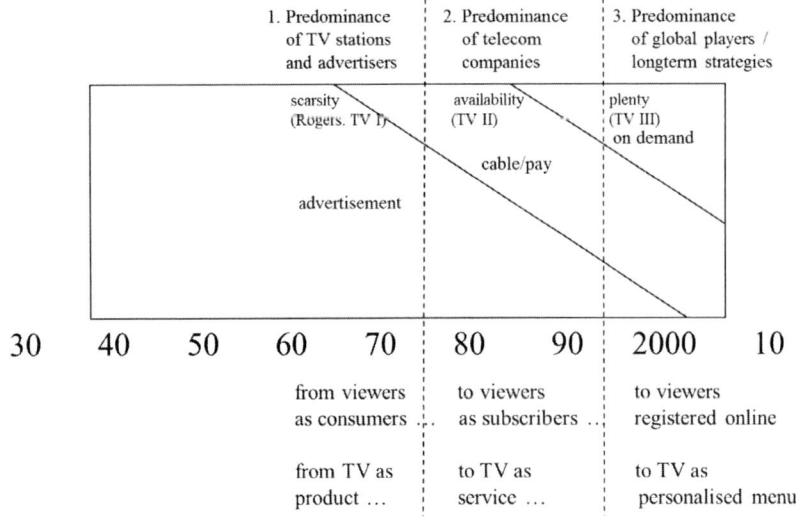

---

[147] These are approximate numbers, with years and phases not to be taken literally. Diagonals indicate the perceived importance of concepts, at a given time.

While there were few television programs available for European viewers during the "era of scarcity", there was only *relative* (outlet, program and frequency) scarcity in terms of what US viewers could receive in their home at about the same time. At stake was not a restriction of watchable programs out there, but instead a "familiar menu, chiseled stonily in TV Guide [that] consisted of a trio of generically similar programs in any given time slot, one each on the local CBS, NBC and ABC stations" (as Marc / Thompson put it, 2004, 67).[148]

In the beginning all television fiction was performed live and enacted in front of the television cameras. There is an debate among television historians about the reasons why the earlier form of live performed anthology theatre (in the tradition of Orson Welles' "radio theatre on the air" and similar ventures) gave way to the filmed television series as default format. Some researchers (such as Stempel 1992) claim that the demise of the live anthologies was due to their unpredictability and the uncontrollable handling of controversial issues. Others simply doubt their potential to cater to larger audiences' – and, in consequence, sponsors' – interests. Jeffrey Sconce (2004, 97) summarises the debate:

> "In popular accounts of the medium, this was the era dominated by the genius of Serling, Chayefsky, and other TV playwrights, serious authors who each week created an individual drama on a par with that of the theatrical stage. More recent scholarship in television history has greatly revised this rather idealized fable, demonstrating that the live anthology was a doomed (and often mediocre) genre almost from the moment of its interception."

Whatever reason prevailed – lack of control, lack of interest and / or the insight that a saturated appliance market no longer needed the high culture argument to woo a wealthy consumer base into buying costly television sets – it lead to the rigid schedule of assorted half-hour and hour-long formats and the organisational structure of prime time as a streamlined bouquet of weekly episodic series perpetuating those well-known generic formulas from the "pulps" and newspaper cartoons further.

Most European television system did undergo significant changes in-between the late 1970's and up to the mid-1980's, while developing various adaptation techniques for responding to a deregulated "dual" system that allowed for commercial stations to co-exist with the traditional public service providers. Van Zoonen (1994) gives an overview on how national public service broadcasters coped with the new situation, either by partial competition (in Denmark one public station went popular, while

---

[148] For more detailed overviews regarding the development of US television up to the "TV II" era see Comstock / Scharrer (1999, 3-20), and Murray (2003).

others stuck to the public service mission), by direct competition (in England, and later Finland, the public stations started to mix popular with more traditional fare in response to what was programmed by the competitor), by practically copying the competitor's strategies (in the case of Italy's dual system and those "neo" TV programs Eco describes) or by consolidation and thus affirmation of the predominant service public mission (Germany).

The significant changes within the US television system, at about the same time, were also related to enhanced competition from some "newer" kind of television ... as the claim by premium cable provider Home Box Office proudly stated ("It's not TV – it's HBO"). Here, greater availability resulted from the successful implementation of narrowcasting techniques such as the (basic and prime) cable services and satellite technologies that catered more directly to specific (subject-related or generic) audience interests.

While in Europe advertisement became a main issue and distinctive factor, over the course of the 1980's and 1990's, in the United States the debates turned around the "client" state of sponsors on the one hand and more directly addressed audiences on the other. What resulted as identity crisis of the established three networks (... or what ABC programming executive Brendan Tartikoff subsequently termed the *three blind mice* in his autobiography (Auletta, 1991) was not so much related to publicly discussed "mission" problems but instead to questions of internal schedule organisation and focus.

Once the prime time schedules began to lose their influence on what was conceived as a somewhat coherent, "programmable" mass audience, targeting became key. Changes can be attributed to rapidly expanding and increasingly personalised offers in a deregulated institutional context (for the development of the free basic cable and the subscription-based premium cable channels see Mullen 2003, for the strategic reuse of existing program libraries in terms of a more extensive "feeding off the past" Spigel 1995, Phil Williams 2000, and Kompare 2005). According to Mittell (2006, 31) these shifts in the television industry were essential for reinforcing strategies of complexity within the prime time drama:

> "Traditional industry logic dictated that audiences lacked the weekly consistency to allow for serialized narratives, and the pressures of syndication favored interchangeable episodes of conventional sitcoms and procedural dramas. But as the number of channels has grown and the size of the audience for any single program has shrunk, networks and channels have grown to recognize that a consistent cult following of a small but dedicated audience can suffice to make a show economically viable."

In part such strategies developed also from the television set's tranformation into a multimedia outlet for non-scheduled, individually "consulted" sources of entertainment such as video cassettes and computer games.[149] However, these changes were not only technology-inferred but mirror larger social issues such as the questioning of established gender roles, mutations within the work force and implications on family structures and the everyday. All of this made it increasingly difficult to assign particular timeslots (such as: nondescript "daytime") to particular audiences (i.e.: nondescript "housewives").

If schedulers could no longer rely on their desired market segments to "wait for them" within predefined timeslots assigned to either "domestic" audiences or "breadwinners", they needed to adapt. One answer to the problem is what Eco describes as generic hybridity. Another answer lies is the strategic delivery of programs to limited (i.e.: upwardly mobile, urban and well-educated) target audiences which could then be delivered to interested advertisers. Both measures have contributed to the "quality" discourse which was to become so important later on.[150]

Jeffrey Sconce (2004, 98) refers back to Horace Newcomb (1974, and 1985) when describing the new narrative modes as balancing "... episodic treatments of a program's story world with larger arcs of long-term narrative progression". While such strategies were already present within (the MTM school of) half-hour comedies, the

---

[149] Feuer (1995, 3) lists the following devices for remote access to broadcast and other materials that were implemented during the 1980's: the videocassette recorder; the electronic remote control; videodisc, camcorder, video games, and home computers; and pay-per-view for wired households. VCR penetration increased from 4% of US households in 1982 to 60% in 1988, with time shifting (the individual recording of programs for later use) becoming more common within the second half of the decade. Cable penetration increased from roughly 17 to 57 percent in-between 1978 and 1989.

[150] For the term and its various applications Feuer / Kerr / Vahimagi (1984), Brower (1992), Feuer (1996 and 2003), Thompson (1996), Betsy Williams (2000), Thomas (2002), Jancovich / Lyons (2003), Sconce (2004), and Nelson (2008). For a summary of criteria distinguishing "quality" programming from other types of prime time content see Thompson (1996, 13-15): To him Quality TV is not "regular" TV (1). has a quality pedigree (2), attracts a well-educated audience (3), is daring, and thus usually "the result of fights with the airing network" (4), tends to have a large ensemble cast (5), has a memory (6), creates a new genre by mixing old ones (7), tends to be literary and writer-based (8), and its writing is usually more complex than in other types of programming (9). Quality TV is self-conscious, and the subject matter at stake tends toward the controversial (10) and aspires toward "realism" (11). And: Series exhibiting those traits are, usually, "enthusiastically showered with awards and critical acclaim".

novelty was introduction of narrative continuity (... and its complement, narrative memory) into the hour-long drama series (ibid.):

> "Three of the most influential series in this regard (appearing in the 1980's) would be *Magnum, P.I., Hill Street Blues,* and *St. Elsewhere,* each of which reinvented long-standing television genres (the detective, cop and medical shows) by focusing less on episodic treatments of crooks and patients and more on the serial development of melodrama involving the private eye, cops, and doctors."

As for the history of repeated and remote access to broadcast prime time fiction, the era of "plenty" (or: TV III) refers by its very definition to an economic necessity for increased redundancy just as it depends on novelty. Broadcast prime time fiction gets now more aggressively (or: desperately) proposed as "more of the same" within its various outlets; and that goes for daytime as well as late night programming.

Since the mid-1990s television series became available to their viewers also in many outlets outside the original schedule. Mittell (2006, 31) discusses the aspects of "rewatchability" with regards to serialised prime time series in an era that is (to say it in Ellis' terms) demand-led rather than offer-led:

> "While reruns proliferated in syndication, typically, programs were shown out of other, encouraging episodic narratives to accommodate an almost random presentation of a series. Since the mainstreaming of cable and the VCR in the early 1980's, the balance has shifted more toward viewer control – the proliferation of channels has helped routinize repeats, so that viewers can catch up on a program in chronologically aired reruns or view missed premium cable shows multiple times throughout the week. Time-shifting technologies like VCRs and digital video reorder enable viewers to choose when they want to watch a program, but, more important for narrative construction, viewers can rewatch episodes or segmnets to parse out complex moments. While select series have been sold on videotape for years, the compact packaging and visual quality of DVDs have led to a boom in a new mode of television viewing, with fans binging on a show a season at a time [...] and encouraging multiple viewings of what used to be a mostly ephemeral form of entertainment."

As for the increased access to episodic fiction in the TV II and TV III eras, canonical as well as more obscure outlets for reruns, re-recordings and subsequent re-readings emerged ever since, be it in the form of timed access to streaming videos on a network's official websites, be it with the possibility to download episodes on handheld devices. All of this nourished respective expectations on all levels of observation. And it had recursive repercussions for scheduling practices that forfeited the traditional "summer rerun" (in terms of repeats of already broadcast seasons) in favour of more flexible short-term seasons with packages of 13 episodes instead of the traditional 22-24 episodes per year.[151]

Sconce (2004, 97) summarises the development of US network and post-network television fiction as following: "Cable's fragmentation of the network audience, the growth of 'reality television,' and the concurrent reduction of more expensive narrative-based programming has created an environment of increasingly specialised narrative vehicles, allowing smaller audience groups the potential for targeted and intensive narrative investment."

However: prime time fiction remains, even in its variously hailed forms of "quality television", a cultural commodity for most of the responsible, directly involved communication partners. It is worth noting that all of the characteristic forms of historical and contemporary US-American television fiction drew from older, and likewise commercial, storytelling traditions – the anthology drama from the tradition of the Broadway theatre, and prime time series and serials from the newspaper cartoons, from early cinema and radio.

As for the past, and the future of the currently dominant "serialised series" there are many open questions, with answers sought best from all three observational stances mentioned earlier:

- from the macro perspective of the "social project" at stake,
- from the meso perspective of production and distribution, with a closer look at scheduling practices,
- from the micro perspective that focuses on narrative communication at various stages of more or less initiated readership.

For this, let me refer to John Fiske, and to his description of television being foremost a cultural experience (1987, 59):

> What television delivers is not programs but a semiotic experience. This experience is characterized by its openness and polysemy. Television is not quite a do-it-yourself meaning kit but neither is it a box of ready-made meanings for sale. Although it works within cultural determinations, it also offers freedoms and the power to evade, modify, or challenge these limitations and controls. All texts are polysemic, but polysemy is absolutely central to television's textuality.

---

[151] For the history of the prime time season and how commissioned instalments dropped from 39 per year to an average of 22 see Anderson (1990) and Schatz (1990); for the strategic role of the Hollywood studios in this Anderson (1994).

PART II
EPISODIC FICTION AS ART

> We need to keep people guessing. We only give away fragments.
> The viewer has to put the pieces of the puzzle together.
> When it comes to *The X-Files*, you can't be a passive viewer.
> (Chris Carter in Gradnitzer / Pittson 1999)

> The truth, the truth! There's no truth.
> These men, they make it up as they go along.
> (Alex Krycek in "Tunguska")

7 THE GAPS OF WHICH EPISODIC TELEVISION FICTION IS MADE

This chapter leads over from a series of reflections on episodic narrative fiction as communication to a series of reflections on how meaning is negotiated within such communication as art.

Narratives were so far presented as chains of events and episodes based on (explicit or inferred) relations of cause and effect, with mutually shared narrative knowledge determining the outcome of events, episodes and stories. This means that storytelling is seen as a constructivist process of meaning-making, with various dimensions (factual, temporal and social, in the words of Niklas Luhmann) prefigured, configured and critically reassessed during the course of a telling. Prefiguring, in all three cases of events, episodes and stories, relates to expectations that were engendered within earlier narrative experiences. Configuration equals the Aristotelian mimetic stance and realises narrative events as the telling moves on, and refiguring constructs, or "recognises", in hindsight what happened so far, with the reflexive stance alimenting expectations as to what is left to be told – right there, or maybe later on.

At stake is what co-tellers intend to make each other know, but also what is withheld at what point, for whatever reason. Branigan distinguishes paradigmatic, *declarative* knowledge (of a "this" or "that", or "yes" or "no" kind) from syntagms of *procedural* knowledge that advances in stages from knowing less (... than before, and with regards to what others know) to knowing more – until an equal state of knowledge an all sides is reached, with nothing more to be added for clarity.[152]

From a conversational perspective, storytelling relies on alternating auctorial voices and different perspectives to choose from. The story evolves not gradually from a linear plot but must be reassembled from what is a) contributed over time and b) remembered as happening at different moments in time. As Walter Ong (1980) pointed out, storytelling in oral cultures depends heavily on "memory devices" to structure the ongoing narrative flow, since there is no way of safekeeping and storing what may have been told outside of the circle of those actually present. There is, in other words, no tale beyond the telling, and since nobody can control, and thus authorise, the tale at hand, stories need to be told in segments that are more easily memorable than the story as a whole – and they need to be repeated in order to remain on the participants' play list.

Storytelling within time-in culture (to which mass-mediated "news" and "reportages" importantly contribute) is expected to produce more determinate meanings, in terms of a shared understanding of what information was uttered how, and to what commonly shared gain of knowledge. Narratives as leisurely time-out culture are – similarly to vanguard art, and in many ways similarly to religion – exempt from this kind of pressure; they can allow for a larger range of interpretation and allusive play. These are by default stories based on redundancies, and on indeterminacies – of which the syntagmatic gaps (*vacancies* as well as *blanks*) are of particular interest here.

Episodic narrative communication is by default littered with gaps and produces variant stages of competent readership over time. What results as narrative competence ranges from "ingenuous" to "expert" and varies in relation to access granted (to story material and initiated circles of knowledge) but also in relation to the participants' sustained interest and investment in the telling.

Episodic narratives in broadcast television are remarkably close to oral storytelling, since they
- are unpredictable with regards to duration and outcome,
- depend on what everyone involved bring to the table, in terms of prior narrative knowledge and (personal or mass mediated) memories,

---

[152] See Branigan (1992, 65); Spivey (1997) suggests to distinguish between *topic* (or *content*) knowledge and *discourse* knowledge.

– produce expendable as well as sustainable second worlds, as result of the collective storytelling efforts over time.

Taken into account here are the changes over various "eras" of increasingly demand-led television that saw the convergence of daytime and prime time serials happen and extended use made of storage and replay technologies. This arguably culminated in a process that is described by McGrath (2000) as "novelisation" of episodic television fiction – with contents increasingly available within material or virtual "libraries" and extended access granted to episodes as "chapters" of more focused narratives. This, and the ongoing "quality" debate that fosters recognition of auctorial voices, indicates that television narratives are not (only) headed towards greater expressive freedom and extended collaborative intertextuality but maybe also towards greater textual control, by various institutional players at different communicative levels.[153]

7.1   Vacancies and blanks within broadcast television fiction

As was stated earlier, narrative fiction as art oscillates between the playful disposition to "suspend disbelief" (against all odds. and voluntarily) and the self-reflexive stance of knowing already (... if only to limited extent) what lies ahead. With regards to the gaps that narrative fiction addresses and simultaneously produces conventional wisdom is needed to make sense of what is withheld or willingly obscured as "vacancy" while personal as well as collective memories of former experiences need to be constantly recalled in order to make sense of "blanks".

According to Hagedorn the complexity of episodic fiction stems from the "fact dimension" of meaning, in terms of a significantly enhanced variety of what can happen to particular characters as performing *agents* within the second world at stake,[154] under particular circumstances at particular moments in time. Such "fact dimensions" granted, for instance, the original *Star Trek* premise (i.e.: spaceships

---

[153]   For this see Rifkin (2000). Symptomatic for the ongoing conflicts over access and control are the recurring Hollywood "writers' strikes" (for instance 1980, 1988 and 2007) which result from fights over fair shares of residuals that studios and networks ought to grant their officially licensed storytellers. Such conflicts do regard the profits from advertisement that is placed within repeats and recordings and can further extend to the domestic home front where readers, listeners and viewers must choose either to buy legitimate copies or to peruse bootlegged copies / downloaded content from peer-to-peer networks instead.

[154]   For the *agency* of characters as well as co-imaginating readers as "interactors" within the story world see Branigan (1992, 106), and Murray (1997, 152 ff.).

travelling from planet to planet, but also through time and space) remarkable "extended narrative fluidity" (as C. Johnson puts it, 2005a, 821) while the episodic structure (of individual missions following each other) remained intact.[155]

This study focuses not on the paradigmatic fact dimension of series' premises but instead on the temporal dimension of meaning-making, and analyses the syntagmatic indeterminacies allowing for similarly extended "narrative fluidity" with regards to patterns of continuity and change. Notably contributing to this kind of fluidity is the characteristic unpredictability at both ends of the ongoing (or: frequently renewed) communication. On the authors' end this is due to the precarious production conditions that were described earlier in part I and, in consequence, to the rigidly timed production and distribution cycles also known as the prime time season. No legitimate narrator of weekly broadcast television fiction can ever assume the omniscient viewpoint regarding an evolving overall story that is conventionally attributed to (other) authors of narrative fiction, in terms of control over the story world. Such control is merely given to the proprietors of the narrative franchise (distributing studios and commissioning networks) while the authors are usually just a few steps ahead of what their implied viewers already anticipate as "off-the-shelf" content and plotted course of action.

The creative function of vacancies and blanks that "invite to imagine" within narrative fiction is illustrated best by examples. The following ones stem from generic hybrids as typically "postmodern", poststructuralist film and television fare – and are thus somewhat susceptible to violate, or tamper with, narrative conventions.

The erotic cinema thriller *Wild Things* (John McNaughton, 1998) tells two different crime stories based on how vacancies, in terms of *ellipses*,[156] are recursively connected – first imaginatively and in response to (seemingly accidental) indetermina-

---

[155] There is a widespread misunderstanding about what is to expect within repeatedly accessed second worlds, in terms of an alleged uniformity stemming directly from the premises of serial production. While mass communication as programmed program may indeed depend on long-term expectations and predictability (... of more, and similarly formatted programs to follow) this does by no means determine the outcome of what is communicated and co-constructed as "story". Because, as Iser notably argued (with more rhetoric backup provided elsewhere), all meaning is refigured, and again prefigured, in-between episodes, and in-between "acts" and "seasons" – by many participants in the telling and with just as many possible outcomes.

[156] For the term see Chatman ([1978] 1993, 67-68); for its application to television fiction Kozloff (1992, 87-88).

cies and then again (but only within the rolling credits of the film) in more explicit terms. As it turns out, crucial story events were cunningly withheld from the unsuspecting audience and told off-screen, by way of suggestive sounds such as pistol shots and screams. In hindsight alone are we made knowledgeable about what "really" happened – and have to cope with radical shifts of previous knowledge with regards to causes and effects, and the narrative roles assumed by the main characters over the story's subsequent course of action.

The X-Files played, as a prototypical "serialised series", continuously with audiences' hopes (or, maybe: fears) to find the two investigating partners Fox Mulder and Dana Scully entangled in a romantic relationship. What built over time as *unresolved sexual tension*, or UST (for the term see Sabucco 2000, 69), culminated in well-orchestrated moments of indeterminacy which had the two FBI agents confined to tight locations in situations of heightened emotion. Such a moment occurred in the episode "Operation Paperclip" (Fox, originally broadcast 29-09-1995) right after a climactic encounter between the main protagonists, and while both were about to recover from the loss of family members, and overwhelming feelings of guilt:[157]

> Mulder: There are truths out there that aren't on that tape. (He walks out. She glares at Skinner, then puts his gun on the desk and walks out. Skinner looks at the tape and puts it in his pocket. Down the hall, Mulder presses the down button for the elevator and looks at Scully, who walks up to him. She stares at him for a second, then looks down, smiling.)
> Scully: Mulder, I am ...
> Mulder: Scully, whatever you're going to say ...
> Scully: I went to your father's funeral. I told your mother that you were going to be okay.
> Mulder: How did you know?
> (The elevator dings.)
> Scully: I just knew.
> (The door opens and Scully walks past him into the elevator. He follows and presses a button. The door closes.) [Etc.]

What is clearly designed as a vacancy (we don't need to see Mulder and Scully stepping out of the elevator in order to "know" that the elevator journey took only seconds) opens up a "gap" that promptly lead to gleeful gossiping and wild speculations among fans with regards to *what exactly* happened in that elevator. What follows is the beginning of an NC-17 fan fiction by Doyle Srader; the three parts of the story ("Going Down I", "Going Down II", and "Going Up") are accessible on the

---

[157] The reference is accessible at *www.insidethex.co.uk/transcrp/scrp302.htm*, courtesy of Vic Vega (18-08-2017).

Usenet group archive *rec.arts.tv.mst3k.misc*.[158] The speculative tale is interspersed with consenting as well as ironically commenting response from co-tellers (reproduced here in italics):

> This story takes place during Operation Paperclip at the beginning, as they head into the elevator. Enjoy!
>
> GOING DOWN
>
> "I just knew," Scully murmured, as she crossed smoothly into the waiting elevator. Mulder flashed
> *All: AAAAAAGHH!!*
> briefly on the Eves, and then just sighed and followed her docily inside.
> *Mike: * whew **
> *Crow: He must've imprinted on her docily when he was just a duckling.*
> He absently pressed 1,
> *Servo: (as Han Solo) Push the button, Chewie, but pretend you're absent.*
> *Mike: (as Chewbacca) Raawwwwwr?*
> *Servo: (Han Solo) I don't know, press casually.*
> then turned to find Scully staring at him with an unfathomable expression. "What is it?"
> *Crow: (Scully voice) "It's a contortion of my facial muscles that you're unable to interpret. But that's not important right now."*
> he asked softly. "What's wrong?" Suddenly she smiled, lightening his heart a hundred-fold.
> *Servo: Sending it hurtling up his throat and out his mouth.*
> *Mike: Mullaraam, sullaraam! Mullaraam, sullaraam!*
> "Nothing now. I'm just glad to have you back." Mulder bit
> *Mike: His necktie in half.*
> back his standard sardonic reply and instead opened
> *Crow: His pocket flask?*
> *Servo: His petals sunward?*
> *Mike: His very own chain of low-cal fondue restaurants?*
> his arms to engulf her in a warm hug.
> *All: Ohhhhhh.* [Etc.]

As for an example of a "blank" I refer instead to the episode 3x4 of the same series ("Clyde Bruckman's Final Repose"; Fox, 13-10-1995), with a highly improbable dialogue taking place between Dana Scully and the episode's main protagonist (an infallible clairvoyant named Clyde Bruckman):[159]

---

[158] See *https://groups.google.com/forum/#!topic/rec.arts.tv.mst3k.misc/_hvtIHghJ9c* (18-08-2017).

[159] The reference is accessible at *www.insidethex.co.uk/transcrp/scrp304.htm* and was, again, transcribed by Vic Vega (18-08-2017).

(Bruckman and Scully are playing poker. Bruckman has three Aces and two eights, constituting a full house known as a "Dead Man's Hand.")
Scully: So, Ahab mistakes the prophecy and as a result, dies. A similar fate happens to Macbeth.
Clyde Bruckman: Still, you're not the least bit curious? (There is a knock on the door.)
Scully: That must be Mulder. Time for the midnight shift. (She puts her cards down and stands up. She goes towards the door, but then walks back up to Bruckman.)
Alright. So how do I die?
Clyde Bruckman: You don't.
(He smiles as she stares at him. There is more knocking. She looks through the peephole and opens the door. Mulder holds up a folder.) [Etc.]

The riddle as to how someone *won't die* was never fully resolved, over the course of the original series.[160] But the indeterminacy lead up to entertaining online debates about how exactly Dana Scully might indeed "not die" – within the premise of this particular hybrid sci-fi / detective series, that is.

For examples of subsequent fan speculation see the discussion on Usenet (group *alt.tv.x-files*; all postings from 19-06-1996 / 20-06-1996):[161]

> QUESTION: *I've been wondering about the exchange between Scully and C.B. when she asks: "OK, how I am going to die" and he responds "You're not." What's the consensus on this?*
>
> ANSWER: *The best I could come up with is that there may be some clones of Scully around after her abduction. This is improbable, as the clones would not be around forever. I'd guess that CB would also get a view of the original Scully's death even if there were clones. Hmmm ... Any ideas?*

Viewer proposals included:

– *Clones, with the chance to live on forever.*

– *Scully's DNA ideal for creation of a new hybrid life-form, half human / half alien.*

– *General cosmic statement: Nobody really dies.*

– *She lives on in syndication and movies.*

– *She's not who she claims she is.*

---

[160] While the issue of Scully's unlikely death was brought up in the episode 6x09 ("Tithonus", January 24th, 1999), the question of who does and does not die became a staple topic on the series; see episode 4x01 ("Herrenvolk", October 4th, 1996), or fans debating within various Internet billboards if – and how – on *The X-Files* "nobody really dies".

[161] For more in-depth analysis of these comments see Ganz-Blättler (2000a, 2000b).

- *He just lied.*
- *It's probable that we'll never know [...] I would like to have some hints from the writers.*
- *If a clone, please not Mulder's sister Samantha!*

The respective ideas range from the application of expert knowledge and metaphysical musings to some production-oriented reflection ("She lives on in syndication and movies") but also to humorous speculations about Bruckman lying and intertextual cross-references to the *Star Wars* franchise. One sole contributor asked for auctorial help since otherwise "… we'll never know".

As these examples show, textual gaps invite for a wide, and wildly playful range of reader response. However, propositions will remain within a predefined spectre of possibilities that are "decodable" for co-tellers.

Blanks, on the other hand, provide the occasion to close, but also to open up, particular events and episodes as "unities of action" within an overarching, focused (=plotted) chain of cause and events. They halt whatever is underway as story-in-progress, and thus provide a state of (preliminary or temporary) stasis.

7.2 Openings and closures of segments

According to common sense a story is over when the last contributing event falls into place and provides us with the chance to recognise what "it all means", ultimately. Closure brings the narrative voyage to its end and releases us (back) into our own life course. Stories end, and so does the process of storytelling.

As may be guessed by now, this is not what happens to stories told within ongoing narrative communication. Here the question remains as to how stories "end", paradoxically, while being already expected to resume actions, events and states at a later stage. A constructivist viewpoint has no problem to conceive the process of storytelling as a kind of a communicative *perpetuum mobile*, with endless possibilities of contract renegotiation later on. New meanings can emerge from a repeated (and necessarily more "knowing") reading or, alternatively, from an insertion of more puzzle pieces that become meaningful units in the overall context. Pauses, in terms of intervals between narrative segments, can be read as endings but just as well as temporary lay-offs before some dormant story is resumed.

All of this suggests that narratives can go on forever, potentially, while only the telling of stories stalls, and stops – in wait to be resumed, at one point or another.

This is certainly the case with the soap opera where stories go on as long as there are co-tellers left to take over from former co-tellers and carry on the torch (or light it for some nostalgic "reunion" episode, as happened repeatedly on *Dallas*). However, even with soaps the plotted action will stall and stop, occasionally, with storylines laid off for good, or waiting to be resumed some other day.

To the ingenuous viewer all stories told within each and every soap opera may appear as "lookalikes", with confusingly similar-looking characters stuck in an endless "middle" with nothing (... of notable worth) *really* happening. This impression is not shared by the sophisticated readers, however who register a multitude of openings and closures, and many irreversible as well as reversible outcomes in-between.

Edward Branigan (1992, 67) points to the multiple knowledge disparities that are negotiated not only among co-tellers of a particular soap opera but also, and typically, among the characters within the soap: "It is no accident that flamboyant genres, such as melodramas and television soap operas, are filled with excessive forms of narration whereby characters spy upon, eavesdrop, and gossip about other characters, producing a chain of tellings and retellings based on various disparities." Soap opera action is, in other words, to a great extent *talk* about actions, happenings and states –and may for that very reason appear less "plotted" to the unaccustomed onlooker.

But there is plot; breathtakingly dense plot, even. The only aspect missing (if one insists to compare the daily soap opera's action to the more linearly plotted action of the prime time drama series) is that determining moment when, finally, "enough" narrative knowledge has been imparted among co-tellers so that participants in the telling can call it quits. According to Cohan-Shires (1988, 65),

> "[a] given story [...] organizes a transformation of events within the syntagmatic space of a sequence. [W]hen a story sequence combines more than two events (and most do), the addition of other events advances or amplifies the sequence to widen the space between opening (i.e. the possibility of an outcome) and ending (i.e. the realization of an outcome). In delineating this space as a temporal movement from one event to another, a story sequence moves towards its *closure*, or point of termination, and yet necessarily postpones it, usually by raising an enigma and delaying its solution. The open-ended structure of TV soap operas makes the importance of syntagmatic postponements quite obvious. Serial structures organize several macrosequences, embedding or combining the final point of one sequence with the opening or middle points of another one in order to defer the final moment of closure."

Within a *simple narrative* (or, "a series of episodes collected as a focused chain", as Branigan 1992, 20, puts it), closure is reached when all causes and effects have been delineated by the participants in the telling, so that some cyclic, or "closed" structure appears in hindsight (ibid.):

> "Not only are the parts themselves in each episode linked by cause and effect, but the continuing center is allowed to develop, progress and interact from episode to episode. A narrative ends when its cause and effect chains are judged to be totally delineated. There is a reversibility in that the ending situation can be traced back to the beginning; or, to state it another way, the ending is seemingly entailed by the beginning. This is the feature of narrative often referred to as *closure*."

In classic narrative theory the course of a linear, dramatic plot is often represented as a triangle or pyramid, with a clear-cut beginning, a middle (aka "turning point") and an ending depicted as apexes. A prominent example is the model triangle found in Gustav Freytag's "Technique of the drama" which was originally published in 1863 (see here, Figure 17):

Figure 17: The plotted drama's "unity-of-action" structure (Freytag 1863, 102)[162]

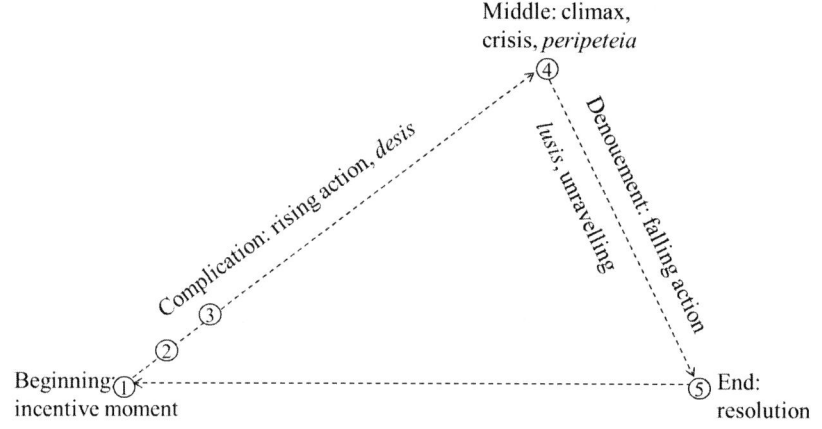

---

[162] For the original model illustration see the online link at *www.einladung-zur-literaturwissenschaft.de/index.php?option=com_content&view=article&id=368:7-1-5-die-technik-des-dramas&catid=42:kapitel-7* (18-08-2017). For a revised version of the Freytag triangle see also *www.englishbiz.co.uk/extras/freytagtriangle.htm* (18-08-2017). Eberhard Lämmert (1997, 63) requires from a main dramatic plot that it be succinct and focalised. In German he asks for a "Straffung und Geschlossenheit des Gesamtvorgangs [...], bei dessen Bildung kausalverknüpfte und endkulminierende Stränge durchaus die Oberhand besitzen müssen."

The "three-act structure" is usually accredited to Aristotle's *Poetics*. A slightly shorter "broadway version" is instead attributed to various sources (ibid., 27):

First act: *Get your hero up a tree* (= rising action / complication).

Second act: *Throw rocks at him* (= middle / climax).

Third act: *Get him down* again (= falling action / denouement).

Tzvetan Todorov (cit. Lacey 2000, 29) suggests instead to view the dramatic action in five stages (included here, Figure 17): An initial state of equilibrium (1) is disrupted by some disturbing event (2). Any attempt to repair the disruption (4) can be undertaken only after the disruption has been recognised as such (3). The five-act structure refers thus to an additional stance of assessment, or recursive connectivity: Realising the need for action is indispensable for the action to get going, and as requirement for some climactic revelation, or collision that will shift positions, turn the tables and allow for an (old, or new) equilibrium to be (re-)instated (5).

The plotted action, in this model, is supposed to gain momentum as tension rises from zero to maximum, in terms of *peripeteia* (greek for "moment of reversal"). From there on tension diminishes until all there is to know is fully disclosed, and the story ends. The beginning and end of the movement delineate moments of rest, or *stasis*, and therefore resemble each other. Depending on genre and narrative intention the end can signify *absolute* stasis and lead right back to the beginning (of another picaresque adventure, for example)[163] or, instead, propel the involved character(s) slightly forward to another level of consciousness (within the coming-of-age story or "Bildungsroman", for instance).[164]

Frank Kermode ("The Sense of an Ending", 1967) compares the dramatic structure of classic narratives to the "tick-tock" of a clock and points to mythic and religious traditions (in the case of Christianity: the *tick* and *tock* of genesis and apocalypse) and how they inspired the literary convention of stories displaying of a beginning, a middle, and an end. Between the "tick" and the "tock" time appears in its plotted and therefore "humanized" form (ibid., 45) – in Luhmann's terms there is a double

---

[163] Genre-wise, the *picaresque* adventure story translates into the satirical "Schelmenroman". The term is also used to describe adventurous travel stories that are told in autonomous segments or episodes. Other typical attributes are the protagonists' lower social status and the frequent use of soliloquy as self-centered monologue (I am indebted to Paul Michel for pointing this out).

[164] The dramatic structure of *Harry Potter* works that way, as Thierfelder (2006) notes.

contingency of expectations based on the mutually shared trust that a "tock" will undoubtedly follow upon the promise of a "tick".

How story endings are handled, and interpreted depends, in Kermode's view, on notions of time in general – and particularly on the differences that are made, or not made between (greek) *chronos* and *kairos* (ibid., 47-48):

> "The Greeks [...] thought that even the gods could not change the part; but Christ did change it, rewrote it, and in a new way fulfilled it. In the same way the End changes all, and produces, in what in relation to it is the past, these seasons, *kairoi*, historical moments of intemporal significance. The divine plot is the pattern of *kairoi* in relation to the End. Not only the Greeks but the Hebrews lacked this antithesis; for Hebrew [...] had no word for *chronos*, and so no contrast between time which is simply "one damn thing after another" and time as concentrated in *kairoi*. It is the New Testament that lays the foundation for both the modern sense of epoch [...] and the modern distinction between times: the coming of God's time (*kairos*), the fulfilling of the time (*kairos* – Mark i.15), the signs of the times (Matt. xvi.2,3) as against passing time, *chronos*. The notion of fulfilment is essential; the *kairos* transforms the past, validates Old Testament types and prophecies, establishes concord with origins as well as ends. The *chronos-kairos* distinction is therefore relevant to the typological interests of some modern theologians, and also some modern literary critics [...]."

There is an epistomological problem lurking within the interval between a "tock" and another "tick" (... possibly following) because it represents that "purely successive, disorganized time of the sort that we need to humanize" (Kermode, ibid.). It is an interval (aka: gap) which challenges both religious and artistic (here: literary) time-out culture for particular reasons: Because in such blank, unaccounted-for spaces nihilism looms large.[165]

Tudor Oltean (1993) analyses the gaps between segments of episodic fiction based on the presumption that both narrative forms of the *series* and the *serial* do not just

---

[165] See Kermode (1967, 89, for mythic solutions): "To close that great gap we use fictions of complementarity. They may now be novels or philosophical poems, as they once were tragedies, and before that, angels." And again (ibid., 101-102), for the notion of "permanent crisis" as a literary device developed in response to the enhanced social mobility of modern man: "The fiction of transition is our way of registering the conviction that the end is immanent rather than imminent; it reflects our lack of confidence in ends, our mistrust of the apportioning of history to epochs of this and that. [...] Since we move from transition to transition, we may suppose that we exist in no intelligible relation to the past, and no predictable relation to the future."

organise the episodes as such, but "the episodes and the intervals in between them" (ibid., 13):

> "*Le Juif Errant* (Eugene Sue's family serial novel), the radio soaps of America in the 1930s, or, more recently, *Dallas*, control the whole interval within which they take place – whether this occurs in written, audio or audiovisual form, and whether this varies from 14 months and 175 episodes [in the case of Eugene Sue] to 14 years [sic!] of *Dallas*."

Oltean then asks for "the ways in which both series and serial make use of this interval", and he presents a model of analysis based on significantly different modes of how *movement* (in terms of what is explicitly depicted within the episodes) and *stasis* (in terms of "what happens between the episodes") are handled.

What Kermode identifies as the transition from a "tock" to another "tick", appearsin Oltean's theory as conventionalised "narrative programme" that involves the audience as knowing readership which is accustomed to make sense of the "transitional stages" (aka: the gaps) that episodic fiction is made of.

While Oltean's paradigmatic model is not followed here (since it focuses on oppositional positions within subsequent chains of events rather than on the syntagmatic patterns of continuity and change) his terminology (with *movement* and *stasis* as complemented by "non-movement" and "non-stasis", to indicate what is not explicitly shown but needs to be conventionally inferred) to describe what does (... not) happen within the institutional, regular "leaves of absence" that the licensed storytellers regularly take from their audience.

According to Oltean "non-movement" is what happens to characters of the (procedural) drama series once all case-oriented knowledge is successfully disclosed, with nothing more to add ... and nothing more to imagine and guess, either (ibid., 16):

> "The goings-on of *Kojak, Derrick* and all the army of uniformed or non-uniformed actors cast as subjects of detective shows or police series are of no relevance to the audience. The marionettes stay put in a cabin placed outside the fictional reality. It is very important that the show continues; the subjects step again inside the fictional world where a variety of objects (thieves, murderers, villains) are at their disposal."

Contrary to the series' typical transitional state of "non-movement" the serial's more typical transitional state is that of "non-stasis"; in Oltean's definition a state that has no more events, or happenings actively depicted but remains highly relevant for the audiences involved in the telling (ibid., 17):

> "For the public it is the non-stasis that is relevant, the successive transitional stages that are inserted by the serials. What characters are doing meanwhile

(in-between the episodes) is important; they remain fictitiously active, even though fiction makes it impossible for them to be seen. [...] The stage of non-stasis in the serial is a kind of non-visible fiction or segment of narration, the meanings of which are initially for the audience to determine. [...] This explains why the serial as serialized narration always places its readers *in medias res*, why it never begins and never ends and why any clear resolution of the conflict is avoided [...]."

Oltean's analogies – the string puppet hanging motionless (and: consciousless) in the closet of the puppeteer, and the fictitiously active soap ensemble that "shuts us out" of their domestic lives while the plotting, and our respective guessing, continues behind closed doors – illustrates not only how episodic fiction conventionally handles the apocalyptic "gaps" in-between tocks and those yet untold ticks. It also indicates, on a more pragmatic and functionalist level of double contingency, how different ways of observing vacancies and blanks evolved over time.

A good example of how seemingly similar formal solutions can indicate closure or, instead, a temporary lay-off at the end of a narrative segment is the *freeze* – described by Feuer (1994, 557) more precisely as "shot reverse-shot cuts between the actors' locked gazes, [which is] usually accompanied by a dramatic burst of music".

Within the soap opera this translates into the "blank" stare of protagonists signalling the end of a "beat" or segment, but at the same time also a moment of heightened knowledge disparity. Some secret is about to be revealed, and we better stay alert and tune back in – be it right after the break, or tomorrow, or next week, or – with the seasonal cliffhanger typical for the prime time soap – when next season's premiere episode is about to begin.

The conventionally applied *freeze* technique of the soap opera (Hayward 2000, 205, note 18, speaks of an acting skill that needs to be learned, and trained) deliberately leaves audiences in the dark about what just happened, or is about to happen. It also deprives the excited viewers of the emotional reaction some upcoming breaking news undoubtedly entails. Both forms of the cliffhanger – the sustained secret's mystery, but also the uncertainty about how characters are afflicted and react – keeps our imagination busy until we are invited back into the homes and tribulations of these lively, albeit "fictitious" agents.

For the potentially upsetting effect of the lay-off see Allen (1985, 79):

"Each episode of a soap opera is, of course, separated from the next by a twenty-four-hour 'gap' during the week and an even longer one over the weekend. Soap opera writers take advantage of this hiatus in reading activity by leaving a major narrative question unanswered at the end of each episode, saving the greatest narrative indeterminacy for the end of Friday's episode. The anticipation thus provoked produces in some soap opera readers the modern-day equivalent of Dickens's American readers greeting the packet at the dock: when Pope John Paul II was wounded in an assassination attempt in May 1981 the Associated Press reported that a St. Louis television station received three hundred calls from irate soap opera fans protesting the preemption of regular afternoon programming in favor of press coverage of events in Rome."

Classic prime time series close instead each segment with a just as conventional *freeze frame* – that is, a narrative "pause" which puts an end to the episode and "drives the moral home" (Kozloff 1992, 88). There is an important difference between the two seemingly similar ending moments: While the soap's *freeze* is situated within the second world at stake (characters do "freeze" while holding each other's gaze), the *freeze* within at the end of the series' segment is nondiegetic (for the discussion of the term see here, p. 258 ff.) and belongs to the same paratextual reality of the episode's fringes as the rolling end credits do. This "blank" signifies that there is nothing more to be told: The puppeteers' auctorial stance removes the fictitious agents from the scene and lets them hang loose, literally, until a new episode – and with it some new adventure, some new dilemma – demands the heroes' full attention. Meanwhile, all remaining knowledge disparities among authors and interested viewers are declared obsolete. Closure has been attained and confirmed: Time to bow, and to applaud.

While the classic drama series (of the TV I era) finds closure within each and every segment, overall closure remains just as much suspended as it is on the soap opera. According to John Ellis the series insists on a nagging problem as premise that is perpetuated, week after week, while the recurring closure provides only temporary solution (1982, 154):

> "Fundamentally, the series implies the form of the dilemma rather than that of resolution and closure. This perhaps is the central contribution that broadcast TV has made to the long history of narrative forms and narrativised perception of the world."

This means that the "equilibrium" of the episode's beginning and ending is only temporary: There is some relative *stasis* while the underlying problem persists.

What results from such narrative conventions has repercussions on the narrative communication: Choices need to be made as to either accept or reject the meaning entailed in the convention. Ingenuous viewers may "obey" and read the ending of a series' segment according to the auctorial suggestion. However, the "blanks" at the end of a segment can just as well invite for further imaginative investments by the more sophisticated readers with some inside knowledge how to bend the rules. Within the soap opera's temporary lay-off and indefinite deferral of closure (the "continual postponement of the final resolution", as Geraghty puts it, 1981, 11, with argumentative support by Seiter / Wilson 2005, 143-144), however, time is remarkably malleable and passes according to the mutual narrative needs of both authors and viewers. Within the soap temporal intervals vary and can just as well encompass the exact 24 hours or 7 full days of the programmed hiatus (… that is, until the next segment is broadcast), or easily entail more diegetic time, or less (Geraghty 1991, 10):

> "Serials [...] use a set of unresolved puzzles to carry viewers across the time gap from one episode to another but the length of the fictional time which is deemed to have passed between episodes depends on the demands of the narrative: it may be a minute, a month, a year; it may be no time at all if the following episode returns to the moment of drama on which the preceding episode ended."

The *serialised series* of the post-network era draws, as the term already indicates, from both sets of narrative conventions which were established at both ends of the series-serial continuum: Its conventional ending is, not coincidentally, the *fade-out*, be it in terms of a gradual *fade to black* or, less commonly, some gradual *fade to white*. The closing of the camera lens corresponds with the closing of one's eyes (as in: going to sleep, or fainting, or concentrating on other matters) and signifies an ambivalent state of transition from movement to non-movement, as Oltean would say. We are courteously asked to leave the scene while characters are left alone to ponder their fate, with or without a spoken commentary or more pensive soliloquy.

Some things come to an end and halt – while others, apparently, do not.

7.3   Acts and beats within segments of broadcast TV fiction

The prime time series, or serial, does not only "control" the time span provided by the commercial break but also any larger interval between "clusters" of episodes resulting from the tight production schedules. On broadcast network television so-called "preemptions" of planned episodes did frequently happen in late autumn when time ran out on production, and postproduction of already scheduled episodes. More episodes were usually "pre-empted" in spring when screenwriters were busy writing spec scripts for new series' proposals (Anderson 2005, 81). Series on cable network television, however, follow their own seasonal cycles and are usually broadcast during summer.

In "Speaking of soap opera" Robert C. Allen combines Iser and Eco with a hefty dose of feminist criticism, when assessing the narrative structure of the radio and television daytime serial (1985, 75-84). He confirms that gaps are constituent parts "of any communication" (ibid., 78) before highlighting the particular role of commercially induced indeterminacy within the segments of the soap opera (ibid., 79 f.):

> "Within each episode the syntagmatic structure of the soap opera is regulated by the gaps inserted in the text at regular intervals to allow for commercial messages. [...] [T]he repetition of ads leaves plenty of room in the commercial gap for soap opera readers to fill it with retensive and protensive ruminations about the soap opera text. [...]
>
> Commercial 'gaps' [also] provide additional opportunities for the development of an interreader social discourse. More competent readers can acquaint new viewers with portions of the text the latter might not have seen. A reader's private interpretation of an action, scene, or line of dialogue can be compared to that of other readers, with the result that new expectations are formed and new paradigmatic relationships actualized. Ironically, the subjects of many soap opera commercial messages – laundry products, diapers, household cleaners – encourage the use of commercial gaps for social soap opera reading among college-age viewers, since these products are largely irrelevant to their life-styles."

The prime time drama series of the network and post-network era is, in theory, structured by the exact same institutional gaps as serial daytime programming is, and notably the ad breaks bought by program sponsors as space for breaking commercial messages. However, these gaps are not necessarily used for the exact same narrative purpose. While in both cases (of the series and the soap) breaks work as "mini cliffhangers", increasing tension and making audiences guess about what to expect from upcoming actions, happenings, or states, the ad breaks within the series' segments also work as "act breaks", and thus similarly to the curtain's opening, and closing, during an opera, or theatre play.

In his study on "Television. Technology and Cultural Form" ([1974] 1992), Raymond Williams describes the advertisement break not as an "interruption" but points to its function as second program flow that interacts with the scheduled program and, in part, with the station's auto-promotional clips (ibid., 84).[166]

What is described by Williams as a series of contingent, parallel "flows" of program segments from various sources is, of course, far from random. The original ad

---

[166] It should be mentioned that ad breaks on US broadcast TV do not require some identification, as ads in the printed press do – and most ads on European TV.

breaks provide the series' segment with its dramatic structure; they are consistent with what screenwriting guides usually describe as "plot points" – moments of partial revelation (of characters recognising what is at stake, according to Todorov) or partial climax. The convention of the ad break as "curtain" is so deeply rooted within the production logic of commercial prime time television that some series even dare to poke fun at it. A good example is the ambitious yet short-lived IRS "tax fraud" series *Push, Nevada* (eight segments broadcast, ABC, September 17th – October 24th, 2002): Here a particularly tense moment ends with the rhetorical question "What can possibly be worse than this?" right before the ad break sets in.

The following model of the four-act structure (here, Figure 18) is taken from Hal Himmelstein ("Television Myth and the American Mind", 1994); the interest of the author lied here with the dramatic use of music in terms of how "an intense buildup of the background music and ambient sound [...] create the smooth transition to the often frenetic, high-pitched ads" (ibid., 201).

Figure 18: The classic drama series' four-act structure (Himmelstein 1994, 202)

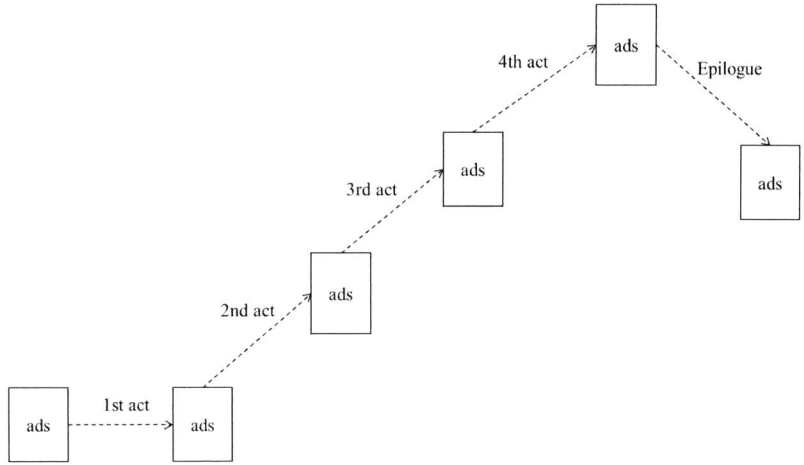

Beginnings and endings are handled flexibly, with a trailer (a short summary of the episode's events) provided to lead over from one program to the next, or maybe a "teaser" (an appetizer that leads audiences right in the middle of the story). A short message of the program's sponsor ("*Magnum P.I.* is brought to you by ...") then introduces to the successive "flow" of program, network identification, trailers for upcoming programs, and advertisement.

On *The X-Files* a more formulaic "monster-of-the-week" episode did not end with the resolution of the case but instead with the mystery pending. Delasara (2000, 43) counts four acts plus a "teaser", while the dramatic development of rising and falling action is described as "a skewed bell-shaped curve, with the long slope to the left representing the rising action of approximately ¾ to 9/10 of a narrative."

According to Pamela Douglas (2007, 19) current drama programming verges towards more than four acts, with more time consequently given to advertisement: "[M]any network shows now use five acts [...] even a rare seven-act structure has surfaced".

Kristin Thompson (2003, 43 ff.) provides examples of act analysis on US-American drama series and (American as well as British) situation comedies, focusing on quantity, length and narrative function. She notes that, meanwhile, these acts do not just structure the series' episodes on commercial free to air television (where ad breaks are *de rigeur*), but episodes on ad-free prime cable services too, as the examples of *The Sopranos* (HBO, 1999-2007) and *Sex and the City* (ibid., 1998-2004) show.

For the situation comedy (see ibid., 51, and here, Figure 19; and similarly Cobley 2001, 189 f.) Thompson states: "The action builds to a point where the initial problem seems to be solved, and then a turning-point event shows that the resolution has not really been achieved: moreover, this event ratches up the level of conflict. [...] The second act increases the general antagonism and then reconciles everyone."

Figure 19: The classic sitcom's two-act structure (adapted from Thompson 2003, 51)

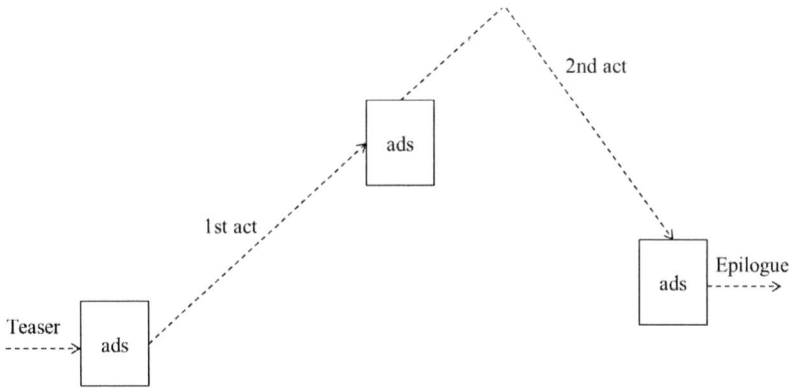

A good example of the similarly "skewed bell-shaped curve" within the dramatic structure of sitcom is provided by ABC's *Life according to Jim*. In episode 6x03 ("Guinea Pygmalion", January 10th, 2007) the following takes place

Fluffy, the family's beloved house guinea pig, is seriously ill and in need of surgery. The first act sees Jim trying to explain to the rest of the family that Fluffy is dead meat, given the exorbitant cost (2'100 $) of the operation. In response to the outcry he gives in and agrees to the operation, and the original problem is resolved. Or so it seems: What follows in the second act is a series of unexpected complications after Jim's family is convinced that he let Fluffy die and bought another guinea pig for 8 $ instead. The action culminates in climactic attacks on the poor rodent's life *after* surgery that extend from homemade guinea pig food going up in flames to some hungry birds of prey.

Here, as in the drama series, protagonists are *chased up on trees*, and sizeable rocks are thrown at them before they are allowed to come down and go on with their life.

Besides "acts", series and soaps have "beats". However, "beats" on commercial television signify two very different things: On the pages of a film or television script the expression [*beat.*] indicates a suspended moment of hesitance and asks the reciting actor to hold his or her breath. On the other hand "beats" are used in screenwriting terms to define some minimal (... unfocused or focused) unity of action.

According to Michael Z. Newman (2006, 17) the beat is nothing else than a "scene" (the term used by Porter et al., 2002) and is described as "television's most basic storytelling unit". Beats are, in other words, "the rather short segments, often less than two minutes in length" that "situation comedies, episodics, and serial dramas" are made of.

The term was originally coined with regards to daily soaps that had staff writers work collaboratively on continuous, parallel storylines. These storylines were then broken down into acts or scenes (see Rouverol 1983, 16, for how the "One-Week Breakdown" on the daily soap works). The idea was to let viewers "tune in", subsequently and alternatively, into the various storylines proceeding simultaneously.

When screenwriters on the newly introduced serialised series (or PTS, which is short for *prime-time serial*) started to write for specific characters and their ongoing storylines rather than segments, the storyline became one of the basic units within the evolving narrative. Stories were now developed over longer periods of time, in terms of "futures" (Geraghty 1981, while Rouverol ibid., 15, speaks of "projection"), and then collaboratively "broken down" to fit the individual segment's dramatic needs. According to Newman who goes into details of the process (ibid., 18), "[e]ach episode has a total of between twenty and forty beats; the average might be twenty-five. This means that each of the four acts in an hour-long show has around six beats." The ensemble drama reassembles various storylines that are developed simultaneously in terms of "A plots", "B plot" and "C plot", etcetera. Here, "[e]ach act ideally includes at least one beat from all of the episode's plots."

It comes as no surprise that the concordance of "act" and "beat" within the serialised series recalls the conventions of soap opera once more. Newman writes (ibid., 21):

> "As in a stage melodrama, a television program's curtains crystallize the dramatic developments of the act and sometimes introduce a surprise or *coup de théâtre* [...]. Like the PTS's beat structure, its curtains function to rivet the audience to the screen. [...] It is thus standard that writers save their strongest beats for the curtains. It is also typical for a curtain to fall on a reaction shot of the main character, a classic soap opera device that intensifies our interest in character psychology."

7.4   Story arcs that extend beyond segments

In the following paragraph I refer to the two terms of the "storyline" and the "story arc" as synonyms, with the *storyline* used as the more general term that describes ongoing narrative "threads" – or, what Martínez / Scheffel (2006) identify as *episodes* that evolve alongside each other.

The earliest "story arcs" on television drama were, arguably, introduced on British television screens with the highly popular adventure serials of the 1960s (for this see Ellis 1982, 154 and Tulloch / Alvorado 1983, ix-xi). Steven Cannell is, on the other hand, accredited with the "invention" of the narrative arc in the context of the US-American adventure series. Cannell did indeed establish the form of the multi-part episode on *Wiseguy* (CBS, 1987-1990; for a formal analysis Marc 1992, 205):

> "A *Wiseguy* story might extend for eight or ten weeks by making use of direct, episode-to-episode narrative continuity. This 'arc' would then come to narrative climax. It would be followed by one or two self-contained episodes, usually concerning the hero's personal life, which in turn would be followed by another extended story, or arc. In a sense, Cannell had created a generic formula for presenting fresh miniseries concepts within secure continuing series structures."

Another form of "arc" is found within serialised series that do employ larger ensemble casts: In this particular case several character-oriented arcs progress alongside each other, with or without cross-references.

According to Newman (2006, 23) such a narrative arc is to be understood as "a character's journey from A through B, C, and D to E" – or again, in Edward Branigan's terms, as a *simple* story, that is "a series of episodes collected as a focused chain".

Steven Bochco (creator of *Hill Street Blues* ; cit. in Krogerus 2006b, 30-31, and trad. ugb.) explains how he employed the structure of the arc to solve a problem his "soap-like" shows (... in Oltean's terminology, 1993, 19) obviously shared with the just as heavily populated daily soap. The problem he addresses is the institutionally allotted time frame which is never large enough to introduce each and every one of the relevant characters within one and the same instalment:

> "Of every episode's sixty minutes runtime 17 are reserved for advertisement and the credits. If I want to tell a complex story with many characters I cannot introduce all of these persons at once. I cannot introduce them one by one either because the viewer that tunes into episode 7 has no clue who 'Billy' from episode 3 might be. Instead I write a complete story in about 20 scenes for every character. These stories are held together by various storylines that I weave into each other. Each segment is provided with a beginning, a middle and an end. Each segment also contains the beginning of a new storyline to which the next segment will provide the middle and the subsequent one the end. I develop all of my stories in this manner."

Sue Turnbull and Vyvian Stranieri (2003, 13-16) give the most detailed account on how story arcs within the serialised series work, drawing from the example of *Buffy the Vampire Slayer* (WB, 1997-2003). They distinguish not only between "seasonal story arcs" and lengthier "cross-seasonal story arcs" that extend beyond seasons (as the term says) but also between arcs that are character-driven (ibid., 13: "Seasonal story arcs usually arise out of Buffy's role as a slayer whose function is to save the world") and arcs which are relationship-driven (ibid., 14: "Relationship arcs can be both seasonal or cross-seasonal but they differ from the seasonal arc ... in that they usually address the ongoing relationships of the characters").

According to Steven Johnson's absolving manifesto with regards to the, often underestimated, wisdom of contemporary pop culture ("Everything bad is good for you", 1995) the use of story arcs – or what he calls *multithreading* – is the most characteristic structural element of contemporary television drama.

7.5   Seasonal endings and series' runs

While daily soaps can virtually "go on and on", presenting new instalments ready for consumption each working day of the week and each week of the year, the traditional prime time drama of the network era was structured in seasons, and broadcast weekly. What was identified earlier on as production cycle reverberates here directly with the distribution cycle, with the "programmed programming" of the broadcast schedule referring both to short-term decisions (of networks that commission a limited number of segments to evaluate audience numbers and reactions) and long-term scheduling traditions (of a "first run" that is followed up by some contractually accorded "second run" of the same number of episodes, usually over the summer).

As Marc Dolan notes (1995, 34), near the end of the 1980's most television series on prime time displayed of season-endings that were cliffhangers. This practice was since extended to, and conventionalised for, the serialised series as such.

The basic rule has some main storyline kept hanging in the air while other (= secondary) storylines wrap up. However, this basic rule is no longer just valid for PST episodes within a network season (of 22-24 segments) but applies to full seasons too, in terms of "macro episode". That is where Turnbull / Stranieri's distinction between "seasonal story arcs" (that conclude with a season's end) and "cross-seasonal story" comes into play (2003, 15-16): the latter displays of "open" arcs which propel the action further, and beyond the summer hiatus as seasonal gap.

Jason Brett, a *showrunner* (that is, a responsible writer / producer with the obligation to oversee some series' continuity and dramatic consistency), recounts the particular high points within the prime time season as if it were a dramatic "quasi arc" (Brett 1993, 32-33, cit. in Thompson 2003, 62):

> "A show-runner arcs a season's worth of shows like a writer structures a script. With a season opener, a beginning, a first-act ending, which is your holiday show that in America would either be a Thanksgiving or a Christmas show; a mid-point two-parter which comes during something called "sweeps week", which is where the advertising agencies see their rates on the basis of the popularity of a show, so you're going to do a really high-concept show during sweeps week; and a season's closer, which is an intriguing development to make sure the audience returns to the show in the fall."

This dramatic "act" structure of the season is addressed again by Newman (2006, 24) who adds that "[...]across these larger segments of story – call them 'season acts' – definable problems are introduced, developed, and resolved."

As such, the series' finale is an innovation of Eco's *neo TV* era just as much as the seasonal cliffhanger was. According to Ellis (1982, 154) there was no overall resolution to be provided at the end of some last segment of some classic series of *paleo TV*; that is, right before the characters were "put back" in the closet by the licensed puppet players. Because an overall solution to *all* of the presented problems would have asked from the licensed authors as well as from their audiences to let go and call it quits. It would have suggested that the characters were put to rest, and never ever taken out once more for another performance of their skills and bravery.

Sarah Kozloff remarks (1992, 91) that "[o]nly on red-letter occasions will a series reach an Aristotelian *end*." She refers to the last episode of *M*A*S*H* (CBS, 1972-1983; see Wittebols 1998) attracting national attention since the show ended in a new state of affairs (ibid.): "The Korean War ended and everyone got to go home."

The counterintuitive practice of actually, "really" concluding a series and tying up eventual loose ends was arguably introduced on the situation comedies of the MTM studios (Feuer / Kerr / Vahimagi 1984 and Newcomb 2005, 31), the very first example being the *Mary Tyler Moore Show* itself (CBS, 1970-1977).[167] From there the innovation of the series' finale spread over to other situation comedies (Morreale, 1993), and to the hour-long drama.

In conclusion of this overview of the "gaps" that conventionally structure(d) the classic series, the soap opera and, more recently, the serialised prime time drama this table helps to tell the terms and their respective uses apart (here, Table 7).

Table 7: The intervals structuring broadcast television fiction

	Daytime soap	Prime time drama	Serialised series	Prime time serial
Micro level	beats	acts	acts, beats	beats, scenes
Episode = segment	part of several serialised storylines	case of the week; ev. part of two-parter	case(s) of the week; part of story arcs and / or storylines	part of several story arcs; ev. theme of the week
Macro level	lingering storylines with partial closure	two-parters, ev. series' finale (rare!)	story arcs and storylines; seasonal arcs, series' finale	story arcs, seasonal arcs, cross-seasonal arcs, with series' finale
Segment's end	*freeze technique* (=locked gaze)	*freeze frame* (=fixed image)	*fade out*	*fade out*

---

[167] Apart from *The Fugitive*, that is (ABC, 1963-1967; see Newcomb 1974, 159 and http://en.wikipedia.org/wiki/The_Fugitive_%28TV_series%29, 18-08-2017). English adventure serials of the same era provided "their" heroes regularly with a conclusive series' finale (Tulloch / Alvarado 1983).

8 THE SERIALISED SERIES: A STATE OF THE ART

8.1 What happened until now

Two forms of episodic fiction were so far identified as shaping industrialised so-called "mass" culture, with both developing their own communication style, and addressing modes within popular literature of the 19th century. Spilling over from there, the *series* and the *serial* successfully infiltrated 20th century's mass media before blending into each other as serialised series within prime time television programs of the *neo, cable, plenty* or (... to say it with Amanda Lotz) *multichannel transition* era. Theories were presented as to what structural changes prompted the transition from series to serial right there, and then. Some open questions remain as to what inspirational impulses carried over from similar narrative program strands within other contemporary media (say, newspaper cartoons, or radio serials ... with *Amos'n'Andy* being a particular promising contender for early serialisation).[168]

However, in this thesis I am focusing on broadcast television alone, and focusing on the TV II era introducing "plenty of programs" for "narrower casted" audiences with more media outlets, and more distinctively customised viewing modalities at their command. In this context I sustain the argument that the mutations from offer-led to demand-led programming (... in Ellis' terminology) provided just the right framework for institutionalising the serialised series as hybrid mix between the series (as a long-established staple on prime time TV) and the serial (as cultivated earlier within the less-respected fringes of prime the time, namely the afternoon, and early evening).

The two forms, or formats, are often distinguished in reference to particular "properties": on the one end of the spectre we find the segment of the *series*, understood as telling a complete story, and thus conveying sufficient knowledge for (a) the respective narration to achieve closure and (b) the respective readers, listeners and viewers to call it quits. The *serial*'s segment, on the other hand, suspends disclosure and ends each time, instalment by instalment, on a mystery: Someone is left up

---

[168] For the history of this show see Hilmes (1993). For updates regarding TV series' history (and serial narrative structure in general), I suggest to consult the bulk of work assembled in the "Popular Serialty" research program series (Göttingen 2010-2017; see *http://gepris.dfg.de/gepris/projekt/68338857/ergebnisse*, and also the research team's actualised website at *www.popularseriality.de/*; 18-01-2018).

there on the tree while somebody else is just about to throws rocks. Or, to say it in the words of Tudor Oltean and Frank Kermode: Life is suspended not in a closet but on a "tick".

With the serialised series assuming more and more fluidity and ambivalence as to which storylines achieve closure within what narrative interval (while other storylines are merely laid off, or left hanging suspended in mid-air) the characteristic "ticks" and "tocks" of episodic fiction were to be conceived as sequences of floods and ebbs rather than punctuation marks, while the "focused chains of causes and effects" from the past can now be interpreted as chapters in an ongoing tale.

Following this argumentation further, one can assume the two narrative "types" of *series* and *serial* to be the result of discursive conventions rather than of text-inherent structural features. Seen from this angle, they indicate an observer's stance rather than properties of some observed entity. In other words: One can choose to concentrate on a particular storyline, or "arc", and decide to *go with it* while relegating the other story strands that develop alongside to a position of less importance. Depending on the length and focus of the chosen storyline the segment will appear "episodic" (= part of a series) or "serialised". With this in mind some *serialised series* can be read as centred on an acute problem or dilemma (such as: a murder mystery, some other professional challenge) – or, instead, as focusing on the main characters' personal lives that lurk in the background and will progress in the undergrowth, with respective vacancies and blanks providing ample bonus material for more extensively involved audiences.

As may by now have become evident (and I refer to chapters 6 and 7 in particular), the television broadcast series and its counterpart, the ongoing serial, are not conceived here as epistemologically different and mutually exclusive forms of narrative stratagems and plotted structure but rather as two extremes within a series / serial-continuum that features mixes of episodicity and seriality, both in terms of format (as "programmed program") and in terms of formula (as "presumed presumption").

Another consequence is that the series / serial dichotomy gives way to what is better described as a "series / serial observational mode": One point of view perceives (and tells) the single segment as autonomous "story" (with subsequent stories following), while the other perceives them as the sum of all (past, and upcoming) episodes as "story" (or, more precisely, the story *so far*).

Newcomb agrees to this decisively audience-oriented shift in perspective when discussing the more flexible narrative strategies employed over the course of the

1980s with Hoke-Kahwati (1990, 28): "Whether or not a show is a soap becomes a question of how much interest there is in the main character. It may be an audience definition. If they're interested in plot, it's arc. If they're interested in character, it's soap – although that is changing as soaps become more involved with plot."

Michael Newman defines the *character arc* as the dominant mode of storytelling for contemporary prime time serials (Newman 2006, 23) suggesting that "[a]rc is to character as plot is to story." His claim is backed up by Christen / Ganz-Blättler's analysis of *Ally McBeal* (Fox, 1997-2002) from the same year (2006): While the professionally handled court cases clearly followed classic four-act structure as *plot*, with the closing argument and the verdict usually delivered in act three, the legal studio staff's lives and tribulations went on as unfocused arcs, meandering in and out of the (thematically related) court cases.[169]

An antagonistic reading of one and the same series as "plot-driven" or, instead, "character-driven" reveals two completely different notions: *Magnum, P.I.* is often conceived as a *paradigmatic* series based on fairly repetitive (and predictable) patterns. If the CBS show is reduced to the basic narrative formula of "a man and his friends", and a car (... not to forget the gun, the proverbial "Magnum") the show does easily figure as classic, episodic detective series.

Once the telling of "what happens" concentrates on the *syntagmatic* arc structure and takes into consideration the series' overall run as "story", one encounters a notably different show that is (just as legitimately, but not necessarily *more* legitimately) about a man's quest for peace after a difficult and traumatic period of war and sorrow. *This* Thomas Magnum lost his wife in Vietnam and came back disillusioned, and he viewed his day job mostly as a distraction from what robbed his youth. He shares (... and frequently discusses) war-related memories with his friends and with Higgins (who seems to have participated in virtual every war of the 20th century – if we are to believe his extended, and frequently excessive war stories). Over the course of eight years, and eight broadcast seasons, the title character sees his long-lost wife reappear and leave him again; he loses a close friend in an assassination attempt and kills the murderer in cold blood. And he loses another courted love interest under tragic circumstances. He celebrates his fortieth birthday reluctantly, goes home to mourn his half-brother (who died in Vietnam) ... only to

---

[169] For some (post-)feminist soul-searching within *Ally McBeal* see Watson (2006), for a close reading as "beautiful television" Smith (2007); for a theological analysis of the "faces of love" the same series presents Krajewska (2007).

become, in a melodramatic twist of fate not uncommon to serialised television programming, the father of a little daughter that stays with him as the curtain closes, and the end credits roll.[170]

With regards to *The X-Files* the episodic plot of any given "monster-of-the-week" segment is jokingly summarised in an article of the British *Focus* magazine entitled "Bending the Truth" (October 1997, 58-59, cit. in Delasara, ibid., 40):[171]

> "*Step One*: The core of your story should be an idea 'as paranoid and off-the-wall as possible,' and the best place to locate such an idea is in urban legends or by scanning magazines devoted to the paranormal and para-politics or by using news events or people in them with a 'paranoid twist.'
>
> *Step Two*: In the first scene it is advisable to kill a US government employee ('as bizarrely as possible') in order to give the FBI jurisdiction in the case.
>
> *Step Three*: Scully proposes a rational explanation of what happened to the victim ("which is obviously completely barking [up the wrong tree] otherwise you've got no show").
>
> *Step Four*: Mulder responds with a solution involving aliens, government cover-ups or 'obscure psychic experiments.' Local law enforcement officials react in disbelief.
>
> *Step Five*: The agents investigate separately, keeping in touch with their ever-present mobile phones.
>
> *Step Six*: Either or both agents investigate a dark, threatening area carrying 'their extremely bright yet poorly illuminating' flashlights.
>
> *Step Seven*: 'Mulder gets beaten up.'
>
> *Step Eight*: 'Scully gets kidnapped yet again.'
>
> *Step Nine*: 'Explaining it all to [FBI Assistant Director] Skinner.'
>
> *Step Ten*: 'Getting rid of the evidence. ... Incriminating files and other evidence of the paranormal must end up back underneath the Pentagon or go up in smoke.'"

If the same segments are viewed as belonging to the "mythology arc", however (a term coined by the faithful fans, aka the *X-Philes*), they tell more personal stories of loss, and hope. There is:

---

[170] For *Magnum, P.I.* as series "about Vietnam" see Newcomb (1985, and here, further down), and Anderson (1987), Ganz-Blättler (1995a); for the appeal of the series to women Flitterman (1985) and Scherer (2000); for a broadcasting history of the series in Germany Wehn (1996, 1998).

[171] For a more detailed break-down of acts and arcs see Delasara (2000, 43 ff.).

1. the story of Fox Mulder (who lost his younger sister at an early age and und longs to resolve the mystery of her abduction),
2. the story of Dana Scully (who is abducted during the series' second season and ponders subsequent questions of motherhood under mindboggling circumstances), and
3. the overall conspiracy involving not only aliens, the FBI, Fox Mulder's family (hence the abduction scheme) but also the Watergate scandal, and John F. Kennedy's assassination (for this see Graham 1997, and Markley 1997).

Closure is brought upon by what Sconce (2004, 102) terms the "reluctant romance" between the two lead characters – in addition to having Fox Mulder absolved from the allegation of treason, over the course of a rushed two-part series' finale.

8.2   Some preliminary remarks

What follows, in terms of "state of the art" regarding narratological terminology, takes into consideration selected writing on television drama. Included are categorisations based on episodicity and continuity as textual "properties" but also more observation-oriented stances. Considering the growing bulk of scholarly and textbook materials in this area – and the heterogeneous approaches from which they stem – strict choices needed to be made. At stake is:

- prime time television drama of US-American origin,
- reflections on narrative structure of episodic fiction (that may focus on textual, or contextual matters),
- syntagmatic patterns of continuity and change (as contrasted to paradigmatic patterns and multimodal, or multi-perspective, aspects of storytelling).

A further requirement was that the writing acknowledges the *series / serial* dichotomy having subsided in favour to what is more frequently addressed, and examined by now as *series-serial* continuum.

The goal of this breakdown is not to provide readers with an exhaustive summary on the writing done on a rapidly changing, necessarily "fluid" subject of shared interest within the social sciences and humanities. Instead I hope to reline and contextualise some of the arguments that helped shape my own thinking over the past chapters (on narrative as communication, and art) and in view of the forthcoming ones (on *cumulative* narrative as communication, and art). The intersection chosen is that of *television studies* on the one hand and what might be called (... for lack of a more established term) *serial narrative studies* on the other.

Not taken into consideration is writing done on sitcoms, soap opera or telenovelas, studies done on individual programs (with the exception of some writing that addresses narrative structure in the first place) and scholarly work done on other than US-American and, to some extent, British television programs.

Again, the main goal is to trace the series / serial-related nomenclature back to its origins, namely (1) the *series* vs. the *serial*, (2) *episodic* fiction vs. *serial* fiction, (3) *parallel* processing vs. *linear* processing, (4) *unilinear* (simple) story vs. *multilinear* (complex) story, and (5) *modular* narrative vs. *serialised* narrative.

In terms of preamble I take a brief look back at academic critique expressed towards recurringly broadcast fiction over the 1940s and 1950s. Research, then, was interested in daytime serials too, and in the listening / viewing habits of female patrons:

A *Time* magazine article written by psychiatrist Louis Berg (23-03-1942) held daytime soaps such as *The Right to Happiness* (NBC) and *Woman in White* (CBS) responsible for female patients suffering relapses. As proof for his thesis the doctor listened to three weeks of the two radio serials, noting an exaggerated amount of "sexual jealousy, fear, rage, revulsion, frustration, insecurity, as well as excessive situations of "domestic discord, separation, divorce, sickroom scenes", and "courtroom scenes". Among the typical personnel featured in the ongoing narratives he could not single out one happy character: "All present single psychological profiles. They are unrelievedly bad or good." Berg then came to the conclusion that "[t]he cumulative effect of a diet of corrupting melodrama could not fail to produce an 'anxiety state.'"

Herta Herzog's essay "On borrowed experience. An analysis of listening to day time sketches" (1941) was among the first to examine radio soap operas more systematically, including the gratifications expected from such programs. Later, Paul Lazarfeld's wife presented more findings in a follow-up study called "What do we really know about daytime serial listeners?" that was published in her husband's *Radio research series* (Herzog, 1944). Herzog analysed various media consumption profiles of female soap opera listeners and individuated three incentives encouraging the consumption of soaps: 1. *emotional release* (in terms of digression from one's own problems), 2. *wishful thinking* (in terms of escapist daydreaming as to how one's own problems might be magically solved) and 3. *advice* (in terms of help seeked, and eventually found, with regards to some actual problem).

Most reflection on ongoing broadcast narratives during and right after World War II followed in the footsteps of these early examples of radio soap research and emphasised the escapist role of serial radio (and later, television) fiction. Academic criticism was usually based on psychological reflection and symbolic analysis (Warner / Henry 1948, 1950) or addressed ideological questions regarding industrial mass culture, mostly in the vein of the Critical Theory model established by leading exponents of the Frankfurt school such as Adorno ([1954] 1991).

A refreshing alternative to these warning voices is Marshall McLuhan's already mentioned essay included in the "Mechanical Bride" essay collection (1951). His distinction between "horse opera" and "soap opera" fits not only Hollywood cinema as contrasted to radio soaps but also horse-powered "car screetchers" in television prime time when compared to daytime melodrama. McLuhan closes on a somewhat idealistic, if not prophetic note: While acknowledging the gap between the (representation of the) "frontier" and the domestic sphere of the "home town" he insists that this "separation between business and society, between action and feeling, office and home, between men and women" (1951, 157) ought to be a thing of the past and must not be upheld much longer.

However, it took a while for the two modes of storytelling to finally approach the "fusion" McLuhan dreamed about in the early 1950s. In a groundbreaking essay on "Series and Seriality in Media Culture" (1993) Dutch scholar Tudor Oltean saw the two modes of storytelling, one "masculine" and the other "feminine", searching for some common ground (or: niche) within a less rigid, more fluid program schedule than what prevailed in the TV I era. In Oltean's own words (ibid., 19): "A possible conclusion might be that masculine narratives (series) hide, in their depth, some feminine features or that feminine narratives have not been able to free themselves completely from the 'masculinity' of broadcasting."

Roger Hagedorn addresses the "series" vs. "serial" dichotomy in his introduction to Robert Allen's anthology "Soap operas around the world" (1995, 42, italics by ugb.):

> "For the series, there is at most some 'basic story concept' or situation which is broad enough to allow for the creation of a large number of adventures, but these actions or situations bear no consequences for later episodes. In a sense, individual episodes of a series function like *cards in a deck* – they can be shuffled without distorting the deck.
>
> Episodes of a serial, however, are like interlocked *links in a chain* – missing even one risks the integrity of the whole."

Most scholars in television and narrative studies refer to the "series" and "serial" in similar ways. But the English language uses "series" also as an umbrella term for both episodic formats, as narrative modes: the set of cards in the deck, as Hagedorn puts it, and the interlinked elements producing the chain.

The same rule applies to most terminological distinctions made in other languages. The German "Serie" is used both as an umbrella term for (every kind of) serial product and, more particularly, for the episodic "series" as such whereas the noun "serial" translates into the term of the "Langzeitserie" (= long-term serial; for details see Hickethier, 1992). In French "la série" is used both as umbrella term and "series" analogy, while "le feuilleton" (of literary descent) refers more to the clearly serialised versions (Benassi 2000, and 2007). The Italian "telefilm", however, is used as a stand-in term for each and every series' episode within prime time television – no matter if more or less serialised. On the other hand the Anglo-Italian term "(il) serial" has come to complement "(la) serie" in similar ways as the German "Langzeitserie" has the "Serie". To complete the picture there is also a newer programming strategy with regards to Italian procedurals called (la) "serie serializzata" (for the term see Buonanno 2000, 277-278, and 2002, 161-181). The narrative pattern in question asks for overall continuity within limited "mini-seasons" (that is: six episodes per year, broadcast over six consecutive weeks), with each of these short-term seasons added as link to a chain of *miniseries* that inevitably close in on a "tock".

8.3   From series / serial dichotomy to series-serial continuum

John Ellis was among the first to distinguish the narrative structure of the episodic series on US prime time, with its dominant "form of the dilemma rather than that of resolution and closure" (1982, 145-159; similar Feuer 1986, and Kozloff 1992), from the soap opera (with its *cumulative* events) and from the (British) adventure serial such as *The Prisoner* (BBC, 1967-1968) and the original *Doctor Who* series (BBC, 1963-1989). Tulloch / Alvorado (1983, ix-xi) actually describe the latter as "episodic serials" whose narrative continuity "over a limited and specified number of episodes" aligns them with the – much later – developed) US-American "arc show" format.

In the TV II era the boundaries between series and serial arguably began to blur with the MTM school, as Feuer et al. suggest, in their quintessential book on the narrative innovations the MTM studios brought to the contemporary prime time schedule (1984), especially with *Lou Grant* (CBS; 1977-1982, a spin-off of the *Mary Tyler Moore Show*). In her later book "Seeing through the Eighties" (1996, 111) Feuer argues that, "given the sitcom's potential for diachronic development in the direction of character growth and change", one should view "the greater diachronic development of the American sitcom in the 1980's as part of the general movement on American television towards the continuing serial form, not as an abrupt break with the static series format." Sarah Kozloff (1992, 92) comes to a similar conclusion:

> "I am tempted to claim that one of the distinguishing characteristics of American television over the last five years has been its blurring of the distinction between series and serials, or, to be more precise, its increased tendency toward serialization. [...]
>
> *St. Elsewhere, L.A. Law*, and similar shows have ... developed a distinctive, stable amalgam of series and serialization; on such shows, one or more of the half-dozen storylines featured on a given night may conclude, but others will develop over a number of weeks. Perhaps the distinction between serial and series should be seen more as a continuum than as an either/or situation."

While John Lacey emphasises the historical differences between "series" and "serial" more than what they actually have in common (2000, 30-40), Charles McGrath (2000) envisions the contemporary television series as a worthy successor to the serialised 19th century novel. What he labels "prime time novel", consequently, is supposed to adopt a wide range of episodic styles from Aristotelian rigidity (*Law and Order*, NBC, 1990-2010) right to "baroque, mannierist" exuberance (*Murder One* ABC, 1995-1996). Porter et al. (2002) focus instead on the story arc as essential construction principle of the contemporary series / serial hybrids that is said to encourages the audiences' perception that characters do indeed "live on" between segments (ibid., 24):

> "The story arc has an important function in a television narrative. It resists closure and maintains continuity, thus shifting attention from plot to character. The use of the story arc in television series helps to create a sense of realism [...]. Story arcs help create an illusion that the characters have existed before and continue living between and after episodes. [...] And writers often encourage the notion that the characters lead off-screen lives."

In her introduction to "The Contemporary Television Series" (Hammond / Mazdon 2005) Lucy Mazdon (2005, 9) refuses to name the subject matter of the anthology anything else then [quality] "drama series / serial". This is because

> "[...] the traditional distinctions between series (a set of television programmes having the same characters and / or settings but with different stories) and serial (a television narrative presented in a number of separate instalments which may or may not reach a conclusion) are broken down by contemporary programming."

As if to confirm Mazdon's observation the trade magazine *Variety* had, at that time, adopted the term of the "serialised drama series" in order to describe some middle ground between the more episodic "procedurals" (= "series") and the "serials" (for instance Schneider, 2002). A slightly different use of the traditional nomenclature is made by Stéphane Benassi (2007) who proposes four gradual stages of serialisation, ranging from the "série canonique" (= *canonical series*) to the "série feuilletonante" (= *serialised series*) and the "feuilleton sérialisant" (= *serialised serial*) which, finally, blends over into the "feuilleton canonique" (= *canonical serial*).

8.4 From unilinear to multilinear prime time fiction

Starting out with the bulk of analysis published on Steven Bochco's quintessential "quality TV" series *Hill Street Blues* (NBC, 1981-1987) this has remained the research strand most prominently developed further within television studies of the TV II era. Respective work addresses storylines as "arcs" but also the braided storylines leading up to "narrative complexity". Some authors point to the characteristically extended cast of the "ensemble series" (see Schatz 1987, for the example of *St. Elsewhere*, NBC, 1982-1988) while others focus more on the series' multiplying storylines. One of them is Robin Nelson (1997, 21-25; and similarly 2000; 2006); he suggested the term "flexi-narrative" to describe the braided storylines and cross-references made within quality drama series such as *Hill Street Blues*. (ibid., 24) while adding that "[i]t suffices in the interim to note that flexi-narrative has extended into virtually all popular series and serials." The term of the *flexi-narrative* is defined as following (1997, 34)

> "The difference between soaps and popular series with regards to the deployment of flexi-narrative is that new characters and narrative strands are introduced in each episode of a series. Their stories are usually brought to closure within the episode whilst a number of regular characters (smaller than in soaps) is involved in unresolved narratives which give continuity across episodes. The blurring of distinction between the series and serial affords schedulers the joint advantage of an unresolved narrative strand – a cliffhanger to draw the audience to watch the next episode – and a new group of characters and self-contained stories in each episode."

John Corner (1999, 58) opts instead for the term *multistrand* narrative:

> "Series have become flexible in their employment of single episode and multi-episode plot strands and, following American precedents, they have often developed complex multistrand narratives, switching to and from concurrent lines of action during the course of an episode. This is most notable in workplace-based series, those featuring hospitals and police stations in particular,

where both the size of the cast and the nature of the occupation allow for such diversity."

Act structure on the *multithread* dramatic series (... as Steven Johnson calls the phenomenon, 2005) is a central topic addressed both in Kristin Thompson's lecture series on "Storytelling in Film and Television" (Thompson 2003, 36-73) and in Sue Turnbull and Vyvian Stranieri's textbook on "Narrative structures and *Buffy the Vampire Slayer*" (Turnbull / Stranieri 2003).

Narrative elasticity is another key term; it was coined by Jeffrey Sconce (2003, 184) and conceptualised further within Sara Gwenllian-Jones and Roberta Pearson's anthology regarding (earlier as well as contemporary) examples of "Cult Television" (2004). Also in 2004 Sconce introduced the term of the *conjectural narrative* (2004, 107) for stories that make use of hypothetical courses of action within alternate universes. Both Gwenllian-Jones / Pearson and Sconce remind me of an earlier distinction Tudor Oltean made between "linear" and "parallel" processing; they all differentiate between realist genres that are supposed to follow some "chronological temporal progression" (including time-leaps as flashbacks and flashforwards) and fantasy genres, with their often impossible timeframes and parallel, alternative histories played out within a constantly revised "metatext". The term of the "nodal format" (Gwenllian-Jones / Pearson, ibid., 88) refers here to the common ground of fantasy narratives and fantasy (role playing) games: The second world at stake is seen as a three- (or: four-)dimensional space with a nodal centre from which episodic adventures (and the audiences' own performative imaginations) take flight.

Another innovative strand within scholarly thinking on multiple story logic stems from Omar Calabrese (1987, 27-46). He channels Umberto Eco when distinguishing between the quasi-mythical series for children (with no significant character development) and the quest-oriented adventure series for adults (*Star Trek* qualifies here, just as the quintessentially picaresque *Zorro* and *Ivanhoe* series do). Other series with distinctively repetitive patterns (such as *Columbo*) do provide sophisticated audiences with thematic variations of almost *oulipomenic* (= dadaistic, nonsensical) stature.

This is the ground from which Ndalianis (2005, 83-101) develops her own narrative models based on increased complexity and required expertise of audiences. She does not address syntagmatic progression explicitly, but concludes her own overview on narrative structure by stating that "[t]elevision has begun to experiment with the serial, and the result has been some creative scenarios that complicate narrative processes further still" (ibid., 97). The ideal type of such narratives draws from the "hypertextual / hypermediated form familiar to the computer screen" and verges towards neo-baroque polycentric logic."

While *narrative complexity* is more explicitly addressed by Jason Mittell (2006; see also 2010, and 2015)[172] the essays assembled in Allrath / Gymnich (2005) focus on multiple perspective (that is, the invitation to see things from various characters' viewpoints), with examples ranging from *Twin Peaks* (ABC, 1990-1991) to *Ellen* (ABC, 1994-1998), *Die Zweite Heimat* (Zweites Deutsches Fernsehen, 1992) and the British sitcom *Blackadder* (BBC, 1983, 1986-1989). Here, the introduction opts (ibid., 6) for the "series" to be conceived as an umbrella term that encompasses both the traditional series and the serial, but also "all intermediate, hybrid forms", with a series-serial continuum extended from *The Simpsons* to *Murder, She Wrote, Ally McBeal, Buffy the Vampire Slayer, The X-Files*, and to the quintessential soap.

8.5   From "modular" to serialised prime time fiction

Coming back to John Ellis' description of earlier broadcast prime time fiction (1982), the traditional (or, in the terminology of Stéphane Benassi, "canonical") episodic drama presented in each and every segment a similarly structured problem or puzzle in wait to be resolved. Whatever cases were fixed, week after week, the underlining problematic situation persisted, be it criminal energy as social threat, the need to establish order in space as "final frontier", be it the mission to keep some darker underworld at bay in Sunnydale, or the noble call to aid humanity's struggle for health. All of these problems persisted beyond the series' final episode (ibid., 154): "Since [t]he TV series repeats a problematic, [i]t therefore provides no resolution of the problematic at the end of the run of the series."

In his essay on "Television's New Textual Boundaries" (2004) Jeffrey Sconce speaks about the now dominant "hybrid cumulative format", referring to Horace Newcomb (1985, and 2004) and identifying as its most distinct feature that newly found counterbalance of what he describes as (ibid., 98) "episodic treatments of a program's story world with larger arcs of long-term narrative progression". According to Sconce this description fits ground-breaking television shows like *Hill Street Blues* and *Magnum, P.I.* – but also most of U.S. fiction evolving within television's prime time schedule, over the 1980s and 1990s.

---

[172] See Mittell, Jason: Television and American Culture. New York: Oxford University Press 2010. And ibid.: Complex TV. The Poetics of Contemporary Television Storytelling. New York Press 2015.

Within the "cumulative" drama series an evolving story appears as oriented just as much towards the past and to what characters carry with them as personal "baggage" as it it oriented towards some yet untold future. Instead of spanning explicit narrative arc(s) (... of audience expectation) beyond episodes, or seasons, cumulative storytelling works with what was already told, and successfully inferred, earlier on, thus re-collecting existents, events, and episodes as the story progresses.

The Newcomb school of television drama as cumulative narrative had only moderate resonance within academia, up to the turn of the century. Things changed, however, as a growing number of scholarly writing focused on character development and growth.

Newcomb is explicitly quoted in Anderson (1987), Hoke-Kahwati (1990 – this is the *Soap Opera Digest* edition quoted earlier), Feuer (1995; she quotes Newcomb from Hoke-Kahwati, 11-112, and is again quoted by Turnbull / Stranieri, 2003), Reeves / Rodgers / Epstein (1997), Buonanno (2002), Sconce (2004), and Christen / Ganz-Blättler (2006).[173]

Interestingly, the concept's resonance was larger with screenwriting practitioners; here, most screenwriting guides describe both the "arc"-oriented and the "cumulative" strategy as particularly rewarding. Pamela Douglas' "Writing the TV drama series"" (2007) opts for the term of the "modular" drama series (that is, an arrangement of amnesiac card-in-a-deck type of segments) as complement to the various "serialised" series (meaning: an arrangement of chain-in-a-link type of segments) - while clearly verging toward the more serialised end of the spectre (ibid., 10):

> "When a series is well developed, the writers and fans follow the characters and find it hard to resist their history as it inevitably builds over time. In its early seasons, *The X-Files* had a new alien or paranormal event each week, and though the romantic tension between Mulder and Scully simmered, it didn't escalate. Then interest from viewers pushed more and more of a relationship and turned the partners into lovers by the end of the series. Most *X-Files* can still be enjoyed in any order, but serial storytelling is beguiling."

Shortly after she mockingly resumes the old prejudice regarding the (allegedly: inferior) quality of day-time storytelling (ibid.): "Serials: Now there's a dirty word in some minds because it also describes soap operas."

---

[173] For a more recent article on the matter see Lotz, Amanda: The Cumulative Narrative of the Cumulative Narrative of Television Studies. In: *Antenna* (23-07-2013); see *http://blog.commarts.wisc.edu/2013/07/23/the-cumulative-narrative-of-the-cumulative-narrative-of-television-studies/* (18-08-2017).

When Newcomb resumed the subject of "Narrative and Genre" (Newcomb 2005) he confirmed the innovative role soap operas played in bringing (more) narrative complexity to prime time programming (ibid., 30-31):

> "The fact that almost all television genres today exhibit a degree of seriality, and that some are built primarily on this device, suggests that it remains a major factor in television storytelling. Indeed, I suggest that the turn to serial narrative in prime-time television confirmed the value of soap opera strategies and enabled the creation of some of television's most outstanding content. Even those 'series' that deny, or defy, seriality, the *Law & Orders*, the *CSIs*, are defined by their rejection of seriality."

I would like to conclude this overview with one more essay dealing with questions of narrative complexity in view of the shift US-American television underwent in the transition from "TV II" to "TV III". Christopher Anderson's "Television Networks and the Uses of Drama" (2005) analyses auctorial conflicts regarding the writing practices on ongoing (serialised) drama and the scheduling practices of network officials. The example at stake is *Lost* (ABC 2004-2010), one of two serialised series (besides *Heroes*, NBC, 2006-2010) that were widely acclaimed as "typically" complex, hybrid, high-concept, arc driven, cumulative, conjectural state-of-the art prime time drama on US-American broadcast schedules.

Not taken in consideration here is research done with regards to John Caldwell's concept of *convergence television* (for this see Caldwell 1995, 2000, 2004, 2006, and Jenkins 2003, 2006), since the focus of the respective argumentation lies more with cross- or transmedia storytelling in terms of publishing strategy.

Notably absent from this overview and the synthesis presented on the following pages (Table 8), are more specific generic terms like the "serial-thriller soap" by which Linda R. Williams (2005) addresses David Lynch's metaphysics-infused, distinctively soap-reminiscent series-serial hybrid *Twin Peaks* (ABC, 1990-1991).

8.6 Synthetic overview of approaches

The following table (Table 8) resumes scholarly proposals for terms and typologies regarding episodic fiction on (mainly) broadcast television. The timeframe extends from 1951 until 2007, and considered were models taking into account one or both of the following criteria, and respective intermediate stages: unilinearity versus multilinearity, and modular principle versus serial principle.

Table 8: The *serialised series* on broadcast network television. A synthetic overview on terms and concepts

Author (year)	(Type) of series			(Type of) serial	
McLuhan (1951)	horse opera as Western saga (*ex. with regards to motion pictures*)			soap opera as domestic saga (*ex. with regards to daytime radio*)	
Newcomb (1974)	episodic series (*no memory/ change / character history*)		adventure series (*picaresque / quest-oriented*)	continued series (*patterns of growth and continuity*)	
Ellis (1982)	series (*no development at all*)	light drama series (*particular events passed on*)	soap opera (*characters remember, events are cumulative*)	serial (*long slow narrative movement towards conclusion*)	
Tulloch / Alvorado (1983)	episodic series (*discrete episodes*)	sequential series (*enigma posed at the episode's end*)	episodic serial (*narrative continuity over several episodes*)	continuous series (*multiple narrative strands*)	
Feuer et al. (1984)	series	constructive reflexivity and multiple plot lines (*since Lou Grant*)		serial form	
Allen (1985)	closed series (*as in murder mystery*)	open series ?	closed serial (*as in telenovela*)	open serial (*as in soap opera*)	
Newcomb (1985)	series	cumulative narrative (*as introduced on Magnum, P.I.*)	open-ended serial (*ex. Hill Str. Blues / Dallas*)	soap opera	
Feuer (1986)	the episodic series I (*as in sitc. Lear school*)	the episodic series II (*as in MTM school*)		the continuing serial (*ex. Dallas*)	
Calabrese (1987)	distinct episodes (*ex. Tarzan / Lassie*)	single narrative goal (*ex. Zorro / Ivanhoe*)	mutation / progression (*ex. Bonanza*)	thematic variation (*ex. Columbo*)	multiple narrative formations

Fiske (1987)	masculine series (*climax-oriented*)	multiple-plot, with memory (as in *Hill Street Blues*)		feminine serial (*relation-oriented*)	
Schatz (1987)	episodic strategies	ensemble series (*multiple-plot, serialised orientation*)		serial strategies	
Hoke-Kahwati (1990)	episodic show	cumulative narrative (*with sense of history*)	"arc" show (2 to 20 episodes)	multiple-story show	soap opera
Kozloff (1992)	series similar to an anthology of short stories	blurry line between series and serial, hybrid formats (*increased tendency towards serialisation; distinction series vs. serial to be seen more as a continuum than as an either / or situation*)			serial (*like a serialised Victorian novel*)
Oltean (1993)	linear mode	shifts series-serial (as in MTM comedies)	multidimension (ex. *Hill Street Blues*)	"soap noir" (ex. *Twin Peaks*)	parallel mode
Dolan (1995)	episodic series	sequential series (*events in an ep. reverberate with later eps.*, ex. *Cheers*)	episodic-serial detective story (*pointed backwards too*)	episodic serial	continuous serial
Hagedorn (1995)	episodic	intertextual references (ex. *Star Trek*)	unresolved problems (ex. *Cheers*)		soap opera
Feuer (1995) quoting Hoke-Kahwati	episodic show	cumulative narrative (*with sense of history*)	"arc" shows (2 to 20 episodes)	multiple-story show	soap opera

Reeves et al. (1996)	episodic series	episodic / serial straddle with blurred boundaries (ex. *The X-Files*, claimed as being cumulative like *Magnum, P.I.*)		continuous serial
R. Thompson (1996)	trad. series like short story coll.	serial form with slowly accruing stories		soap opera
Nelson (1997, 2000, 2006)	plot / resolution narr., series	flexi-narrative		serial
Corner (1999)	episodic series (*main plot concludes; cross-progr. continuity and familiarity with backgr. storylines which may run through ser.*)	multistrand narrative (*flexible employment of single episode and multi-episode plot strands; most notable in workplace-based series*)	soap opera (*long-term deep-level plots about relationships; middle- and short-term storylines developed*)	
Lacey (2000)	series (*circular narrative structure; occasional developments*)	serial (*cliffhanger-based; overarching narr. runs through all eps.*)	soap opera (*in any one ep. some narr. strands are active, others sleep*)	
McGrath (2000)	primetime novels, ranging from stately Aristotelian fashion to baroque mannerism			
Porter et al. (2002)	series	continuation of storylines (story arcs)		serial
Buonanno (2002)	series	cumulative narrative	serialised series	serial
Variety (2002 ff.)	procedurals	serialised drama series (*considered high concept*)		serials
Sconce (2003)	television's episodic seriality and textual density allows for narrative elasticity			
K. Thompson (2003)	one-hour series program	dramatic serials, multiple-story dramas		soap opera

Author(s)				
Turnbull / Stranieri (2003)	episodic series (*usually 13 or 26 episodes per season*)	hybrid series (*part episodic series, part ongoing serial*)		ongoing serial / soap (*multiple plot lines over unspecified no. of eps.*)
Gwenllian-Jones / Pearson (2004)	realist genres (*chronological temporal progression incl. flashbacks and occasional flashforwards*)	fantasy genres (*range of narr. possibilities enhances cult potential: multiple backstories, parallel histories, revised metatext*)		
Newcomb (2004)	(prime time) series	cumulative narrative	arc-driven narrative	soap opera
Sconce (2004)	episodic amnesia	conjectural narrative (ex. *The X-Files*)		soap opera
Allrath et al. (2005)	series-serial continuum, encompassing ex. *The Simpsons / Murder, She Wrote / Ally McBeal / Buffy the Vampire Slayer / The X-Files*, and soap opera			
Mazdon (2005)	series	(quality) drama series / serial		serial
Ndalianis (2005)	distinct episodes	single narrative goal	expanding series' time, progressive	palimpsest effect, theme var.	multiple narrative formations
Anderson (2005)	episodic series, procedural drama (ex. *Law and Order / CSI*)	serialized prime time drama (ex. *Dallas, Hill Street Blues*)		
Newcomb (2005)	intimacy, seriality, liminality (*"the twisted, enigmatic Mona Lisa-like half grin of melodrama"*)			
Christen / Ganz (2006)	paradigmatic vs. syntagmatic view			
Mittell (2006)		narrative complexity		
Newman (2006)	episodics	prime time serial (PTS)		soap opera?
Benassi (2007)	canonical series (*série canonique*)	serialised series (*série feuilletonante*)	serialised serial (*feuilleton sérialisant*)	canonical serial (*feuilleton canonique*)
Douglas (2007)	modular ser.	drama series		soap opera

PART III
THE CUMULATIVE NARRATIVE AS EPISODIC FICTION

> My aunt Mildred once said that the only difference between men and boys is the kind of games they play.
> (Thomas Magnum in "Little Games")

9 FROM PICARESQUE TO CUMULATIVE NARRATIVE: HORACE NEWCOMB'S THEORY OF *MAGNUM, P.I.* [174]

This chapter provides a more in-depth reflection on the concept of cumulative storytelling, both in terms of narrative structure and programming strategy within broadcast television – and other mass media, presumably. The starting point is Niklas Luhmann's claim that entertaining program strands within these media bring about a "new mythology". Entertainment reimpregnates "what one already is", thus entailing "feats of memory" that are, somewhat paradoxically, "tied to opportunities for learning" (Luhmann 2000a, 58). The question remains as to how one is supposed to learn from *what one already is*.

Cumulative narratives are presented here as providing a possible answer to this question. And, in addition, as a promising strategy for the retrieval of memories that were considered lost and gone.

According to Luhmann the process of "social forgetting" is irreversible, and necessarily so, because without the gift of amnesia we would end up being paralysed by the weight of the past. However: What is forgotten *for now* can always be imaginatively re-membered, later on. What is *no longer* known can be made knowledgeable

---

[174] In a public talk on *Magnum, PI.*, held 17-03-1995 in the Los Angeles Museum of Television and Radio cast and crew members referred to Newcomb's 1985 essay on cumulative narrative. Tom Selleck said: "People who watched our show regularly discovered that there was a continuing thread. The episodes played under themselves, but there was a continuing life. Chris or Charles might be able to – we had actually a guy who gave us credit for something that we were trying to do." Chris Abbott: "Oh, what was that called?" Chas Floyd Johnson: "Cumulative narrative." Selleck nodded: "Horace Newcomb's theory of *Magnum*."

again, in exchange for other knowledge that is, meanwhile, considered obsolete. Fiction – as an art and secondary observation – is seen here as providing the tools for societies to revise their own selective uses of the past. And the cumulative narrative, as described by Horace Newcomb, is a particularly powerful example of this.

Serialised series have developed their own narrative strategies how to expand some imaginatively shared story world at stake. Within what is commonly known as the "arc" show the future of selected characters is collectively explored and "prefigured". In the case of the cumulative narrative, however, the (same) characters' past is at stake and gets collectively explored and "refigured", as the telling moves on.

The question remains as to how narrative memory is employed within episodic (here: broadcast television) fiction that accumulates – or, instead, ablates – knowledge about events and episodes that lay in the past of characters and characters' relations. To answer that question I suggest to identify two key elements of cumulative storytelling. They are:

1. *backstory* (for a definition see Michaela Krützen, 2004), and
2. *dramatic progression* (for this see Laios Egri [1942] 2004, and James W. Chesebro, 1987).

After these two elements have been introduced, three series from the 1980s – 2000s are examined as case studies and illustrative examples for how cumulative strategies were put to use within the serialised prime time drama of the multi-channel transition era. These are: *Magnum, P.I.*, (CBS, 1980-1988), *The X-Files* (Fox, 1993-2002) and *Six Feet Under* (HBO, 2001-2005).

John Ellis inferred the concept of the cumulative narrative back in 1982 while deploring the lack of memory within the classic television series – in contrast to the more "cumulative" soap (see Ellis 1982, 156-157; and here, Table 8):

> "The basic problematic of the series, with all its conflicts, is itself a stable state. The series works on a sense of perpetual tension between individuals, whose causes it routinely does not care to examine. These individuals encounter different incidents that do receive some kind of resolution each episode. Week by week, we choose to forget, as do the characters, the incidents of the week before. [...]
>
> Instead the soap opera 'moves forward, a slow history always in the immediate present; characters remember, events are cumulative'."

His remarks on the episodic series' lack of memory draw significantly from Newcomb's "TV. The Most Popular Art" (1974; especially 253-254):

"The usual episodic pattern of television only gives the illusion of continuity [...]. [T]here is no sense of continuous involvement with these characters. They have no memory. [...] With the exception of soap operas, television has not realized that the regular and repeated appearance of a continuing group of characters is one of its strongest techniques for the development of rich and textured dramatic presentations. [...] The lack of continuity leads to the central weakness of television, the lack of artistic probability."

This study asks if "lack of continuity" (Newcomb) and "lack of history" (Ellis) are related concepts of institutional "forgetting". And it repurposes Newcomb's question regarding the resulting deficit (in terms of "lack of artistic probability") with various cumulative narrative techniques in mind.

According to the American Heritage Dictionary (1992), the term *cumulative* means "increasing or enlarging by successive addition". Narratives are, or become cumulative when they successively accumulate layers of depth (in terms of retrospectively added narrative knowledge) to existents and events, thus enlarging not only the co-tellers' familiarity with the second world in question but the second world as such.

In broadcast television the term of the *cumulative narrative* refers to episodic fiction that employs (selective) memory of characters to accumulate a retroactive history of its own. This is done by deliberate referrals back to narrative existents and events that are tied in either with the protagonists' personal or collectively shared history or draw from former exchanges of story-related knowledge among co-tellers engaged in the respective universe. The accruing continuity – or backstory in progress, to put it more precisely – is necessarily "filled with gaps" and alimented not just by memories that are inherent to the story-world at stake but also by memories that are collaboratively *accumulated* as referential resource by everyone involved in the respective tale's ongoing production, distribution and reception.

In the following three sub-chapters ideas are discussed that regard (a) the concept of cumulative narrative and how it developed over the course of the TV II era, (b) the concept of "backstory" (originally a screenwriter's device, and brought into the spotlight for analysis by German film professor Daniela Krützen) and (c) conceptual ideas that view characters' memories (of earlier events and episodes) as socially constructed and ask for their further, progressive use within particular social contexts (Egri 1942, and Chesebro 1987).

At stake are, by default, vacancies and blanks that lay within the diegetic past of particular characters, with the explicitly mentioned (and: variously inferred) actions, happenings and states used as springboard for later additions and inserts.

9.1 "As characters remember, so do we"

In his 2004 essay on "Narrative and Genre" for the Sage Handbook of Media Studies Horace Newcomb summarised the various narrative strategies employed by licensed authors to make use of the time span allotted to plotted action within the segments of a dramatic prime time series (this is: 43 minutes out of 60 minutes, minus ads and promotion). Newcomb (ibid., 422) confirmed the common use of "arcs" in terms of "plots completed within a few episodes" while explaining that this allowed distributors to sell these episodes neatly "programmed in packages" while leaving authors the option to work with braided storylines and (respectively complex) characters that faded in and out of the dramatic action.

Newcomb went on to describe the various patterns of "serialisation" that lead to characteristic ways of how meaning was generated and negotiated over time (ibid.):

> "Beyond the obvious economic advantage constructed by having audiences return week after week to follow an ongoing narrative, serialization offers potential advantage to the creators of such fictions and potential intensifications of pleasure for viewers. Without the restriction of time imposed in most movies, serial narratives for television have the opportunity to explore events in a far more complicated fashion. The consequences of actions can be played out over weeks, even years in the case of daytime soap opera. Choices made by characters return to haunt or to relieve them in later sequences of events. Relationships are allowed to become more complicated and complex. 'Good characters' can die, adding levels of emotional reaction for viewers."

This description of the cumulative narrative as based on serialisation and a distinct sense of memory resonates with what the author formulated earlier on, in 1974, when addressing the yet underdeveloped storytelling opportunities provided by contemporary television drama (Newcomb 1974, 253-254; also quoted by Sconce 2004, 97):

> "The usual episodic pattern of television only gives the illusion of continuity by offering series consisting by twenty-six individual units. The series may continue over a period of years, revolving around the actions of a set of regular characters. As pointed out, however, there is no sense of continuous involvement with these characters. They have no memory. They cannot change in response to events that occur within a weekly installment, and consequently they have no history. Each episode is self-contained with its own beginning and ending. With the exception of soap operas, television has not realized that the regular and repeated appearance of a continuing group of characters is one of its strongest techniques for the development of rich and textured dramatic presentations."

What episodic storytelling lacks (and could borrow from narrative practices developed for daytime soap opera, obviously) is the "regular and repeated appearance of a continuing group of characters" for whom audiences care enough to develop "a sense of continuous involvement". And therein, just as in the development of a series' collectively shared "history", lies the opportunity for change.

Newcomb's suggestion to introduce bits and pieces of the soap opera technique into the prime time schedule resonates with many of the storytelling conventions that have, since then, become common practice within television drama. Douglas' screenwriting guide (2007) provides many examples, just as other, more recent sources do. The serialised series has, meanwhile, learned how to weave that "rich and textured" canvas Newcomb dreamed about in 1974.

Serialised storytelling has also become largely acknowledged as a collective *work in progress* to which not only the fictional protagonists contribute (... via their backstories and respective memories, as we will see further down) but also the variously involved creators and affiliated story providers – and committed viewers within enlarged, media-savvy viewer communities, too.

In his 2004 essay on narrative and genre Newcomb came back to describing the *cumulative narrative* as a uniquely flexible strategy that took into account reading habits of both accustomed and occasional viewers. Quoting himself, he stated (ibid., 422):

> "I have referred to one version as the 'cumulative narrative' (Newcomb 1985). In this pattern, each episode can 'stand alone.' That is, the plot is completed within the allotted time. Yet it relies on and frequently makes specific reference to aspects of character, motivation, and even story that have occurred in previous episodes. Regular viewers are rewarded with the pleasure of remembering these references, understanding complexities, rising from new character developments, and recognizing the potential for future events and characterizations, whereas single-episode viewers take pleasure in the full completion of a specific plot. The 'cumulative narrative' might be said to encompass something of *meta-plot* that extends over the entire series, in a manner similar to, but distinct from, the fully serialized narrative."

One of the distinct addressing problems arising from the soap opera, but also from the "arc" show is that both demand from viewers to tune in again, day after day and / or week after week, in order to keep track of winding storylines. The cumulative narrative solved this problem by recurring to a *meta-plot* that was supposed to be recognisable (and: rewarding) only to sophisticated readers while it left the more ingenuous (or: less caring) readers' viewing habits undisturbed.

Newcomb mentioned the device of the "arc" show in the tradition of Stephen C. Cannell (that is, "plots completed within a few episodes, which allow the series to move on to another arc in subsequent episodes") besides other, more recent and mixed strategies that catered similarly to more fluid distributing and reading practices. Among them were "clusters of episodes", or mini-seasons in the tradition of the European *serie serializzata*. They were, like these, programmed over a shorter period of time but were, in contrast to these, exempt from the distributive need to obey some prefigured order. Such clusters could be isolated for some subsequent publication later on, and then be re-targeted, and repurposed in conveniently packaged "macrosequences" (as Branigan might have called them, 1992).

Newcomb's original essay on cumulative narrative appeared in the 1985 May / June issue of the communication review *Channels of Communication*. Its provocative title was "*Magnum*: The Champagne of TV?" – and while the openly admitted fan's stance gave its author credibility beyond academia, it also translated in an unusually wide-ranging, and remarkably influential publishing history.

Newcomb starts with the claim that *Magnum, P.I.* (CBS, 1980-1988) was, at the time, "an excellent, even the best, television series" around (ibid., 23). Moreover he suggests that the series helped its US-American viewers to come to terms with the collective traumata caused by the (loss of the) Vietnam War.

Magnum, P.I. receives praise for its wide variety of adopted styles and generic mixes that reach far beyond the classic, action-oriented detective-story, enriching it with elements of slapstick and screwball comedy. Close attention goes then to the innovative use of what Newcomb labels "melodrama of the first order" (ibid., 24) by which affiliated audiences were wooed back, week after week. The recurring insights into the protagonists' thoughts, hopes and fears also invited viewers (ibid.) "to be as concerned about character, values, and emotions as about adventure and mystery".

Newcomb saw this emerging form of storytelling as situated "between the traditional self-contained episodic forms and the soap opera, and alongside the "open-ended serial" (ibid., 24). This is where the term of the *cumulative narrative* is coined:

> "Call it the '*cumulative narrative*'. One episode's events can greatly affect later events, but they're seldom directly tied together. Each week's program is distinct, yet each is grafted onto the body of the series, its characters' past."

The chance to take part not only in the characters' collective present but also in their past, be it via flashbacks or soliloquies or other narrative devices, provides a unique sense of intimacy and familiarity with these characters. While the recollection of former events and episodes within the series' original timeframe is utterly gratifying to those audiences that recall a "first" and can successfully place the memory the gratification with characters sharing insights from their former lives bears confessional traits and resonates with larger issues such as vulnerability and trust. Both types of recall manoeuver provide ample occasions for narrative bits and pieces to make another appearance, and to genuinely haunt – or just as effectively relieve – the already affiliated viewers (1985, 24-25, and similarly 2004, 422):

> "The producers, writers, directors, and, most importantly, the characters they create *remember* events from the fictional past. The past plays an active, significant role in the plots of the present. Nothing is lost. Everything is cross-referenced. And as characters remember, so do we.
>
> What we remember is not merely that something happened. Rather, it is that each moment in an episode I view can reveal something about the show's history. [...] The essential connections are not in the sequence of events, or in their causes and effects, but in their resonance."

Resonance is a key term within the cumulative concept: What authors and audiences imagine in terms of original material (and in terms of reassessed knowledge of the story so far) allows for the second world to expand, and more so in the domain of causes and motivations that than that of effects and outcomes. The term "cumulative" applies to all kinds of narrative that grow "thicker" over time while permitting the participants in its making to explore, share and actualise what lies *behind*.

The cumulative's main function, however, is to suggest alternative readings from various angles and viewpoints, depending on what participants know and remember from previous visits to the second world at stake. What is subsequently revised and reconstructed as characters' past can also serve as incentive, or trigger, for a genuinely interested or affected community's journey into the ideologically charged territory of some traumatic and / or heavily disputed past.

So far scholarly writing on cumulative narrative strategies has been scarce. Christopher Anderson (Anderson 1987; quoted here, p, 232) explored *Magnum, P.I.* and the Vietnam War theme further, emphasising on how history, memory and fiction interacted to revise this conflicted chapter of US-American history further.

Hoke-Kahwati (1990, 26) focused on the differences between cumulative narrative and "arc" show. One is, and she quotes Newcomb, "a show with a memory" that nevertheless allows stories to be wrapped up in one singular episode. The other employs short term ("anywhere from two to ten episodes") storylines, in additionto the continuing storylines involving the main characters. Both Feuer (1995) and Buonanno (2002) emphasise the aspect of memory (Feuer ibid., 112): "According to

Newcomb a better name for the series-with-a-memory concept would be a cumulative narrative."

Reeves et al. (1996) reassess the narrative structure of *The X-Files* as cumulative, quoting Newcomb (1985). Jeffrey Sconce remains so far the only scholar – besides Newcomb – who tried to explore the concept further (2004, 98):

> "Discussing the emergence of this strategy in *Magnum, P.I.* in the mid-1980s Newcomb called this mode 'cumulative' narrative, referring to the form's ability to 'accumulate' nuances of plot and character as a series matures over several seasons. Each installment of ER, for example, features a patient or crisis of the week specific to that episode (i.e., bus crash on the turnpike, hospital power outage, liver transplant) interwoven with long-term story lines that may or may not receive attention that week or even that season (Doug and Carol's romance, Peter's deaf son Reese, Weaver's personality conflicts. As in the serial format, these cumulative story lines lead to often-powerful resolutions (frequently promoted and staged during 'sweeps' periods)."

What Sconce's analysis lacks is the explicit reference to past events that intrinsically motivate an ongoing storyline's crucial conflict, reflexive stance or relational dynamic. Because the main difference between what is viewed as "arc" or as a storyline accumulating knowledge lies in its extended interconnectivity back and forth in time (for models see here, Figure 20, and next page, Figure 21; illustrations my own):

Figure 20: Narrative model of the episodic segment / story arc

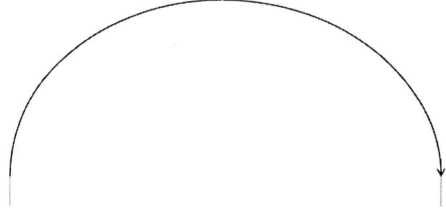

The model shows the bell-shaped curve of dramatic progression from *stasis* to climax and back to (a new state of) stasis in the case of the modular segment, or "arc". Segments build towards a "tick" and supposedly end on a "tock".

Figure 21: Narrative model of the cumulative segment / story arc

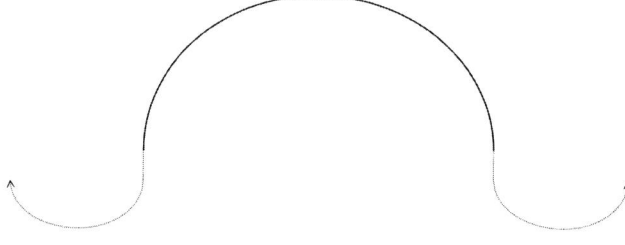

The segment follows the same dramatic, bell-shaped course of action, with casual "hooks" – that is, bits and pieces of memories and anticipations that make initiated co-tellers remember and anticipate as well – thus providing story depth just as importantly as story progression.

One thing needs to be added for clarity: In cumulatives, just as in soap opera, narrative knowledge is handled flexibly. Memories can build towards some consistent "history" or, instead, be skewed, and patchy, and full of (accidental or intentional) inconsistencies. A good example is character memory handled on *The X-Files*: Here the legit authors constantly revised what the protagonist claimed to "remember" in the context of later episodes, thus producing new indeterminacies from assumed determinacies, as the telling progressed, and existents were moved along syntagmatic events and happenings. It is the kind of storyline revision that is called *retcon* within initiated fan circles. Retcon stands for the term of "retro-active continuity" (see *http://en.wikipedia.org/wiki/Retroactive-continuity*; 18-08-2017): Such rewriting is frequent on soap operas where "forgetting" about some character's past is considered just as necessary as the perpetuation of memory (for this Geraghty 1981, 18):

> "Although the accumulated past is important to a serial, one could also say that the ability to 'forget' which has happened in the serial's past is equally crucial. If the serial had to carry the heavy weight of its own past it would not be able to carry on. The stories would grind to a halt while the implications of past events were explained to new viewers / listeners. Instead, the serials, while clearly accepting [...] that they have a past, cannot be bound by it."

Newcomb traces the much more linearly plotted narrative structure of the series back to cinematic traditions, while confirming the soap opera's status as genuine innovation of broadcasting. He refers frequently to the Western and the police procedural – both genres that fit McLuhan's description of the "horse opera" in perfection. See ibid., 421: "Most early fictional television programs did, in fact, follow the classic structure – beginning, middle, end; goal-oriented hero; and equilibrium disturbed but restored in the 'conclusion.' Thus, each week, the central recurring character of a western would defeat the violent intruder, or the police detective would solve the current crime."

9.2 Aspects of intimacy, seriality, and liminality

In the final chapter of his earlier book (Newcomb 1974, 243-264), the author described three characteristics as unique to television – in the sense that they "enable television to be seen as something more than a transmission device for other forms [of content]." The three elements addressed as crucial ingredients to the particular aesthetic of television are (a) intimacy, (b) continuity, and (c) history.

Thirty years later, Newcomb did a reassessment of the same terms (Newcomb 2005, 30-33), retaining only *intimacy* as the defining trait of "neo" and "post" television – in coincidental accordance with Umberto Eco and Jean Missika – while replacing "continuity" with *seriality*, and "history" with *liminality*. In the following subchapters I synthesise the respective arguments, and motives.

9.2.1 Intimacy

When analysing the Western genre back in 1974, Newcomb distinguished the television westerner as bearing significantly more "domestic" traits than his cinematic counterpart (Newcomb 1974, 248-250; for the *Bonanza* series Newcomb 1997). He tied this need for intimacy to an economic rather than cultural logic (1974, 249-250):

> "Even when landscape and chase become part of the plot, our attention is drawn to the intensely individual problems encountered, and the central issue becomes the relationships among individuals.
>
> This physical sense of intimacy is clearly based in the economic necessities of television production. It is far more reasonable, given budgetary restraints, to film sequences within permanent studio sets than on location, when the Western is the subject. But certainly the uses of intimacy are no longer exclusively based on that restriction. The soap operas, most financially restricted of all television productions, have developed the idea from the time when audiences were made to feel as if they were part of a neighborhood gossiping circle until today, when they are made to feel like probing psychiatrists."

In his reassessment of "The most popular art" (2005) the author confirmed "intimacy" as being one of the central concerns of contemporary television (ibid., 30):

> "'Intimacy' I would retain, despite some reliance in the initial description on the size of the television screen [that was of course significantly smaller in 1974 than the average screen of 2005]. I maintain that television fiction, [but also] news, documentary, and recent versions of programming known as 'reality' continue to be fascinated with and reliant on narratives recounting intimate matters in intimate ways. In some instances intimacy has been extraordinarily intensified. We have been made privy to decisions regarding 'marriage,' 'birth,' and 'death,' that could alter lives. We have observed as individuals are ridiculed and embarrassed. We have been allowed to witness alterations of the body, procedures that in many cultures might be considered sacred. We have been afforded the voyeur's perspective, even as we are aware that the 'real' people we observe are equally aware of their exhibitions, are 'performing' for us."

So, while retaining *intimacy* as crucial for establishing familiarity with particular characters over time Newcomb now suggested to substitute his earlier concepts of a series' "continuity", and "history", by referring to its *seriality*, and *liminality* instead.

9.2.2 Seriality (was: Continuity)

In 1974 Newcomb wrote (ibid., 253-254):

> "The usual episodic pattern of television only gives the illusion of continuity by offering series consisting of twenty-six individual units. The series may continue over a period o years, resolving around the actions of a set of regular characters. As pointed out, however, there is no sense of continuous involvement with these characters. They have no memory. They cannot change in response to events that occur within a weekly installment, and consequently they have no history. Each episode is self-contained with its own beginning and ending. With the exception of soap operas, television has not realized that the regular and repeated appearance of a continuing group of characters is one of its strongest techniques for the development of rich and textured dramatic presentations."

In view of the recent inflation of this term's use, Newcomb now suggested to replace "continuity" with *seriality* as the more precise term (2005, 31):

> "'Continuity', however, should give way to seriality. This is what I attempted to elevate as narrative device in admiration of soap opera and miniseries. In the earlier work the praise was pointed toward 'realism,' toward 'probability,' and the goal was to place (force, guide) audiences into a more immediate encounter with content. Believing serious treatment of contemporary issues to be somehow diminished by narrative closure (a common assumption among far harsher critics of television than I), I considered continuity a rhetorical strategy of great significance."

Following the author's reconsideration "continuity" is easily misunderstood as referring simply to some economic need for prosecution, obscuring the storytellers' intrinsic, legitimate desire for closure – in terms of that "sense of an ending" which all contemporary serialised series (and notably the *telenovela*) do indeed convey.

9.2.3 Liminality (was: History)

Because Newcomb's original 1974 analysis focused on the Western genre, the reflection necessarily took into account the televisual uses of a (conflicted) part of US-American "history" (1974, 256). What he predominantly addressed was the generalised, "mythical" notion of history which emanated from these tales:

> "The importance of history to the popular arts has been carefully dealt with by John Cawelti in an essay, 'Mythical and Historical Consciousness in Popular Culture' (unpublished essay, 1971). The root of this distinction, which Cawelti takes from myth theorists such as Mircea Eliade, lies in the perception of time. In the mythical consciousness 'time is multidimensional. Since mythical events exist in a sacred time which is different from ordinary time, they can be past and present and to come all at the same time' (ibid., 11). For

modern man, however, history is unilinear and moves 'from the past, through the present, and into the future' (ibid.)."

Following Cavelti (... and walking with him in Eliade's footsteps),[175] Newcomb distinguished the adventurer's handling of temporal matters as depending on larger concepts of myth, with the relational shift from *cosmic time* (relevant to archaic societies) to *ordinary time* (or *social time*, as Schütz calls it) radically altering the purpose of the "hero's journey" as such.

As Kermode would relate the difference, modern man's conception of time is more distinctively goal-oriented and structured as a series of events with conventionally anticipated "tocks" that mark the progress made from one (heroically mastered) level to the next. In contrast the cosmic timeframe allows the mythical hero to mark his presence everywhere at (roughly) the same time. The archaic concept leaves the hero's interfering options forever intact while the more "civilised", occidental version shifted the emphasis to expectations for a conclusion – not necessarily with each and every segment but inevitably at some time further up along the journey.

The ideologically charged concept of "history" as the logical result of a (somewhat foreseeable) course of events is commonly assumed to inspire all entertainment culture – for corroborating evidence see Luhmann, and Bleicher, earlier on. When Newcomb revised the concept he had gained more insight in anthropology explaining how myth, conceptions of the past and everyday experience interact (2005, 32):

> "The term 'history' must also be replaced in a description of television's common characteristics. Already in 1974 its application was fragile, artificial. Had the Western not so recently been so central to television programming, or had the first successful miniseries imports [in the wake of BBC's *The Forsyte Saga*, 1967] not traded so heavily on historical topics, the device I was attempting to describe might have been differently named. It was not until the preparation of the 'Cultural Forum' essay, following increased attention to symbolic anthropology, that a more appropriate description became evident."

This term he now preferred as fitting particular uses of a past was *liminality* (ibid.):

> "The work of Victor Turner, Clifford Geertz, and Mary Douglas was a crucial opening in this regard. Most specifically, Turner's exploration of 'liminal' and 'liminoid' occasions, spaces, and events provided a different way to think about the manner in which television narratives both remove us from and place us inside social and cultural events, problems, topics, themes."

---

[175] Cawelti's reference is to Mircea Eliade's "The Sacred and the Profane. The Nature of Religion", engl. publ. New York: Harcourt 1959.

And he added (2005, 32-33):

> "When intimacy, seriality, and liminality are merged and concentrated, as in *The Sopranos* or *Six Feet Under*, in *Scrubs* or *The Office*, even at times, in *Frasier* and *Friends*, television rich's possibilities are exhibited. The past merges with the present – special makeup and memory sequences reveal the 'fat Monica' [on *Friends*] and explain much about her obsession and professions. Dreams inform 'reality', but it is in the reality of 'fiction.' Fathers die but continue to appear [on *Six Feet Under*], playing key roles in the lives of sons and daughters."

What comes into play, here, are differences made between various observational stances on past events as still present or actually bygone, but also differences made between some acknowledged history as universal „truth" and the more personalised, repeatedly revised discursive versions of „what happened". History is still seen as relevant, but not as *per se* relevant to the aesthetics, or truthfulness of fiction. Because there is no final logic of how past events are ever to be framed, for once and for good. And: In the realm of artistic probability (not just of fiction, but of all tales told) mythical conceptions of what is acknowledged as "truth" do have a lot to say.

In the following two sections I will concentrate on the concept of *liminality* as established by Victor Turner, adapting it to "backstory wounds" and dramatic progression (of the series' protagonists, that is). Three case studies will later be examined as illustrative examples: *Magnum, P.I.* (CBS, 1980-1988), *The X-Files* (Fox, 1993-2002) and *Six Feet Under* (HBO, 2001-2005).

9.3 Backstory wounds and character growth

To begin with another, more detailed reflection on *liminality* I quote Newcomb / Hirsch's *Cultural Forum* essay([1983] 1987, 459); they in turn quote Victor Turner on passage rituals.

According to Newcomb / Hirsch, Turner sees ritual "as process rather than as product". There is the *liminal* stage of the ritual process in terms of (ibid.) "'in-between' stage, when one is neither totally in nor out of society. It is a stage of license, when rules may be broken or bent, when roles may be reversed, when categories may be overturned." The essence of the liminal stage ...

> "is to be found in its release from normal constraints, making possible the deconstruction of the 'uninteresting' constructions of common sense, the 'meaningfulness of ordinary life,' [...] into cultural units which may then be

reconstructed in novel ways, some of them bizarre to the point of monstrosity. [...] Liminality is the domain of the 'interesting' or of 'uncommon sense'."[176]

Turner distinguishes between the *liminal*, existential (and often life-threatening) experience that adolescent tribe member in pre-modern societies undergo as *rite de passage* towards adulthood, and the *liminoid* passage we choose to undergo in time-out culture, alongside (here:) fictional characters that effectively undergo liminal experiences in "their" second world.[177]

Newcomb / Hirsch identify the creator as *bricoleur*, with the focus set on the *uncommon sense* granted by the imaginary freedom of television, both as a cultural forum and as "liminal" realm for some program's protagonists which, in turn, becomes a "liminoid" realm for participants engaged in wilful suspension of disbelief.

Once we step onto that collectively shared "liminoid" stage of meaning-making and enter a *playful* intermediary state (... that allows us to regulate cognitive and affective investment according to narrative needs) we oscillate between participatory performance and "knowing" second-order observation just as actual participants within some *rite de passage* do. In the words of Newcomb, and in reference to Turner's conceptual ambiguity regarding "liminal" and "liminoid" occasions, spaces, and events (2005, 32), "[e]ven the most immediate detective program, such as those in the *Law & Order* franchise, makes urban space and headline narratives into something removed from our experience but touching us directly."

The following addresses more specifically what "liminal" stages are explored in popular, generic fiction and what kinds of *rites de passage* (of fictional characters) emerge during the course of a telling and / or in hindsight.

The term "backstory" derives not from scholarly analysis but, like the "beat" (in terms of *scene*) mentioned in chapter 8, from the screenwriter's practice. On soap opera *backstory* simply describes "events which happened before our story began" (Rouverol 1984, 206). Mittell (2007, 36) uses the term in similar ways to indicate events which are set before the plotted (= narrated) action but maybe be told later on in flashback, for instance "as a detective narrates the solution to a crime".

---

[176] The original quote is from Turner, Victor: Process, System, and Symbol. A New Anthropological Synthesis. In: *Daedalus* (Summer 1977, 68).

[177] See Turner, Victor: Liminal to Liminoid, in Play, Flow, and Ritual. An Essay in Comparative Symbology. In: *Rice University Studies* 60 (1974, 3).

According to Wikipedia (*http://en.wikipedia.org/wiki/Backstory*, 18-08-2017), "backstories are usually revealed, sketchily or in full, chronologically or otherwise, as the main narrative unfolds. However, a story creator may also create portions of a backstory or even an entire back-story that is solely for his or her own use in writing the main story and is never revealed in the main story". As these references indicate, backstory events can be explicitly stated or depicted, at one moment or another, or instead infuse the characters' actual state of being in more implicit ways.

Two more aspects are of particular interest here: the recurring appearance of (serialised) drama series that allows for the introduction of some characters' backstory at any given moment in time, to any particular purpose. And the suggestion (... which goes back to Aristotle's *Poetics*, as so many other dramatic narrative devices do) that "[t]he dramatic revelation of secrets from the backstory is a useful term for forming the story" (as the Wikipedia article puts it, ibid.).

In terms of summary, backstories do reach back to some moment in time before the actual, plotted action sets in. They are used to disclose some important clue that was missing from the picture until now or serve to motivate a character's actions and reactions. Backstories can be made explicit, hoover in the background or remain fully unpublished, in the latter case serving screenwriters to adequately, and consistently, flesh out their acting *personae*.

Despite of its importance for dramatic storytelling, "backstory" is only seldom, and casually, addressed within academic writing on film and television. This may have to do with its alleged origin from the melodrama and thus with a status problem. Many film theorists consider flashbacks to be a clumsy and disruptive narrative device (for their use see Turim, 1989), and the same goes for knowledge that is disclosed "after the fact" within extensive talk rather than sophistically plotted action. Many screenwriting guides recommend to use hindsight revelation with caution.

John Corner considers background storylines to be highly characteristic of the more recent drama series, referring to storylines that extend not (only) to the characters' future but also to their more or less recent past (1999, 57):

> "In the television series, although the end of each episode conventionally concludes a main plot, cross-programme continuity is achieved by an increasing familiarity with the main characters, with the setting, and with background story-lines which may run throughout the entire series."

In its ultimate consequence a "backstory" lets its addressees know where someone originates or comes from. In myths (and superhero cartoons, for that matter) the *origin story* (see Wikipedia: *http://en.wikipedia.org/wiki/Origin_story*; 18-08-2017) "can refer to narratives of how the world began, how creatures and plants came into existence, and why certain things in the cosmos have certain qualities". However, such story details are often revised and altered to the point where they seem to belong (ibid.) to an "altogether different character".

What the protagonists of episodic prime time drama just like Thomas Magnum or Fox Mulder "accumulate" over their respective series' run is not only narrative knowledge derived from the story as *told so far* but also narrative knowledge from these protagonists' earlier, former life. Such backstories often entail a climactic event that motivates the hero's quest as such. Backstory in popular Hollywood movies is accumulated to provide characters with depth rather than change. It lets the protagonists *mature*, rather than *age*.

Krützen (2004, 24 ff.) analyses character progression within classic Hollywood cinema while recurring, in part, to Christopher Vogler's adaptation of Joseph Campbell's "Hero with a thousand faces" (see Vogler 1993, and Campbell 1949). Her analysis focuses on the dramaturgical device of the "backstory wound", with examples drawn from the psychological thriller (*Silence of the Lambs*, 1991) and the action adventure genre (*Twister*, 1996). Both movies feature female heroines that lost their fathers under tragic circumstances, and both remember (in flashback) what happened at the time. In the case of Clarice Lecter the *backstory wound* makes her want to solve the cases of the kidnapped girls, while Jo Harding seeks to survive what her father did not. Krützen (ibid., 89) sees the overcoming of the backstory wound as a central step within some hero's individual journey.

Krützen distinguishes four types of backstory wounds as common to Hollywood dramaturgy: Death, Separation, Violence, and Failure (Krützen ibid., 34-39, Hamami 2007, 28). She claims, however, that characters within episodic fiction – in terms of the "amnesiac", episodic series – cannot assume a backstory wound (ibid., 320; trad. ugb.): "The more serial a character, the more difficult the construction of an interior development. This is why the conception of a backstory wound is practically unthinkable for the TV series' protagonists."[178] Hamami disproves that argument in her master thesis on *Six Feet Under* (2006) for the cases of two of the series' main protagonists, Nate and David Fisher.

---

[178] In German: "Je serieller eine Figur wird, umso schwieriger wird die Konstruktion einer inneren Entwicklung der Figur. Entsprechend ist die Anlage einer Backstorywound bei den Hauptfiguren von TV-Serien nahezu unmöglich. "

As far as soap opera goes, Krützen's argument is valid to some extent: What is learned in hindsight about some character's past – be it a child born out of wedlock, or a long lost love, or relative – is seldom there to motivate a quest or shed light on some deeply rooted guilt. It motivates instead some upcoming major turn in the ongoing narrative's course of action. At stake is the characters' *future*, rather than their newly illuminated past. In contrast, an accumulated past in a serialised series with modular structure is there to shed light both on what lies ahead and what lies behind the character's actual whereabouts.

Within the adventure genre, however, the adventurer's travel is already infused with some kind of a (larger) cause that motivates the hero's actions and serves as narrative backbone. Many of the popular (male) protagonists within the action adventure drama of the TV I era do share a similar past of an "absent father" – and quite a few chose the path of law enforcement only after their dads were "killed in action" when professionally, and heroically fighting crime (for examples see Ganz-Blättler 1995a).

The significant difference lies in the uses of such a past as being relevant or not. Backstory wounds are present both in the lives of Thomas Magnum (his father's death in the Korean War, two tours of duty during the Vietnam War) and Fox Mulder (his sister's abduction). In *Six Feet Under* all three children of Nathaniel Fisher need to come to term with their own father's sudden demise – as well as many later events that easily count as Separation, Violence, or Failure. But this is not a novelty *as such* – at least not for the heroes of police / detective procedurals.

The genre of the *picaresque* narrative, as evoked by Newcomb in reference to the adventure series (1974, 179; among the examples quoted are *The Fugitive* and *Star Trek*) shares even more traits with the cumulative narrative, thus rendering its protagonists ideally suited for featuring backstory wounds as well as the required reflexive stance. *Picaresque* here refers to generically indebted narratives featuring:

- adventurers as quest-oriented heroes,
- "episodic amnesia" (the term borrowed from Sconce 2004, 102),
- a marginalised perspective (protagonists are underdogs by definition),[179]
- irony, with protagonists frequently uttering self-reflexive comments.

---

[179] For the *picaresque* genre in literature Fludernik (1996); additional information was kindly provided by Paul Michel.

Why did earlier, "canonical" television drama series (as Benassi labels them, 2007) not make use of the "hooks" brought to the dramatic stage by intimacy, seriality, and liminality? The reasons relate both to scheduling principles (that encouraged character amnesia) and to the competition over "big" audience numbers (encouraging modular viewing habits). But they also relate to generic conventions asking from the adventure-seeking hero to remain stagnant rather than progressive and to rely on existing bonds rather than to allow for new ones. For this see Ellis (1982, 124-125):

> "The format series is matched by the fictional series, which operates across all the modalities of fiction from farce to tragedy. It is characterised by the constant repetition of basic narrative situations and characters: a family, a business enterprise, a hospital, etc. Each week the characters encounter a new situation which has no permanent effect upon them: the following week they will be in the same relation one to another. The repetitions are very marked, to the extent of some series (from USA chiefly) ending their weekly narrative with a kind of coda in which the basic relations between characters are reaffirmed outside of any narrative context. Subordinates joke with boss; children outwit their parents over some domestic chore. The formula, the basic situation, receives a final statement in a segment that tends to echo the title sequence. This has the effect of reaffirming the stasis from which the next episode will depart: a stasis that is more a basic contradiction or power relation than a zero degree. The series, then, relies on repeating a basic problematic which is worked through on each occasion without a final resolution. In a police series, the police catch the criminals in each individual instance of the series, but two things still remain: criminality itself (the episode ends with another call, a trivial assignment, etc.) and the particular relationships between the police involved (*Starsky and Hutch*'s spiky mutual dependency; *The Sweeney*'s blend of antagonism to authority and respect for justice)." [Etc.]

This mirrors some aspects already adressed in Newcomb's earlier essay (1974, 159):

> "Inherent in the adventure formula [...] is the fact that the central premise, the reason for the adventures to occur, cannot be concluded, ended, solved, in a single hour-long performance. The motivating problems must not be solved, or the series will cease to exist."

The potential for characters to grow and develop is acknowledged by both authors (Newcomb, ibid., 158): "While the adventure shows are presented as self-contained episodes, they also create a sense of continuity, of relatedness, which makes their world less fantastic [...]." In Ellis' argumentation (1982, 156; here, p. 210) the classic series was amnesiac not by default, but more out of habit since "[w]eek by week, we choose to forget, as do the characters, the incidents of the week before." He even uses the term of "habitual forgetting" to explain why the classic series counted so many more incidents per episode than (British) adventure serials and soap operas did. Which leads me back to quoting him on the soap's habit to let (ibid., 157) "characters remember, [while] events are cumulative" – at the price of audiences having to remember, too.

For the characteristic amnesia of the series' classic hero see also Kozloff (1992, 91):

> "One truism of television criticism is that series characters have no memory and no history: amazingly, they don't notice that they said and did exactly the same things the previous week. (However, although past events disappear into a black void, characters' interrelationships grow from week to week)."

Not surprisingly, Douglas pictures a very different situation, 15 years later (2007, 26):

> "Characters continue over many episodes instead of concluding a dramatic arc. [...] Storylines may evolve over many episodes, especially in serials. Emphasize increments or instalments of a series-long quest rather than tying up a plot. However, most shows have some stories that 'close' (resolve) within an episode while other dramatic arcs continue."

"Marginalisation" and "irony" are two more traits typical for picaresque adventures that don't resonate readily with the classic prime time drama of the TV I (or: network) era. Except for that larger canvas looming behind most heroes' quests for truth (or justice) – and I refer to Newcomb, again (1974, 159):

> "[W]hile the heroes can solve the problems that form the content of individual episodes, they are reminded by a number of factors that they are less than heroic. They have yet to solve the problems of their own lives, whether those problems be wanderlust, the threat of injustice and death, or the necessity to explore the reaches of space. The structure is that of the picaresque, a series of adventures within a larger framework."

A closer look at the more serialised prime time drama of the 1980s and 1990s brings both properties to the foreground, marginalisation as well as irony: Thomas Magnum (of *Magnum, P.I.*) is an underdog who depends forever on the generosity of his landlord and feels embarrassed by his less-than-suitable day job. Many of his cases are hilariously funny to watch, and he regularly uses the characteristic voice-overs to poke fun at us, the viewers, or at himself. On *The X-Files* the two lead figures may be "armed and dangerous", but they are at the lowest level of the pecking order (Mulder's office is in the basement, while Scully never even gets an office of her own) and completely "at the whim" of more or less cooperative brass and sinister conspiracy forces. At least some of their cases are hilariously funny feasts of *angstlust* and glee (as Reeves et al. reluctantly admit, 1997, 35), while irony is played out by way of innumerable convention benders, tongue-in-cheek-jokes and allusions to other popular artefacts "out there".

The serialised series also provided the occasion for characters to mature, and for characters' relations to recall true, believable "life-like" dilemmas. James W. Chesebro (1987, 22) quotes Kenneth Burke's "dramatistic process" that sees all human dramas carried out in distinct stages that lead (here, in the case of the series' protagonists) from

- *pollution* (what norms are violated and cast as *disruptive* to the social system involved?) to
- *guilt* (who or what is generally *held responsible* for the pollution?) to
- *purification* (what kinds of acts are generally initiated to *eliminate* the pollution and guilt?) and finally to
- *redemption* (what *social system or order* is created as a result of passing through the pollution, guilt, and purification stages).

Chesebro thus suggests an analysis of television fiction that focuses less on the characters' (external as well as internal) journey but more on the communicative systems played out between characters. The ironic stance of the picaresque adventurer appears here as one of several communicative "modes" of how protagonists (as underdogs, everyday people, leaders, "romantic agents", or mythical heroes) resolve their dilemmas and / or overcome their backstory wounds, on their way to "purification." Important here is the characters' bond among each other – they work in teams, switch alliances and (must) learn to relate on each other's strengths.

Chesebro's model resonates with what Newcomb identifies as *motivation* (1974, 137):

> "[F]or characters in the adventure series the motivation is the result of character rather than of role. Role is a function of formula. Motivations rise from a required set of actions and events. Audience expectations are shaped by the strict limitations in which the roles are defined. Characters approach the status of invention, their motivations are internal, and the audience is willing to wait and see what happens in the course of events. The adventure series quickly makes a role of the internally motivated character, of course."

And (ibid., 139-140): "Values that determine the outcomes of various encounters are directly related to the attitudes that motivate the movement of the characters in the first place. The values that make it necessary for the characters to move are those that prevent their lives from becoming formulaic, their personalities from becoming roles."

In consequence cumulative narratives draw from their protagonists' backstory not for motivational reasons alone but also for the prevention of formulaic repetition:

The characters' colourful past provides them with "a sense of density" (ibid., 256) that keeps – in our case: not necessarily all but the more loyal – audiences alert.

As Sconce sums it up (2004, 95), referring to character growth as well as character interplay and expanded story-worlds:

> "Television, it might be said, has discovered that the cultivation of its story worlds (diegesis) is as crucial an element in its success as is storytelling. What television lacks in spectacle and narrative constraints, it makes up in depth and duration of character relations, diegetic expansion, and audience investment."

While the classical prime time TV series in the tradition of the picaresque adventure story already saw their (slightly downbeat and / or outcast) heroes struggle with basic human dilemmas apart from their timeless quest for a greater good it is the cumulative narrative's particular merit to have opened a whole toolbox of possibilities of how to address (and: resolve) these basic dilemmas by way of (a) accumulated character backstories adding layers of *depth* and by way of (b) progressively expanding – or, instead: constantly questioning – the story arcs whose "hooks" foresee more complex (and possibly: more domestic) human relationships to form and more hindsight revelations to make themselves known, over the allotted runtime.

9.4   The example of *Magnum, P.I.* (CBS, 1980-1988)

Magnum, P.I. went on air in December 1980 after a writers' strike had halted production for several months. Initially *Magnum, P.I.* was produced by Donald P. Bellisario and Glen A. Larson for the Universal Studios. Later, when Bellisario went on to develop new program concepts alongside the – still highly successful –*Magnum* franchise, Tom Selleck took responsibility, founding his own production company for the purpose.[180] The detective drama was part of CBS' Thursday line-up and received constantly good ratings over the first four years. The following plunge in viewership is generally accredited to NBC's *Cosby Show* making its first appearance alongside *Magnum, P.I.* in the same Thursday evening slot, from 20-09-1984 onwards.

The fierce competition lasted for two years before *Magnum, P.I.* was shifted to Wednesdays where it stayed on for two more, and final seasons. There were even doubts if CBS might concede the series an eighth run, beginning October 1987. After

---

[180] For the transition as well as other business-related matters Reich (1987).

12 more segments the series concluded with a special episode broadcast on Sunday, 01-05-1988 (see here, Table 9):

Table 9: Broadcast history of *Magnum, P.I.* (CBS, 1980-1988)

Seasons	Run	Number of episodes
First season	11-12-1980 to 16-04-1981	17 segments
Second season	08-10-1981 to 01-04-1982	21 segments
Third season	30-09-1982 to 01-04-1983	22 segments
Fourth season	29-09-1983 to 03-05-1984	21 segments
Fifth season	27-09-1984 to 04-04-1985	22 segments
Sixth season	26-09-1985 to 10-04-1986	20 segments
Seventh season	01-10-1986 to 15-04-1987	21 segments
Eighth season	07-10-1987 to 01-05-1988	12 segments

plus one stand-alone "Plot-It-Yourself" novel: *Maui Mystery 1#*, published in 1983

When Horace Newcomb's *Champagne* essay appeared in the May / June 1985 issue of *Channels of Communication*, the scholarly nod to the series' innovative narrative structure and "moral complexity" of its protagonists was promptly noticed by the *Magnum* producers and Universal Studios. The in-depth analysis came at a crucial moment of network struggle over the "lead" on Thursday night – and it hit home, apparently. The essay caught the attention of the *Magnum, P.I.* producers, and a larger part was published as full-page ad in the *Daily Variety* (18-07-1985). From there it migrated from into an issue of the *Little Voices* fanzine (1985 #3).[181]

It is safe to assume that the cumulative structure became even more of a trademark of the series in response to Newcomb's analysis, as the 1995 MTR talk suggests (see transcript here: p. 209, note 176) and my own research interviews conducted with producers Don Bellisario (10-11-993) and Chas. Floyd Johnson (12-11-1993) confirm.[182]

---

[181] Thanks to David Romas at *Magnum Memorabilia*, Detroit, for a complete set of the *Little Voices* fanzine provided. For an Italian version of Newcomb's Champagne essay see: *Magnum P.I. Lo champagne della TV?* In: Ibid.: *La televisione da forum a biblioteca*. Milano: R.C.S. Libri (1999, 95-103).

[182] Bellisario said the article inspired the series' writing profoundly, and positively: "We all cut that article out and saved it." Tom Selleck mentioned *Magnum, P.I.*'s

In comparison to most other US police and detective series of the 1980's serialisation and that "sense of density" describe *Magnum, P.I.* in ideal terms. The resulting "sense of continuous involvement with these characters" (in the words of Sconce 2004, 97), relied not on bundled storylines or expanded story arcs, but came with frequent hints at past experiences that were shared by protagonists and guest characters and were commonly addressed in terms of backstory reference.

In the case of *Magnum, P.I:* links to earlier instalments were as frequent as recurring guest characters or memories from a distant childhood. The most important references regarded the Vietnam War, in various and changing contexts. Thomas Magnum himself appeared as the traumatised Vietnam veteran, but also as a surviving family member and mourning lover, seeking revenge as well as redemption. This is why Newcomb identified the series as being *about memory and history* – but more explicitly *about Vietnam* (1985, 24-25):

> "For the most part the show takes what I believe is a widely acceptable view of the war: Vietnam was a mistake. Good people were lost. The troops were thwarted by the ineptitude and ambition of politicians and high-ranking officers. Soldiers may have no business there, but once committed they fought for their buddies. In keeping with this critique of the war, clearly less political than those of the '60s, the program deliberately tries to counter the all-too-easy representation of Vietnam veterans as crazies, victimized and haunted by the war. [...]
>
> Politics has invaded the characters' lives. Their present experience spins out of war – the most brutal of human interactions, the most distorted of political choices. In this context, even occasional slapstick and silliness are tinged with the knowledge that everything may suddenly slip into pain, and even the strongest sense of honor eventually must be humbled. All this explains why *Magnum, P.I.* is, for me, the best show on television."

Newcomb had to admit that a "warrior past" was by far not the most innovative historical background devised for the character of a fictional private detective. But the authors grasped the chance to provide the main characters with further layers of depth (ibid.): "[F]or those familiar with the accumulated stories, a sudden revelation is an exercise in characterisation and motivation. [...] New information may, for example, have something to do with why Magnum seems unable to settle into a conventional post-Vietnam life."

In short, *Vietnam* was the series' *leitmotif* and backbone (again Newcomb 1985, 25):

---

cumulative structure in a more recent *CBS News* interview on the *Jesse Stone* TV movies (May 2007, see *www.youtube.com/watch?v=JVidPmZup-s*; 18-08-2017).

"Magnum hates Navy bureaucrats, official policy, and public posturing. His motivation for being a detective, like that of many fictional detectives before him, seems to relate to the disillusionment, the anger, and the violence of war. Because his war is the war of our own most recent past, it is quite possible to say that in being about memory and history, *Magnum* is about Vietnam."

The particular use of a contested "history" fuelled the protagonist's screen existence even more than his detective work did, according to Christopher Anderson (1987, 123-124):

"Slowly, over the course of four years' episodes, a sense of Magnum's past has emerged to reveal a man tortured by sadness and guilt. [...] Vietnam plays a crucial role in Magnum's memories. Initially, the Vietnam War might have seemed to be a topical gimmick, a novelty to distinguish the series. Over the course of time, however, it has become a vital symbolic force, and perhaps the most complex representation of the Vietnam War in popular culture. Nearly all of Magnum's most painful memories – in fact, most of his defining experiences – revolve around the war. While serving in Naval Intelligence in Vietnam, he gained his friends, Rick and T.C., and lost his wife, who was killed on the day they were to evacuate Saigon (later she returns, alive, to betray him). In fact, the memories of all the major characters affix themselves to crucial war or war-time experiences: for Magnum, Rick, and T.C., the Vietnam War; for Higgins, the British major domo, his decades of service in the British Army. The fact that the memories of these individuals are bound up within events central to social memory, begins to suggest the symbolic function of the characters and the cultural function of the series. By identifying personal narratives of individual memory with social historical narratives, the series links its characters' efforts to resolve past and present with society's similar efforts. Individual memory becomes a metaphor for collective history."

Anderson went as far as identifying the series' central premise as a reflexive inner monologue constantly verging on history, fiction, and memory (ibid., 124-125):

"Thomas Magnum himself is more generally concerned with sorting out his own past than with solving cases: in fact, he is an inept detective throughout the series. The overwhelming burden of his memory, combined with his struggle to master the past, make Magnum the first tragic character on prime-time television."

In the end Thomas Magnum emerged as somewhat "purified", nevertheless. The *Vietnam* storyline finds closure as the protagonist goes back into the Navy, in the festive context of a friend's wedding. When walking down the aisle in his white Navy uniform he resembles more the bride-to-be more than a seasoned veteran. He comes back full circle, reassuming responsibility as a Navy official while assuming new responsibilities as father of a little girl – both in a melodramatic twist of fate not uncommon to soap opera.

9.5 The example of *The X-Files* (Fox, 1993-2002)

The X-Files was the first TV series produced by Chris Carter, a former journalist and screenwriter for the Disney Studios. What became one of the Fox network most renowned franchises besides *The Simpsons* and a cult classic to devoted fans worldwide started out as a more than modest *sleeper hit*: The genre mix of parapsychology with alien folklore and conspiracy thriller elements seemed felt just as odd as the pairing of a soft-spoken, nerdy introvert with a no-nonsense female coroner did – which is why sceptic network officials considered the less than popular Friday night timeslot to be fitting for a try-out.

Audiences built slowly but steadily to the point where reviewers and nomination committees took notice, and the series was shifted to Sunday night, during its fourth season. Due to the show's very dark look, plenty of gore and the habit to leave viewers with unresolved puzzles (all borrowed from horror movies as well as German expressionism, arguably)[183] the first two seasons featured additional, explanatory segments in documentary *National Geographic* style. Once it became clear that fans rooted for the *mythology arc* just as much as for the odd couple's complex relationship, the alternation of stand-alone *monster-of-the-week* episodes with serialised conspiracy-oriented segments became one of *The X-Files*' distinct trademarks.

According to many fans the series became, over the years, too successful for its own good. For them audience numbers grew out of proportion just as (... the network's expectations for) spectacular show pieces did, and production costs in general. After David Duchovny asked for the show's facilities to be moved from their original Vancouver setting to Los Angeles, Fox Mulder's basement office was effectively torched in the season 5 finale ("The End"), as a pretext for the set's reconstruction at the start of season 6 ("The Beginning").

Two programming strategies stand out with regards to the successful nine year run of *The X-Files*. One is the crossmedia stunt of having a two-hour feature film spanning the narrative events between season 5 and 6. The other is the publication of VHS cassettes with selected episodes from past seasons, from 1996 onwards; it al-

---

[183] For *The X-Files*' particular *film noir* look, and the use of flashlights Probst (1995).

lowed the global fanbase of the series (that referred to electronic bulletin boards rather than handcopied fanzines, by then) to procure new episodes from their local videostore instead of having to wait for them to be broadcast on local / national TV. Also to be mentioned is *The X-Files'* tentative – and short-lived – spin-off series *The Lone Gunmen* (Fox, 04-03-2001 to 01-06-2001). For the scheduling details of *The X-Files* original series see here, Table 10:

Table 10: Broadcast history of *The X-Files* (Fox, 1993-2002)

Seasons	Run	Number of episodes
First season	10-09-1993 to 13-05-1994	23 segments
Second season	16-09-1994 to 19-05-1995	25 segments, plus "Secrets of the *X-Files*"
Third season	22-09-1995 to 10-05-1996	24 segments, plus "More secrets of the *X-Files*"
Fourth season	04-10-1996 to 18-05-1997	24 segments
Fifth season	02-11-1997 to 17-05-1998	20 segments
Feature film, connecting seasons 5 and 6 as midsequel: *Fight the Future*, released 01-06-1998		
Sixth season	08-11-1998 to 16-05-1999	22 segments
Seventh season	07-11-1999 to 21-05-2000	22 segments
Eighth season	05-11-2000 to 20-05-2001	21 segments
Ninth season	11-11-2001 to 19-05-2002	20 segments

plus video game with additional information on the mythology arc: *Unrestricted Access*, 1997

plus video game, set between seasons 3 and 4: *The X-Files*, 1998

plus game, set within season 7: *Resist or Serve*, 2004

plus feature film, set after season 9: *I Want to Believe*, released 23-07-2008

In terms of *cumulative narrative* The X-Files continuously presented new mysteries as the mythology arc (... of the conspiracy involving the FBI, the US government and extraterrestrial forces) moved on. Narrative knowledge was accumulated but also frequently questioned and constantly revised. As Reeves / Rogers / Epstein (1997, 33) state:

> "*The X-Files*, like *Magnum*, walks an intermediate path between the episodic series and the open-ended serial, one that is for the most part episodic but in which certain ongoing plotlines carry across episodes and even seasons. Consequently, *The X-Files* qualifies as a cumulative narrative (or what Marc Dolan terms a 'sequential series'). [...]
>
> By shifting gears between the serial and the episodic, *The X-Files* self-consciously rewards avid fans by drawing on the continuity of previous episodes, hence validating their diligent viewing, while at the same time welcoming new audience members since most of the plotlines don't rely on previous knowledge of the series."

True to its premise that no one was to be trusted, history was presented as a forever contested minefield (see Markley 1997, for the paranoid structure of history regarding Alien lifeforms and governmental cover ups). Historical events like the Kennedy assassination or the Watergate scandal were replayed in true conjectural *What-if-* mode. And even the most trustful of sources – the main characters' own personal memories – were repeatedly addressed as skewed, severely distorted, and tampered with. The epistomological "truth" Fox Mulder was searching for remained thus far from evident, over the course of the series.

The X-Files is arguably the first serialised series that built a "backstory" while constantly revising the past of the protagonists, to the point where they were forced to doubt their own memory, if not their sanity. This signature trait of enhanced indeterminacy rewarded some of the more (inter-)active fans while discouraging many others that hoped for some consistency, and maybe an explanatory final "tock".

The biggest innovation of the series lies within its enhanced connectivity as television franchise, though. As mentioned before, *The X-Files* was the first US-American cult series to strategically employ VCR "reruns" which made more recent episodes available in video stores before they were even rebroadcast in domestic / foreign television. Just as innovative was the use of feature films and video games to purposefully tell the story of the series' characters further, instead of just providing another plot-driven *stand-alone* segment. As for the protagonists' redemption and "purification", this happened in rather conventional style, though – with the two protagonists becoming romantically involved, and with "truth", as well as "belief", "love" and "hope" re-established – at least to some extent, and for the time being.

9.6 The example of *Six Feet Under* (HBO, 2001-2005)

The basic idea for a TV series picturing the lives and deaths of a somewhat weird, dysfunctional family of undertakers came from the HBO cable network, not from its creator and showrunner, Alan Ball. He was only asked to produce the show, and after some initial hesitation he agreed, apparently enticed by the prospect to throw many of the common precautions that governed free to air TV, in terms of family friendly program fare, over board. True to the cable program's slogan "It's not TV, it's HBO", the series juggled a wide array of taboo subjects right from the beginning: a gruesome death in the family (... for starters), graphic sex scenes, a gay couple (that would adopt children, later on), crystal meth, and a more than unconventional workplace – for a workplace drama series.

Even more so than HBO's other, highly successful original series such as *Sex and the City* and *The Sopranos* the slowly evolving ensemble show displayed distinctly serialised, braided storylines. The only sign of episodicity was that in each and every segment's opening a person would die (... in order to provide the week's business matter handled by the Fisher family's Funeral Home), with tension considerably rising whenever the opening displayed familiar faces instead of the usual guest stars, thus heightening expectations for some major, tragic plot twist to occur. Since HBO forewent ad breaks altogether, there was no act structure notable within segments.

True to cable TV standards, most of the show's cropped 13-episode seasons were programmed over the summer hiatus of regular TV (June to September), with two seasons (2 and 3) running from March to June instead (for details see here, Table 11):

Table 11: Broadcast history of *Six Feet Under* (HBO, 2001-2005)

Seasons	Run	Number of episodes
First season	03-06-2001 to 19-08-2001	13 segments
Second season	03-03-2002-06 to 02-06-2002	13 segments
Third season	02-03-2003 to 01-06-2003	13 segments
Fourth season	14-06-2004 to 13-09-2004	12 segments
Fifth season	06-06-2005 to 21-08-2005	12 segments
plus website with additional information: www.hbo.com/sixfeetunder		
plus scrapbook, adding backstory details: *Better Living Through Death*, 2004		

The series began with a death, and it concluded with another death. In-between the two tragic demises, people died on a regular base, since the premise of the series was set within the family business of undertakers. Clearly a "multistrand" narrative, *Six Feet Under* nevertheless employed cumulative backstory to give its many protagonists "density" and to let them grow (see Hamami 2007, for the accumulated past of the two brothers Nate and David).

If we are to count not only the series' events of what "explicitly happened" but also all the additional narrative knowledge provided within a fictitious photo album of the Fisher family (compiled by Ball / Poul, 2004), the story can be said to span no less than 120 years and three generations. The scrapbook's backstory begins with Nathaniel senior and Ruth getting married and includes all the childhood memories of the couple's three children – two sons and one daughter.

On the other hand the series also allowed for unusual glimpses into the future of its protagonists when concluding with a series of *flashforwards* to how everybody was going to die, over the years and decades to come.

Claire's story, for instance, starts out with her birth as represented in the (recursively linked, report-like) scrapbook, then gives us detailed and privileged access into her coming of age (over the course of the five consecutive seasons of the *Six Feet Under* serial) and finally grants us glimpses into her future private live as sister, sister in law and spouse, over the very last minutes of the last episode ("Everyone's Waiting") that propel us forward into the year 2085.[184]

What we came to witness over the course of the characters' "observable" life on screen (2001–2005) and were made to imagine and willingly infer with regards to their former and further life "off-screen" (with hints provided for the 1983-2085 time period, in Claire's case) resonates with what Douglas (2007, 10) addresses as the most compelling trait of serialisation:

> "When a series is well developed, the writers and fans follow the characters and find it hard to resist their history as it inevitably builds over time."

In the last two chapters of this thesis the concept of "diegesis" (in terms of storyworld, but also as province of meaning, as Schütz's might claim) is re-examined, addressing the cumulative narrative as serialised television fiction "with a memory".

Special attention is given to matters of of indeterminacy (chapter 10) and reader response (chapter 11).

---

[184] The series' four-minutes long finale is underscored by Sia's „Breathe Me" and accessible at *www.youtube.com/watch?v=eNwARV9tPUw* (18-08-2017, video by yuuy999).

> Le texte, par exemple, est une utopie.
> Text, for example, is an utopia.
> (Barthes on Barthes, vol. 3, 153)

10 QUESTIONS OF DIEGESIS

This chapter explores how characters' memories and backstories, understood here as dramatic, retroactive progression of story-related knowledge, can significantly expand the "second world" at stake.

Characters within serialised series are defined here as socially relevant "personae" (to use Luhmann's terminology), and as the "most important agents of continuity", according to Oltean (1993, 15) who argues "from the point of view of a functionalistic approach" (where characters fulfil particular *roles*, following Vladimir Propp) and "from that of structural semantics" (where characters are seen as *actants*, following Algirdas J. Greimas).[185]

10.1 Preliminaries

Structuralist literary studies (from which narratology emanated) focused predominantly on narratives displaying singular voices / perspectives, anticipating a story to follow an unilinear logic, with presumed knowledge disparities stemming from an author's auctorial, omniscient God like viewpoint. These studies did, however, not take into account dialogic narrative activities within everyday life, as performances deeply rooted in oral culture. It is no wonder, then, that poststructuralist approaches on narrative communication have come to rely (again) on concepts that were established with regards to oral and dialogical narrative discourses.

With regards to language as a world-explanatory skill and system, Edward Sapir and Benjamin Lee Whorf asked the important question if language was to be understood as a mere means to grasp and understand the world in its unfolding – or if we do, in fact, constantly constitute and shape the world(s) we inhabit, by way of language use (this would be: by describing the world and ascribing meaning).

Sapir wrote in 1929 (cit. in Chandler 1995, 31): "The fact of the matter is that the 'real world' is to a large extent unconsciously built upon […] language habits […]. We see and hear and otherwise experience very largely as we do because the language hab-

---

[185] For a critical assessment of these conceptions see Kermode (1979), 80 f.

its of our community predispose certain choices of interpretation." According to Whorf's own reflections on the subject (1940, cit. Chandler 1995, 32), these ascribing processes do necessarily generate *different* worlds depending on language use:

> "We dissect nature along lines laid down by our native languages. The categories and types that we isolate from the world of phenomena we do not find there because they stare every observer in the face; on the contrary, the world is presented in a kaleidoscopic flux of impressions which has to be organised by our minds [...]. We cut nature up, organise it into concepts, and ascribe significances as we do, largely because we are parties to an agreement to organise it in this way – an agreement that holds throughout our speech community and is codified in the patterns of our language."

If narrative is to be understood as a kind of language that works on specific levels of meaning-making, the linguistic relativity hypothesis formulated by Sapir and Whorf does have its merit: Narrative communication emerges not just as one of many tools we routinely use in order to grasp and understand what we call "our world". Instead it constitutes as well as organises, by its very nature and temporal logic, the world(s) we routinely live in.

As for the analytical differences between narrative "text" and "discourse", Mary M. Talbot suggests to perceive the former as a cultural activity which results in the latter as cultural artefact (1995, 24):

> "In linguistics, the term *discourse* is sometimes used interchangeably with *text*. More often the two are set in opposition, to make some kind of distinction between two views or aspects of language. I use text to mean the observable product of interaction: a cultural object; and discourse to mean the process of interaction itself: a cultural activity. The distinction between *text* and *discourse* I am making is an analytical one between the observable materiality of a completed product and the ongoing process of human activity. [...]
>
> Text is the fabric in which discourse is manifested, whether spoken or written, whether produced by one or many participants."

Once texts are conceived as a "cultural fabric" in which discourses manifest themselves, the discursive practices can be seen as "weaving" that fabric. Discourses constitute text(s), but not as the result of an author's activity (or: the author's discursive practices) alone but, instead, as the collaborative result of an interaction between authorship and readership. The interpretive activities do not so much confront a "finished" text to be wholeheartedly embraced or refused; instead they respond to a textual offer as *text in the making*.

In other words: If texts – and by this I mean fictional narrative texts, for the time being – are conceived as invitation for collaborative and imaginative efforts in making (some) meaning (instead of dispensers of ready-made meaning offered by a circle of properly authorised producers and distributors) then texts are, by default, more or less "open", and the text's narrative "closure" is never the privilege of one party alone.

What can be closed, however – and also needs to be at least temporarily closed, or *achieved* so that it can be offered up for distribution to publicly addressed audiences, and assure the text's recognition as cultural artefact and product – is the work. Works permit to denominate a given text within a given medium as "completely told for the moment"; they also allow for identification and recognition of an author's intellectual property rights, and thus for the "authorisation" of a given text as such. In our case, the work is congruent with the instalment that is achieved to the point where it can be offered up for distribution to publicly addressed audiences. The reader can expect an authorised version (more precisely: a co-authorised version issued by authors and distributors) and thus a more or less finite "province of meaning" (not counting later revisions such as a "director's cut" or versions repurposed for particular audiences, or particular media formats).

Both Roland Barthes and Umberto Eco contributed important arguments for the potential "openness" both of works and texts in the early 1970s, in the context of (and: in opposition to) more restrictive opinions about the legitimacy of interpretation and the negotiation of an artwork's meaning. As mentioned before, John Fiske (1987) borrowed from Barthes (1974) the distinction between "writerly" and "readerly" texts when referring to the degree of collaborative effort a textual offer demanded from its readers, while Umberto Eco discussed questions of closure with regards to popular literature in his reflections on the "role of the reader" (Eco 1979) and the "open work" (Eco ibid., and 1989). Eco looked at cases of deliberately unfinished works of art which invite for an interactive intervention as completion, and thus for a kind of encouraged co-authorship rather than extended interpretive activities.

In all of these reflections the *text* was more focused upon than the *work in progress* because it was here – with regards to the text – that any reader currently "at work" and in the course of completing a story could imaginatively change certain parameters and even the outcome of the story in question. Meanwhile the work "as such" was supposed to remain affiliated to its original author. Eco saw this premise validated also for serially produced texts published in instalments.[186]

---

[186] It is no coincidence that prolific authors such as Umberto Eco do not seem to care much for the integrity, or "continuity" of their original books and essays.

10.2 Paradigms and syntagms

Structuralist narrative analysis in the tradition of Tzvetan Todorov, Gérard Genette and many others suggests that the formal aspects of a social phenomenon are best described when comparing them (as a whole and in their constitutive parts) to similar structures of other social phenomena. A structuralist's aim is (Sturrock 2003, 24) "... to demonstrate that beneath the superficial variety of its existing forms there is an underlying unity". With regards to such ideas of underlying unity both literary and anthropological structuralisms use (ibid.) "a common method and a common set of principles, by which a text or a body of anthropological data may be similarly 'read'."

Structuralist thinking is closely related to semiotics in the tradition of Ferdinand de Saussure's language-oriented "semiology" (see Spivey 1997, 98-101): When it comes to texts conveying meaning structuralism assumes that some universal guiding principles can be studied in terms of grammar based, conventionally conceived and also conventionally read linguistic features. A leading figure of French structuralism was the anthropologist Claude Lévy-Strauss who detected similar structures of significance with regards to cultural practices in different parts of the world. He suggested to describe these characteristics as either "-emic" (traits that were culturally shared) or as "-etic" (traits that were culture-specific). Structuralism is also indebted to formalistic thinking.

Russian formalism was founded between 1915 and 1920 in Moscow and Petrograd by a group of literature and film theorists such as Vladimir Propp and Victor Shklovsky and was, right from its beginning, more interested in exceptional textual features than universal norms and guidelines, and more in the divergent possibilities of narrative development than in the description of common textual traits and conventional narrative life-courses (see Spivey ibid., 101-102; for a history of the short-lived Formalist movement Erlich 1955). Formalist thinking is interested both in the life course of narratives and turns and twists, and in the corresponding roles or "narrative functions" characters assume within a narrative over time.

When narrative composition is at stake, analytical questions arise with regards to similarities and dissimilarities of narrative elements locked in a paradigmatic relationship (what oppositions are to be found in the narrative text, and which biases

---

Bondanella (1997) describes the agony he repeatedly underwent when trying to put into chronological order Eco's textual drafts in different languages, or to tell apart later, not necessarily finalised text versions from earlier ones.

result, based on either stereotypical views or strategic omission?) and with regards to the chronological order of the same narrative elements and their placement in time (what is described as "before" and "after" some specific moment in time, and which might be alternative successions instead, with different outcomes, maybe?).

The objective of such an analysis can be grammar-oriented and ask for specific uses of stylistic devices. Another goal can be the understanding of the meaning-making process as such; in this case questions are asked about encoding and decoding processes and about the corresponding social functions of (particular) narratives within larger communication frameworks. The analysis of narrative bias can lead to questions about formulaic representations and agendas (who generalises and leaves out, to what possible purpose?), the analysis of narrative order to questions about cause and effect, and the prevailing of some formulaic ending (what kind of rhetoric logic prevails, to what end and to which moral consequence stated or implied?).

The paradigmatic, existent-oriented aspects of media narratives address the relation between protagonists and antagonists or, instead, generic preferences regarding narrative settings; they are usually described in terms borrowed from the structuralist school of analysis. Whereas the syntagmatic aspects (such as: the dynamics of a narrative's development over time, and the specific relation between *syuzhet* and *fabula*, or "plot" and "story" that determines its organization in time) goes back to formalist research traditions.[187]

Both schools can also be seen as representing two complementary approaches within the same structuralist paradigm that attempts to define a narrative by its grammar and basic operative principles. In consequence both formalism and structuralism have been criticised for considering a text's characteristics as "properties" rather than external ascriptions. The poststructuralist movement as represented by Roland Barthes, Umberto Eco and Philippe Bourdieu but also Kristin Thompson and David Bordwell has since adapted these concepts further: They all suggested to reflect all textual analysis in the light of the culture-specific circumstances of the particular

---

[187] For the difference Shklovsky made between *plot* and *story* see Hawkes (1977, 65-66): "'Story' is simply the basic succession of events, the raw material which confronts the artist. Plot represents the distinctive way in which the 'story' is made strange, creatively deformed and defamiliarised." In other words: Just as signs are composed of representative "signifiers" that – more or less arbitrarily – design something which is represented or "signified", narratives present themselves in the form of "plots" which – more or less strategically – signify what is actually at stake and can be reconstructed (or "refamiliarised") as "story".

text's social relevance and (individual or collective) reception – and thus contributed importantly to the interdisciplinary toolbox of Cultural Studies.[188]

The two complementary sides of narrative grammar – paradigm and syntagm – are presented in the following Table (Cohan and Shires 1988, 14; see here, Table 12):

Table 12: Paradigms and syntagms (Cohen / Shires 1988, 14)

Paradigms organise	Syntagms organise
vertical relations of	horizontal relations of
similarity / difference at the	continuity / proximity at the
systemic level of	discursive level / in actual situations of
language competence / linguistic activity	language performance / language use

This is to say: If we seek to understand what a narrative sequence conventionally means we do actualise some prior, narrative or situation-bound knowledge that draws from existing language competence (... what is the usual significance of such an element, and what might be its meaning in this particular instance?). On the other hand we need to reconfigure the same element's position within the actual development of the narrative at hand (... what happened until then; and what happened / will happen next?). The same narrative sequence allows thus for a description (or close analysis) of *what is there*, in relation to something else and / or in contrast to what is missing and might be inferred. Or, instead for a description of *what goes on* – in relation to what comes beforehand and / or what is to be expected next – and in the light of what overall consequences.

A useful concept for the analysis of paradigmatic and syntagmatic story elements stems from Seymour Chatman's "Story and Discourse" ([1978] 1993^6; and mentioned here: p. 13, footnote 32): Chatman distinguished the existents of a narrative, and notably the narrative's characters and settings, from the events of the emerging story, in terms of actions (what characters do) and happenings (what characters experience).

Structuralist narrative theory places the story's characters at the centre of what is told: Their role and interplay – or narrative "function" – determines the paradigmat-

---

[188] For a description of neo-formalist film theory see Thompson (1988), for a critique of neo-structuralist approaches in film studies Bordwell (2004).

ic structure of "what is" and the syntagmatic progression in terms of "what will be". Within the communication between authors and readers characters act as intermediaries: They convey knowledge as well as emotions and invite for sustained engagement and / or identification. When focusing on actions and happenings within serialised narratives, we individuated the story's characters as providing depth: It is with their progression (in terms of coming of age) and their struggles (in terms of coming to terms with difficulties) that our affective alliances and discords most likely lie, grow and develop – rather than with some plotted twist, or action stunt.

10.3   Story and plot

With syntagmatic story analysis being about how narratives progress, take form and change, the main question is as to how an ongoing process of telling relates to (and interferes with) the evolution of what is about to be told.

So the problem at stake is (a) how plot is accumulated into story, as time passes, and (b) how an expanding second world, as diegesis in progress, is negotiated over time.

When formalist narrative theories were developed within literary and (later) film studies narrative progression was assumed to be necessarily guided by some kind of enlightened reasoning and therefore following some more or less linear path (such as: from the beginning to the end, from a conflict to its resolution, from cause to effect, from questions to answers, or from a mystery to its solution). "Sense" was seen as derived from the tale's explanatory logic and only fully realised within the readers' gratification, thus linking it to some (... foreseeable or surprising) story outcome – as if there were no implicit hints and guesses strategically placed along the line to entice our playful imagination and wet our appetite. This general assumption puts the emphasis on story endings rather than story progression. It is an observational mode typical for canonical and formulaic narrative genres in Western culture, be it children's bedtime stories or Hollywood action movies, and is expected also to be valid for more fragmentary or randomly arranged narrative chains of events: for works yet in progress and stories that go around in cycles, leaving an imaginative door open for guesses about the outcome *by default*.

It is the outcome, exactly – or rather some shared assumption about a specific outcome *to be* – that distinguishes "reports" (with an ordering principle that is mostly chronological) from "stories" (with an ordering principle that allows for an explanatory logic beyond the simple passing of time).[189] Most popular fiction, as developed in Western mythology and later adapted into the Hollywood blockbuster model,[190] is oriented towards significantly "plotted" events, with the course of these events being pushed forward by protagonists and antagonists, their actions being evoked or implied by a narrator and, first of all, thought up and skillfully shaped by some creative agency claiming authorship and reserving the corresponding authors' rights.

It is with regards to such stories that the dichotomy between "plot" versus "story" – or *syuzhet* versus *fabula*, in the terminology of the Russian formalists – was developed. The terms describe two complementary ways of how to look at one and the same narrative text, and they help to explain the difference between what we, as readers, experience first as narrative in progress and then, through ongoing combination and in hindsight, as overall story. Thompson (1988, 38-39) explains the difference with regards to audiovisual media:

> "Basically, the *syuzhet* is the structured set of all causal events as we see and hear them presented in the film itself. Typically some events will be presented directly and others only mentioned; also, events often will be given to us out of chronological order, as when flashbacks occur or when a character tells us of earlier events which we did not witness. Our understanding of these syuzhet events often involves rearranging them mentally into chronological order. Even when the film simply presents events in their 1–2–3 order, we need to grasp their causal connections actively. This mental construction of chronologically, causally linked material is the *fabula*."

Once we participate in a narrative conversation we are at the same time confronted with an ongoing process of telling (the configuration of a *syuzhet*, or plot) and the anticipated result of this telling in the form of "causally linked material" (what has been told so far, in therms of *fabula*, or story). That double nature of the "told" versus the "telling" and thus the co-existence of two possible viewpoints on the same narrative as story or as plot applies, however, not just to the end of a prospective tale, but to any given moment within its narrative progression.

---

[189] See Fludernik (1996, 58): "Much narrative in conversation does not develop into a proper 'story' but simply provides a summary of the speaker's doings, of certain events or developments." Fludernik goes on to differentiate between *report-like narrative*, which (318) "basically summarises action or event sequences", and *experiental narrative*, which (ibid.) "renders one's own or another's experience within an evaluative frame".

[190] See Campbell (1949) for the example of mythical *quest* adventures, and Vogler (1993) for adaptations based on the Hollywood adventure formula.

According to Bordwell and Thompson ([1986] 2003, 70-71) the common ground of both story and plot consists of what is explicitly manifested within the narrative (be it as sound or writing or visual representation). But there is also implicit story material which we as listeners, readers and viewers need to continuously add up to what we actually hear, decipher and observe: A car mentioned twice within different settings or seen abruptly transferred from the one setting to the other does usually indicate a change of place for the characters transported and / or the passing of time. And the same goes for other seemingly "unmotivated" jumps that bring us from one (geographical and / or temporal) point in the narrative to another.

This narrative convention is called an *ellipsis* (and recalls Iser's concept of *vacancy*, of course):[191] Some part of the narrative is omitted in favour of another part considered more relevant, or convenient, maybe. While the omission helps to speed up the tale, it can also generate more specific expectations as to what has was left out, and for what eventual strategic or protective reason. Ellipses are an effective means for withholding story-relevant information, be it a too obvious clue to some problem's resolution or the explicit rendering of a graphic scene of sexual or violent content. At the same time they efficiently trigger our narrative imagination and thus contribute in essential ways to what both James Carey and Noël Carroll might term "shared beliefs", here in the sense of collective, socially shared assumption.[192] Narrative communication is made to an important degree of such gaps that invite us to come up with our own solutions as to how some character got from A to B or how other things evolved in-between two moments that are explicitly mentioned, put down on paper or played out for us to see, and believe.[193]

But there is more: As addressees of an unfolding narrative we are confronted with plot material that does not belong to the represented story world but instead gives us – the listeners, readers and viewers – privileged access to additional background

---

[191] Originally: the leaving out of words considered less important for the understanding of what is actually described.

[192] The erotic thriller *Wild Things* (John McNaughton, 1998) achieved this by deliberately withholding story elements which were revealed only as the credits rolled. What could be interpreted both as a misleading stunt or as invitation for some shared guessing among initiated readers bore traits of an educational lesson in conjectural storytelling too: The authors contributed their own five cents as to how things might, or might not have evolved, and to what consequences.

[193] For the uses of ellipsis and other conventional ways of condensing plot time with regards to story time see Genette (1990, 86-112) and Chatman (1978, 67-68), who completed Genette's model by the possibility of extending, or "stretching" plot time with regards to story time.

information. The narrative device is "out of the story" just as the theatre prompter is "out of the stage": It is there to whisper to us exclusively and present us with clues such as a missing link, some hint with the fence post or an emotional cue. The respective conventions need to be learned (or *refamiliarised*, as the formalists would say) before they can be considered perfectly "natural" again.

Such added material is called *nondiegetic* and extends from an external narrator's voice to a similarly "telling" musical score; from written credits, prologues and epilogues to inter- and / or subtitles; and from flashbacks / flashforwards that are not tied in with a character's subjective perspective (and thus become part of his or her story) right to the more recent cutscenes used in quest-oriented computer games.[194]

The main difference between things that are explicitly represented within the story world at stake or explicitly presented "out of story" refers to our privileged position as onlookers or lurkers in the wings: What we can overhear, read as superimposed writing or observe without any of the story characters being aware and responding, does indeed participate in the plotting activity of the agents responsible (understood as authors, and producers and / or distributors of the text). It just does not, at the same time, contribute to the story world as the characters get to experience it.[195]

What was said earlier leads to two possible interrelations between an emerging story and its constitutive plot(s):

- Stories as *reports* are the result of a chronological re-ordering of events that were more or less randomly arranged and publicly presented earlier on. At the narrative's end we face a probable reconstruction of events that are not necessarily interlinked between each other (as in: the possible answer to a riddle).
- Stories as *tales* imply that there is more to the emerging story than just a revelation of some ordering principle: What has been "plotted" appears based on some

---

[194] Salen / Zimmerman (2004, 408) describe the cutscene as an *"embedded* narrative element – a scripted narrative sequence which is integrated into the formal structure of the ... game. [...] As a kind of narrative in miniature, they help fill out the larger narrative frame of the game, playing a crucial role in establishing the fictive world of a game's story."

[195] The strict separation between the characters' world and the audience's world implies, again, that fictional tales should not let the two overlap. However, trespassing of the "fourth wall" was a frequent defamiliarising device all through modernity, developing its own conventions– such as when individual characters seek eye-contact and address their listeners, readers and viewers more directly, or when scripting and / or staging processes becomes transparent as such.

kind of logic which strategically propels the action forward (or just as strategically retards it) until the *story* as such reveals itself in its final stages. If ever there was a riddle (such as in a classical detective story), then there is only one winning answer, only one solution to the case in question.

Stories can thus be viewed as a *possible* outcome or as the *only possible* outcome of what was explicitly presented (and skilfully veiled) during the course of some plot's telling. The two terms again describe two complementary perspectives with regards to (the same) narrative: A given tale can be retold from its beginning to the end and stick to the original event presentation – or it can be retold from the end and take into consideration all the information by then absorbed as to how things turned out, along the way.

As mentioned earlier formalist film theory was developed in view of stories that were supposedly conceived in an author's mind (as representation of a fully developed series of events *before* the plot was put down and made public. This implied that the creators of a given narrative know more than their audiences about what is going to happen; they are in full control of the telling (... as the transmission model of narrative communication suggests). But this is not normally the case: Narrators can, at any given moment and for a variety of reasons, invest their ongoing tale with a shift of perspective, a sudden turn in the course of events or just some doubt about the eventual outcome. As long as its publication is pending, no one notices: This is still the draft stage. With episodic fiction evolving over time, however, the "legit" telling instances are forced to lay bare (some of) the drafting process – to the point where they may seem just as clueless, or left in the dark about the course of the story just as their devoted listeners, readers and viewers are.

This means that not everything which is told as plot must take a strategic position within a story-related "master plan". While a structuralist design would expect the narrative'sevents to contribute in some way or another to the progression (or retardation) of the *fabula* as mental construction, more recent narrative theories question the necessity for stories to reach a final conclusion altogether. They even challenge the idea that every story should be a "plotted" one. A good example is Mark S.

Meadows' claim (2002, 5) whereas "[i]n the context of storytelling, perspective may be the only thing that exists."[196]

According to Monika Fludernik (1996) a plot (or: a set of given plotlines) is only one of various possibilities how some characters' actions (or states of mind) contributes to an evolving story. More important than plot is *experientiality* (ibid., 26): "Actants in my model are not defined [...] by their involvement in a plot but, simply, by their *existence* (their status as existents)." And (ibid., 310): "Narrative at its fullest manifestation [...] correlates with human experientiality."

A similar suggestion comes from Joseph Hillis Miller whose essential ingredients for an emerging narrative include (a) an initial situation which is disrupted by some intervention or by a situation's reversal, (b) some kind of *personification* which determines and fleshes out the narrative's characters, and (c) some repetitive pattern which allows for recognition of the type of narrative at stake. Personification and plot may be related, but personification is more decisive (Hillis Miller cit. in Salen / Zimmerman 2003, 380): "Second, there must be some use of personification whereby character is created out of signs – for example, the words on the page in a written narrative, the modulated sounds in the air in an oral narrative. However important plot may be, without personification there can be no storytelling."

An applied version of the rather abstract narrative models presented by Fludernik and Hillis Miller is found in the popular distinction between narratives (or: narrative sequences) as being *plot-driven* or *character-driven*.[197] What is plot-driven builds on deeds instead of words and thus to an important degree on *action* sequences involving bodily performance and (often spectacular) stunt-work. Examples are fights, car chases and other situations where sheer physicality or materiality prevails.[198] Whereas character-oriented sequences rely more heavily on (both monologic and dialogic) *talk* and introspective silence; they emphasise a character's inner turmoil and mood development and / or mutual face-to-face interaction, indicating some proximity between characters.[199]

---

[196] The concept of perspective, or *focalisation* (which often implies "seeing" through a character's eyes or "speaking" with a character's voice) is not developed further, here.

[197] I came across the distinction back in 1998 when discussing TV movie structure with Swiss film director and producer Samir Jamal Aldin.

[198] For a cognitive approach on narrative action see Jan-Christoph Meister (2003).

[199] As with all narrative conventions this can be played out according to or against the book: *Miami Vice* (ABC, 1984-1988) introduced song texts as voice over

In conclusion *perspective*, as described by Mark S. Meadows, does not just ask from us to choose and follow one character in moments of individual or collective action and maybe switch between different characters' viewpoints. Instead, it asks readers, listeners and / or viewers to invest those characters with an *experientiality* of their own, and thereby *personify* them. On the other hand, if a more obviously "plotted" course of action can significantly speed up or delay a story's progression (in order to enhance its mystery or suspense appeal, for instance), an "experiental" moment of introspection into a character's state of mind can allow for more familiarity with this character's reflections and subsequent actions – and thus make us more fully understand both his or her motivation and progression regarding the story at hand.

Within the interdisciplinary field of narrative theory various sets of corresponding terms have been coined for (a) the *fabula*, in terms of meaningful constitution of plotted (and personified) series of events, and (b) the *syuzhet*, understood as a set of constitutive building blocks resulting in the fabula. Some of the wider known terminologies with regards to narrative levels in literature are reassessed in Fludernik (1993, 62); and here, Table 13 (next page).

While all of the authors taken into account by Fludernik (and by myself, for the sake of neoformalist film studies) do agree on an analytical difference to be made between processes of a telling (as enunciation and / or textual manifestation) and the tale actually resulting from such a telling (with *reports* included or more specifically addressed as such), there are conceptual variations as to where to draw the line between the two, and how to address / where to situate the narrative "text" as such.

This question leads me right back to the *gaps of which serialised series are made*. Because they are by no means different from other narrative gaps (i.e.: vacancies or blanks) except for their repeated, recurring manifestation by which they significantly enlarge the playground for toying with indeterminacies, as Iser himself pointed out. While the episodic mode already provides both authors and readers as co-tellers with reflexive periods of time as imaginative spaces for meaning-making processes, serialisation expands these imaginative spaces even further towards the future of involved characters (in the form of planned, or anticipated "arcs") and also

---

comments (see Buxton 1994) and made frequent shoot-outs sound like sequences of a heated dialogue between parties whose guns had recognisable voices. Action scenes often had an introspective quality about them while the use of colour (bright urban pastels versus the rare earthen tones reminiscent of someone's Vietnam past) allowed to be read as constitutive plot elements.

further towards the past of the same characters (in the form of recursively refigured links).

Table 13: Narrative levels in literary (and film) studies (Fludernik 1993, 62)

Author	Events in chronol. order	Events casually connected	Events ordered artistically	Text on page	Narration as enunciation
Gérard Genette	*Histoire*			*discours (récit)*	narration (voice + focalisation)
Seymour Chatman	story	discourse			
Mieke Bal	*fabula*	story and focalisation		narration (plus language plus voice)	
Shlomith Rimmon-Kenan	story			text	narration
Gerald Prince	Narrated			narrating	
Franz K. Stanzel	story			mediation by teller or reflector + enunciation if teller figure	
(addendum by ugb.) Victor Shklovsky (David Bordwell / Kristin Thompson)	fabula (as story)			syuzhet (as plot)	

Following this logic, cumulative storytelling is to be interpreted as an offer for involved and knowing audiences to transfer pending contingencies of plot into story (... in order to achieve closure) – but also as an offer to dissolve the double contingencies of a story into the indeterminacies of a pending plot, at any given moment during the telling at stake. I cannot think of a stronger incentive and invitation for collaborative tellers as world-makers to put their collectively accumulated narrative knowledge at work within some upcoming narrative task.

In the serialised series of the TV II era, the accumulated backstory of characters' lives assumed meaning both in the episodic "plot" (in terms of sub-plot) and within the ongoing "story" as work-in-progress. While a particular profession – say, the identification of a character as policeman, doctor or lawyer – determined this particular character's actions within earlier eras of television, serialisation allowed for (more) plots to draw as well from the personal lives leading up to that professional prowess and performance. Within the ensemble series as multistrand or "flexi"-narrative, the intertwining of (both professional and personal) relationships increased the potential for new story lines and for further complications regarding already consisting plots and stories.

David Bordwell and Kristin Thompson propose the following model of how story and plot interact within the feature film (see here, Figure 22):

Figure 22: Story and plot (Bordwell / Thompson [1986] 2003, 71)

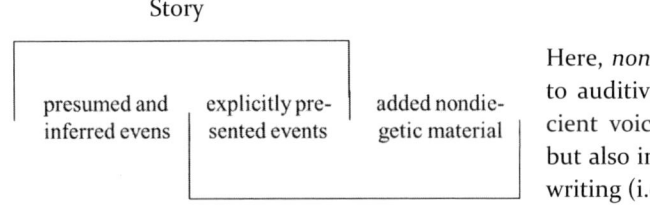

Here, *nondiegetic* material refers to auditive cues such as omniscient voices and musical scores but also intercut / superimposed writing (i.e. credits, or titles).

The presentation of "story" and "plot" as partly overlapping invites for a discussion of "text" and "discourse" in a more flexible way. We can view as "text" only what is inherently plot-relevant (= whatever is explicitly presented and thus consisting of "writerly" stuff). Or we refer instead to both ends of the spectrum, adding the inferred and presumed (= distinctively "readerly") material which then produces the narrative text in imaginative co-authorship, beyond of what is witnessed as plot.[200]

Turnbull / Stranieri (2003, 6-7) use the same model to explain how story and plot interact on the television series – here in the example of *Buffy The Vampire Slayer*.

> "David Bordwell and Kristin Thompson [...] suggest that, as viewers, we make sense of a narrative by identifying its events and linking them by inferring a cause and effect sequence in time and space. We are therefore making sense of a film (or a television series) in terms of what we perceive as both the story and the plot. [These terms] refer to different aspects of the narrative. [...]

---

[200] The difference between the *writerly* (or *producerly*) and the *readerly* text is borrowed from Roland Barthes (1974) and from its application to the television text suggested by John Fiske (1987); see also here, p. 72, and p. 80.

> From the standpoint of the storyteller, the story constitutes the sum total of all the events in the narrative, some of which the audience will see, and some of which they won't. For example, the audience may not see a character travelling from point A to point B in the film, but they know or infer this must have happened in order for the character to have changed location in time and space. Or in *Buffy* terms, Buffy arrives in Sunnydale in episode 1 of Season 1 after being expelled from her last school. We don't see this, but we infer it from what we hear later in the episode. [...]
>
> The plot, on the other hand, constitutes everything that is visibly and audibly present on the screen [...] What we actually see in the first scene of Buffy the television series is Buffy being dropped off at Sunnydale High School by her Mom on the first day of her sophomore year."

The difference between "story" and "plot" is explained by Bordwell / Thompson in relation to how we tell a story – either from the earliest incidence we are made aware of and combining what happened, from there to the end, or by starting with the very first incident we encounter when watching the film. In the words of Turnbull / Stranieri (ibid.), "[v]ersion one (the story) would give you the whole picture, while version two (the plot) would be like a running commentary."

This difference (story = the big picture, plot = synopsis of events as told and witnessed) goes for feature films as well as (serial) television narratives (ibid., 7):

> "As it unfolds on the screen, the plot may therefore be constructed in such a way as to supply or withhold information in order to create curiosity, surprise or suspense. This process of revealing the plot, Bordwell and Thompson describe as 'narration'. Thus when we talk about the narrative structure of a film or television series, we are dealing with the moment-by-moment revelation of the plot which enables us to construct the story as a whole."

According to Bordwell / Thompson both the "explicitly presented" events as well as the "presumed and inferred" ones are diegetic: They belong to the second world of the (evolving) story. For this see the glossary of terms ([1986] 2003, 502):

> "Diegesis: In a narrative film, the world of the film's story. The diegesis includes events that are presumed to have occurred and actions and spaces not shown onscreen."

The same applies to the diegesis of the serialised television series, as Turnbull / Stranieri (2003, 7-8) confirm, in reference to Bordwell / Thompson:

"[T]he diegetic world of *Buffy The Vampire Slayer* [means] the fictional world of the series as a whole, set in the fictional Sunnydale, California. This story world may look like the world we know, but it has its own internal rules and logic, what fans of *Buffy* describe as the 'Buffyverse'.

However, as viewers we often hear and see things in the TV series that the characters in their fictional world do not. For example as regular viewers to the show we might first watch a trailer to the show which catches up with what has happened thus far (Previously on *Buffy* ...). We might then be presented with a pre-title teaser, and then the titles themselves. During the episode, if we are watching on TV, there will be regular interruptions for advertisements. The term used to describe production elements which are extraneous to the story world of the film is *non-diegetic*."

The authors go on to present an example for how diegetic and non-diegetic sound is used on the series: In episode 5x16 ("The Body", February 27th, 2001) Buffy's mother dies from an aneurism. Throughout the segment, there is no sound other than what the characters hear in their diegetic story world. "Because we are accustomed to the use of non-diegetic elements in a film or television series, the suspension of the normal background music has a dislocating effect."

The term *diegesis* stems from Anne and Etienne Souriau's "La structure de l'univers filmique" (published in 1948). The authors suggest to describe "story space" as "diegetic space", or the "space where the story unfolds".[201]

Diegesis is necessarily tied-in with the perception of the characters within the story world: "diegetic" refers to what the characters within the second world witness and behold, in one form or another. Diegetic knowledge is always shared by characters – but not necessarily by all characters, though. And it is shared by characters with the co-tellers of a story (that is, authors and audiences), while additional nondiegetic ("prompted") knowledge is shared only between co-tellers within the fringes of the ongoing narrative, without the characters becoming aware of the telling.

The concept of "diegesis" is thus a necessarily fluid and ambivalent one. What characters tell the audience within a self-reflexive comment or maybe a visualised "fantasy sequence" must break the fourth wall (of the delineated fictional stage of the telling). When Thomas Magnum repeatedly addresses the audience, and when Meredith Grey (of *Grey's Anatomy*, 2005 ff.) yields the same right to comment to her roommates George O'Malley and Cristina Yang, this can be read both as diegetic

---

[201] In original French "l'espace diégetique" or "l'espace où se passe l'histoire" (for the subject and its terminological use see Souriau / Souriau 2004).

(because it belongs to the story world) and as non-diegetic (because other characters will not be able to hear and see what we indeed can).

In other words: Diegetic material is necessarily tied-in with the perception of particular characters within the story at stake. And "their" second world is not that different from "our" everyday reality when it comes to conveying knowledge ... be it to us, the viewers, or to their own colleagues, friends and foes.[202]

Within complex multistrand narratives featuring larger ensemble casts "diegetic" elements must always be negotiated among characters (since not all members of some fictional ensemble may be knowledgeable of the same things). The theoretical problem of how to describe diegetic consistency, then, can be resolved by identifying as "diegetic" not just *everything* happening within some story world at stake (which would presume that the narrative's complete ensemble shares one and the same fictitious "paramount reality") but rather as (... particular characters' preferred) *story world memory*.

This could help to reassess the divergent story perceptions assigned to various characters, and it would also help to describe what the recurring characters of a modular, or *amnesiac* series experience (... in their own extradiegetic space) while they are off duty, temporarily frozen in the limbo of some *stasis* and "hanging in there", as Tudor Oltean frames it.

10.4   Narrative memory as diegesis

Let me now turn back to episodic fiction (in terms of modular or serialised series) and the organisation of cumulative second worlds in terms of diegetic space, and time.

In an earlier article dealing with the differences between cinema and TV fiction (1986, 104) Jane Feuer claimed that the very concept of diegesis was "unthinkable on television". By this she referred to the disruptive nature of the televisual "flow" and also, presumably, to a film buff's unconditioned love for the cinematic experience as depending on the immersive quality of some uninterrupted screening.[203] Her state-

---

[202] However, with second worlds establishing their own "internal rules and logic" (Turnbull / Stranieri 2003, 7), the rules of communication vary and the system borders of characters as "psychic systems" shift towards the permeable.

[203] For the definition of "immersion" I refer to Murray (1997). The handling of (extradiegetic) ad breaks is a good example for the underlying conceptual difference made here between television and cinema: While the ads on network tele-

ment alludes of course to the televisual flow's particular mix of program strands that are viewed here as interacting to the point where they merge into one overarching "province of meaning" (to quote Schütz). Feuer indeed presumed that all material presented in sequence would be experienced as consistently diegetic: as one second world, so to speak. However, to the initiated readers of some particular narrative universe the diegesis is not that of some overarching "televisual flow". The diegesis of *Buffy the Vampire Slayer* – for instance – is consistent with the series' second world as *Buffyverse* (Turnbull and Stranieri, 2003): It is an imaginatively co-created world that is (... still, to this day) played out and cultivated by the series' original authors, cast and crew, and also by fans worldwide.

Kozloff (1992, 93; in response to Feuer's argument) grants television – and the emerging *serialised series* in particular – the status of "permeable diegesis". By this, she refers once more to the phenomenon of characters' partial amnesia (ibid. 91):

> "One truism of television criticism is that series characters have no memory and no history: amazingly, they don't notice that they said and did exactly the same things the previous week. (However, although past events disappear into a black void, characters' interrelationships grow from week to week.)"

"Permeable diegesis" has since become the dominant structure for second worlds emerging from episodic fiction on broadcast television, with the development of character- and relationship-related "arcs" a telling example. Here I just elaborate what "permeable diegesis" – in the sense of negotiated character memory – means for cases of retroactively accumulated, continuously reassessed (in short: cumulative) narratives.

According to Sconce (2004, 95) television learned (over the course of its history as *leitmedium*) how to cultivate expectations and conventions regarding its many and multivariated story worlds. The acknowledgement of the audiences' contribution to TV fiction was a crucial step in this, and Sconce points out the pioneering role of *Star Trek* fans that "supplemented and expanded the original diegetic boundaries" of the show in significant ways (ibid., 99).

This brings me back to Horace Newcomb and his notion of the adventure series as *picaresque* narrative that provides closure to each episodic segment while constantly "reminding" the protagonists that they have yet to solve the basic problems of their own lives (Newcomb 1974, 159). And it brings me back to Tudor Oltean and his

---

vision are seen as constitutive for the enjoyment of episodic fiction the same ads are considered disruptive for the enjoyment of the cinematic work in question.

suggestion to see the construction of the story world as either "parallel processing" or "linear processing". By this he means that within the episodic (or: amnesiac) series a new and parallel story world is established with each modular segment, while in the serialised series the continuously "activated" memory of characters holds together the story world of all the segments, told and pending.

When the gazes lock on soap opera, life goes on. Once the frame on the classic episodic series' segment "freezes" and the puppets are put back into their closet, however, their story world shrinks and disappears. One might say that the series' *amnesiac* characters are sentenced to suffer from recurring Alzheimer – just like Lucy in the romantic comedy *50 First Dates* by Peter Segal (2004) who must fall in love with the same person over and over, every day anew, for the rest of her life. Every day is a new episode, and every new episode inaugurates a new story space. In contrast, the characters on the serialised drama series do remember what brought them there – at least selectively, and strategically.

This is why I suggest to define *diegesis* as "what characters remember", not just as "what characters experience".

When narratives are, or become cumulative they provide (some of) their principal characters with privileged memory functions regarding past events that are shared to some extent with other characters (... in the case of some shared Vietnam fighting experience, for instance) but also shared, more exclusively, with the audience (by the means of a voice-over, or flashback, perhaps). Such processes of memory-building allow for complex alliances to form between favourite characters and their initiated readership within some particular story extension– just as it allows to recursively connect narrative events and episodes (or: stories) ... and to deliberately "forget" and discard whatever connection there was. This is exactly what the term *permeable diegesis* entails, here in allusion to sustained (= ongoing) communicative operations of memory negotiation.

> I read an article about the Holocaust that said
> with history we reshape the truth, and
> with the death of memory we lose the truth.
> (Chris Carter in *Cinefantastique*, 1996)

> I was there, you know. – Where? –
> Nuremberg. During the trials.
> (Jonathan Higgins in "Never Again")

11 CUMULATIVE NARRATIVE AS MEMORY IN PROGRESS

11.1 Diegetic memory and expanding story worlds

As Newcomb observed (1974, 159, in reference to *Star Trek*) the generic structure of the picaresque adventure story did entail larger, presumed and inferred frameworks of meaning: "These shows approach a form that might be called novelistic. A larger world is tentatively created in which the episodes appear. The sense of continuity brings the problems of those episodes closer to our own sense of probability." It is this kind of aesthetic probability, exactly, that broadcast television fiction tentatively explored over the course of the TV II era and in view of more dramatic institutional challenges to follow.

As the – particularly prolific – example of *Star Trek* shows, such progressively built second worlds are intimately co-created in exchange with the series' fans. In Newcomb's words (... and this is 1974, ibid.): "The starship *Enterprise* did suddenly cease to appear, but its audience has not allowed it to die. It runs in many areas in perpetual reruns, and an ever-expanding group of fans have formed associations, are publishing magazines on the subject and are even holding conventions."

Over the course of this thesis "cumulative" narratives were identified as employing selective memory in order to establish a history as "series of causes and effects" of its own. Whoever contributes to some emerging narrative does so by way of referring back to what characters are believed to know while drawing significantly from *their* remembered past and accumulated knowledge. But the contributions stem also, obviously, from the accumulated past as referential resource of everyone involved in a particular episode's production, distribution and reception.

This chapter starts out with another digression into literary studies, by referring to the doctoral thesis "Vernetzte Texte" (= networked texts) of Swiss playwright and novelist Brigitte Helbling (1995). Her study dealt with expanded narrative worldmaking in the literary work of Ingeborg Bachmann and Uwe Johnson – in the cartoon universe of Garry Trudeau's *Doonesbury* strips. All three fictional oeuvres (and by "oeuvre" I refer here to the "Gesamtwerk", meaning all published writings of an author) were taken in consideration for an analysis of the same strategies that were here identified as cumulative narrative strategies.

In all three literary universes of Bachmann, Johnson and Trudeau characters don't disappear from the author's agenda at the end of a particular novel / panel in terms of instalment. Instead they resurface later on within thematically related stories.

According to Helbling Uwe Johnson lets Gesine Cresspahl become the main contemporary witness of German history over a series of several crosslinked novels that cover ninety years and several wars, from 1888 until 1978. Ingeborg Bachmann's protagonists run into (... and occasionally miss) each other quite regularly. They are allowed to grow and mature – and they reveal bits and pieces of burdening secrets as *blind spots* which appear far too unspeakable to be ever addressed in full.[204]

Garry Trudeau's *Doonesbury* cartoon series is also examined in terms of case study; here the emphasis lies with the strategic concept change from modular panels (that would be Tudor Oltean's cards in a deck) to more serialised panels as links in a chain. Until 1982 the cartoons were only implicitly cross-referenced. This allowed for the occasionally published *Doonesbury* anthologies to select and regroup events and stories according to overarching themes. In 1984, following a two years' hiatus, Trudeau reassumed the strip, but now the characters went on "living" in-between episodes. From now on they were allowed to grow up, grow old and die, eventually.

Helbling's observations regarding the uses of memory functions within literature and serial cartoons correspond in many important aspects with the theory of the cumulative narrative explored here. For once they confirm the importance for long-term communicative alliances to be formed between authors and their initiated readership before some meaningful as well as gratifying recognition of a character's

---

[204] See Helbling (1995, 144; trad. ugb.): "'Wissen' und 'sehen' [...] erscheint nie anders als in einem *Gegensatz* zu 'Erzählen'. Diese Unmöglichkeit zu sagen, 'wie es war', kann nur im Fragen danach aufgehoben werden, in einem unablässigen, nicht beantwortbaren Fragen, das auf die Leerstellen verweist, indem es sie umkreist [...]." – "What characters 'know' and 'see' [...] is by default opposed to some 'telling'. The impossibility to disclose some happening as a given fact leads to ceaseless, unanswerable questioning that points straight to the gaps, circling around them."

Cumulative narrative as memory in progress

resurfacing name or mannerism can occur from which even more sophisticated intertextual (or is it: intratextual?) cross-referencing can originate. The resulting oevre's "permeable diegesis" invites for all participants in the process of some telling to bring their own (observed / lived) events, episodes and stories to the table, complete with presumptions, inferences and those *unspeakable secrets* that Ingeborg Bachmann's novels hinted at.

11.2 Narrative models

What follows is a series of models that illustrate various possibilities how to adapt the basic concept of the classic episodic series while drawing from serialisation processes – and thus from "diegetic permeability" and other forms of communicative contextualisation described earlier in chapters 9 and 10. Representations refer to the *amnesiac* series built from "modular" segments (Figure 23), the serialised series as (both modular and multistrand) "arc" show (Figures 24 and 25), the "cluster of episodes" (also termed *narrative cycle*, see Figure 26), the fully serialised soap opera (Figures 27-29) and the serialised series as cumulative narrative (Figure 30).

The models refer to variations of the hour-long drama series of the TV I and TV II era and integrate earlier reflections and adaptations regarding Ricoeur's mimetic cycle (see here, chapter 3: p. 56 ff.) and structuralist narrative theory (chapter 7: p. 176, 184 for narrative act structure; chapter 10: p. 216, 217 for story arcs, and p. 252 for aspects of diegesis, in terms of "plotted" as well as "inferred" narrative events).

Figure 23: Narrative model of the "modular" segment

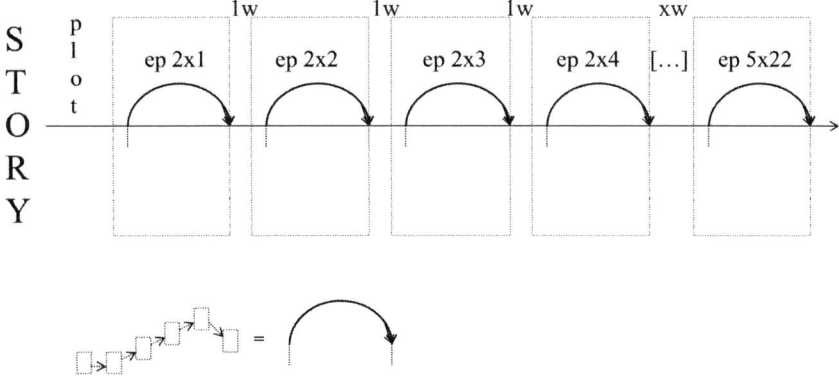

Figure 23 represents the classic series' archetype: Each additional segment provides another variation as "token" of the original type (as Eco would say) and as "cards in the deck" (in Oltean's terms). In-between segments the diegetic world shuts down, and the amnesiac condition of extended *stasis* freezes characters in a catatonic state.

Each recurrent instalment (represented here as episodes 1-22 of season 2) opens up a new story world within a given, well-known setting. This allows for segments to be published out of order (and guest actors to be cast in different roles without the regular characters "remembering" them from an earlier appearance). The protagonists' (... partial) forgetting does not necessarily extend to the viewing expertise of loyal audiences, though, since the institutional blanks between segments do invite for imaginative (solitary, or collectively shared) daydreaming ventures *by default*.

Figure 24: Narrative model of the "modular" arc show

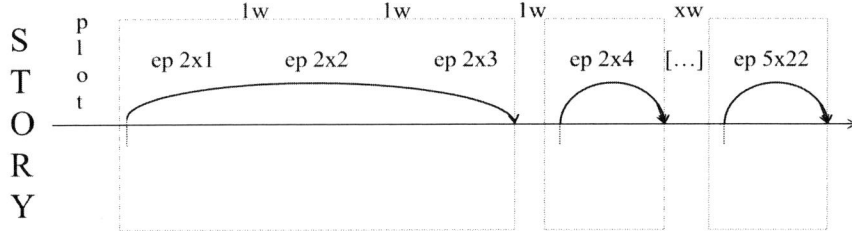

The "arc" show comes in many variations (see here, Figures 24 and 25). Symbolised above is the "Cannell"-type of series that employs short, unilinear storylines to tell an episodic tale over multiple instalments (here: as three-parter that introduces the series' second season). Segments close in mid-air on a "tick" – and usually some reassuring note confirming the pending story as "to be continued". Example: *Wiseguy* (CBS, 1987-1990). In contrast the multistrand flexi-narrative features parallel arcs that are presented here (Figure 25) as intertwined (= braided):

Figure 25: Narrative model of the multistrand arc show

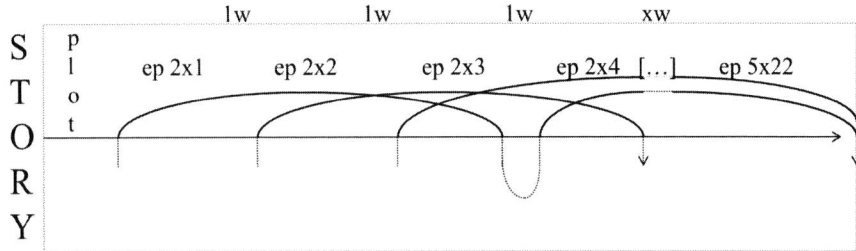

The model of the multistrand arc show applies to serialised series featuring complex ensemble casts such as many medical dramas like *ER*, or *Grey's Anatomy* do. The (character-, and often relationship-driven) arcs extend over multiple episodes, with individual diegeses merging and separating as the collective tale moves on. The "arc" structure establishes a strong sense for events to extend into the protagonists' (looming or yet far-away) "future".

The dotted line indicates a *vacancy* in terms of event presumed to occur in-between week 3 and 4 – with the week's interval corresponding to 7 days passed in the ensemble's lives, in reference to the action or happening at stake.

Figure 26: Narrative model of the episodic "cluster"

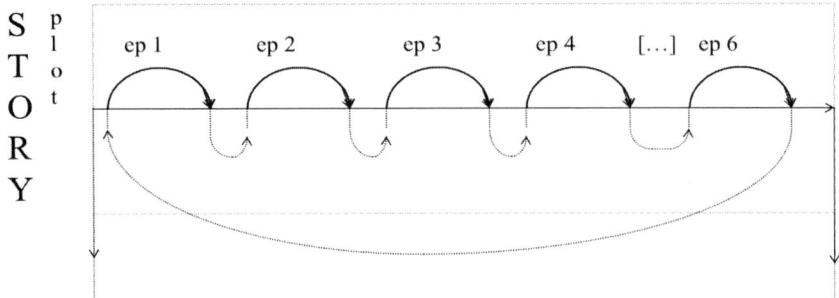

The "cluster" model (here, Figure 26) follows the literary tradition of the "narrative cycle" (for this see Besson 2004, and Mielke 2006) and is popular as *serie serializzata* with fiction departments of many European public service networks. Represented here is a random season of 6 consecutively screened episodes (depicted are episodes 1-4 and the season's ending); more such *standalone* cycles may follow depending on the pubcaster's demand and publishing strategy.

The cluster's (or cycle's) characteristic double structure as modular series with a distinct seasonal arc allows for flexible (re-)scheduling packages while asking from recurring characters (and from initiated readers) to please remain on their toes and wait for the overarching seasonal plot to close. The main difference regarding the classic modular series relates to the uses of blanks and vacancies as ordering principle: Episodes within a season's are consecutive while the seasons within a series are not – or not necessarily so. Since the *serie serializzata*'s overarching seasonal plot is often distinctively character-driven, the structure invites for audience involvement and readerly or writerly co-narration on many levels of story-world expansion.

Typical examples are *Il Maresciallo Rocca* (RAI, 1996-2005; for the series' narrative structure see Buonanno 2000, 2002) and *Montalbano* (RAI, 1999 ff.; see Marrone, 2003).

Figure 27: Narrative model of the classic (daytime or prime time) soap opera

The unilinear representation of the soap opera's many parallel storylines (above, Figure 27) can only approximatively illustrate what actually "happens" on the various levels of plot and story depicted here because the multistrand structure requires more complex analogies that preferably draw from web, or rhizome like structure rather instead of some chronologically ordered, consecutive course of events. For a telling example of the latter see Ryan 1987, 60-61, quoted in Oltean 1993, 20 (here, Figure 28):

Figure 28: The complex diegetic web woven on soaps (Ryan, quoted in Oltean 1993, 20)

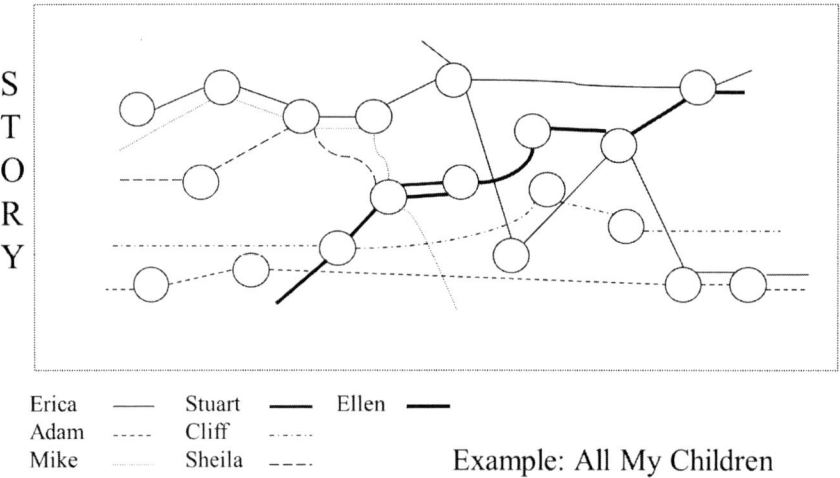

The narrative model developed by Marie-Laure Ryan translates into the following actions and happenings, in terms of refigured *story-so-far* (see Oltean, ibid.; and here, Figure 29):

Cumulative narrative as memory in progress

Figure 29: What the soap's characters actually do, and say (quoted ibid.)

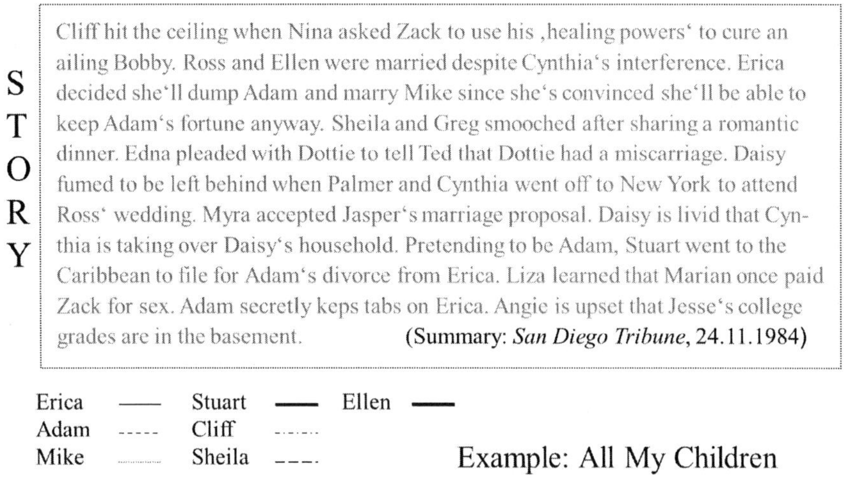

S
T
O
R
Y

> Cliff hit the ceiling when Nina asked Zack to use his ‚healing powers' to cure an ailing Bobby. Ross and Ellen were married despite Cynthia's interference. Erica decided she'll dump Adam and marry Mike since she's convinced she'll be able to keep Adam's fortune anyway. Sheila and Greg smooched after sharing a romantic dinner. Edna pleaded with Dottie to tell Ted that Dottie had a miscarriage. Daisy fumed to be left behind when Palmer and Cynthia went off to New York to attend Ross' wedding. Myra accepted Jasper's marriage proposal. Daisy is livid that Cynthia is taking over Daisy's household. Pretending to be Adam, Stuart went to the Caribbean to file for Adam's divorce from Erica. Liza learned that Marian once paid Zack for sex. Adam secretly keps tabs on Erica. Angie is upset that Jesse's college grades are in the basement. (Summary: *San Diego Tribune*, 24.11.1984)

Erica ——— Stuart ——— Ellen ———
Adam ----- Cliff ·-·-·-·
Mike ············ Sheila ---.

Example: All My Children

In contrast to the forever indeterminate and distinctively "tick"-oriented soap opera structure cumulative series adhered, from their very beginning within US broadcast television of the 1980s and 1990s, to the classic episodic structure established for earlier prime time drama series. The novelty consisted in a – just as distinct – sense of time passing between episodes which associates this US-American prototype (and the respective treatment of diegetic continuity) with the prototype of the episodic cluster common to European schedules from the early 2000s onward (see the following Figure 30, in comparison to Figure 26, p. 263).

Figure 30: Model of the episodic cumulative narrative

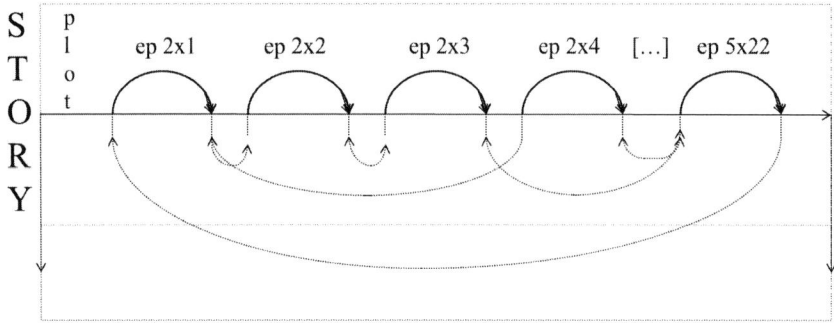

As was repeatedly addressed here (chapter 9 and 10) both forms of *serialised series* rely significantly on their characters remembering actions and happenings that were represented, or alluded, to earlier on in foregoing episodes. In addition they bring in diegetic (= memorable) backstory material from the characters' earlier lives

265

and tribulations that, in turn, invites for being recursively reconnected (= temporarily ordered) and thus refigured as belonging to a historical (or: mythical) past of presumed relevance to the pending course of events.

As indicated earlier, cumulative narratives come in two distinct flavours: One adds consistent layers of knowledge as the telling proceeds, thus deepening our knowledge of the story-that-was and fostering our understanding for what the protagonists are struggling to overcome, step by step. The other subtracts bits and pieces from whatever knowledge was hitherto accumulated, thus questioning the reliability of individually just as collectively provided memories and pointing to history as being forever precarious and provisional.

Both narrative strategies – retroactive continuity just like retroactive discontinuity – play with diegetic knowledge as being not just *permeable* but *malleable*, in the sense of what characters will (in complicity with their involved co-tellers in the fringes) learn about their whenabouts ... or may choose to discard / unlearn instead, at particular moments of backstory reflection that shape the tale-to-be.

What is refigured by way of some retrocumulative reassessment is necessarily triggered by an explicit "hook" placed within some plotted storyline of the here and now. But there is practically no limit to the narrative realms the *other* hook may take us – and to particular uses of particular, distinguished pasts within an imaginatively expanded story world at stake.[205]

The analysis of the picaresque adventure genre, once it provides the canvas for such narrative ventures back in time, reveals the added layers as telling us more about pain and loss, and guilt and redemption, predominantly – which brings me back to Krützen's observations regarding the adventurous hero's backstory wound. While the domestic world of soap opera provides its everyday heroes with what Mimi White aptly described as "memory without nostalgia" (here, chapter 6, p. 158) the picaresque narrative's protagonists struggle with the shadows of earlier events and episodes that tie them in with some publicly debated, political agenda of relevance.

When thinking back to Luhmann's enigmatic opening of this chapter it is here, possibly, and in relation to the heroes' more personal (= intimate, and liminal)

---

[205] While a more accurate terminology might ask for calling such refiguring operations "retrocumulative" rather than cumulative, I stand with the original wording; thanks to Ethel Wiener for bringing up the argument.

encounters with some presumed "history" (and / or: mythology), where the learning potential lies for *what one already is*.

11.3   Expanded story worlds and narrative involvement

As can be assumed from Brigitte Helbling's analysis of diegetic interplay cumulative storytelling did originate from literary traditions and respective generic preferences just as importantly as it did from format traditions on particular *leitmedia* and respective scheduling practices. When classic broadcast prime time fiction first experimented with target-oriented "narrowcasting" strategies there were, arguably, other models available, besides the domestic soap opera identified here as major influence. Newspaper cartoons come to mind that toyed with new, fan-oriented formats such as the graphic novel.

This is not the place to write the cumulative narrative's history, as tempting as it might be. Let me just point to one more entertaining playground where cumulative storytelling "with a memory" brought depth to characters and their serialised storylines. By this I refer to adolescent literature "coming of age" in the 1990s and 2000s, with the acclaimed *Potter* series of Joanne K. Rowling inspiring one of the most prolific "second worlds" ever to be collectively built and maintained (Thierfelder 2006).

There are many indicators for how such narratively engendered second worlds gain relevance and plausibility as time moves on. One is permeable diegesis (as Sarah Kozloff termed it) allowing for all kinds of interferences to be built between various "provinces of meaning" involved in a telling. Possibilities entail an author's backstory wound to be reworked as motivating premise for a fictitious *alter ego*, child actors growing up on soap operas (and: the *Potter* film series) and family members of recurring stars making guest appearances as characters' "extended family" in telling flashbacks, dream sequences and other instances of acutalised memory. But this is only part of the story.

On the medical drama series *ER* (NBC, 1994-2009) Luca Kovac, played by the Croatian actor Goran Visnijc, was introduced as a new addition to the doctoral staff in the pilot episode of season 6 ("Leave it to Weaver", originally broadcast 30-09-1999). Kovac came fully equipped with a backstory wound since he lost all of his family back home in the Croatian war.

In episode 14 and 15 of the series' 8th season Dr. Kovac's traumatic past came around for a haunting reminder ("A Walk in the Woods", 15-02-2001, and "The Crossing",

22-02-2001), prompting him to ask advice as well and absolution for his loss of faith from a dying Bishop. Both instalments were conceived as seasonal highlights and part of the (heavily publicised) Nielsen February *sweeps* period. Here is what the local *Toronto Sun* preview by Bill Brioux announced (as published 22-02-2001):[206]

> "A horrifying train wreck, an early labour, the quiet death of a bishop, a devastating loss during the war in Croatia. Those are just some of the storylines in tonight's incredibly ambitious 150th episode of TV's top-rated series [...]."

In an interview quoted in the same article the screenwriter of the episodes (Jack Orman) said that "tonight we learn through haunting flashbacks the tragic details of how Kovac lost his wife and young children. We saddled him with a heavy back story and wanted to offer a little more insight into his character."

The article promptly circulated within two Usenet billboards (*soc.culture.croatia* and *soc.culture.usa*), alerting people with a Croatian background or history to watch. For a typical example of this see B.M.'s "Crossing"-related posting:[207]

> "Hello all. This coming thursday 2-22-01 on ER, at 10pm on NBC, the Croatian actor Goran Visnjic will have flashbacks to Vukovar and his wife (a Croatian actress from Croatia will play the part). This is not in the TV guide, but we know it is the 150th show and this Croatian segment is supposed to happen this week. Please spread the word to all. On last weeks show he already had a flashback and our Croatian pastor's voice from Los Angeles was heard on the program."

The wording is interesting here: While the person circulating the message is clearly aware of the fact that it is the fictitious Luca Kovac having flashbacks (and not the actor Goran Visnjic), it is the *actor* who is believed to share with the *character*, and with th *audience members*, a similar background – namely the intimacy, the serialised recurrence, and the played-out liminality of the "heavy back story" that the segment's author refers to in the *Toronto Sun* interview.

What happened at "Vukovar" became the subject of many co-imagined fan stories on the Internet that addressed not so much the war with its historical events but rather the struggle of the series' hero to overcome his painful flashbacks before he was ready to get involved in a further romantic relationship.

---

[206] Brioux, Bill: *E.R. Gets Ambitious For 150th episode*. In: *Toronto Sun* (22-02-2001). Accessible via *soc.culture.croatia* and the link here, footnote 209 (18-08-2017).

[207] Source: https://groups.google.com/forum/#!search/Goran$20Visnjic$20will$20have $20flashbacks$20to$20Vukovar$20/soc.culture.croatia/8T4aXeEvD-U/EWZyEdtX4 BUJ (18-08-2017)

Cumulative narrative as memory in progress

It is also notable that "Vukovar" remained one of the *leit* themes on all further *ER* storylines involving Luka Kovac. And so, during his stay in the Congo as a member of the *médecins sans frontières* , he got involved in a war-related argument with his medical colleague John Carter (played by Noah Wyle) over what wars are all about (episode 9x22, "Kisangani"; season finale screened 03/05/15 – transcript by ugb.):

> Kovac: These people just want what everyone else wants. Their kids to have something to eat, to grow up laughing and happy. They don't care where the border is, or who is president. They just want this to stop.
> Carter *(sighs. Then)*: I don't even pretend to understand the politics of it.
> Kovac: You're an American, Carter. You believe that if people are given a chance to convert to democracy the world will be a better place.
> Carter: What's the alternative? Military dictatorship?
> Kovac: You fight wars from the sky, with bombs and missiles. Then your planes land back on their aircraft carriers and the pilots watch *Drew Carey* on satellite TV.
> Carter *(gets defensive)*: American soldiers died in Iraq.
> Kovac: Yeah, but your children don't starve to death as your men fight. Your women aren't raped.
> Carter *(Silence.)*
> Kovac *(sighs. Then adds)*: I remember reading the newspapers, watching the TV, certain that we had to fight. And then my family was gone. I couldn't remember why it was all so important, what difference did it all make. My children were dead.

Needless to say that this explicit conversation on war-related topics lead up to another round of heated debate between posters on various bulletin boards opting for or instead against the (further) presence of American soldiers in Iraq.

As the example shows, the segments with a cumulative structure can still work as "cards in a deck" within the serialised series, and to more ingenuous readers – while they also work as *cross-referenced index cards* for audience communities that remember and recognise the "hooks" back to earlier episodes and incidents.[208]

The aim is to handle contingencies in a flexible manner that allows for optional transfers of open contingencies into closed contingencies, and similarly optional transfers of closed contingencies into open contingencies. The characters' memories can then be used to expand the diegesis towards far-away places and local communities with similar memories (Vukovar, Congo, the Iraq; or the former wife that is played by a "Croatian actress from Croatia") or refer instead to fictitious events, far-

---

[208] See Newcomb (1985, 24): "Nothing is lost. Everything is cross-referenced."

away places and persons whose shared memories merge into one overarching diegesis via some *cross-over* episode or a *spin-off*.[209]

The optional "hooks" on the cumulative segment can be used for various narrative purposes, then. They can invite for imaginative (deferred, or alternative) endings or for the introduction of a liminal experience as backstory wound *later on*. Implied references can be made explicit, and explicit references made to mean something else. The trick is still how to do "things with words"; here, more specifically, "things with anticipations and memories".

11.4 The example of *Magnum, P.I.*

The earliest instance of explicit inter-episodic memory shared by recurring characters was, arguably, about an unnamed goat roaming free on the Hawai'i-located estate of Robin Masters. The animal left a trail of destruction, and the incident led Jonathan Higgins (the estate's housekeeper) to repeatedly accuse Thomas Magnum (the estate's security manager) of negligence on the job even with the goat long past and gone. Other instances of (selective) continuity referred to props that could be spotted in the background as being intact, then damaged, once more painstakingly fixed and finally ruined for good (... and I am referring to the ongoing Magnum-Higgins' banter, once more).

Because consistency mattered the producers of the series employed what is known in television screenwriting as a *show bible*: a series of documents sampling all of the protagonists' preferences and affiliations but also memorable events from episodes that could be used as an indicator of changes to happen.[210] Over the course of the series the continuity aspect grew stronger, and ongoing "arcs" emerged. The most far-reaching had the protagonist spending a night with his long-lost former wife in episode 2x05 / 2x06 ("Memories are forever", 05-11-1981) and pondering the possibil-

---

[209] Crossovers are a popular stunt strategy during Nielsen sweeps periods, while spin-offs try to expand a franchise further: *Magnum, P.I.* joined episodes with *Simon & Simon* and *Murder She Wrote*, just as the (fictitious) detectives of *Remington Steele* guest-starred on *Moonlighting*, thus merging the respective second worlds. While *The X-Files* were spun off into the (short-lived) derivate *Lone Gunmen* in 2001, a more recent example of a spin-off was ABC's *Private Practice* (26-09-2007 to 22-01-2013) that featured Derek Shepherd's ex-wife from *Grey's Anatomy* (Addison Montgomery, played by Kate Walsh) as protagonist in another medical ensemble cast.

[210] For the term and its use see *https://en.wikipedia.org/wiki/Bible_(screenwriting)* (18-08-2017).

ity of having become a father five seasons later in episode 7x07 ("Little Girl Who", 05-11-1986). Another indicator for increased serialisation is the hero's week-long phase of mourning after a love interest died (at the end of episode 5x02: "Echoes of the Mind", 04-10-1984). Instead of shuffling the deck the producers had the protagonist come to terms with another painful link in an unbroken chain of significant losses.

"Vietnam" proved to be the series' backbone and *leit* theme over its entire run and on many levels of plotted action and reflection. Early on in episode 1x06 ("Skin Deep", 15-01-1981) Theodore Calvin's chopper is seen flying from a combat scene right into a peaceful beach scene full of sunbathing people while the gunfire noise fades. The sequence is identified first as Thomas Magnum's flashback but ends on the beach as being T.C.s flashback memory (= instead / as well?). Not coincidentally the episode ended on the following exchange, before the closing freeze frame:[211]

> Magnum: Hey T.C.
> T.C.: Yo!
> Magnum: You ever think about 'Nam? I mean have memories flash through your head without really even thinking about it?
> T.C.: Naw, never.
> Magnum: Uh-huh, that's kinda what I thought.
> T.C.: How about you?
> Magnum: Who me? No.

While "'Nam" was ever-present but not openly discussed by Magnum and sidekicks T.C. and Rick – who all wore their common team ring from serving in Da Nang [212] – Jonathan Higgins' war anecdotes made for extensive – and mostly humoristic – interplay between characters. His was an overtly colonial past, spanning from, roughly, British military school entered in 1927 to being sent with the UN peace corps to Congo right after the Mau Mau Rebellion (1952-1960).[213] The irony was, of course, that nobody ever seemed to believe the little man's colourful, way too long memories from old times.

---

[211] Source: *Magnum,P.I.* episode guide accessible at *http://magnum-mania.com/*; here: *http://magnum-mania.com/Episodes/Season1/Skin_Deep.html* (18-08-2017). A flight accident on that particular shoot killed camera technician Robert Van Der Kar to whom the episode is dedicated.

[212] For the ring (and the Lorraine cross worn by members of the French resistance) see *http://magnum-mania.com/Articles/The_Team_Ring.html* (18-08-2017).

[213] For details of Higgins' extended backstory see Gary Holmes on *alt.tv.magnum-pi* (04-07-1999); post accessible at *http://groups.google.com/group/alt.tv.magnum-pi/msg/300d7bbe2316e606?&q=gary+holmes+higgins* (18-08-2017).

As for the basic, repeatedly addressed premise / backstory of the Vietnam war *Magnum, P.I.* earned praise but also criticism. For a comparison of Vietnam veteran portrayals in *Magnum, P.I.* and the *Rambo* series see Harry W. Haines (in Richard Morris' and Peter Ehrenhaus' anthology dealing with the cultural legacies of Vietnam, 1990). Vivid examples of how actual veterans of the war responded to the various perspectives on "Vietnam" offered over the eight-season run of the series are provided by Richard H. Owens (2001; see ibid., 87):

> The author (himself a former veteran) points to all the yet unresolved issues that *Magnum, P.I.* dealt with, "[...] including MIA's, U.S. diplomatic and trade relations with Vietnam, war children, Vietnamese-Americans, post-traumatic [delayed] stress syndrome, and the ongoing effect of the Vietnam experience on American foreign and domestic policy from international peacekeeping to illegal government surveillance"). Even more important was the repeated confrontation [...] with the effect of the Vietnam War on the lives of the characters, some of whom were people like us."

Owen closes on an urgent appeal to "not forget" (ibid.):

> "Because the issues are real and present today, the series *Magnum, P.I.* has relevance. Magnum, P.I. repeatedly reminds us that the Vietnam war never truly ended for many people; and its lessons and impact must be recognized and understood today if we are to prevent the mistakes of the past from being the basis for decisions regarding the future of our country and our world."

The examples of *Magnum, P.I.* and *ER* are not brought up here in terms of textbook recommendation as to how some difficult or haunting past is ideally addressed / handled in broadcast television fiction. The point is that expanded diegesis provides vacancies and blanks for narrative conversation on relevant matters brought up within entertaining fiction to take precedence over some pending (here: legal or medical) problem at stake.

11.5 The example of *The X-Files*

Since the series' original premise was that of a forever futile mission to seek the truth about all kinds of gossiped-upon urban folklore the respective treatment of "the past" as a contested, biased and contaminated research area was only fitting.

Cases handled by FBI special agents Mulder and Scully were "classified" by default and related to paranormal phenomena of all sorts while the *mythology arc* addressed some hidden agenda suspected to pave the way for Alien invasion and colonisation, via genetic engineering and the establishing of a mixed breed of "super soldiers".[214]

The *leit* theme on *The X-Files* led back into the childhood of male protagonist Fox Mulder and, in consequence, back to the eavesdropping scandals surrounding the Watergate affair and Richard Nixon's subsequent resignation as US-American president. The producers also had the recurring character of the enigmatic "Cigarette-Smoking-Man" (played by Bill Davis) telling his own backstory in the 7th episode of season 4 ("Musings of a Cigarette Smoking Man", 17-11-1996) which revealed him to be the original mastermind behind the assassination of John F. Kennedy (22-11-1963). Or was he?[215]

Instead of having the series' screenwriting staff consult a regularly updated *show bible* the series' creator / producer Chris Carter preferred a more improvisational approach – as he told *Entertainment Weekly's* staff in 2013:[216] "When people say, 'You should create a bible for your show,' I say, 'You don't want a bible. It'll prevent you from making discoveries along the way.' And that's what happened on *The X-Files*." The resulting inconsistencies matched the series' conspiracy-oriented premise and motto ("Trust No One") and contributed significantly to the heavily biased states of affairs the heroes stumbled upon, with a gleefully guessing (and: gossiping) audience on their tail.

The series' protagonists were clearly modelled on earlier examples of reverse gender stereotyping in film and television: FBI agent Dana Scully shared the earnest, no nonsense approach and dedication to forensic science with Clarice Sterling (played by Jody Foster in Jonathan Demme's *Silence of the Lambs*, 1991) while Fox Mulder owed much of his soft-spoken yet headstrong personality – and David Duchovny's unmistakable physique – to transgender special agent Denise / Dennis Bryson occasionally appearing on the earlier mystery series *Twin Peaks* (ABC, 1990-1991).

---

[214] For a recent synopsis of the series' nine-season run-as conspiracy-related mythology arc see Janey Tracey's Infographic on the *Outer Places* website (20-01-2016), accessible at *www.outerplaces.com/science-fiction/item/10969-9-seasons-of-the-x-files-mythology-explained-in-one-infographic* (18-08-2017).

[215] As usual there was no proof. The episode in question could be viewed "in canon" or "out of canon"; either as belonging to the series' conspiracy-themed story-so-far or, instead, as a somewhat amateurish attempt at novel-writing by the Cigarette-Smoking Man himself.

[216] Source: Interview conducted by staff writers (= n.n.) for the *Entertainment Weekly* double issue 1282 / 1283 (25-10-2013); the online version is accessible at *http://ew.com/article/2013/10/31/x-files-1993-2002/* (18-08-2017).

The ambivalence of what underwent frequent revisions on *The X-Files* (in terms of shared memory of the series' recurring characters) produced interesting oscillations between *fact* and *fiction,* and *truth* and *denial.* There were many self-referential episodes exploring the basic question of how we know what we *believe to* know via tongue-in-cheek interplay with narrative improbabilities. And there were episodes making strategic use of historical tropes to allude to such unspeakable atrocities as an Alien genocide.

The respective liberties taken with historical – as well as other scientific – "truths" promptly reverberated within the comment sections on various TV-related Usenet boards: There were expert-led debates on all kinds of knowledge disparities brought up over the course of the series' run ... and there was the occasional meta-level analysis of Bakhtinian laughter and the *carnivalesque* on episodes such as "Humbug" (2x20, originally aired 31-03-1995).[217]

As mentioned before, the series' consequence to "Deny All Knowledge" to its protagonists as well as their (increasingly online-based) fellowship left many of its initiated readers feeling duped and growing tired of trying to make ends meet, narratively – over nine seasons of extended indeterminacy and forever holey diegetic memory.

11.6 The example of *Six Feet Under*

While the show's original idea (= slice-of-life episodes from a family-owned funeral home on the outskirts of Los Angeles) came from the commissioning cable network HBO the series' author / producer Alan Ball brought his own personal memories as backdrop to the premise. As he explained in his foreword to the scrapbook anthology "Better Living Through Death (Ball / Poul 2004, p. 4) – and told audiences of a public talk held at the 2016 New York Tribeca film festival – he lost both his sister and his father during his teenage years. Which is why he modelled the personality of the series' matriarch (Ruth Fisher, played by Frances Conroy) in homage to his real-life mother:[218] "There's a lot of my mother in Ruth. [...] She went through a long

---

[217] For a directory to *The X-Files*-related fandom see *https://fanlore.org/wiki/The_X-Files* (18-08-2018); for the specific discussion on episode "Humbug" consult the *alt.tv.x-files* archive at *https://groups.google.com/forum/#!searchin/alt.tv.x-files/carnivalesque/alt.tv.x-files/XZVM5kh-g_Y/t9lobfeFqikJ* (18-08-2017).

[218] Source: Liz Shannon Miller, in: *IndieWire* (19-04-2016); the synopsis of the talk is accessible at *www.indiewire.com/2016/04/tribeca-six-feet-under-creator-alan-ball-reveals-just-how-personal-the-hbo-drama-was-for-him-289680/* (18-08-2017).

period of just being destroyed. She eventually came out of it, but what do you do when you lose a child?"

In his role as the series' executive producer and *showrunner* [219] Ball was responsible for all of the main characters' ongoing storylines as well as the show's many diegetic twists and turns. They included dream sequences (sometimes in the guise of musical numbers) and the occasional reappearance of some long deceased loved-one for another round of helpful advice (or: sardonic wit) from beyond the grave.

Six Feet Under was to be understood as *memento mori* and post-modern *dance macabre*, but also as a celebration of ordinary life. The photographs tracing back the Fisher family history in Ball / Poul 2005 were provided by the actors playing the parts (in particular: Richard Jenkins, p. 12, 28; Peter Krause, p. 34, 39; Michael C. Hall, p. 34, 49, and Lauren Ambrose, p. 78-79) which contributed to the readers' impression of sharing some privileged, exclusive access to an "authentic", biographically relined collection of memorable Fisher Trivia. Collective authorship for the artful rearrangement of bits and pieces of backstory material goes to eight of the regular screenwriters on *Six Feet Under*, with lyrical support by novelist C.S. Lewis (1898-1963) and essayist / poet / funeral home director Thomas Lynch (1948*).

11.7 Narrative uses of the past

This concluding paragraph on diegetic memory leads me back to the study's underlying theme of narratively explored contingencies in societies' *leitmedia* and what their (necessarily ambivalent, provisory) *status quo* contributes to communicative operations of meaning-making. Its goal is to (briefly) summarise the main results regarding serial storytelling and the particular uses of diegetic memory and cumulative narratives in broadcast television fiction – and to consider possible reverberations in other meaning-making provinces of emergent narrative communication.

As the backstory examples derived from various series of the TV II era tried to show the *extended diegesis* of popular fiction relies on conversational efforts on many levels of narrative co-authorship. The increased familiarity with recurring characters as friends, or foes, and the intimate, personalised attachment to some permeable narrative text as diaphragm allows for the textual canvas to gain in density – and

---

[219] For the term and its common use see here, p. 189, and (more in general) *https://en.wikipedia.org/wiki/Showrunner* (18-08-2017).

that, in turn, invites for even more co-telling expertise to be jointly applied as the backdrop thickens.

As Iser argued earlier on, such meaning-making processes do not mend any gaps. While they may convert open contingencies in closed contingencies, other contingencies become manifest and invite to be quizzically addressed. And the same goes for collective processes of joint forgetting that gradually strip layers of meaning from a text's density, be it for strategic purposes or simply to allow for new memories to overwrite what is no longer considered relevant. Because, and I quote Luhmann again on another analogy of memory as "flow" (1998, 579; and here, earlier on, p. 53, note 66): "The main function of memory is to forget; to avoid the blocking of the systems once the results from former observations clot together."

Here is not the space to explore the theoretical implications of what Horace Newcomb described as the advent of the cumulative narrative on US-American broadcast television further to other research areas within academic memory studies. I just wish to turn back to one important intersection between "memory" and "history" which is narrative identity. Marie-Laure Ryan (2005; and quoted here, p. 3) described the formation of autobiographical *life stories* as a "continuous act of self-creation" and as "book-in-progress" to which new chapters are constantly added. The respective re-writing processes entail just as much reflection as action, and they require collective efforts of meaning-making.

I consider autobiographical narratives to be a particular rewarding venue for exploring the various uses of diegetic memory further. And by this I mean: outside of the more obvious application of the concepts discussed here to popular fiction that oscillates between oral modes of remembering and more "canonical" forms of written *show bibles*, by this producing necessarily contested versions of what "actually happened" at a particular site as (imagined or documented) *lieu de mémoire*.[220]

When it comes to long-term uses of some repeatedly revised past (here: of fictional characters within expanding, leisurely explored second words as provinces of meaning) there are remaining questions as to how expanded diegesis may interact with our own perception of some event, or episode as "past and gone". Alfred Schütz insisted on second worlds (in terms of fictionally co-created, daydreaming "provinc-

---

[220] The term coined by French historian Pierre Nora. For a state of the art regarding basic memory studies concepts (in German language) see Erll (2005); for applications of what is called "communicative memory" (in the tradition of Maurice Halbwachs and Jan / Aleida Assman) Welzer (2002), and Welzer / Moller (2002).

es of meaning") as being *closed* (= border-proofed), with a minimal risk for adult readers seeing their paramount reality invaded by some world of phantasms while they are *wide-awake*. When studying war-related German family anecdotes, however, Harald Welzer (Welzer 2002, 185 ff.) found many of the tales circulating among descendants of Second World War veterans to be suspiciously close to episodes from popular war-themed movies such as "All Quiet on the Western Front" (Lewis Milestone, 1930; Delbert Mann, 1979) and "Die Brücke" (Bernhard Wicki, 1959). Here, apparently, fact and fiction interacted to the point where backstories merged into one overarching "collective memory arc" of survival, and resistance.

Another far-reaching application of the concept of cumulative storytelling to the re-minding (and: re-mending) of precarious life stories is found in dementia treatments that employ popular memory as source of contentment and training ground for cognitive rehabilitation and the conserving of social skills. The respective therapy programs range from the New-York based "Music and Memory" program to memory care facilities that are structured as *dementia villages*.[221]

They all refer to shared, familiar fragments of backstory material that is used for diegetic purposes at the intersection of "memory" and "history", once more.

---

[221] For the respective uses of popular music see *https://musicandmemory.org/* (18-08-2017); for the idea (and: realisation) of *dementia villages* in the Netherlands and elsewhere *www.dementiavillage.com/* (18-08-2017).

> We reach across the gap, and sometimes
> against all odds, against all logic, we touch.
> (Meredith Grey in "Some Kind of Miracle")

12   CONCLUSION: END OF STORY?

12.1   Research interest and answers

As for the research questions raised in the introduction to this thesis the following answers were found:

Cumulative narratives allow for serialisation of episodic fiction without necessarily robbing the "card in the deck" of its narrative autonomy. An important resource for episodic fiction on television to become more serialised (and: cumulative) was identified with characters' diegetic memory (which was, at the time, a common staple featured on daytime soap opera) applied to the narrative structure of more classical adventure stories within the prime time schedule of TV II and TV III as "neo" television. As for the (economic, cultural, but also political) potential of episodic narratives with a "wayback" function the examples quoted here – and particularly *Magnum, P.I.* and Doctor Kovac's Croatian-war "arc" on *ER* – might easily be explored further within the context of academic memory studies.

As for the negotiation of popular narrative knowledge and the collective "mending" of gaps the examples quoted here might also be explored further within other and variously relevant / significant reality domains as "provinces of meaning".

Every biography works as *cumulative* life story and makes imaginative uses of variously retold everyday experiences from one's own – or someone else's – first-hand experience as "paramount reality" (Schütz 1945, 549). Other imaginative uses of narrative configurations stem arguably from what Schütz suggested to distinguish as "daydreaming" territories and the respective second-order observation. What we *are* (or choose to become, rather) is necessarily shaped by both observational stances – by what we learn to distinguish as everyday reality just as much as what we encounter, and keep in mind, as "fiction".

In the words of John Durham Peters, the gaps (of which communication is made, arguably) define human relationships for better or worse, and face-to-face communication just as much as mass-mediated (here: broadcast) communication. Niklas Luhmann pointed to the different operations of double contingency that engender expectations between psychic systems (that *perceive*, via their consciousness) and, respectively, expectations between persons that "interpenetrate" with social systems (and by this *communicate*) in order to achieve the mutually shared goal of "making sense". He described communication as a precarious, quite "improbable" endeavour but also as a necessary autopoietic operation of social systems with the function to define and maintain the respective system's borders. Seen from this perspective the cumulative narrative, as described first and foremost by Horace Newcomb, is just one (more) puzzle piece in an ongoing attempt to make "ends meet".

An ultimate step to be taken here is a reflection on how extended memory of characters, and respectively expanded second worlds, can be related back to narrative and genre as communication.

Christopher Anderson argued that within the cumulative television series "individual memory becomes a metaphor for collective history" (1987, 124 – and similarly Creeber, 2001). Personal recollection of past events builds on that of fictional characters, and vice versa. In the communicative attempts to apprehend reality, the independent existence of any of these three levels of discourse cannot be upheld because "[n]o single expression of the past takes precedence over the others; no single expression can stand alone."

When memory, fiction and history interact, the stories that we tell each other entail the chance to become "mythic" as well as "ironic" or "mimetic", "romantic" or a tale of (successful) "leadership." Redemption can be sought and found. Memories can be altered, and history revised.

In the realm of fiction as second-order observation this is done playfully, but also purposefully, as the two reactions to the expanded Vietnam discourse on *Magnum, P.I.* illustrate. One is the critical, self-reflexive stance towards the ideology expressed within the "history" as established for the series (expressed by Haines, 1990). This is countered by the appreciation for the series' Vietnam-related "truth" uttered by the Vietnam veteran claiming that *Magnum, P.I.* dealt with hitherto unresolved issues "[...] including MIA's, U.S. diplomatic and trade relations with Vietnam, war children, Vietnamese-Americans, post-traumatic [delayed] stress syndrome, and the ongoing effect of the Vietnam experience on American foreign and domestic policy from international peacekeeping to illegal government surveillance" [...] "And most importantly, [...] with the effect of the Vietnam War on the lives of the characters, some of whom were people like us" (Owens 2001, 87).

Fiction, then, attains "relevance" (ibid.) not because of its arguable verisimilitude to actual events and episodes but because the addressed issues are considered of importance – and are *therefore* "... real and present today". The sustainable story world of fiction remains within the realm of suspended disbelief. What is accumulated as story knowledge, however, is used to "mend" the gaps – and so, indeed, works as proof of their existence.

Cumulative storytelling is, in other words, a particularly "telling" example of how narrative fiction provides the tellers of a story with a "second chance" – be it for the purpose to explore liminality or that to reflect. In both cases backstory works as set of "personally" refigured *blanks*, with insight provided, or withheld, just as much from the teller's communicatively shared perspective as from that of the characters.

Within *neo* television of the TV II era cumulative patterns of storytelling emerged in an institutional context marked by media deregulation and generic hybridisation. Prime time soaps such as *Dallas* and *Dynasty* brought ongoing storylines as well as characters "with a memory" to prime time. The early cumulative protagonists – such as Thomas Magnum, and Chris Cagney and Mary Beth Lacey of *Cagney and Lacey* – were private detectives or police(wo)men with a hefty baggage of backstory that helped to explain where the main characters came from and what did motivate their recent career moves. The respective narrative threads as "episodes" (Martínez / Scheffel, 2006) often explored traumatic experiences and verged towards melodramatic soap opera territory, such as when a love interest or spouse was introduced, or maybe some surprising offspring that was subsequently added to the ever-expanding list of principal characters.

What remains to be analysed further is the notable potential of cumulative narratives to act as catalyst for collective memories that are shared by larger communities of readers, listeners and viewers. This is where Horace Newcomb, and especially Christopher Anderson, saw the potential for broadcast television within the early 1980s, with *Miami Vice*, *China Beach*, *Quantum Leap*, *The X-Files* and more procedural series such as *Cold Case* soon making similar use of US-American history as heavily contested "memorial" territory. Depending on the protagonists' interplay and reflective stance (which are factors heavily indebted to generic conventions) these collectively shared memories invite to be further explored, be it as referring to various "public" as well as "domestic" arenas and subjects, or as referring to larger frameworks of (national) storytelling traditions.

12.2 Where to go from here?

As mentioned earlier, this study finds its (final?) ending only after a decade of not entirely voluntary hanging in-there in some remote drawer as "closet". The ten-year interval saw television series come and go (... and return for the occasional, celebrated reunion episode), and it saw cumulative narratives thicken and wane.

Instead of aligning the findings of this thesis with more recent serial successes of US-American origin – and the many important contributions to the analysis of serial television that saw the light of publication in-between 2007 and 2017 – I prefer to stick to my own national hometurf for an outlook and turn back to where I started:

Public service television in Switzerland (in its German-speaking variety as *Schweizer Radio und Fernsehen* SRF) adopted the model of the *serie serializzata* over the last few years, after two successful attempts at workplace-themed prime time soaps (in the mould of *Dallas* and *Dynasty*) that were broadcast on Sundays as *Motel* (40 instalments, 08-01-1984 ff.) and *Lüthi und Blanc* (8 seasons, 10-10-1999 to 13-05-2007).

"Der Bestatter" (The Undertaker, 6x6 instalments so far, 08-01-2013 ff.) has its main protagonist Luc Conrad (played by Mike Müller) struggling with a backstory wound that made him leave the police force and take over his parents' funeral home instead. Conrad's father is played in dream sequences by the actor's father.

"Wilder" (2x6 instalments so far, 07-11-2017 ff.) leaves its main protagonist Rosa Wilder (played by Sarah Spale) stuck in the wintery outback of her (fictitious) hometown Oberwies where she attempts to solve a recent murder case that might or might not be tied-in with her own burdened family history and some *unspeakable secret* from older times.

Both drama series do employ cumulative strategies in order to allow for contingencies to open up, and be closed over the course of the protagonists' investigation. Only time will tell where Conrad and Wilder are heading, as *picaresque* heroes with a distinctive (and motivating as well as demotivating) personal past. And what their initiated audiences will draw from their recursively linked findings and insights, in terms of observational stance and fodder for thought.

13   ABBREVIATIONS

- ABC   American Broadcasting Company
- AWOL   Absence Without (Official) Leave
- CBS   Columbia Broadcasting System
- e.g.   "for example" (*exempla gratia*)
- E.R.   Emergency Room
- HBO   Home Box Office (cable TV provider)
- i.e.   "that is" (*id est*)
- IRS   Income Tax Ruling Series
- MIA   Missing in action
- MTM   Mary Tyler Moore Production Studios
- NBC   National Broadcasting Company
- NYPD   New York Police Department
- O&O   "owned and operated"
- PBS   Public Broadcasting Service
- P.I.   Private Investigator
- Retcon   Retroactive Continuity
- RPG   Role-Playing Game
- VP   Vice President
- ZDF   Zweites Deutsches Fernsehen

14 BIBLIOGRAPHY

14.1 Dictionaries and encyclopaedias

Articles quoted from *www.wikipedia.org* and *www.wiktionary.org*:

"Backstory"; see *http://en.wikipedia.org/wiki/Backstory* (18-08-2017).

"Chuck Norris Facts"; see: *http://en.wikipedia.org/wiki/Chuck_Norris_Facts* (18-08-2017).

"*The Fugitive*; see *http://en.wikipedia.org/wiki/The_Fugitive_%28TV_series%29* (18-08-2017).

"Midquel"; see *https://en.wiktionary.org/wiki/midquel* (18-08-2017).

"Origin story"; see *http://en.wikipedia.org/wiki/Origin_story* (18-08-2017).

"Prequel"; see *https://en.wikipedia.org/wiki/Prequel* (18-08-2017)

"Retroactive continuity"; see *http://en.wikipedia.org/wiki/Retroactive-continuity* (18-08-2017).

"Sequel"; see *https://en.wikipedia.org/wiki/Sequel* (18-08-2017).

"Show bible"; see *https://en.wikipedia.org/wiki/Bible_(screenwriting)* (18-08-2017)

"Slash fiction"; see *http://en.wikipedia.org/wiki/Slash_fiction* (18-08-2017).

"Sidequel"; see *https://en.wiktionary.org/wiki/sidequel* (18-08-2017).

"Showrunner"; see *https://en.wikipedia.org/wiki/Showrunner* (18-08-2017).

American Heritage Dictionary, Based on the New Second College Edition (Paperback Version). Boston et al.: Houghton Mifflin 1983.

American Heritage Dictionary of the English Language. Boston et al.: Houghton Mifflin 1992³.

HERMAN, David / JAHN, Manfred / RYAN, Marie-Laure (eds.): Routledge Encyclopedia of Narrative Theory. London / New York: Routledge 2005.

NEWCOMB, Horace M. / O'DELL, Cary (eds.): Museum of Broadcast Communications' Encyclopedia of Television. 3 vol., Chicago et al.: Fitzroy Dearborn 1997 (see *www.museum.tv/eotv/eotv.htm*, 18-08-2017).

NEWCOMB, Horace (ed.): Encyclopedia of Television. 4 vol., New York / London: Fitzroy Dearborn 2004².

14.2   Primary resources

BALL, Alan / POUL, Alan: *Six Feet Under*. Better Living Through Death. New York: Simon & Schuster 2004.

CORNWELL, Patricia: The Body Farm. New York: Scribner 1994, and London: Little, Brown and Company 1994.

FABRI, Felix: Evagatorium. Stuttgart 1556 (vol. 1-3). All volumes online accessible via:

www.literature.at/webinterface/library/ALO-BOOK_V01?objid=10897 (18-08-2017).

www.literature.at/webinterface/library/ALO-BOOK_V01?objid=11028 (18-08-2017).

www.literature.at/webinterface/library/ALO-BOOK_V01?objid=11029 (18-08-2017).

Grey's Anatomy (USA 2005- date; produced by Shonda Rhimes for ABC).

HOLMAN, Sheri: A Stolen Tongue. [Historic crime novel, adapted from the travel accounts of friar Felix Fabri and fellow pilgrim Hans Tucher]. New York: Atlantic Monthly Press 1997.

The Lone Ranger. Original radio series accessible at the Old Time Radio Researchers Group; see *https://archive.org/details/OTRR_Certfied_Lone_Ranger* (18-08-2017).

LYNCH, David: The Angriest Dog in the World. Examples of the cartoon series accessible at *www.lynchnet.com/angrydog/* (18-08-2017).

Magnum, P.I. (USA, 1980-1988; produced by Belisarius / T.W.S. Prod. for CBS).

Push, Nevada (USA, 2002; produced by ABC Studios in association with LivePlanet).

ROTSLER, William: *Magnum, P.I.* Maui Mystery #1. New York: Simon & Schuster 1983 (= Wanderer Books).

ROWLING, Joanne K.: Harry Potter Series. 7 vol., London: Bloomsbury 1997-2007.

SCHULZ, Charles M.: The Complete Peanuts. Seattle: Fantagraphics Books 2004 ff.

The Shadow. For the original pulp magazines see the online archive accessible at *www.thepulp.net/theshadow.html* (18-08-2017).

Six Feet Under (USA, 2001-2005); produced by Alan Ball / The Greenblatt Janollari Studio for HBO). For the official website see *www.hbo.com/sixfeetunder/*; for the series' finale *www.youtube.com/watch?v=el4eUKmLujg* (18-08-2017).

The X-Files (USA, 1993-2001; produced by Ten Thirteen Prod. for Fox).

14.3   Secondary and tertiary resources

alt.tv.magnum-pi (selected postings from the *Magnum, P.I.* Usenet group).

alt.tv.x-files (selected postings from the *X-Files* Usenet group).

https://fanlore.org/wiki/The_X-Files (online hub for *X-Files*-related fan activities, 1993- today).

soc.culture.croatia and *soc.culture.usa* (selected postings).

BANG, Derrick: The Football Gags (*Peanuts*). For the original cartoons and respective background information see *www.fivecentsplease.org/dpb/football.html* (18-08-2017).

BRIOUX, Bill: *E.R. Gets Ambitious For 150th episode*. In: *Toronto Sun*, 22-02-2001. Accessible via *soc.culture.croatia* (18-08-2017).

CICIEREGA, Neil: *Potter Puppet Pals* (2003-; for the respective series of videos see *www.youtube.com/user/potterpuppetpals*; 18-08-2017).

GANZ-BLÄTTLER, Ursula: Interview with Don P. Bellisario, recorded at the Belisarius offices, Los Angeles, 10-11-1993.

GANZ-BLÄTTLER, Ursula: Interview with Chas. Floyd Johnson, recorded at the Universal back lot, Los Angeles, 12-11-1993.

HERZ, Randall: "Die Reise ins Gelobte Land" Hans Tuchers des Älteren, 1479-1480. Untersuchungen zur Überlieferung und kritische Edition eines spätmittelalterlichen Reiseberichts. Wiesbaden: Ludwig-Reichert-Verlag 2002 (= Wissensliteratur im Mittelalter 38).

HOLMES, Gary: Jonathan Higgins' war-related backstory; for the original Usenet version see the archive link at *http://groups.google.com/group/alt.tv.magnum-pi/msg/300d7bbe2316e606?&q=gary+holmes+higgins* (18-08-2017).

Illemonati. For the Neil Cicierega fanpage see *https://illemonati.com/* (18-08-2017).

Little Voices 1985 – 1987 (volumes 1-14 of the *Magnum, P.I.* fanzine; courtesy of David Romas at *Magnum Memorabilia*, Detroit).

MILLER, Liz Shannon: *Six Feet Under* Creator Alan Ball Reveals Just How Personal the HBO Drama Was For Him. In: *IndieWire*, 19-04-2016; online version accessible at *www.indiewire.com/2016/04/tribeca-six-feet-under-creator-alan-ball-reveals-just-how-personal-the-hbo-drama-was-for-him-289680/* (18-08-2017).

N.N.: *Magnum, P.I.* episode guide and trivia accessible at *http://magnum-mania.com* (18-08-2017).

N.N.: *The X-Files* (1993-2002). In: *Entertainment Weekly* double issue 1282 / 1283, 25-10-2013; online version of the article accessible at *http://ew.com/article/2013/10/31/x-files-1993-2002/* (18-08-2017).

OSTWALD, Susanne: Ende gut, alles gut. In: *Neue Zürcher Zeitung*, 13-04-2002, p. 75.

Public talk on *Magnum, P.I.* (with Chris Abbott, Don Bellisario, Chas. Floyd Johnson, John Hillerman and Tom Selleck) held at the Museum of Television and Radio (now the Paley Center for Media), Los Angeles, 17-03-1995; video accessible on site.

Public talk on *The X-Files* (with Gillian Anderson, Chris Carter, David Duchovny) in the Museum of Television and Radio (now the Paley Center for Media), Los Angeles, 04-03-1995; video accessible on site.

REINHOLD, Robert: Television. Tom Selleck Stalks his Future. In: New York Times, 20-12-1987, accessible at *www.nytimes.com/1987/12/20/arts/television-tom-selleck-stalks-his-future.html?pagewanted=all* (18-08-2017).

SELLECK, Tom: Interview on *CBS News*, May 2007, on behalf of the CBS *Jesse Stone* series; see *www.youtube.com/watch?v=JVidPmZup-s* (18-08-2017).

SIMON, Ulrike: Interview with SSR director Roger de Weck. In *Report Marktplatz Schweiz* 3 (2016), pp. 34-35; the online version of the interview is accessible at *www.horizont.net/epaper/HORX_38_2016eReportSchweiz/html5* (18-08-2017).

SRADER, Doyle: Going Up I, II, Going Down. *X-Files* fan fiction, accessible at *https://groups.google.com/forum/#!topic/rec.arts.tv.mst3k.misc/_hvtIHghJ9c-*(18-08-2017).

TRACEY, Janie: 9 Seasons of the *X-Files* Mythology Explained in One Infographic (20-01-2016), accessible at *www.outerplaces.com/science-fiction/item/10969-9-seasons-of-the-x-files-mythology-explained-in-one-infographic* (18-08-2017).

VEGA, Vic: Transcripts of *The X-Files* episodes "Operation Paper Clip" and "Clyde Bruckman's Final Repose" accessible at *www.insidethex.co.uk/transcrp/scrp302.htm* (18-08-2017).

VITARIS, Paula: Family Ties. The [*X-Files*] basic premise turns on a family tragedy. Tracing Mulder and Scully's Backstory. In: *Cinefantastique* 26/27 (1995), pp. 43-44.

VITARIS, Paula: Interview with Chris Carter on *The X-Files* episodes "The Blessing Way" and "Paper Clip". In: *Cinefantastique* 28 (1996) 3, pp. 19-20, 62.

YUUY: Sia. Breathe Me (*Six Feet Under* Finale); the last minutes of the series' ending accessible at *www.youtube.com/watch?v=eNwARV9tPUw* (18-08-2017).

14.4 Playwriting / screenwriting resources

DOUGLAS Pamela: Writing the TV Drama Series. How to Succeed as a Professional Writer. Los Angeles: Michael Wiese Production 2005, 2007^2.

EGRI, Lajos [1942]: The Art of Dramatic Writing. Its Basis in the Creative Interpretation of Human Motives. New York et al.: Simon & Schuster 2004.

ROUVEROL, Jean: Writing for the Soaps. Cincinnati: Writers Digest Books 1984.

VOGLER, Christopher: The Writer's Journey. Mythic Structure for Writers. Los Angeles: Michael Wiese Production 1993, 1998^2.

14.5 Secondary literature

14.5.1 Television and broadcast series / television fiction in general

ADALIAN, Josef: Eye Spinning a Wilder Web. CBS Shifts From Crime to Creeps. In: *Variety*, 30-04-2007, pp. 14-16.

ADALIAN, Josef: Nets Doing Split. Divide Seasons Costly, but Effective. In: *Variety*, 22-01-2007, pp. 16.

ADALIAN, Josef / SCHNEIDER, Michael: The New Mantra: Think Big. Next Fall's Pilots Still Copying Hits – But at Least They're Bold Hits. In: *Variety*, 28-11-2005, pp. 21, 75.

ADALIAN, Josef: TV Tests Its Tentpoles. New Dramas Flout Old Biz Rules. In: *Variety*, 19-11-2005, pp. 1, 85.

AKASS, Kim / MCCABE, Janet (eds.): TV To Die For. Reading *Six Feet Under*. London: I.B. Tauris 2005.

ALLEN, Robert C.: Speaking of Soap Operas. Chapel Hill / London: University of North Carolina Press 1985 (for the series-serial continuum see "Soap opera narrative structure", pp. 69-84).

ALLEN, Robert C. (ed.): To Be Continued ... . Soap Operas Around the World. London / New York: Routledge 1995 (for the series-serial continuum, with emphasis on the serial types, see Introduction, pp. 17-24).

ALLEY, Robert S. / BROWN, Irby B.: *Murphy Brown*. Anatomy of a Sitcom. An Inside Look at a Classic in the Making. New York: Bantam Doubleday 1990.

ALLRATH, Gaby / GYMNICH, Marion (eds.): Narrative Strategies in Television Series. London: Palgrave Macmillan 2005.

ALLRATH, Gaby / GYMNICH, Marion / SURKAMP Carola: Towards a Narratology of TV Series. In: Gaby Allrath / Marion Gymnich (eds.): Narrative Strategies in Television Series. Basingstoke / London: Palgrave Macmillan 2006, pp. 1-43.

ANDERSON, Christopher: Reflections on *Magnum, P.I.* In: Horace M. Newcomb (ed.): Television, The Critical View. New York / Oxford 1987^4, pp. 112-125.

ANDERSON, Christopher: Television Networks and the Uses of Drama. In: Gary Edgerton / Brian Rose (eds.): Thinking Outside the Box. Television Genres in Transition. Lexington: University of Kentucky Press 2005, pp. 65-87.

BENASSI, Stéphane: Séries et feuilletons TV. Pour une typologie des fictions télévisuelles. Liège: Editions du Céfal 2000.

BENASSI, Stéphane: Transfictions. In: Eric Maigret / Guillaume Soulez (eds.): Les raisons d'aimer ... les séries télé. Paris: Armand Colin 2007 (= MédiaMorphoses, hors série), pp. 158-162.

BLEICHER, Joan Kristin: Fernsehen als Mythos. Poetik eines narrativen Erkenntnissystems. Habilitation Thesis Wiesbaden: VS Verlag für Sozialwissenschaften 2002.

BLEICHER, Joan Kristin: Television as Myth. Poetics of a Narrtive Epistomological System. In: William Uricchio / Susanne Kinnebrock (eds.): Media Cultures. Heidelberg: University of Heidelberg Press 2007 (in print), pp. 117-128.

BONNER, Frances: Ordinary Television. London et al.: Sage 2003.

BRETT, Jason: Development Hell. The Process of Creating TV in the US. In: Julian Friedmann / Pere Roca (ed.): Writing Long-Running Television Series. Lectures from the first PILOTS workshop. Madrid: Media Business School 1993, pp. 25-49.

BUONANNO, Milly: Le formule del racconto televisivo. La sovversione del tempo nelle narrative seriali. Milano: Sansoni 2002.

BUONANNO, Milly: *Il Maresciallo Rocca*. The Italian Way to the TV Police Series. In: Horace Newcomb (ed.): The Critical View. New York / Oxford: Oxford University Press 2000^6, pp. 266-281.

BUXTON, David: From *The Avengers* to *Miami Vice*. Form and Ideology in Television Series. Manchester / New York 1990 (= Cultural Politics).

BUXTON, Rodney: *Magnum, P.I.* In: Horace Newcomb (ed.): Encyclopedia of Television. New York / London: Fitzroy Dearborn 2004^2, vol. 3, S.1397-1398.

CALABRESE, Omar: L'età neobarocca. Roma: Ed. Sagittarius Laterza 1987, 1992^3. English version: Neo-Baroque. A Sign of the Times. New Jersey: Princeton University Press 1992.

CANTOR, Muriel G. / CANTOR, Joel M.: Prime-Time Television. Content and Control. Thousand Oaks / London: Sage 1980, 1992 (= CommText Series 3).

CANTOR, Muriel G. / PINGREE, S.: The Soap Opera. Beverly Hills et al.: Sage 1983 (= CommText Series 12).

CHISHOLM, Brad: Difficult Viewing. The Pleasures of Complex Screen Narratives. In: *Critical Studies in Mass Communication* 8 (1991) 4, pp. 389-403.

CHRISTEN, Thomas / GANZ-BLÄTTLER, Ursula: Segments in an Endless Flow. Narrative Gaps and Partial Closure in *Ally McBeal*. In: Elwood Watson (ed.): Searching the Soul of *Ally McBeal*. Critical Essays. Jefferson / London: McFarland 2006, pp. 219-237.

CREEBER, Glen (ed.): Serial Television. Big Drama on the Small Screen. London: British Film Institute 2004.

CREEBER, Glen: "Taking our personal lives seriously". Intimacy, Continuity and Memory in the Television Drama Serial. In: *Media, Culture and Society* 23 (2001), pp. 439-455.

D'ACCI, J.D.: Defining Women. Television and the Case of *Cagney and Lacey*. Chapel Hill: University of Northern Carolina Press 1994.

DEMING, Caren J.: *Hill Street Blues* as Narrative. In: *Critical Studies in Mass Communication* 2 (1985), pp. 1-22.

DOLAN, Marc: The Peaks and Valleys of Serial Creativity. What Happened to / on *Twin Peaks*. In: David Lavery (ed.): Full of Secrets. Critical Approaches to *Twin Peaks*. Detroit: Wayne State University Press 1995, 30-50.

DUPONT, Florence: Homère et *Dallas*, Introduction à une critique anthropologique, Paris: Hachette 1991.

DURZAK, Manfred: *Kojak, Columbo* und deutsche Kollegen. Überlegungen zum Fernseh-Serial. In: Helmut Kreuzer / Kurt Prümm (eds.): Fernsehsendungen und ihre Formen. Typologie, Geschichte und Kritik des Programms in der BRD. Stuttgart: Reclam 1979, pp. 71-93.

ESSLIN, Martin: Aristotle and the Advertisers. The Television Commercial Considered As a Form of Drama. In: Horace Newcomb (ed.): Television. The Critical View. New York 1987[4], pp. 304-318.

ESSLIN, Martin: The Television Series as Folk Epic. In: C.W.E. Bigsby (ed.): Superculture, American Popular Culture and Europe. Bowling Green: Bowling Green State University Popular Press 1975, pp. 190-198.

FEUER, Jane: Melodrama, Serial Form and Television Today. In: *Screen* 25 (1984) 1, pp. 4-16. Reprint in: Manuel Alvarado / John O. Thompson (eds.): The Media Reader. London 1990, pp. 253-264, and in: Horace M. Newcomb (ed.): Television, The Critical View. New York / Oxford: Oxford University Press 1994[5], pp. 551-562.

FEUER, Jane / KERR, Paul / VAHIMAGI, Tise (eds.): MTM (*Mary Tyler Moore*), Quality Television. London: British Film Institute 1984.

FEUER, Jane: Narrative Form in American Network Television. In: Colin MacCabe (ed.): High Theory / Low Culture. Analyzing Popular Television and Film. Manchester: Manchester University Press 1986, pp. 101-114.

FEUER, Jane: Seeing Through the Eighties. Television and Reaganism. Durham / London: Duke University Press 1996 (for the series-serial continuum see "Serial form, melodrama, and Reaganite ideology on Eighties TV", pp. 111-130).

FEUER, Jane: Quality Drama in the US. The New "Golden Age"? In: Michele Hilmes (ed.): The Television History Book. London: British Film Institute 2003, pp. 98-102.

FISKE, John: British Cultural Studies. In: Robert C. Allen (ed.): Channels of Discourse, Reassembled. Television and Contemporary Criticism. Chapel Hill / London: University of North Carolina Press 1992[2], pp. 284-326.

FISKE, John: *Cagney and Lacey*, Reading Character Structurally and Politically. In: *Communication* 9 (1987), pp. 399-426.

FISKE, John: Popularity and Ideology. A Structuralist Reading of *Dr. Who*. In: Willard D. Rowland jr. / Bruce W. Watkins (eds.): Interpreting Television. Current Research Perspectives. Thousand Oaks / London: Sage 1984, pp. 165-198. Reprint in: Leah Vande Berg / Lawrence A. Wenner / Bruce E. Gronbeck (eds.): Critical Approaches in Television. Boston: Houghton Mifflin 2004², pp. 86-109.

FLITTERMAN-LEWIS, Sandy: All's Well That Doesn't End. Soap Opera and the Marriage Motif. In: Lynn Spigel / Denise Mann (eds.): Private Screenings. Television and the Female Consumer. Minneapolis: University of Minneapolis Press 1992, pp. 217-226.

FLITTERMAN-LEWIS, Sandy: Thighs and Whiskers. The Fascination of *Magnum, P.I.* In: *Screen* 26 (1985) 2, pp. 42-58.

GANZ-BLÄTTLER, Ursula: From Multiple to Cumulative Narrative. Thoughts on Syndication and Episodicity in Film and Broadcast Media. In: Anna Antonini (ed.): Il film e i suoi multipli / Film and Its Multiples. Udine: Forum 2003, pp. 317-323.

GANZ-BLÄTTLER, Ursula: Gedächtnis – Erinnerung – Geschichte. Überlegungen zur Zeitstruktur von Fernsehserien. In: *medien und erziehung* 42 (1998) 6, pp. 367 - 371.

GANZ-BLÄTTLER, Ursula: Der Krimi als Sport und Spiel. Das Verfolgen von Spuren und Tätern als "Infinite Game". In: Brigitte Frizzoni / Ingrid Tomkowiak (eds.): Unterhaltung. Konzepte – Formen – Wirkungen. Zürich: Chronos 2006, pp. 197-218 [2006a].

GANZ-BLÄTTLER, Ursula: Scripted and Staged Media Realities. In: *Studies in Communication Sciences* 4 (2004) 1, pp. 111-128.

GANZ-BLÄTTLER, Ursula: Serienhelden auf der Suche nach sich selbst. Ein paar Überlegungen zu deutschen Detektivserien. In: Christiane Hackl / Elizabeth Prommer / Brigitte Scherer (eds.): Models und Machos? Frauen- und Männerbilder in den Medien. Konstanz: Constance University Press 1996 (= kommunikation audiovisuell 21), pp. 151-181.

GANZ-BLÄTTLER, Ursula: Shortcuts and Detours. Der Fernsehserientext als Itinerar. In: Daniel Ammann / Heinz Moser / Roger Vaissière (eds.): Medien lesen. Der Textbegriff in der Medienwissenschaft. Festschrift Christian Doelker. Zürich: Verlag Pestalozzianum 1999, pp. 198-219.

GANZ-BLÄTTLER, Ursula: Vietnam, Väter und andere Vergangenheiten. Geschichte(n) in "crime-adventure"-Serien. In: Brigitte Scherer / Ursula Ganz-Blättler et al.: Morde im Paradies. Amerikanische Detektiv- und Abenteuerserien der 80er Jahre. Konstanz: Constance University Press 1995² (= kommunikation audiovisuell 19), pp. 68-103 [1995a].

GERAGHTY, Christine: The Continuous Serial. A Definition. In: Richard Dyer et al.: *Coronation Street*. London: British Film Institute 1981, pp. 9-26.

GERAGHTY, Christine: Women and Soap Opera. A Study in Prime Time Soaps. Cambridge: Polity Press 1991.

GRADNITZER, Louisa / PITTSON, Todd: X Marks the Spot. On Location with the *X-Files*. Vancouver: Arsenal Pulp Press 1999.

GRAHAM, Allison: "Are You Now or Have You Ever Been?" Conspiracy Theory and the *X-Files*. In: David Lavery / Angela Hague / Marla Cartwright (eds.): "Deny All Knowledge". Reading the *X-Files*. Syracuse: Syracuse Univ. Press 1996, pp. 52-62.

GRASSO, Aldo: Buona maestra. Perché i telefilm sono diventati più importanti dei libri e del cinema. Milano: Mondadori 2007.

GRAY, Jonathan / MITTELL, Jason: Speculation on Spoilers. *Lost* Fandom, Narrative Consumption and Rethinking Textuality. In: *Particip@tions* 4 (2007) 1 (see *www.participations.org/Volume%204/Issue%201/4_01_graymittell.htm*; 18-08-2017).

GRIGNAFFINI, Giorgio: La mappa dei generi televisivi. In: Ibid.: I generi televisivi. Rome: Carocchi 2004 (= Le bussole).

GWENLLIAN-JONES, Sara / PEARSON, Roberta E. (eds.): Cult Television. Minneapolis: University of Minnesota Press 2004.

GWENLLIAN-JONES, Sara: Histories, Fictions and *Xena, Warrior Princess*. In: *Journal of Television & New Media* 1 (2000) 4, pp. 403-417 [2000a].

GWENLLIAN-JONES, Sara: Starring Lucy Lawless? (*Xena*) In: *Continuum* 14 (2000) 1, pp. 9-22 [2000b].

HAGEDORN, Roger: Doubtless to Be Continued. A Brief History of Serial Narrative. In Robert C. Allen (ed.): To Be Continued ... . Soap Operas Around the World. London / New York: Routledge 1995, pp. 27-48.

HAGUE, Angela: Infinite Games. The Derationalization of Detection in *Twin Peaks*. In: David Lavery (ed.): Full of Secrets. Critical Approaches to *Twin Peaks*. Detroit: Wayne State University Press 1995, pp. 130-143.

HAINES, Harry W.: The Pride is Back. *Rambo, Magnum, P.I.*, and the Return Trip to Vietnam. In: Richard Morris / Peter Ehrenhaus (eds.): Cultural Legacies of Vietnam. Uses of the Past in the Present. Norwood 1990, pp. 99-123.

HAMAMI, Amira: Figurenentwicklung und Backstory in Quality TV-Serien am Beispiel von *Six Feet Under*. Master thesis, University of Fribourg 2007.

HAMMOND, Michael / MAZDON, Lucy (eds.): The Contemporary Television Series. Edinburgh: Edinburgh University Press 2005.

HÄUSERMANN, Jürg: Und dabei liebe ich euch beide .... Unterhaltung durch Schlager und Fernsehserien. Wiesbaden 1978.

HICKETHIER, Knut: Die Fernsehserie und das Serielle des Fernsehens. Lüneburg 1991 (= Lüneburger Beiträge zur Kulturwissenschaft 2).

HOKE-KAHWATI, Donna: Is Your Favorite Primetime Show a Soap? Shows Like *L.A. Law* and *Thirty-Something* Don't Think So. Do You? In: *Soap Opera Digest*, 11.12.1990, pp. 24-29.

JANCOVICH, Mark / LYONS, James (eds.): Quality Popular Television. Cult TV, the Industry and Fans. London: British Film Institute 2003.

JENKINS, Henry: "Do You Enjoy Making the Rest of Us Feel Stupid?" *alt.tv.twinpeaks*, the Trickster Author, and Viewer Mastery. In: David Lavery (ed.): Full of Secrets. Critical Approaches to *Twin Peaks*. Detroit: Wayne State University Press 1995, pp. 51-69. Reprint in: Ibid.: Fans, Bloggers, and Gamers. Exploring Participatory Culture. New York / London: New York University Press 2006, pp. 115-133.

JENKINS, Steve: *Hill Street Blues*. In: Jane Feuer / Paul Kerr / Tise Vahiamgi (eds.): MTM. Quality Television. London: British Film Institute 1984, pp. 183-199.

JOHNSON, Catherine: Quality / Cult Television. *The X-Files* and *Buffy the Vampire Slayer* in US Television of the 1990s. In: Ibid.: Telefantasy. London: British Film Institute 2005, pp. 95-123 [C. Johnson 2005b].

JOHNSON, Catherine: Regulated Innovation. *Star Trek* and the Commercial Strategy of US Television of the 1960s. In: Ibid.: Telefantasy. London: British Film Institute 2005, pp. 68-94 [C. Johnson 2005a].

JOHNSON, Steven: Everything Bad Is Good for You. How Today's Popular Culture Is Actually Making Us Smarter. New York: Riverhead Books 2005 [S. Johnson 2005].

JURGA, Martin: Fernsehtextualität und Rezeption. Opladen: Westdeutscher Verlag 1999.

KELLNER, Douglas: TV Spectacle. Aliens, Conspiracies, and Biotechnology in *The X-Files*. In: Ibid.: Media Spectacle. New York: Routledge 2003, pp. 120-159.

KELLNER, Douglas: *The X-Files* and the Aesthetics and Politics of Postmodern Pop. In: *Journal of Aesthetics and Art Criticism* 57 (1999) 2, pp. 161-176.

KOZLOFF, Sarah Ruth: Narrative Theory and Television. In: Robert C. Allen (ed.): Channels of Discourse, Reassembled. Television and Contemporary Criticism. Chapel Hill / London: University of North Carolina Press 1992, pp. 67-100.

KRAJEWSKA, Anna: Des visages de l'amour à travers la série télévisée Ally McBeal. Pour une pastorale du téléspectateur. Paris: L'Harmattan 2007.

KROGERUS, Mikael: Der Serientäter (Steven Bochco). In: *NZZ Folio*, October 2006, pp. 28-32 (Krogerus 2006b, accessible at *www.nzzfolio.ch/www/d80bd71b-b264-4db4-afd0-277884b93470/showarticle/1175e94c-60a9-4147-9a80-2bec03b40a64.aspx* (18-08-2018).

LAVERY, David / HAGUE, Angela / CARTWRIGHT, Marla (eds.): "Deny All Knowledge". Reading the *X-Files*. Syracuse: Syracuse University Press 1996.

LAVERY, David (ed.): Full of Secrets. Critical Approaches to *Twin Peaks*. Detroit: Wayne State University Press 1995.

LIN, C.A.: Network Prime-Time Programming Strategies in the 1980s. In: *Journal of Broadcasting and Electronic Video* 39 (1995) 4, pp. 482-495.

LOWRY, Brian: Alphabet's *Lost* Needs an Exit Strategy. In: *Variety*, 27-11-2006, p. 17.

LOWRY, Brian: ... And Next Up. Serial Sitcoms. In: *Variety*, 12-06-2006, pp. 16, 18.

MARC, David: Demographic Vistas. Television in American Culture. Philadelphia: Univ. of Pennsylvania Press 1984, 1996^2.

MARC, David / THOMPSON, Robert J.: Prime Time, Prime Movers. From *I Love Lucy* to *L.A. Law* - America's Greatest TV Shows and the People Who Created Them. Boston / Toronto / London: Syracuse University Press 1992, 1995.

MARKLEY, Robert: Alien Assassination. The *X-Files* and the Paranoid Structure of History. In: *Camera Obscura* 40 / 41 (1997), pp. 77-102.

MARRONE, Gianfranco: *Montalbano*. Affermazioni e trasformazioni di un eroe mediatico. Roma: RAI-ERI 2003.

MAZDON, Lucy: Introduction. Histories. In: Michael Hammond / Ibid. (eds.): The Contemporary Television Series. Edinburgh: Edinburgh University Press 2005, pp. 3-10.

MCGRATH, Charles: The Triumph of the Prime-Time Novel. In: Horace M. Newcomb (ed.): Television, The Critical View. New York / Oxford: Oxford University Press 2000^6, pp. 242-252.

MCLUHAN, Marshall: Horse Opera and Soap Opera. In: Ibid.: The Mechanical Bride. Folklore of Industrial Man. New York: Vanguard Press 1951, Boston: Beacon 1964, and Corte Madera: Gingko Press 2001, pp. 155-158.

MILLS, Brett: Television Sitcom. London: British Film Institute 2005.

MITTELL, Jason: Genre and Television. From Cop Shows to Cartoons in American Culture. New York / London: Routledge 2004.

MITTELL, Jason: Narrative Complexity in Contemporary American Television. In: *The Velvet Light Trap* 58 (2006), pp. 29-40.

MORREALE, Joanne: Sitcoms Say Good-Bye. The Cultural Spectacle of *Seinfeld*'s Last Episode. In: Ibid.. (ed.): Critiquing the Sitcom. A Reader. Syracuse: Syracuse University Press 2003.

Museum of Radio and Television (ed.): Worlds Without End. The Art and History of the Soap Opera. New York: Harry N. Abrams, Inc. 1998.

NDALIANIS, Angela: Television and the Neo-Baroque. In: Michael Hammond / Lucy Mazdon (eds.): The Contemporary Television Series. Edinburgh: Edinburgh University Press 2005, pp. 83-101.

NELSON, Robin: Analysing TV Fiction. How to Study Television Drama. In: Glen Creeber (ed.): Tele-Visions. An Introduction to Studying Television. London: British Film Institute 2006, pp. 74-92.

NELSON, Robin: TV Drama. "Flexi-Narrative Form" and "a New Affective Order". In: Eckart Voigts-Virchov (ed.): Mediated Drama, Dramatized Media. Trier: Wissenschaftlicher Verlag 2000 (= Contemporary Drama in English 7), pp. 111-118.

NELSON, Robin (ed.): State of Play. Contemporary High-End TV Drama. Manchester: Manchester University Press 2008.

NELSON, Robin: TV Drama in Transition. Form, Values and Cultural Change. Houndsmills / New York: Macmillan 1997.

NEWCOMB, Horace M.: *Cagney and Lacey*. In: Ibid. / Cary O'Dell (eds.): Museum of Broadcast Communications' Encyclopedia of Television. Chicago: Fitzroy Dearborn 1997, vol. 1, pp. 274-277. And in: Ibid. (ed.): Encyclopedia of Television. London / New York: Fitzroy Dearborn 2004^2, vol. 1, pp. 400-403.

NEWCOMB, Horace M.: Evaluation, Analysis, Reform, and the Peabody Awards. In: *Flow* 2 (2005) 8, 26-07-2005; see *http://flowtv.org/?p=590* (18-08-2017).

NEWCOMB, Horace: From Old Frontier to New Frontier. In: Lynn Spigel / Michael Curtin (eds.): Revolution Wasn't Televised. Sixties Television and Social Conflict. London: Routledge 1997, pp. 287-302.

NEWCOMB, Horace M.: *Magnum*. The Champagne of TV? In: *Channels of Communication* (1985) May / June, pp. 23-26. Italian version: *Magnum P.I. La champagne della TV?* In: Ibid.: La televisione da forum a biblioteca. Milano: R.C.S. Libri 1999, pp. 95-103. Also reprod. in *Daily Variety* (18-07-1985), and *Little Voices* (1985 #3).

NEWCOMB, Horace M.: Media Institutions. The Creation of Television Drama. In: Klaus Bruhn Jensen / Nicholas W. Jankowski (eds.): A Handbook of Qualitative Methodologies for Mass Communication Research. London / New York: Routledge 1991, pp. 93-107.

NEWCOMB, Horace M.: Narrative and Genre. In: John D.H. Downing (ed.): The Sage Handook of Media Studies. Thousand Oaks / London: Sage 2004, pp. 413-428.

NEWCOMB, Horace M.: Reflections on TV. The Most Popular Art. In: Gary Edgerton / Brian Rose (eds.): Thinking Outside the Box. Television Genres in Transition. Lexington: University of Kentucky Press 2005, pp. 17-36.

NEWCOMB, Horace: Studying Television. Same Questions, Different Contexts. In: *Cinema Journal* 45 (2005) 1, pp. 107-111.

NEWCOMB, Horace M. / HIRSCH, Paul M.: Television as a Cultural Forum. Implications for Research. In: *Quarterly Review of Film Studies* 8 (1983) 2, pp. 45-55. Reprint in: H.M. Newcomb (ed.): Television, The Critical View. New York: Oxford University Press 2000^6, pp. 561-573.

NEWCOMB, Horace M.: TV. The Most Popular Art. New York: Doubleday 1974.

NEWMAN, Michael Z.: From Beats to Arcs. Towards a Poetics of Television Narrative. In: *The Velvet Lighttrap* 58 (2006), pp. 16-28.

OLTEAN, Tudor: Series and Seriality in Media Culture. In: *European Journal of Communication* 8 (1993) 1, pp. 5-31.

OWENS, Richard H.: Perspectives on the Vietnam War in the TV Series *Magnum, P.I.* In: *Vietnam War Generation Journal* 1 (2001) 1, pp. 81-87.

PORTER, Michael J. / LARSON, Deborah L. / HARTHCOCK, Allison / BERG NELLIS, Kelly: Re(de)fining Narrative Events. In: *Journal of Popular Film and Television* 30 (2002) 1, pp. 23-30.

PROBST, Chris: Darkness Descends on *The X-Files*. Cinematographer John Bartley, CSC Lends Weekly Series an Eerie Ambience. In: *American Cinematographer* (June 1995), pp. 28-32.

REEVES, Jimmy L., EPSTEIN, Michael / ROGERS, Mark C.: Postmodernism and Television. Speaking of *Twin Peaks*. In: David Lavery (ed.): Full of Secrets. Critical Approaches to *Twin Peaks*. Detroit: Wayne State University Press 1995, pp. 173-195.

REEVES, Jimmy L. / ROGERS, Mark C. / EPSTEIN, Michael: Rewriting Popularity. The Cult Files. In: David Lavery / Angela Hague / Marla Cartwright (eds.): "Deny All Knowledge". Reading the *X-Files*. Syracuse: Syracuse Univ. Press 1996, pp. 22-35.

ROGERS, Mark C. / EPSTEIN, Michael / REEVES, Jimmy L.: *The Sopranos*. HBO Brand Equity. The Art of Commerce in the Age of Digital Reproduction. In: David Lavery (ed.): Investigating *The Sopranos*. New York: Columbia University Press / London: Wallflower Press 2002, pp. 42-57.

SANDOZ, Thomas: Derrick. L'ordre des choses. Grolley: Les Éditions de l'Hèbe 1999.

SCHATZ, Tom: *St. Elsewhere* and the Evolution of the Ensemble Series. In: Horace M. Newcomb (ed.): Television, The Critical View. New York / Oxford: Oxford University Press 1987^4, pp. 85-100.

SCHERER, Brigitte: Das Beispiel *Magnum P.I.* In: Peter Hoff / Dieter Wiedemann (eds.): Serie, Kunst im Alltag. Berlin: Vistas 1992 (= Beiträge zur Film- und Fernsehwissenschaft), pp. 99-104.

SCHERER, Brigitte / GANZ-BLÄTTLER, Ursula / GROSSKOPF, Monika / WAHL, Ute: Morde im Paradies. Amerikanische Detektiv- und Abenteuerserien der 80er Jahre. München: Oelschläger 1994 and 1995² (= kommunikation audiovisuell 19).

SCHERER, Brigitte: Thomas Magnum und die Frauen. Produktion und Rezeption einer US-Serie. Doctoral Thesis Tübingen / Konstanz: Constance University Press 2000 (= kommunikation aktuell 27).

SCHNEIDER, Michael: Serials Get Soggy. In: *Variety*, 12-06-2006, pp. 16, 18.

SCHNEIDER, Michael: Serials Losing Pop at Webs. In: *Variety*, 06-05-2002, p. 33.

SCONCE, Jeffrey: Dickens, Selznick, and *South Park*. In: John Glavin (ed.): Dickens on Screen. Cambridge: Cambridge University Press 2003, pp. 171-187.

SCONCE, Jeffrey: What if? Charting Television's New Textual Boundaries. In: Lynn Spigel / Jan Olsson (eds.): Television After TV. Essay on a Medium in Transition. Durham / London: Duke University Press 2004, pp. 93-112.

SEITER, Ellen / WILSON, Mary Jeanne. Soap Opera Survival Tactics. In: Gary Edgerton / Brian Rose (eds.): Thinking Outside the Box. Television Genres in Transition. Lexington: University of Kentucky Press 2005, pp. 136-155.

SIMON, Ron: Serial Seduction. Living in Other Worlds. In: Museum of Radio and Television (ed.): Worlds Without End. The Art and History of the Soap Opera. New York: Harry N. Abrams, Inc. 1998, pp. 11-39.

SMITH, Greg M.: Beautiful TV. The Art and Argument of *Ally McBeal*. Austin: University of Texas Press 2007.

THIERFELDER, Ulrike: The Magical Formula of *Harry Potter*. Master thesis, University of Lugano 2006.

THOMPSON, Kristin: Storytelling in Film and Television. Cambridge: Harvard University Press 2003 (for the series / serial continuum see pp. 36-73).

THOMPSON, Robert J.: From *Hill Street Blues* to *ER*. Television's Second Golden Age. New York: Continuum 1996.

TORRES, Sasha: War and Remembrance: Televisual Narrative, National Memory, and *China Beach*. In: *camera obscura* 33/34 (1994/95), pp. 146-165.

TULLOCH, John / ALVARADO, Manuel (eds.): *Doctor Who*. The Unfolding Text. London: Macmillan, and New York: St. Martin's Press 1983 (for the series-serial continuum see "Terms", pp. ix-xi).

TURNBULL, Sue / STRANIERI, Vyvyan: Bite me. Narrative Structures and *Buffy the Vampire Slayer*. Melbourne: Australian Center for the Moving Image (ACMI) 2003.

WATSON, Elwood (ed.): Searching the Soul of *Ally McBeal*. Critical Essays. Jefferson / London: McFarland 2006.

WEHN, Karin: Die deutschen Synchronisation(en) von *Magnum, P.I.* Rahmenbedingungen, serienspezifische Übersetzungsprobleme und Unterschiede zwischen Original- und Synchronfassungen. Master Thesis Halle: Martin-Luther-Universität 1996 (= Hallische Medienarbeten 2).

WEHN, Karin: Redubbings of US-American Series for German Television. The Case of *Magnum, P.I.* In: Yves Gambier (ed.): Translating for the Media. Papers from the International Conference Languages and the Media. Berlin / Turku: Centre for Translation and Interpreting 1998.

WHITE, Mimi: Crossing Wavelengths. The Diegetic and Referential Imaginary of American Commercial Television. In: *Cinema Journal* 25 (1986) Winter, pp. 51-64.

WHITE, Mimi: Television. A Narrative, a History. In: *Cultural Studies* 3 (1989) 3, S. 228-300.

WITTEBOLS, James H.: Watching *M*A*S*H*, Watching America. A Social History of the 1972-1983 Television Series. Jefferson: McFarland & Co. 1998, 2003.

14.5.2 Television studies / broadcast studies in general

ADORNO, Theodor W.: How to Look at Television. In: *Quarterly of Film, Radio and Television* 3 (1954), pp. 213-235. Reprint in: J.M. Bernstein (ed.): The Culture Industry. Selected Essays on Mass Culture. London / New York: Routledge 1991, pp. 158-177.

ALLEN, Robert C. (ed.): Channels of Discourse, Reassembled. Television and Contemporary Criticism. Chapel Hill / London: University of North Carolina Press 1992².

ANDERSON, Christopher: Hollywood TV. The Studio System in the Fifties. Austin: University of Texas Press 1994.

ANDERSON, Christopher: Negotiating the Television Text. The Transformation of *Warner Bros. Presents*. In: Robert J. Thompson / Gary Burns (eds.): Making Television. Authorship and the Production Process. New York / Westport / London: Praeger 1990, pp. 95-116.

AULETTA, Ken: Three Blind Mice. How the TV Networks Lost Their Way. New York 1991.

AUTER, Philip J.: TV That Talks Back. An Experimental Validation of a Parasocial Interaction Scale. In: *Journal of Broadcasting and Electronic Media* 36 (1992) 2, pp. 173-181.

BLEICHER, Joan Kristin: Fernsehen als Mythos. Poetik eines narrativen Erkenntnissystems. Habilitationsschrift Wiesbaden: Westdeutscher Verlag 1999.

BUONANNO, Milly: L'età della televisione. Esperienze e teorie. Rom: Ed. Laterza 2006. English version: The Age of Television. Experiences and Theories. Bristol: Intellect Ltd. 2008.

CALDWELL, John Thornton: Convergence Television. Aggregating Form and Repurposing Content in the Culture of Conglomeration. In: Lynn Spigel / Jan Olsson (eds.): Television After TV. Essays on a Medium in Transition. Durham / London: Duke University Press 2004, pp. 41-74.

CALDWELL, John Thornton: Critical Industrial Practice. Branding, Repurposing, and the Migratory Patterns of Industrial Texts. In: *Television and New Media* 7 (2006) 2, pp. 99-134.

CALDWELL, John Thornton: Modes of Production. The Televisual Apparatus. In: Robert Stam / Toby Miller (eds.): Film and Theory. An Anthology. Oxford: Blackwell 2000, pp. 125-143.

CALDWELL, John Thornton: Televisuality. Style, Crisis and Authority in American Television. New Brunswick: Rutgers University Press 1995 (Communication, Media and Culture). Extract in German published as: Televisualität. In: Ralf Adelmann / Jan O. Hesse / Judith Keilbach / Markus Stauff / Matthias Thiele (eds.): Grundlagentexte zur Fernsehwissenschaft. Theorie – Geschichte – Analyse. München: UTB-Taschenbuch 2002, pp. 165-202.

COMSTOCK, George / SCHARRER, Erica: Television. What's On, Who's Watching, and What It Means. San Diego et al.: Academic Press 1999.

CORNER, John: Critical Ideas in Television Studies. Oxford: Clarendon Press 1999 (for the series-serial continuum see pp. 57-58).

DIETRICH-BERTINI, Sonia: La nascita della televisione della Svizzera Italiana. Un problema di federalismo. Fribourg: Institut d'histoiere moderne 1983.

Eco, Umberto: TV. La trasparenza perduta. In: Ibid.: Sette anni di desiderio. Cronache 1977-1983. Milano: Bompiani 1983, pp. 163-179. English, slightly abridged version: A Guide to the Neo-Television of the 1980s. In: *Framework* 25 (1988), pp. 18-27.

Edgerton, Gary / Rose, Brian (eds.): Thinking Outside the Box. Television Genres in Transition. Lexington: University of Kentucky Press 2005.

Ellis, John: Seeing Things. Television in the Age of Uncertainty. London: I.B. Tauris 2000.

Ellis, John: Visible Fictions. Cinema – Television – Video. London: Routledge & Kegan Paul 1982, and Routledge 1992² (for the series-serial continuum see "Broadcast TV narration", pp. 145-159).

Esslin, Martin: Aristotle and The Advertisers. The Television Commercial Considered As a Form of Drama. In: Horace Newcomb (ed.): Television. The Critical View. New York 1987⁴, pp. 304-318.

Feyles, Giuseppe: La televisione secondo Aristotele. Rom: Editori Riuniti 2003.

Fiske, John: Television Culture. Popular Pleasures and Politics. London / New York: Methuen 1987, Routledge 1999.

Fiske, John / Hartley, John: Reading Television. London / New York: Routledge 1984.

Gripsrud, Jostein: Broadcast Television. The Chances of its Survival in a Digital Age. In: Lynn Spigel / Jan Olsson (eds.): Television After TV. Essay on a Medium in Transition. Durham / London: Duke University Press 2004, pp. 210-223.

Gripsrud, Jostein: Television, Broadcasting, Flow. Key Metaphors in TV Theory. In: Christine Geraghty / David Lusted (eds.): The Television Studies Book. London / New York: Arnold 1998, pp. 17-32.

Hall, Stuart [1974]: Encoding / Decoding. Reprint in: Ibid. / Dorothy Hobson / Andrew Lowe / Paul Willis (eds.): Culture, Media, Language. Working Papers in Cultural Studies, 1972-79. Birmingham / London: Hutchinson 1980, pp. 128-138.

Hallenberger, Gerd: TV Fiction in a Reality TV Age. In: *Studies in Communication Sciences* 4 (2004) 1, pp. 169-181.

Hilmes, Michele: Invisible Men. *Amos'n'Andy* and the Roots of Broadcast Discourse. In: *Critical Studies in Mass Communication* 10 (1993) 4, pp. 301-321.

HILMES, Michele: The Origins of the Commercial Broadcasting System of the United States. In: Edgar Lersch / Helmut Schanze (eds.): Die Idee des Radios. Von den Anfängen in Europa und den USA bis 1933. Konstanz: Constance University Press 2004 (= Jahrbuch Medien und Geschichte), pp. 73-81.

HILMES, Michele: Radio Voices. American Broadcasting, 1922 – 1952. Minneapolis / London: University of Minnesota Press 1997.

HILMES, Michele (ed.): The Television History Book. London: British Film Institute 2003.

HIMMELSTEIN, Hal: Television Myth and the American Mind. New York / Westport / London: Praeger 1984, 1994².

HOLT, Jennifer: Vertical Vision. Deregulation, Industrial Economy and Prime-Time Design. In: Mark Jancovich / James Lyons (eds.): Quality Popular Television. Cult TV, the Industry and Fans. London: British Film Institute 2003, pp. 11-31.

JANKOWSKI, Gene F. / FUCHS, David C.: Television Today and Tomorrow. It Won't Be What You Think. New York: Oxford University Press 1995.

JENSEN, Klaus Bruhn: Super Flow, Channel Flows, and Audience Flows. A Study of Viewer's Reception of Television as Flow. In: *Nordicom Review of Nordic Mass Communication Research* (1994) 2, pp. 1-13.

KOMPARE, Derek: Publishing Flow. DVD Box Sets and the Reconception of Television. In: *Television and New Media* 7 (2006) 4, 335-360.

KOMPARE, Derek: Rerun Nation. How Repeats Invented American Television. London et al.: Routledge 2004.

KRUMMENACHER, Theo: Rundfunkfreiheit und Rundfunkorganisation. Doctoral thesis, Berne: University of Berne 1988.

LOTZ, Amanda: The Television Will Be Revolutionized. New York: New York University Press 2007.

MARC, David / THOMPSON, Robert J.: Television in the Antenna Age. A Concise History. Malden / Oxford: Blackwell 2005.

MEDHURST, Jamie: A (Very) Brief History of Television. In: Glen Creeber (ed.): TeleVisions. An Introduction to Studying Television. London: British Film Institute 2006, pp. 115-123.

MISSIKA, Jean Louis: La fin de la télévision. Paris: Seuil 2006.

MULLEN, Megan: The Rise of Cable Programming in the United States. Revolution or Evolution? Austin: University of Texas Press 2003 (= Texas Film and Media Studies Series).

NDALIANIS, Angela: Neo-Baroque Aesthetics and Contemporary Entertainment. Cambridge: MIT Press 2004.

NEWCOMB, Horace M. / HIRSCH, Paul M.: Television as a Cultural Forum. Implications for Research. In: *Quarterly Review of Film Studies* 8 (1983), pp. 45-55. Reprint in: Horace M. Newcomb (ed.): Television, The Critical View. New York / Oxford: Oxford University Press 1987[4], pp. 455-470, and ibid. 2000[6], pp. 561-573.

NEWCOMB, Horace M. (ed.): Television, The Critical View. New York / Oxford: Oxford University Press 1987[4].

NEWCOMB, Horace M. (ed.): Television, The Critical View. New York / Oxford: Oxford University Press 1994[5].

NEWCOMB, Horace M. (ed.): Television, The Critical View. New York / Oxford: Oxford University Press 2000[6].

RÜHL, Manfred: Rundfunk publizistisch begreifen. Reflexionstheoretische Überlegungen zum Primat programmierter Programme. In. *Publizistik* 40 (1995) 3, pp. 279-304.

SCANNELL, Paddy: Public Service Broadcasting. The History of a Concept. In: Andrew Goodwin / Gary Whannel (eds.): Understanding Television. London / New York: Routledge 1990, 1995, pp. 11-29.

SPIGEL, Lynn: Make Room For TV. Television and the Family Ideal in Postwar America. Chicago / London: University of Chicago Press 1992.

SPIGEL, Lynn / CURTIN, M. (eds.): Revolution Wasn't Televised. Sixties Television and Social Conflict. London: Routledge 1997.

STEMPEL, Tom: Storytellers to the Nation. A History of American Television Writing. New York: Continuum 1992.

VANDE BERG, Leah / WENNER, Lawrence A. / GRONBECK, Bruce E. (eds.): Critical Approaches to Television. Boston: Houghton Mifflin 1998, 2004[2].

WILLIAMS, Raymond: Television. Technology and Cultural Form. Hanover / London Wesleyan 1992[2], and London / New York: Routledge 2003[3].

WILLIAMS, Phil: Feeding Off the Past. The Evolution of the Television Rerun. In: Horace Newcomb (ed.): Television. The Critical View. New York: Oxford University Press 2000^6, pp. 52-73.

ZACCONE, Teodosi A. / MEDOLAGO, Albani F.: Con lo stato e con il mercato? Verso nuovi modelli di televisione pubblica nel mondo. Milano: Mondadori 2000.

14.5.3 Episodic narratives in other media / in general

BACHLEITNER, Norbert: Kleine Geschichte des deutschen Feuilletonromans. Tübingen: Gunter Narr 1999.

BESSON, Anne: D'Asimov à Tolkien. Cycles et séries dans la littérature de genre. Paris: CNRS 2004.

DE FOREST, Tim: Storytelling in the Pulps, Comics and Radio. How Technology Changed Popular Fiction in America. Jefferson et al.: McFarland 2004.

DYER, Richard: Kill and Kill Again (*Copycat, Seven, Millennium*). In: *Sight and Sound* (1997) 9, pp. 14-17.

MCCRACKEN, Scott: Pulp. Reading Popular Fiction. Manchester / New York: Manchester University Press 1998.

MIELKE, Christine: Zyklisch-serielle Narration. Berlin / New York: de Gruyter 2006.

OSTWALD, Susanne: Ende gut, alles gut. In: *Neue Zürcher Zeitung*, 13.4.2002, p. 75.

SINGER, Ben: Fiction Tie-Ins and Narrative Intelligibility, 1911-1918. In: *Film History* 5 (1993), pp. 489-504.

SINGER, Ben: Melodrama and Modernity. Early Sensational Cinema and Its Contexts. New York: Columbia University Press 2001.

THOMAS, Scott: The Making of the Potterverse. A Month-by-Month Look at Harry's First Ten Years. Toronto: ECW Press 2007.

14.5.4 Narratology / ludology / genre theory / gender theory

AARSETH, Espen: Genre Trouble. Narrativism and the Art of Simulation. In: Noah Wardrip-Fruin / Pat Harrison (eds.): First Person. New Media as Story, Performance, and Game. Cambridge, Mass.: MIT Press 2004, pp. 45-55 [Aarseth 2004a].

AARSETH, Espen: Quest Games as Post-Narrative Discourse. In: Marie-Laure Ryan (ed.): Narrative Across Media. The Languages of Storytelling. Lincoln / London: University of Nebraska Press 2004, pp. 361-376 [Aarseth 2004b].

ADAM, Jean-Michel / REVAZ, Françoise: L'analyse des récits. Paris: Seuil 1996.

AGGER, Ben: Gender, Culture and Power. Toward a Feminist Postmodern Critical Theory. Westport / London: Praeger 1998.

BILANDZIC, Helena / KINNEBROCK, Susanne: Persuasive Wirkungen narrativer Unterhaltungsangebote. Theoretische Überlegungen zum Einfluss von Narrativität auf Transportation. In: Werner Wirth / Holger Schramm / Volker Gehrau (eds.): Unterhaltung durch Medien. Theorie und Messung. Köln: Herbert von Halem 2006, pp. 103-126.

BORDWELL, David / THOMPSON, Kristin: Film Art. An Introduction. New York: Alfred A. Knopf 1986, 2003^7.

BORDWELL, David: Neo-Structuralist Narratology and the Fractions of Filmic Storytelling. In: Marie-Laure Ryan (ed.): Narrative Across Media. The Languages of Storytelling. Lincoln / London: University of Nebraska Press 2004, pp. 203-219.

BOURDIEU, Pierre: La domination masculine. Paris: Seuil 1998. English version: Masculine Domination. Stanford: Stanford University Press 2002.

BRANIGAN, Edward R.: Narrative Comprehension and Film. London / New York: Routledge 1992.

CAILLOIS, Roger: The Detective Novel as Game. In: Glenn W. Most und William W. Stowe (Hrsg.): The Poetics of Murder. Detective Fiction and Literary Theory. New York, London 1983, 1-12.

CAWELTI, John G.: Adventure, Mystery, and Romance. Formula Stories as Art and Popular Culture. Chicago / London 1976.

CAWELTI, John G.: The Question of Popular Genres Revisited. In: Gary R. Edgerton / Michael T. Marsden / Jack Nachbar (eds.): In the Eye of the Beholder. Critical Perspectives in Popular Film and Television. Bowling Green: Bowling Green State Univ. Popular Press 1997, pp. 67-84.

CAWELTI, John G.: The Six-Gun Mystique. Bowling Green: Bowling Green State University Popular Press 1970, 1974.

CAWELTI, John G.: The Six-Gun Mystique Sequel. Bowling Green: Bowling Green State University Popular Press 1999.

CHATMAN, Seymour: Story and Discourse. Narrative Structure in Fiction and Film. Ithaca / London: Cornell University Press 1978, 1993⁶.

CHRISTEN, Thomas: Das Ende im Spielfilm. Vom klassischen Hollywood zu Antonionis offenen Formen. Marburg: Schüren 2001 (= Zürcher Filmstudien 7).

COBLEY, Paul: Narrative. London / New York: Routledge 2001, 2005.

COHAN, Steven / SHIRES, Linda M.: Telling Stories. A Theoretical Analysis of Narrative Fiction. London / New York: Routledge 1988.

COLERIDGE, Samuel Taylor: Biographia Literaria. Reprint Princeton: Princeton University Press 1985.

COLERIDGE, Samuel Taylor: Coleridge's Poetry and Prose. Authoritative Texts, Criticism. New York: Norton 2004.

CORNER, John: What Can We Say About Documentary? In: *Media, Culture and Society* 22 (2000) 5, pp. 681-688.

COSTE, Didier: Narrative as Communication. Minneapolis: University of Minnesota Press 1990.

COVER, Rob: Audience inter/active. Interactive Media, Narrative Control and Reconceiving Audience History. In: *New Media & Society* 8 (2006) 1, pp. 139-158.

CREEBER, Glen / MILLER, Toby / TULLOCH, John (eds.): The Television Genre Book. London: British Film Institute 2001.

CULLEN, Jim (ed.): Popular Culture in American History. Malden: Blackwell 2001.

CULLER, Jonathan: Fabula and Sjuzhet in the Analysis of Narrative. Some American Discussions. Reprint in: Susana Onega / José Angel García(eds.): Narratology. An Introduction. London: Longman 1996, pp. 93-102.

CURRIE, Gregory: The Nature of Fiction. New York / Cambridge: Cambridge University Press 1992.

DARST, David High: Converting Fiction. Counter Reformational Closure in the Seculare Literature of Golden Age Spain. Chapel Hill: Univ. of North Carolina 1998.

DERY, Mark: Culture Jamming. Hacking, Slashing and Sniping in the Empire of Signs, originally published 1993 (= Open Magazine Pamphlet Series 25; for an annotated version see *http://markdery.com/?page_id=154* (18-08-2017).

FEUER, Jane: Genre Study and Television. In: Robert C. Allen (ed.): Channels of Discourse, Reassembled. Television and Contemporary Criticism. Chapel Hill / London: University of North Carolina Press 1992², pp. 138-160.

FLEISCHMANN, Suzanne: Tense and Narrativity. From Medieval Performance to Modern Fiction. Austin: University of Texas Press 1990.

FLUDERNIK, Monika: Einführung in die Erzähltheorie. Darmstadt: Wissenschaftliche Buchgesellschaft 2006.

FLUDERNIK, Monika: The Fictions of Language and the Languages of Fiction. London / New York: Routledge 1993.

FLUDERNIK, Monika: Towards a "Natural" Narratology. London / New York: Routledge 1996.

FREYTAG, Gustav: Die Technik des Dramas. Leipzig: S. Hirzel 1863, Reclam 1983. English version: Technique of the Drama. An Exposition of Dramatic Composition and Art. New York: Benjamin Blom 1968.

HARTMANN, Bernd: Literatur, Film und das Computerspiel. Münster: LIT 2004 (= Beiträge zur Medienästhetik und Mediengeschichte 22).

HELBLING, Brigitte: Vernetzte Texte. Ein literarisches Verfahren von Weltenbau. Mit den Fallbeispielen Ingeborg Bachmann, Uwe Johnson und einer Digression zum Comic Strip *Doonesbury*. Doctoral Thesis Hamburg / Würzburg: Königshausen und Neumann 1995 (= Epistemata: Reihe Literaturwissenschaft 138).

HERMAN, David: Story Logic. Problems and Possibilities of Narrative. Lincoln / London: University of Nebraska Press 2002, 2004.

HILTUNEN, Ari: Aristotle in Hollywood. Bristol: Intellectbooks 2002.

JERSLEV, Anne (ed.): Realism and "Reality" in Film and Media. Copenhagen: Univ. of Copenhagen / Museum Tusculanum Press 2002 (= Northern Light Series).

KAFALENOS, Emma: Overview of the Music and Narrative Field. In: Marie-Laure Ryan (ed.): Narrative Across Media. The Languages of Storytelling. Lincoln / London: University of Nebraska Press 2004, pp. 275-282.

KERMODE, Frank: The Sense of an Ending. New York: Oxford University Press 1967.

KOZLOFF, Sarah Ruth: Invisible Storytellers. Voice-Over Narration in American Fiction Films. Berkeley / Los Angeles 1988.

KRÜTZEN, Michaela: Dramaturgie des Films. Wie Hollywood erzählt. Frankfurt: Fischer 2004.

KUREISHI, Hanif: The Carnival of Culture. In: *The Guardian*, 04-08-2005; see www.theguardian.com/world/2005/aug/04/religion.uk (18-08-2017).

LABOV, William / WALETZKY, Joshua: Narrative Analysis. Oral Versions of Personal Experience. In: June Helm (eds.): Essay on the Verbal and Visual Arts. of Washington Press 1967, pp. 12-44.

LABOV, William: Transformation of Experience in Narrative Syntax. In: Ibid: Language in the Inner City. Studies in the Black English Vernacular. Philadelphia: University of Pennsylvania Press 1972, pp. 354-396.

LACEY, Nick: Narrative and Genre. Key Concepts in Media Studies. New York: St. Martin's Press 2000 (for the series-serial continuum see pp. 30-40).

LÄMMERT, Eberhard: Bauformen des Erzählens. Stuttgart 1988, 1997^8.

LAUREL, Brenda: Computers as Theatre. Reading et al.: Addison-Wesley 1993, 1998.

LEHTONEN, Mikko: The Cultural Analysis of Texts. Thousand Oaks / London: Sage 2000.

LEVINSON, Jerrold: Film Music and Narrative Agency. In: David Bordwell / Noël Carroll (eds.): Post-Theory. Reconstructing Film Studies. Madison: The University of Wisconsin Press 1996, pp. 248-282.

LIMA, Luiz Costa: Control of the Imaginary. Reason and Imagination in Modern Times. English version: Minneapolis: University of Minnesota Press 1988.

LIPPMANN, Walter: Stereotypes. In: Ibid.: Public Opinion. London: George Allen and Unwin 1922, pp. 79-94. Reprint in: John Corner / Jeremy Hawthorn (eds.): Communication Studies. An Introductory Reader. London / New York et al.: Arnold 1980, 1993^4, pp. 133-139.

LOTHE, Jakob: Narration in Fiction and Film. An Introduction. Oxford: Oxford University Press 2000.

MEADOWS, Mark S.: Pause and Effect. The Art of Interactive Narrative. London: Pearson Education 2002.

MEISTER, Jan Christoph: Computing Action. A Narratological Approach. Berlin / New York: De Gruyter 2003.

MINCHIN, Elizabeth: Similes in Homer. Image, Mind's Eye and Memory. In: Janet Watson (ed.): Speaking Volumes. Orality and Literacy in the Greek and Roman World. Leiden et al.: Brill 2001, pp. 25-52.

MIZEJEWSKI, Linda: Hardboiled and High-Heeled. The Woman Detective in Popular Culture. London / New York: Routledge 2004.

MIZEJEWSKI, Linda: Picturing the Female Dick. *The Silence of the Lambs* and *Blue Steel*. In: *Journal of Film and Video* 45 (1993) 2-3, pp. 6-23.

MOOY, Jan Johann Albinn: Fictional Realities. The Uses of Literary Imagination. Amsterdam: Benjamins 1993.

MURRAY, Janet: Hamlet on the Holodeck. The Future of Narrative in Cyberspace. New York et al.: The Free Press 1997.

NEITZEL, Britta: Narrativity in Computer Games. In Joost Raessens / Jeffrey Goldstein (eds.): Handbook of Computer Game Studies. Cambridge, Mass.: MIT Press 2005, pp. 227-245.

NELSON, William: Fact or Fiction. The Dilemma of the Renaissance Storyteller. Cambridge: Harvard University Press 1973.

NEUPERT, Richard: The End. Narration and Closure in the Cinema. Detroit: Wayne State University Press 1995 (= Contemporary Films and Television Series).

NORRICK, Neal R.: Conversational Narrative. Storytelling in Everyday Talk. Amsterdam: Benjamins 2000.

OCHS, Elinor / CAPPS, Lisa: Living Narrative. Creating Lives in Everyday Storytelling. Cambridge: Harvard University Press 2001.

ONEGA, Susana / GARCÍA, José Angel (eds.): Narratology. An Introduction. London: Longman 1996.

PEARSON, Roberta E. / SIMPSON, Philip (eds.): Critical Dictionary of Film and Television Theory. London / New York: Routledge 2001.

RICOEUR, Paul: Narrative Time. In: J.W.T. Mitchell (ed.): On Narrative. Chicago: University of Chicago Press 1980, pp. 165-186. Reprint in: Mieke Bal (ed.): Narrative Theory. Critical Concepts in Literary and Cultural Studies. London / New York: Routledge 2004, vol. 3, pp. 327-347.

RICOEUR, Paul: Temps et récit. 3 vol., Paris: Seuil 1983-1985. English version: Time and Narrative. 3 vol., Chicago: University of Chicago Press 1984-1988.

RIMMON-KENAN, Shlomith: Narrative Fiction, Contemporary Poetics. London 1983, 2000².

RYAN, Marie-Laure: Avatars of Story (Electronic Mediations). Minneapolis: University of Minnesota Press 2006.

RYAN, Marie-Laure: Narrative: In: David Herman / Manfred Jahn / Ibid. (eds.): Routledge Encyclopedia of Narrative Theory. London / New York: Routledge 2005, pp. 344-348.

RYAN, Marie-Laure: Narrative as Virtual Reality. Immersion and Intertextuality in Literature and Electronic Media. Baltimore: John Hopkins University Press 2003.

SALEN, Katie / ZIMMERMAN, Eric: Games as Narrative Play. In: Ibid: Rules of Play. Game Design Fundamentals. Cambridge, Mass.: MIT Press 2004, pp. 377-417.

SALEN, Katie / ZIMMERMAN, Eric: Rules of Play. Game Design Fundamentals. Cambridge, Mass.: MIT Press 2004.

SCHATZ, Thomas: Hollywood Genres – Formulas, Filmmaking, and the Studio System. Philadelphia: Random House 1981.

SEITER, Ellen: Stereotypes and the Media. A Re-Evaluation. In: *Journal of Communication* 36 (1986) 2, pp. 14-26.

SHELDON, Lee: Character Development and Storytelling For Games. Boston: Thomson Course Technology PTR 2004.

SIMON, Anne: Sigmund Feyerabend's Das Reyssbuch dess heyligen Lands. A Study in Printing and Literary History. Wiesbaden: Dr. Ludwig Reichert Edition 1998 (= Wissensliteratur im Mittelalter 32).

SLATKIN, Laura M.: Composition by Theme and the *Metis* of the *Odyssey*. In: Seth L. Schein (ed.): Reading the *Odyssey*. Selected Interpretive Essays. Princeton: Princeton University Press 1996, pp. 223-237.

TALBOT, Mary M.: Fictions at Work. Language and Social Practice in Fiction. Burnt Mill: Longman 1995.

TANNEN, Deborah: That's Not What I Meant. How Conversational Style Makes or Breaks Relations. New York: Ballantine 1986.

TANNEN, Deborah: You Just Don't Understand. Women and Men in Conversation. New York: Ballantine: 1990.

THOMPSON, Kristin: Breaking the Glass Armor. Neoformalist Film Analysis. Princeton: Princeton University Press 1988.

TRÖHLER, Margrit: Offene Welten ohne Helden. Figurenkonstellationen im Film. Habilitation Thesis Zürich / Marburg: Schüren 2007.

TURIM, Maureen Cheryn: Flashbacks in Film. Memory and History. London / New York: Routledge 1989.

WARDRIP-FRUIN, Noah / HARRISON, Pat (eds.): New Media as Story, Performance, and Game. Cambridge, Mass.: MIT Press 2004.

WRIGHT, Will: Six Guns and Society. A Structural Study of the Western. Berkeley: University of California Press 1975.

14.5.5 Fan studies / audience studies in general

ABERCROMBIE, Nicolas / LONGHURST, Brian (eds.): Audiences. A Sociological Theory of Performance and Imagination. Thousand Oaks / London: Sage 1998.

ALASUUTARI, Pertti (eds.): Rethinking the Media Audience. The New Agenda. Thousand Oaks / London: Sage 1999, 2000.

ANG, Ien: Desperately Seeking the Audience. London / New York: Routledge 1991.

ANG, Ien: Het Geval *Dallas*. Uitgeverij SUA 1982. English version: Watching *Dallas*. Soap Opera and the Melodramatic Imagination. New York / London: Methuen 1985, and Routledge 1989 [cit. as Ang 1985].

ANG, Ien: Melodramatic Identifications. Television Fiction and Women's Fantasies. In: Mary Ellen Brown (ed.): Television and Women's Culture. The Politics of the Popular. Thousand Oaks / London: Sage 1990, pp. 74-88.

BACON-SMITH, Camille: Enterprising Women. Television Fandom and the Creation of Popular Myth. Philadelphia: Contemporary Ethnography 1991.

BAKHTIN, Mikhail: The Dialogic Imagination. Austin: University of Texas Press 1981.

BANKS, John: Gamers as Co-Creators. Enlisting the Virtual Audience. A Report from the Netface. In: Mark Balnaves / T. O'Regan / Jason Sternberg (eds.): Mobilising the Audience. St. Lucia: Queensland University Press 2002. Reprint in: Virginia Nightingale / Karen Ross (eds.): Critical Readings. Media and Audiences. McGraw-Hill: Open University Press 2002, pp. 268-278.

BASCH, Françoise: Relative Creatures. Victorian Women in Society and the Novel, 1837-1867. New York: Shocken 1974.

BAYM, Nancy K.: Interpreting Soap Operas and Creating Community. Inside an Electronic Fan Culture. In: Sara Kiesler (ed.): Culture of the Internet. Mahwa: Lawrence Erlbaum 1997, pp. 103-120.

BAYM, Nancy K.: Tune In, Log On. Soaps, Fandom, and On-Line Community. London et al.: Sage 2000.

BELGUM, Kirsten: Popularizing the Nation. Audience, Representation, and the Production of Identity in Die Gartenlaube, 1853-1900. Lincoln / London: University of Nebraska Press 1998.

BILANDZIC, Helena / KINNEBROCK, Susanne: Persuasive Wirkungen narrativer Unterhaltungsangebote. Theoretische Überlegungen zum Einfluss von Narrativität auf Transportation. In: Werner Wirth / Holger Schramm / Volker Gehrau (eds.): Unterhaltung durch Medien. Theorie und Messung. Köln: Herbert von Halem 2006, pp. 103-126.

BRAUERHOCH, Annette: Männliche Stars der 80er Jahre - Objekte weiblicher Schaulust? In: *TheaterZeitSchrift* 30 (1989), pp. 19-26.

BROWER, Sue: Fans as Tastemakers. Viewers for Quality Television. In: Lisa A. Lewis (ed.): Adoring Audience. Fan Culture and Popular Media, London / New York: Routledge 1992, pp. 163-184.

BROWN, Mary Ellen: Soap Opera and Women's Talk. The Pleasure of Resistance. Thousand Oaks / London: Sage 1994 (= Communication and Human Values).

CLERC, Susan J.: DDEB, GATB, MPPB, and Ratboy. The *X-Files*, Media Fandom, Online and Off. In: David Lavery / Angela Hague / Marla Cartwright (ed.): "Deny All Knowledge". Reading the *X-Files*. Syracuse: Syracuse University Press 1996, pp. 36-51.

COVER, Rob: Audience inter/active. Interactive Media, Narrative Control and Reconceiving Audience History. In: *New Media & Society* 8 (2006) 1, pp. 139-158.

DAYAN, Daniel: Les mystères de la réception. In: *Le débat* 71 (1992), pp. 146-162.

DELASARA, Jan: Poplit, Popcult and the *X-Files*: A Critical Explanation. Jefferson: Mc Farland 2000.

DYER, Richard: Heavenly Bodies. Filmstars and Society. Houndmills / London 1987.

DYER, Richard: Stars. London 1979, 1982^2.

FINE, Gary Alan: Shared Fantasy. Role-Playing Games as Social Worlds. London / Chicago: University of Chicago Press 1983, 2002.

FISKE, John: The Cultural Economy of Fandom. In: Lisa A. Lewis (ed.): Adoring Audience. Fan Culture and Popular Media. London / New York 1992, pp. 30-49.

GANZ-BLÄTTLER, Ursula: Die (Fernseh-)Fiktion als Gemeinschaftswerk(en) und kulturelle Teilhabe. In: Andreas Hepp / Rainer Winter (eds.): Kultur – Medien – Macht. Cultural Studies und Medienanalyse. Wiesbaden: Verlag für Sozialwissenschaften 2006^3, pp.285-298 [Ganz-Blättler 2006b].

GANZ-BLÄTTLER, Ursula: Knowledge Oblige. Genrewissen als Statussymbol und Share-Ware. In: Udo Göttlich / Rainer Winter (eds.): Politik des Vergnügens. Zur Diskussion der Populärkultur in den Cultural Studies. Köln Herbert van Halem 2000 (= Fiktion und Fiktionalisierung 3), pp.195-214 [Ganz-Blättler 2000a].

GANZ-BLÄTTLER, Ursula: The Medium is the Audience. Successive Talk as Narrative Pleasure. In: Kathleen Loock (ed.): Serial Narratives. Special edition of *Literatur in Wissenschaft und Unterricht* 47 (2014) 1/2, pp. 175-189.

GANZ-BLÄTTLER, Ursula: Risiken und Nebenwirkungen von Missverständnissen. Interkulturelle und intermediale Texte im erweiterten Bedeutungsspektrum. In: Caroline Y. Robertson-Wensauer / Carsten Winter (eds.): Kulturwandel und Globalisierung. Baden-Baden: Nomos 2000, pp. 239-250 [Ganz-Blättler 2000b].

GANZ-BLÄTTLER, Ursula: Shareware or Prestigious Privilege? Television Fans as Knowledge Brokers (1999); see *http://web.mit.edu/m-i-t/articles/index_ganz.html* (18-08-2017).

GERRIG, Richard J.: Experiencing Narrative Worlds. New Haven: Yale University Press 1993.

GLEDHILL, Christine (ed.): Stardom. Industry Of Desire. London / New York: Routledge 1991.

GÖTTLICH, Udo: Medienkultur. In: *quadratur Kulturbuch* 5 (2004) 1, pp. 32-37.

GÖTTLICH, Udo: Die Kreativität des Handelns in der Medienaneignung. Habilitation thesis, Konstanz: Constance University Press 2007.

GREEN, Melanie C. / BROCK, Timothy C. / KAUFMAN, Geoff F.: Understanding Media Enjoyment. The Role of Transportation Into Narrative Worlds. In: *Communication Theory* 14 (2004) 4, pp. 311-327.

GREEN, Shoshanna / JENKINGS, Cynthia / JENKINS, Henry: Normal Female Interest in Men Bonking. Selections from "The Terra Nostra Underground" and "Strange Bedfellows". In: Cheryl Harris / Alison Alexander (eds.): Theorizing Fandom. Fans, Subculture and Identity. Cresskill: Hampton 1998, pp. 9-38.

HARRINGTON, Catherine Lee / BIELBY, Denise B.: Soap Fans. Pursuing Pleasure and Making Meaning in Everyday Life. Philadelphia: Temple University Press 1995.

HARRIS, Cheryl / ALEXANDER, Alison (eds.): Theorizing Fandom. Fans, Subculture and Identity. Cresskill: Hampton 1998.

HAYWARD, Jennifer Poole: Consuming Pleasures. Active Audiences and Serial Fiction From Dickens to Soap Opera. Lexington, Kentucky: The University Press of Kentucky 1997.

HERZOG, Charlotte Cornelia / GAINES, Jane Marie: "Puffed Sleeves Before Tea-Time" (*Letty Lynton*). In: Christine Gledhill (ed.): Stardom. Industry Of Desire. London / New York: Routledge 1991, pp. 74-91.

HERZOG, Herta: On Borrowed Experience. An Analysis of Listening to Day Time Sketches. In: *Studies in Philosophy and Social Science* 9 (1941) 1, pp. 65-95.

HERZOG, Herta: What Do We Really Know about Daytime Serial Listeners? In: Paul F. Lazarsfeld / Frank Stanton (ed.): Radio Research, 1942-43. New York: Duell, Sloan and Pearce 1944, pp. 2-23.

HILLS, Matt: Fan Cultures. London / New York: Routledge 2002 (= Sussex Studies in Culture and Communication).

HORTON, David / WOHL, R. Richard: Mass Communication and Para-Social Interaction. Observations on Intimacy at a Distance. In: *Psychiatry* 19 (1956) 3, 215-229. Reprint in: *Particip@tions* 3 (2006) 1; the online version of the article is accessible at *http://www.participations.org/volume%203/issue%201/3_01_hortonwohl.htm* (18-08-2017).

HORTON, David / STRAUSS, Anselm: Interaction in Audience-Participation Shows. In: *The American Journal of Sociology* 62 (1957) 6, 579-587.

ISER, Wolfgang: Der Akt des Lesens. Theorie ästhetischer Wirkung. München: Wilhelm Fink 1976, 1994[4]. English version: The Act of Reading. A Theory of Aesthetic Response. Baltimore: Johns Hopkins University Press 1978.

ISER, Wolfgang: Die Appellstruktur der Texte. Unbestimmtheit als Wirkungsbedingung literarischer Prosa. Konstanz: Constance University Press 1970 (= Konstanzer Universitätsreden 28). English version: Indeterminacy and the Reader's Response to Prose Fiction. In: Joseph Hillis Miller (ed.): Aspects of Narrative. Selected Papers from the English Institute. New York: University of Columbia Press 1971, pp. 1-45.

ISER, Wolfgang: Der implizite Leser. Kommunikationsformen des Romans von Bunyan bis Beckett. München: Wilhelm Fink 1972, and Konstanz: Constance University Press 1994. English version: The Implied Reader. Patterns of Communication in Prose Fiction From Bunyan to Beckett. Baltimore: Johns Hopkins University Press 1974.

ISER, Wolfgang: The Reading Process. A Phenomenological Approach. In: *New Literary History* 3 (1972) 2, 279-299. Reprint in: Ibid.: The Implied Reader. Patterns of Communication in Prose Fiction From Bunyan to Beckett. Baltimore: Johns Hopkins University Press 1974, pp. 274-294.

JENKINS, Henry: Confessions of an Aca-Fan; see *www.henryjenkins.org/* (18-08-2017).

JENKINS, Henry: Interactive Audiences? In: Virginia Nightingale / Karen Ross (eds.): Critical Readings. Media and Audiences. McGraw-Hill: Open University Press 2002, pp. 279-295.

JENKINS, Henry: The Poachers and the Stormtroopers. Cultural Convergences in the Digital Age. In: Philippe Le Guern (ed.): Les cultes médiatiques. Culture fan et oeuvres cultes. Rennes: Presses Universitaires de Rennes 2002, pp. 343-378.

JENKINS, Henry: "Strangers No More, We Sing". Filking and the Social Construction of the Science Fiction Fan Community (*Star Trek*). In: Lisa A.Lewis (ed.): Adoring Audience. Fan Culture and Popular Media, London / New York: Routledge 1992, pp. 208-236.

JENKINS, Henry / TULLOCH, John: Science Fiction Audiences. London: Routledge 1995.

JENKINS, Henry: *Star Trek* Rerun, Reread, Rewritten. Fan Writing as Textual Poaching. In: *Critical Studies in Mass Communication* 5 (1988) 2, pp. 85-107.

JENKINS, Henry: Textual Poachers. Television Fans and Participatory Culture. New York / London: Routledge 1992.

JENSON, Joli: Fandom as Pathology. The Consequences of Characterization. In: Lisa A. Lewis (ed.): Adoring Audience. Fan Culture and Popular Media, London / New York 1992, pp. 9-29.

LE GUERN, Philippe (ed.): Les cultes médiatiques. Culture fan et oeuvres cultes. Rennes: Presses Universitaires de Rennes 2002.

LEWIS, Lisa A. (ed.): Adoring Audience. Fan Culture and Popular Media. London / New York 1992.

LIEBES, Tamar: On Herzog's "Borrowed Experience". Its Place in the Debate Over the Active Audience. In: Elihu Katz / John Durham Peters / Ibid. / Avril Orloff (eds.): Canonic Texts in Media Research. Are There Any? Should There Be? How About These? Cambridge / Oxford: Polity Press 2002.

LIEBES, Tamar / KATZ, Elihu: The Export of Meaning. Crosscultural Readings of *Dallas*. Cambridge: Polity Press 1990, 1993^2.

LIVINGSTONE, Sonia M.: Interpreting a Television Narrative: How Different Viewers See a Story. In: *Journal of Communication* 40 (1990) 1, pp. 72-85.

LIVINGSTONE, Sonia M.: Interpretive Viewers and Structured Programs: The Implicit Representation of Soap Opera Characters. In: *Communications Research* 16 (1989) 1, pp. 25-58.

LIVINGSTONE, Sonia M.: Making Sense of Television. The Psychology of Audience Interpretation. Oxford 1990 (= Internat. Ser. in Experimental Social Psychology 18).

LONG, Elizabeth: Book Clubs. Women and the Uses of Reading in Everyday Life. Chicago: University of Chicago Press 2003.

MACKAY, Daniel: The Fantasy Role-Playing Game. A New Performing Art. Jefferson / London: McFarland 2001.

MARTÍNEZ, Matias / SCHEFFEL, Michael: Einführung in die Erzähltheorie. München: Beck 1999, 2003^6.

MCQUAIL, Denis: Audience Analysis. Thousand Oaks / London: Sage 1997.

MILLER, Daniel: *The Young and the Restless* in Trinidad. A Case of the Local and the Global in Mass Consumption. In: Roger Silverstone / Eric Hirsch (eds.): Consuming Technologies. London / New York 1992, pp. 164-182.

MODLESKI, Tania: Loving With a Vengeance. Mass-Produced Fantasies For Women. London: Routledge 1982, 1990.

PASQUIER, Dominique: La culture des sentiments. L'expérience télévisuelle des adolescents (*Hélène et les garçons*). Paris: Ed. de la Maison des sciences de l'homme 1999.

REEVES, Jimmie L.: Television Stardom. A Ritual of Social Typification and Individualization. In: James W. Carey (ed.): Media, Myths and Narratives. Newbury Park et al.: Sage 1988 (= Sage Annual Reviews of Communication Research 15), pp. 146-160.

ROSS, Karen / NIGHTINGALE, Virgina: Media and Audiences. New Perspectives. Maidenhead: Open University Press 2003.

SABUCCO, Veruska: Shonen Ai. Il nuovo immaginario erotico femminile tra Oriente e Occidente. Roma: Castelvecchi 2000.

SCAGLIONI, Massimo: TV di culto. La serialità televisiva americana e il suo fandom. Milano: Vita e pensiero 2006.

SCHICK, Lawrence: Heroic Worlds. A History and Guide to Role-Playing Games. Prometheus Books 1991.

SJÖBERG, Lore: Hierarchy of Geeks. Originally published on Sjöberg's Brunching Shuttlecocks website (January 2002); an archived online copy is accessible at *web.archive.org/web/20160710215816/http://brunching.com/geekhierarchy.html* (18-08-2017).

STACEY, Jackie: Star Gazing: Hollywood Cinema and Female Spectatorship. London et al.: Routledge 1994.

STAMP, Shelley: Ready-Made Customers. Female Movie Fans and the Serial Craze. In: Ibid..: Movie-Struck Girls. Woman and Motion Picture Culture After the Nickelodeon. Princeton: Princeton University Press 2000, pp. 102-125.

STEMPEL MUMFORD, Laura: Love and Ideology in the Afternoon. Bloomington / Indianapolis: Indiana University Press 1995.

THOMAS, Scott: The Making of the Potterverse. A Month-by-Month Look at Harry's First Ten Years. Toronto: ECW Press 2007.

VERON, Eliséo: L'analyse du "contrat" de lecture. Une nouvelle méthode pour les études de positionnement des supports presse. In: Ibid.: Les médias. Expériences, recherches actuelles, applications. Paris: Institut de recherches et études publicitaires 1985, pp. 203-229.

VERON, Eliséo: Les médias en réception. Les enjeux de la complexité. In: *Médiaspouvoirs* 21 (1991), pp. 166-172.

VINCENT, David: The Rise of Mass Literacy. Reading and Writing in Modern Europe. Cambridge: Polity Press 2000. Italian version: Leggere e scrivere nell'Europa contemporanea. Bologna: Il Mulino 2006.

VOLLI, Ugo (ed.): Culti TV. Il tubo catodico ed i suoi adepti. Milano: Sperling & Kupfer 2002.

VORDERER, Peter / KLIMMT, Christoph / RITTERFELD, Ute: Enjoyment. At the Heart of Media Entertainment. In: *Communication Theory* 14 (2004) 4, pp. 388-408.

VORDERER, Peter (ed.): Fernsehen als "Beziehungskiste". Parasoziale Beziehungen und Interaktionen mit TV-Personen. Opladen: Westdeutscher Verlag 1995.

VORDERER, Peter: Fernsehen als Handlung. Fernsehfilmrezeption aus motivationspsychologischer Perspektive. Berlin: Ed. Sigma 1992 (= Empirische Literatur- und Medienwissenschaft 1).

VORDERER, Peter: Involvementsverläufe bei der Rezeption von Fernsehfilmen. In: Louis Bosshart / Wolfgang Hoffmann-Riem (eds.): Medienlust und Mediennutz. Unterhaltung als öffentliche Kommunikation. München: Ölschläger 1994 (= DGPuK-Schriftenreihe 20), pp. 333-342.

VORDERER, Peter: Kommunikationswissenschaftliche Unterhaltungsforschung. Quo Vadis? In: Werner Wirth / Holger Schramm / Volker Gehrau (eds.): Unterhaltung durch Medien. Theorie und Messung. Köln: Herbert von Halem 2006, pp. 47-58 [Vorderer 2006a].

VORDERER, Peter / KNOBLOCH, Silvia: Parasoziale Beziehungen zu Serienfiguren. Ergänzung oder Ersatz? In: *Medienpsychologie* 8 (1996), pp. 201-216.

VORDERER, Peter: Picard, Brinkmann, Derrick und Co. als Freunde der Zuschauer. Eine explorative Studie über parasoziale Beziehungen zu Serienfiguren. In: Ders. (ed.): Fernsehen als "Beziehungskiste". Parasoziale Beziehungen und Interaktionen mit TV-Personen. Opladen: Westdeutscher Verlag 1995, pp. 153-171.

WATSON, Victor: Reading Series Fiction. From Arthur Ransome to Gene Kemp. London: Falmer Press 2000.

WINTER, Rainer: Der produktive Zuschauer. Medienaneignung als kultureller und ästhetischer Prozess. München: Quintessenz 1995.

WINTER, Rainer: Der produktive Zuschauer. Zur Medienkompetenz von Horrorfans. In: *medien praktisch* 20 (1996) 2, pp. 33-36.

14.5.6   Memory studies

BITTNER, Günther: Ich bin mein Erinnern. Über autobiographisches und kollektives Gedächtnis. Würzburg: Königshausen und Neumann 2006.

CARR, David: Time, Narrative, and History. Bloomington / Indianapolis: Indiana University Press 1986.

ERLL, Astrid: Kollektives Gedächtnis und Erinnerungskulturen. Eine Einführung. Stuttgart / Weimar: Metzler 2005.

ESPOSITO, Elena: Soziales Vergessen. Formen und Medien des Gedächtnisses der Gesellschaft. Frankfurt: Suhrkamp 2002.

IRWIN-ZARECKA, Iwona: Frames of Remembrance. The Dynamics of Collective Memory. New Brunswick: Transaction Publishers 1994.

LEWIS, Bernard.: History. Remembered, Recovered, Reinvented. Princeton: Princeton University Press 1975.

MARC, David: Bonfire of the Humanities. Television, Subliteracy and Long-Term Memory Loss. Syracuse: Syracuse University Press 1995.

MEUTER, Norbert: Narrative Identität. Das Problem der personalen Identität im Anschluss an Ernst Tugendhat, Niklas Luhmann und Paul Ricoeur. Doctoral Thesis Düsseldorf / Stuttgart: M+P, Verlag für Wissenschaft und Forschung 1995.

ROSEN, Philip: Change Mummified. Cinema, Historicity, Theory. Minneapolis: University of Minnesota Press 2001.

WELZER, Harald: Das kommunikative Gedächtnis. Eine Theorie der Erinnerung. München: Beck 2002, 2005 [cit. as Welzer 2002].

WELZER, Harald / MOLLER, Sabine: „Opa war kein Nazi". Nationalsozialismus und Holocaust im Familiengedächtnis. Frankfurt: S. Fischer 2002 [cit. as Welzer / Moller 2002].

WHITE, Mimi: Tele-Advising. Therapeutic Discourse in American Television. Chapel Hill / London: University of North Carolina Press 1992.

WHITE, Mimi: Women, Memory and Serial Melodrama. In: *Screen* 35 (1994) 4, pp. 336-353.

14.5.7 Linguistics / semiotics / (post-)structuralism

BARTHES, Roland: Mythologies. Paris: Seuil 1957. English version: Mythologies. New York: Hill & Wang 1972.

BARTHES, Roland: Oeuvres complètes. 3 vol., Paris: Seuil 1993-1995.

BARTHES, Roland: S/Z. Paris: Seuil 1970. English version: S/Z. An Essay. New York: Hill & Wang 1974.

BONDANELLA, Peter: Umberto Eco and the Open Text. Semiotics, Fiction, Pop Culture. Cambridge: Cambridge University Press 1997.

CHANDLER, Daniel: Semiotics – the Basics. London: Routledge 2002; see *www.wayanswardhani.lecture.ub.ac.id/files/2013/09/Semiotics-the-Basics.pdf* (18-08-2017).

ECO, Umberto: A Theory of Semiotics. London: Macmillan 1976.

ECO, Umberto: Lector in fabula. La cooperazione interpretativa nei testi narrativi. Milano: Bompiani 1979 und 1997^4. English version (published as sketch only): Lector in Fabula. Pragmatic Strategy in a Metanarrative Text. In: Ibid.: The Role of the Reader. Explorations in the Semiotics of Text. Bloomington: Indiana University Press 1979, pp. 200-262.

ECO, Umberto: Opera aperta. Milano: Bompiani 1962 und 1997^4. English version: The Open Work. Cambridge, Mass.: Harvard University Press 1989.

ECO, Umberto: The Poetics of the Open Work. In: Ibid.: The Role of the Reader. Explorations in the Semiotics of Texts. Bloomington: University of Indiana Press 1979, pp. 47-66.

ECO, Umberto: The Role of the Reader. Explorations in the Semiotics of Text. Bloomington: Indiana University Press 1979.

ECO, Umberto: Sei passegiate nei boschi narrativi. Milano: Bompiani 1994. English version: Six Walks in the Fictional Woods. Cambridge (Mass.): Harvard University Press 1994.

Eco, Umberto: Tipologia della ripetizione. In: Francesco Casetti (ed.): L'immagine al plurale. Serialità e ripetizione nel cinema e nella televisione. Venezia: Marsilio 1984, pp. 19-36. English, slightly abridged version: Innovation and Repetition. Between Modern and Post-Modern Aesthetics. In: *Daedalus* 114 (1985) 4, pp. 161-184. A revised version appeared as: Interpreting Serials. In: The Limits of Interpretation. Bloomington: Indiana University Press 1990, pp. 83-100.

Erlich, Victor: Russian Formalism. History – Doctrine. The Hague: Mouton 1955, 1969³.

Hawkes, Terence: Structuralism and Semiotics. Berkeley / Los Angeles: University of California Press 1977.

Hediger, Vinzenz / Vonderau, Patrick (eds.): Demnächst in Ihrem Kino. Grundlagen der Filmwerbung und Filmvermarktung. Marburg: Schüren 2005.

Hediger, Vinzenz: Self-Promoting Story Events. Serial Narrative, Promotional Discourse and the Invention of the Movie Trailer. In: Anna Antonini (ed.): Il film e i suoi multipli / Film and Its Multiples. Udine: Forum 2003, pp. 295-305.

Hediger, Vinzenz: Verführung zum Film. Der amerikanische Kinotrailer seit 1912. Doctoral thesis Zürich / Marburg: Schüren 2001 (= Zürcher Filmstudien 5).

Seiter, Ellen: Semiotics, Structuralism, and Television. In: Robert C. Allen (ed.): Channels of Discourse, Reassembled. London 1992 ², pp. 31-66.

Stam, Robert / Burgoyne, Robert / Flitterman-Lewis, Sandy: New Vocabularies in Film Semiotics. Structuralism, Post-Structuralism and Beyond. London / New York: Routledge 1992.

Sturrock, John: Structuralism. Malden / Oxford: Blackwell 1986, 2003.

14.5.8 Communication studies / cultural studies / media economics

Agger, Ben: Cultural Studies as Critical Theory. London / Washington: The Falmer Press 1992.

Alasuutari, Pertti: Researching Culture. Qualitative Method and Cultural Studies. London et al.: Sage 1995.

Anderson, Chris: The Long Tail. Why the Future of Business is Selling Less or More. New York: Hyperion 2006. Also published als: The Long Tail. How Endless Choice is Creating Unlimited Demand. New York: Random House 2006.

ARISTOTLE: Poetics. Trans. D.W. Lucas. Oxford: Clarendon Press 1968, 1982.

BARALDI, Claudio / CORSI, Giancarlo / ESPOSITO, Elena: GLU. Glossar zu Niklas Luhmanns Theorie sozialer Systeme. Frankfurt: Suhrkamp 1997.

BATESON, Gregory: Steps to an Ecology of Mind. Collected Essays in Anthropology, Psychiatry, Evolution and Epistemology. 3 vol., London: Paladin Books 1972.

BAUMAN, Zygmunt: From Pilgrim to Tourist, or a Short History of Identity. In: Stuart Hall / Paul du Gay (eds.): Questions of Cultural Identity. London et al.: Sage 1996, pp. 18-36.

BAUMOL, William J.: The Free-Market Innovation Machine. Analyzing the Growth Miracle of Capitalism. Princeton: Princeton University Press 2002.

BAUMOL, William J. / BOWEN, William J.: Performing Arts. The Economic Dilemma. Cambridge (Mass.) / London 1966, 1977^2.

BAUMOL, Hilda / BAUMOL, William J.: The Mass Media and the Cost Disease. In: William S. Hendon / Nancy K. Grant / Douglas V. Show (eds.): The Economics of Cultural Industries. Akron: Association for Cultural Economics 1984, pp. 109-123. Reprint in: Ruth Towse (ed.): Cultural Economics. The Arts, the Heritage and the Media Industries. Cheltenham / Lyme: Elgar 1997 (vol. 2), pp. 304-318.

BAUMOL, William J.: Performing Arts. Reprint in: Ruth Towse (eds.): Cultural Economics. The Arts, the Heritage and the Media Industries. Cheltenham / Lyme: Elgar 1997 (vol. 2), pp. 287-289.

BECHMANN, Gotthard / STEHR, Nico: The Legacy of Niklas Luhmann. In: *Society* (2002) Jan. / Feb., pp. 67-75; see www.itas.fzk.de/deu/Itaslit/besto2a.pdf (18-08-2017).

BECKER, Karin: Media and the Ritual Process. In: *Media, Culture, & Society* 17 (1995), pp. 629-646.

BERGER, Peter L. / LUCKMANN, Thomas: The Social Construction of Reality. Garden City, New York: Anchor 1966.

BERNSTEIN, J.M. (eds.): The Culture Industry. Selected Essays on Mass Culture [by Adorno and other representants of the Frankfurt School]. London / New York: Routledge 1991.

BOSSHART, Louis / MACCONI, Ilaria (eds.): Media Entertainment. In: *Communication Research Trends* 18 (1998) 3, pp. 1-38.

BOSSHART, Louis: Theorien der Medienunterhaltung. Aus dem Nichts zur Fülle. In: Brigitte Frizzoni / Ingrid Tomkowiak (eds.): Unterhaltung. Konzepte – Formen – Wirkungen. Zürich: Chronos 2006, pp. 17-30 [Bosshart 2006a].

BOSSHART, Louis: Zur Genese der Unterhaltungsforschung in der deutschsprachigen Medien- und Kommunikationswissenschaft. In: Werner Wirth / Holger Schramm / Volker Gehrau (eds.): Unterhaltung durch Medien. Theorie und Messung. Köln: Herbert von Halem 2006, pp. 12-24 [Bosshart 2006b].

BOURDIEU, Pierre: La distinction. Critique social du jugement. Paris: Les éditions de minuit 1979. English version: Distinction. A Social Critique of the Judgment of Taste. Cambridge, MA: Harvard University Press 1984.

BRÄNDLI, Sibylle: Der Supermarkt im Kopf. Konsumkultur und Wohlstand in der Schweiz nach 1945. Ph.D. Basel / Wien: Böhlau 2000.

BRANTLINGER, Patrick: Bread and Circuses. Theories of Mass Culture as Social Decay. Ithaca: Cornell University Press 1983.

BRYANT, Jennings / VORDERER, Peter (eds.): Psychology of Entertainment. Mahwah: Lawrence Erlbaum 2006.

CALHOUN, Craig J. (ed.): Habermas and the Public Sphere. Cambridge, Mass.: MIT Press 1992.

CAMPBELL, Joseph: The Hero With a Thousand Faces. Princeton: Princeton University Press 1949, 1968^2.

CAREY, James W.: A Cultural Approach to Communications. In: *Communications* 2 (1975) 2, pp. 1-22. Reprint in: Ibid: Communication as Culture. Essays on Media and Society. Boston: Unwyn Hyman 1989, and New York / London: Routledge 1992 (= Media and Popular Culture 1), pp. 13-36.

CAREY, James W.: Communication as Culture. Essays on Media and Society. Boston: Unwyn Hyman 1989, and New York / London: Routledge 1992 (= Media and Popular Culture 1).

CAREY, James W.: Political Ritual on Television. Episodes in the History of Shame, Degradation and Excommunication. In: Tamar Liebes / James Curran (eds.): Media, Ritual and Identity. London / New York: Routledge 1998, pp. 42-69.

CARROLL, Noël: A Philosophy of Mass Art. Oxford: Clarendon Press 1998.

CARSE, James P.: Finite and Infinite Games. A Vision of Life as Play and Possibility. New York: Ballantine 1986, 1994.

CHESEBRO, James W.: Communication, Values, and Popular Television Series. A Four-Year Assessment. In: Horace M. Newcomb (ed.): Television, The Critical View. New York / Oxford 1987⁴, pp. 17-51.

DAYAN, Daniel / KATZ, Elihu: Media Events. The Live Broadcasting of History. Harvard: Harvard University Press 1992.

DORAY, Bernard: Le taylorisme. Une folie rationelle? Paris: Dunod 1981 English version: From Taylorism to Fordism. A Rational Madness. London: Free Association Books 1988.

DUBIED, Annik: Les dits et les scènes du fait divers. Doctoral thesis Geneva / Paris: Librairie Droz 2004.

DUBIED, Annik (ed): L'information-peuple. Laval: Laval University 2009 (= Special Issue of *Communication* 27,1).

DUBY, Georges: Youth in Aristocratic Society. In. Ibid.: The Chivalrous Society. London: Arnold 1977, and Berkeley: University of California Press 1981, pp. 112-122.

EINSTEIN, Maria: Media Diversity. Economics, Ownership, and the FCC. Mahwah: Lawrence Erlbaum 2004.

ENGELL, Lorenz: Ausfahrt nach Babylon. In: Ibid.: Ausfahrt nach Babylon. Essais und Vorträge zur Kritik der Medienkultur. Weimar: Verlag und Datenbank für Geisteswissenschaften 2000, pp. 263-305.

ENGELL, Lorenz: Filmgeschichte als Geschichte der Sinnzirkulation. In: Manfred Mai / Rainer Winter (eds.): Das Kino der Gesellschaft. Die Gesellschaft des Kinos. Interdisziplinäre Positionen, Analysen und Zugänge. Köln: Herbert van Halem 2005, pp. 48-59.

ENGELL, Lorenz: Vom Bild zur Zahl, oder: Wie die Stellen ihre Objekte verliessen. Über die Digitalisierung der Welt durch das Fernsehen. In: Ibid. / Britta Neitzel (eds.): Das Gesicht der Welt. Medien in der digitalen Kultur. München: Wilhelm Fink 2004, pp. 185-201.

FAULSTICH, Werner / KNOP, Karin (eds.): Unterhaltungskultur. München: Wilhelm Fink 2006.

FISKE, John: Popular Discrimination. In: James Naremore / Patrick Brantlinger: Modernity and Mass Culture. Bloomington: Indiana Univ. Press 1991, pp. 103-118.

FISKE, John: Surfalism and Sandiotics. The Beach in OZ Culture. In: *Australian Journal of Cultural Studies* 1 (1983) 2, pp. 120-148. Reprint in: Ibid.: Reading the Popular. London / New York: Routledge 1991, pp. 43-76.

FLUSSER, Vilém: Die kodifizierte Welt. In: Ibid.: Medienkultur. Frankfurt: Fischer 1997, pp. 21-28.

FLUSSER, Vilém: Writings. Minneapolis / London: University of Minnesota Press 2002 (= Electronic Mediations 6).

FOWLES, Jib: Starstruck. Celebrity Performers and the American Public. Washington: Smithsonian Books 1992.

GANZ-BLÄTTLER, Ursula: Andacht und Abenteuer. Berichte europäischer Jerusalem- und Santiago-Pilger (1320-1520). Doctoral thesis Zürich / Tübingen: Gunter Narr 1990, 2000³ (= Jakobus-Studien 4).

GANZ-BLÄTTLER, Ursula: Schichten, Lagen, Webmuster. Überlegungen zur Stratifikation von Kultur. In: Ulrich Saxer (ed.): Medien-Kulturkommunikation. Opladen: Westdeutscher Verlag 1998 (= Special Issue of *Publizistik* 2), pp. 175-186.

GIEGEL, HANS-JOACHIM / SCHIMANK, Uwe (eds.): Beobachter der Moderne. Niklas Luhmanns "Die Gesellschaft der Gesellschaft". Frankfurt: Suhrkamp 2003.

GOFFMAN, Erving: Frame Analysis. An Essay on the Organization of Experience. New York / London: Harper 1974.

GOFFMAN, Erving: Interactional Ritual. Essays on Face-to-Face Behavior. New York: Anchor Books 1967.

GÖRKE, Alexander: Unterhaltung als Leistungssystem öffentlicher Kommunikation. Ein systemtheoretischere Entwurf. In: Siegfried J. Schmidt / Joachim Westerbarkey / Guido Zurstiege (eds.): a/effektive Kommunikation. Unterhaltung und Werbung. Beiträge zur Kommunikationstheorie. Münster: LIT 2001, pp. 53-74.

GRAMSCI, Antonio: Americanism and Fordism. In: Ibid.: Selections From the Prison Notebooks. Engl. New York: International Publishers 1971, pp. 275-299.

GRAMPP, Sven: McLuhmann. Niklas Luhmanns Systemtheorie und die Realität der Medien. In: *Medienwissenschaft Rezensionen* (2006) 3, pp. 260-276.

HABERMAS, Jürgen / LUHMANN, Niklas: Theorie der Gesellschaft oder Sozialtechnologie. Was leistet die Systemforschung? Frankfurt: Suhrkamp 1971.

HABERMAS, Jürgen: Strukturwandel der Öffentlichkeit. Untersuchungen zu einer Kategorie der bürgerlichen Gesellschaft. Berlin: Luchterhand 1962. English version: The Structural Transformation of the Public Sphere. Cambridge, Mass.: MIT 1989.

HABERMAS, Jürgen: Theorie des kommunikativen Handelns. 2 vol., Frankfurt: Suhrkamp 1981, 1995. English version: The Theory of Communicative Action. Vol. 1: Reason and the Rationalization of Society. London: Heinemann 1984 and Reprint Polity Press 1995.

HANSEN, Anders / COTTLE, Simon / NEGRINE, Ralph / NEWBOLD, Chris: Mass Communication Research Methods. Houndmills: Macmillan 1998.

HAVELOCK, Eric Alfred: The Muse Learns to Write. Reflections on Orality and Literacy From Antiquity to the Present. Reprint Yale: Yale University Press 1988 German version: Als die Muse schreiben lernte. Frankfurt: Hain 1992, 2007.

HEILBRUN, James: Baumol's Cost Disease. In: Ruth Towse (ed.): A Handbook of Cultural Economics. Cheltenham / Northampton: Edward Elgar 2003, pp. 91-101.

HONKO, Lauri: Problems of Oral and Semiliterary Epics. In: Walther Heissig (ed.): Formen und Funktion mündlicher Tradition. Vorträge eines Akademiesymposiums in Bonn, July 1993. Opladen: Westdeutscher Verlag 1995, pp. 26-40.

HORSTER, Detlef: Niklas Luhmann. München: Beck 1997.

JENKINS, Henry: Convergence Culture. New York / London: New York University Press 2006.

JENKINS, Henry: Transmedia Storytelling. Moving Characters From Book to Films to Videogames Can Make Them Stronger and More Compelling. In: *Technology Review* (2003) Jan. 15th; see *www.technologyreview.com/Biotech/13052/page1/* (18-08-2017).

JENSEN, Klaus Bruhn: The Social Semiotics of Mass Communication. London et al.: Sage 1995.

JENSEN, Klaus Bruhn: The State of Convergence in Media and Communication Research. In: Ibid. (ed.): A Handbook of Media and Communication Research. Qualitative and Quantitative Methodologies. London / New York: Routledge 2002, pp. 1-11.

KIEFER, Marie Luise: Die ökonomischen Zwangsjacken der Kultur. Wissenschaftliche Bedingungen der Kulturproduktion und -distribution durch Massenmedien. In: Ulrich Saxer (ed.): Medien-Kulturkommunikation. Opladen: Westdeutscher Verlag 1998 (= Special Issue of *Publizistik* 2), pp. 97-114.

KNUDSEN, Morten: Autolysis Within Organizations. A Case Study. In: *Soziale Systeme* 12 (2006), pp. 79-99.

KRACAUER, Siegfried: From Caligari to Hitler. A Psychological History of the German Film. Princeton 1947.

KRACAUER, Siegfried: Theory of Film. The Redemption of Physical Reality. London: Oxford University Press 1960.

KREUTZNER, Gabriele / SEITER, Ellen: Not All 'Soaps' Are Created Equal. Toward a Cross-Cultural Criticism of Television Serials In Robert C. Allen: To Be Continued. Soap Operas Around the World. London / New York: Routledge 1995, pp. 234-255.

LEVINE, Lawrence: William Shakespeare in America. In: Jim Cullen (ed.): Popular Culture in American History. Malden: Blackwell 2001, pp. 32-50.

LIEB, Clauda: Gemütserregungskunst. Der Grenzfall Unterhaltung in funktionalistischen Medientheorien. In: Siegfried J. Schmidt / Joachim Westerbarkey / Guido Zurstiege (eds.): a/effektive Kommunikation. Unterhaltung und Werbung. Münster: LIT 2001, pp. 25-52.

LIEBES, Tamar / CURRAN, James (eds.): Media, Ritual and Identity. London / New York: Routledge 1998.

LOGUE, Cal M. / MILLER, F.: Communication as Mediated Sharing. A Rejoinder to Peters. In: *Critical Studies in Mass Communication* 13 (1996) 4, pp. 380-381.

LOGUE, Cal M. / MILLER, F.: Gap-Bridging, Interaction and the Province of Mass Communication. In: *Crit. Studies in Mass Communication* 13 (1996) 4, pp. 364-373.

LUHMANN, Niklas: Die Form "Person". In: *Soziale Welt* 42 (1991) 2, pp. 166-175.

LUHMANN, Niklas: Die Gesellschaft der Gesellschaft. 2 vol., Frankfurt: Suhrkamp 1998.

LUHMANN, Niklas: Die Kunst der Gesellschaft. Frankfurt: Suhrkamp 1995 und 1999^3. English version: Art As a Social System. Stanford: Stanford University Press 2000 [Luhmann 2000b].

LUHMANN, Niklas [1996²]: Die Realität der Massenmedien. Opladen: Verlag für Sozialwissenschaften 2005³. English version: The Reality of the Mass Media. Stanford: Stanford University Press 2000 (= Cultural Memory in the Present) [Luhmann 2000a].

LUHMANN, Niklas / LENZEN, Dieter: Das Erziehungssystem der Gesellschaft. Frankfurt: Suhrkamp 2002.

LUHMANN, Niklas: Entscheidungen in der "Informationsgesellschaft". Conference Paper Berlin, 28.10.-3.11.1996; an online version of the full text is accessible at *www.fen.ch/texte/gast_luhmann_informationsgesellschaft.htm* (18-08-2017).

LUHMANN, Niklas: Liebe als Passion. Zur Codierung von Intimität. Frankfurt: Suhrkamp 1982. English version: Love As Passion. The Codification of Intimacy. Cambridge: Harvard University Press 1987. Reprint Stanford: Stanford University Press 1998 (=Cultural Memory in the Present).

LUHMANN, Niklas: Soziale Systeme. Grundriss einer allgemeinen Theorie. Frankfurt: Suhrkamp 1984, 1996⁶ (Suhrkamp-Taschenbuch Wissenschaft 666). English version: Social Systems. Stanford: Stanford University Press 1995 (= Writing Science).

LUHMANN, Niklas: Was ist Kommunikation? In: Fritz B. Simon (ed.): Lebende Systeme: Wirklichkeitskonstruktionen in der systemischen Therapie. Berlin 1988, pp. 10-18. Reprint in: Peter Gente / Heidi Paris / Martin Weinmann (eds.): Niklas Luhmann. Short Cuts. Frankfurt: Zweitausendeins 2000, pp. 41-63. English version: What Is Communication? In: *Communication Theory* 2 (1992) 3, pp. 251-259.

MACDONALD, Dwight [1957]: A Theory of Mass Culture. In: John Storey (ed.): Cultural Theory and Popular Culture. A Reader. Hemel Hempstead 1994 und London: Prentice Hall 1998², pp. 29-36.

MCLUHAN, Marshall: Understanding Media. The Extensions of Man. New York: McGraw-Hill 1964 and Cambridge (Mass.): MIT Press 1996.

MCQUAIL, Denis / WINDAHL, Sven (eds.): Communication Models for the Study of Mass Communication. London / New York: Prentice Hall 1993².

MARQUARD, Odo: Zukunft braucht Herkunft. Philosophische Essays. Ditzingen: Reclam 2003.

MASLOV, Abraham H.: Motivation and Personality. New York: Harper& Row 1954, rev. ed. Joanna Cotler Books 1970².

MASLOV, Abraham H.: A Theory of Human Motivation. In: *Psychological Review* 50 (1943), 370-396.

MIÈGE, Bernard: The Capitalization of Cultural Production. London: International General 1989.

MOELLER, Hans-Georg: Luhmann Explained. From Souls to Systems. Chicago / La Salle: Open Court 2006.

NERONE, John C.: Last Rights. Revisiting Four Theories of the Press. Urbana: University of Illinois Press 1995.

NEWCOMB, Horace: On the Dialogic Aspect of Mass Communication. In: *Critical Studies in Mass Communication* 1 (1984) 1, pp. 34-50.

ONG, Walter J.: Orality and Literacy. The Technologizing of the Word. London / New York: Basic Books 1980.

PARSONS, Talcott: The Structure of Social Action. 2 vol., New York et al.: McGraw Hill 1937.

PETERS, John Durham: The Gaps of Which Communication Is Made. In: *Critical Studies in Mass Communication* 11 (1994) 2, pp. 117-140.

PETERS, John Durham: Media as Conversation, Conversation as Media. In: James Curran / David Morley (eds.): Media and Cultural Theory. London / New York: Routledge 2006, pp. 115-126.

PETERS, John Durham: Sharing of Thoughts or Recognizing Otherness? Reply to Logue and Miller. In: *Critical Studies in Mass Communication* 13 (1996) 4, pp. 373-380.

PETERS, John Durham: Speaking Into the Air. A History of the Idea of Communication. Chicago: University of Chicago Press 1999.

PIZZITOLA, Louis: Hearst Over Hollywood. Power, Passion, and Propaganda in the Movies. New York: Columbia University Press 2002.

QVORTRUP, Lars: Society's Educational System. An Introduction to Niklas Luhmann's Pedagogical Theory. In: Seminar.Net. Media, Technology and Lifelong Learning; see *www.seminar.net/files/LarsQvortrup-SocietysEdSystem.pdf* (18-08-2017).

RASCH, William: Niklas Luhmann's Modernity. The Paradoxes of Differentiation. Stanford: Stanford University Press 2000 (= Cultural Memory in the Present).

RASCH, William / KNODT, Eva / WOLFE, Cary: Theory of a Different Order. A Conversation with Katherine Hayles and Niklas Luhmann (21.9.1994). In: *Cultural Critique* 30 (1995) Sept., pp. 7-36.

RIFKIN, Jeremy: The Age of Access. How the Shift From Ownership to Access is Transforming Capitalism. London: Penguin 2000.

ROTHENBUHLER, Eric W.: Ritual Communication. From Everyday Conversation to Mediated Ceremony. London et al.: Sage 1998.

SAXER, Ulrich: Politik als Unterhaltung. Zum Wandel politischer Öffentlichkeit in der Mediengesellschaft. Konstanz: Constance University Press 2007.

SCHÜTZ, Alfred: On Multiple Realities. In: *Philosophy and Phenomenological Research* 5 (1945), pp. 533-567. Reprint in: Collected Papers, Vol. 1: The Problem of Social Reality. Den Haag: Nijhoff 1962, pp. 207-259.

SEARLE, John R.: Speech Acts. An Essay in the Philosophy of Language. Cambridge / New York: Cambridge University Press 1969.

SEITER, Ellen: Sold Separately. Children and Parents in Consumer Culture. Brunswick: Rutgers University Press 1993, 1995.

SELLA, Zohar Kadmon: The Journey of Ritual Communication. In: *Studies in Communication Sciences* 7 (2007) 1, pp. 103-124.

SIEBERT, Frederik / PETERSON, Theodore / SCHRAMM, Wilbur: Four Theories of Press. Urbana 1956, 1973.

SOURIAU, Anne / SOURIAU, Etienne: Vocabulaire d'ésthétique. Paris: Quadrige 2004.

SPIVEY, Nancy Nelson: The Constructivist Metaphor. Reading, Writing, and the Making of Meaning. Baton Rouge: Louisiana State University / Academic Press 1997.

STÄHELI, Urs: Exorcising the "Popular" Seriously. Luhmann's Concept of Semantics. In: *International Review of Sociology* 7 (1997) 1, pp. 127-145.

SCHATZ, Thomas: The Genius of the System. Hollywood Filmmaking in the Studio Era. New York: Pantheon 1988.

STAIGER, Janet: The Studio System. New Brunswick: Rutgers University Press 1995 (= Rutgers Depth of Field Series).

TAYLOR, Hugh: The Hollywood Job Hunter's Survival Guide. Los Angeles: Lone Eagle 1993.

TUNSTALL, Jeremy: The Media Are American. Anglo-American Media in the World. London: Constable 1977, 1994².

TURNER, Graeme: Understanding Celebrity. London et al.: Sage 2004.

URRY, John: The Tourist Gaze. Leisure and Travel in Contemporary Societies. London: Sage 1990, 2002².

VORDERER, Peter: Kommunikationswissenschaftliche Unterhaltungsforschung. In: Werner Wirth / Holger Schramm / Volker Gehrau (eds.): Unterhaltung durch Medien. Theorie und Messung. Köln: Herbert von Halem 2006, pp. 47-58 [2006 a].

VORDERER, Peter: Unterhaltung. Lust, Leiden, Lernen. In: Brigitte Frizzoni / Ingrid Tomkowiak (eds.): Unterhaltung. Konzepte – Formen – Wirkungen. Zürich: Chronos 2006, pp. 69-79 [2006b].

Medialität – Crossmedialität
Beiträge zur Fernseh- und Onlineforschung
Joan Kristin Bleicher

Johanna Leuschen
Internetfernsehen
Eine angebots- und akteurszentrierte Analyse und Kategorisierung onlinevermittelter Bewegtbildinhalte in ihrer Einführungsphase (2005–2011) und ihre Auswirkungen auf die traditionelle Fernsehlandschaft in Deutschland
Nach der Gründung von YouTube (2005) häuften sich Publikationen zum vermeintlichen Ende des Fernsehens. Das „alte" Medium Fernsehen – so die These – hätte ausgedient und würde von den „neuen" Internetvideos abgelöst.
Der Boom dieser Onlinevideos hatte eine stark ausdifferenzierte Angebotslandschaft zur Folge, die im vorliegenden Buch erstmals in ihrer Breite kategorisiert und analysiert wird. Basierend auf der Analyse beschreibt die Autorin die Medialität des Internetfernsehens und untersucht die Auswirkungen auf das traditionelle Fernsehen. Nicht *ob* es Fernsehen in Zukunft geben wird, sondern *wie*, ist dabei Kern der Fragestellung.
Bd. 3, 2017, 508 S., 54,90 €, br., ISBN 978-3-643-13648-0

Joan K. Bleicher; Barbara Link; Vladislav Tinchev
Fernsehstil
Geschichte und Konzepte
Stil ist als Unterscheidungs- und Identifizierungskategorie in Kultur, Gesellschaft, aber auch in der menschlichen Lebenswelt, omnipräsent. Im Bereich der Medien fungiert Stil nicht nur als Unterscheidungsmerkmal etwa zwischen Fernsehen und dem Internet, sondern auch von Institutionen und Angebotsformen.
Dieser Band liefert einen Forschungsüberblick zu zentralen Bereichen der medienwissenschaftlichen Stilforschung sowie eine Darstellung der Stilgeschichte des deutschen Fernsehens. Die spezifischen Funktionen des Stils von Fernsehdesign und Sendungen (am Beispiel von CSI) werden in Hinblick auf Zuschauerbindung, Ökonomie und künstlerische Komplexität analysiert.
Bd. 2, 2010, 120 S., 19,90 €, br., ISBN 978-3-643-10547-9

Joan Kristin Bleicher
Poetik des Internets
Geschichte, Angebote und Ästhetik
Dieser Band befasst sich mit den medialen Besonderheiten des Internets. Er richtet sich an alle NutzerInnen, die sich für das Internet interessieren, sich dort informieren und lernen, mit ihm kommunizieren, spielen, einkaufen oder arbeiten. Die Kapitel vermitteln Einblicke in die technischen Funktionsweisen, die Ordnungsmodelle und Angebotsformen, die Netzästhetik und die Netzwirkung. Dabei werden bisherige Forschungsarbeiten von Medien- und KommunikationswissenschaftlerInnen berücksichtigt.
Bd. 1, 2009, 208 S., 19,90 €, br., ISBN 978-3-8258-1573-8

LIT Verlag Berlin – Münster – Wien – Zürich – London
Auslieferung Deutschland / Österreich / Schweiz: siehe Impressumsseite